Explorer
Australia

Michael Ivory

 Publishing

Front cover
Top: *Sydney at dawn, with the Harbour Bridge in the foreground* (Steve Day); Centre (left to right): (a) *Great Barrier Reef, Queensland* (Australian Tourist Commission); (b) *Lifeguards* (Mike Longford); (c) *Kangaroos* (Simon Richmond); (d) *Detail of the roof the Sydney Opera House* (Paul Kenward); (e) *Sunset from Mount Ainslie, near Canberra* (Paul Kenward)
Spine: *A shoal of fish off Murion Islands* (Steve Watkins)
Back cover
Left: *Nourlangie rock art* (Steve Watkins); Right: *Surfing at Bondi Beach* (Mike Langford)
All pictures from AA World Travel Library except middle left, which is from the Australian Tourist Commission

Written by Michael Ivory
Updated by Anne Matthews

Published by AA Publishing, a trading name of Automobile Association Developments Limited, whose registered office is Fanum House, Basing View, Basingstoke, Hampshire, RG21 4EA. Registered number 1878835.

ISBN: 978-0-7495-4372-3

The contents of this publication are believed correct at the time of printing. Nevertheless, AA Publishing accepts no responsibility for errors, omissions or changes in the details given, or for the consequences of readers' reliance on this information. This does not affect your statutory rights. Assessments of the attractions, hotels and restaurants are based upon the author's own experience, and contain subjective opinions that may not reflect the publisher's opinion or a reader's experience. We have tried to ensure accuracy, but things do change, so please let us know if you have any comments or corrections.

A CIP catalogue record for this book is available from the British Library.

Colour separation: Fotographics Ltd
Printed and bound in Italy by Printer Trento S.r.l.

Find out more about AA Publishing and the wide range of travel publications and services the AA provides by visiting our website at www.theAA.com/travel.

First published 1994
Revised seventh edition 2005
Reprinted June 2005, Feb 2006
Reprinted 2997. Information verified and updated.

Titles in the Explorer series:
Australia • Boston & New England • Britain • Brittany California • Canada • Caribbean • China • Costa Rica • Crete Cuba • Cyprus • Egypt • Florence & Tuscany • Florida France • Germany • Greek Islands • Hawaii • India • Ireland Italy • Japan • London • Mallorca • Mexico • New York New Zealand • Paris • Portugal • Provence • Rome San Francisco • Scotland • South Africa • Spain • Thailand Tunisia • Turkey • Venice • Vietnam

Opposite: *Sydney Harbour Bridge and Opera House*

A02985

How to use this book

ORGANIZATION

Australia Is, Australia Was
Discusses aspects of life and culture in contemporary Australia and explores significant periods in its history.

A–Z
Breaks down the country into regional chapters, and covers places to visit, including walks and drives. Within this section fall the Focus On articles, which consider a variety of subjects in greater detail.

Travel Facts
Contains the strictly practical information vital for a successful trip.

Hotels and Restaurants
Lists recommended establishments throughout Australia, giving a brief summary of their attractions.

ABOUT THE RATINGS
Most places described in this book have been given a separate rating. These are as follows:

▶▶▶   **Do not miss**

▶▶   **Highly recommended**

▶   **Worth seeing**

MAPS
To make each particular location easier to find, every main entry in this book has a map reference to the right of its name. This comprises a number, followed by a letter, followed by another number, such as 176B3. The first number (176) refers to the page on which the map can be found, the letter (B) and the second number (3) pinpoint the square in which the main entry is located. The maps on the inside front cover and inside back cover are referred to as IFC and IBC respectively.

Contents

5

*Above: Palm Valley, Finke Gorge
National Park
Left: Yachts moored in Hobart*

7

Bright flowers of the bottlebrush

My Australia

Michael Ivory has written extensively about the lands of Eastern Europe—his books include AA *Essential Hungary*, AA *Essential Czech Republic*, AA *Explorer Prague* and AA *CityPack Prague*. He welcomed the chance to write a guide to Australia, a place that has always intrigued him. This book reveals something of his pleasure in experiencing this fascinating and diverse country.

Top: Uluru (Ayers Rock);
Opposite: Kalbarri Gorge,
Western Australia

Crossing the interminable Nullarbor Plain aboard the Indian Pacific train, I made the Englishman's mistake of heading for an empty table in the dining car. The steward was shocked: 'Hold on a minute, mate! Why don't you sit over here with these folk? I'm sure you'll have plenty to talk about.' He was right of course. Australia is a place where human contact is easy. Indeed, Australian friendliness is proverbial; first names are used freely and 'mates' are easily made, especially if you show yourself ready to join in, say what a wonderful country it is (not difficult!), and refrain from invidious comparisons with wherever you come from.

   I won't forget that train ride eastward from Kalgoorlie across the Nullarbor Plain, where the scenery doesn't change from one day to the next and it was a real relief to have entertaining companions at the dining table. Australians have long since overcome what one of them called 'the tyranny of distance', the impossibly vast spaces that faced early explorers. Nowadays half the enjoyment of Australia lies in the many different ways there are of getting around. It was a special thrill to get up into the cab of the big truck heading for the Indian Pacific, to marvel at the aching emptiness of the scene and at the single track heading ruler-straight to the far horizon. In utter contrast was the bumpy ride up the Bloomfield Track in Far North Queensland, with rain forest to either side. Rather more relaxing was a trip through the same kind of landscape aboard an amphibious DUKW, which took jungle, rivers and snake-filled pools in its stride. I also joined bushwalkers in their wanderings among the beautiful bush country and eucalypt forest that surrounds most of the big cities. Here, perhaps more than anywhere else, flying comes into its own. Not by comfortable airliner, but in a light plane, tossed around by the thermals bubbling upwards from the hot surface of Uluru, or in a little seaplane skimming the surface of Tasmania's Gordon River gorge. And the most sublime moment of all? Not in the air, but whizzing across Sydney Harbour in a powerboat, 'tinnie' of lager in hand, at the moment when the Opera House came into sight beneath the great span of the Harbour Bridge, and I felt I'd really arrived 'Down Under'.
Michael Ivory

Australia Is

Australia occupies a lonely place on the globe. Apart from the frozen Antarctic, it is the only continent to lie wholly within the southern hemisphere; Papua New Guinea is over the horizon across the Timor Sea, New Zealand is more than 1,984km (1,233 miles) across the Tasman Sea, and the Asian mainland at Singapore is 2,984km (1,854 miles) distant.

Girded by nearly 36,000km (22,370 miles) of coastline, the 'island continent' has a threefold structure.

THE WESTERN PLATEAU Almost two-thirds of the land surface belongs to the Western Plateau, a vast and arid tableland covering most of Western Australia, South Australia, the Northern Territory and part of Queensland. Mostly flat and low-lying, it is interrupted by spectacular individual features like Uluru (Ayers

Mount Warning National Park, New South Wales

Rock) and Kata Tjuṯa (the Olgas), by rocky strongholds like the Kimberley and Arnhem Land, and by rugged ridges like those of the MacDonnell, Flinders and Hamersley ranges.

The plateau is an ancient land whose fertility was leached away by rains that fell millions of years ago, leaving arid wastes with evocative names like the Nullarbor Plain or the Sturt Stony Desert. Similarly, winds that ceased to blow long ago left repetitive patterns of sand dunes. Except in the tropics, rainfall is not only minimal but also irregular; none may fall for years, then sudden downpours will fill the normally vacant river beds, though the rainwater soon disperses to the great salt lakes.

Much of the area is uninhabited or very thinly settled, with a population measured in hundreds of square kilometres per person. Only to the west of the Darling Range, on the relatively fertile coastal plains around the great city of Perth, are there extensive farmlands and a network of settlements linked by roads and railways. Elsewhere, settlements exist in isolation as ports, mining towns and staging posts along endless highways, or, increasingly, as areas for Outback tourism.

THE GREAT DIVIDING RANGE
This mountain range runs down the whole of the eastern coastline from Cape York in the far north to the hills and highlands of New South Wales and Victoria in the south, where it leaps the Bass Strait to reappear in the mountains of Tasmania. The continent's highest peaks are found here: Mount Kosciuszko in New South Wales (2,228m/7,310ft),

Mount Bogong in Victoria (1,986m/ 6,516ft) and Mount Ossa (1,617m/ 5,305ft), Tasmania.

However, much of the area is not made up of mountains but of high plateaus, from which rivers run eastward across the coastal plain. The bulk of the country's population lives here, clustering for the most part in the metropolitan areas around the great coastal state capitals of Sydney (New South Wales), Melbourne (Victoria), Adelaide (South Australia) and Brisbane (Queensland). Rural settlement is relatively dense in the valleys between the uplands and all along the fertile strip extending into the tropics along the Queensland coast. The only inland city of any size is Canberra, the federal capital.

CENTRAL EASTERN LOWLANDS

Between the Western Plateau and the Great Dividing Range, the Central Eastern Lowlands slope down gradually from the east towards the interior. A series of broad basins succeed one another, from the southern rim of the Gulf of Carpentaria through Queensland's Channel Country to the area drained by the country's greatest river system, the Murray/Darling/Murrumbidgee.

Here in the Outback, grazing animals outnumber people by several hundred to one, and rural life depends as much on unreliable rainfall as on the state of world markets. Mineral wealth has created a small number of towns like Broken Hill and Mount Isa, which are linked by interminably long roads and railways to the coast.

South Australian opals

❏ The world's driest continent after Antarctica has a surprisingly small range of climates. The highest rainfall is in the tropical or subtropical north, where temperatures stay high all year round (29°C/84°F in summer and 24°C/75°F in winter). Unlike the north, where the rain falls during the summer, temperate southern Australia experiences its highest rainfall in winter and spring, and there is more variation in average temperatures (24°C/75°F in summer to 10°C/50°F in winter when snow falls on the higher peaks). Much of the interior is arid, with little rain, and temperatures here soar to scorching heights; a maximum of 53°C (127°F) was recorded at Cloncurry in Queensland in 1889, although nights can be very cold. ❏

11

Australia's 40 million years of isolation from the rest of the world resulted in plants and animals that are unique to the continent. Over this long period, both fauna and flora evolved in response to local conditions quite independently of developments elsewhere, resulting in the array of strange creatures and plants that so delighted Joseph Banks as he accompanied Captain Cook aboard the Endeavour *in 1770. Despite subsequent development that had little regard for environmental side effects, Australia was quick to create national parks, some 2,000 of which await today's visitor.*

12

FORESTS The richest habitat in Australia is that of the rain forest. Tropical rain forest is best seen in northern Queensland (see page 222), but also lies in parts of the northern coastlands in the Northern Territory and Western Australia. Temperate rain forest, of great fascination and beauty, spreads over much of the wild country of southwestern Tasmania. This is the domain of the **southern beech** and of one of the longest-lived trees on earth, the **Huon pine**.

Great forests still cloak some of the less accessible areas of the southeast and southwest, but all of Australia's woodland has suffered grievously at the hands of the timber-cutters. The majority of the country's trees are variations on the theme of **eucalyptus** (also referred to as eucalypts and gum trees); they include some of the tallest trees on earth, like the mountain ash of the Victorian coastal forests or the karri of southwestern Western Australia.

SCRUBLAND AND DESERT Away from the coast, the pioneers found impenetrable **mallee** (a dense scrub of low-growing eucalyptus) or more open, park-like woodland. Most of these original plant communities have been cleared for grazing land, while native grasses and herbs have given way to exotic, high-yielding varieties. The desert is perhaps the

The rainbow lorikeet

most intriguing of all Australian ecosystems, where **saltbush**, **spinifex** and the occasional **desert oak** provide shelter for creatures such as scorpions and spiders, themselves food for snakes, lizards and **goannas**. The seeds of many small plants lie in wait for the sparse rain, flowering spectacularly when nourished.

FROM POUCHES TO PLATYPUSES Of all the marsupials that inhabit the island continent, the macropods—**kangaroos** among them—seem to need little introduction, having long

The kangaroo—one of Australia's best-known marsupials

been familiar as one of the country's best-known emblems. But there's a whole world of roos out there; as well as the red kangaroo (reaching 2m/6.5 ft), there are some 50 other varieties, ranging from the equally large Forester kangaroos to the quokkas (mistaken for rats by early explorers) and brush-tailed bettongs. Kangaroos live in most parts of the country, even occasionally on the fringe of towns.

After the kangaroo, it is the endearing **koala** that every visitor wants to see. Koalas spend most of their time asleep and the rest chewing on the leaves of certain eucalypts. The population is recovering after being hunted for its fur, but it is still subject to disease and loss of habitat. As a result, you're more likely to see them in one of the country's excellent wildlife parks than in the wild alongside **wombats**, burrowing marsupials and **possums**, some of which are actually able to glide from tree to tree, thanks to their flight membrane.

Another creature that you are more likely to see in an artificial environment is the **platypus**. This shy, egg-laying mammal with its soft bill was thought to be a hoax when a specimen was first sent to Britain for examination. The spiny anteater, or **echidna**, is less timid, being well defended by its ability to burrow below ground or present an attacker with its array of sharp spines.

NATIONAL PARKS Australia declared its first national park (Sydney's **Royal National Park**) as early as 1879. Today more than 2,000 such areas are protected and managed in order to conserve their natural beauty, protect their wildlife and make them accessible to visitors. The outstanding quality and global importance of the country's natural treasures has also been recognized by the designation of no fewer than 13 World Heritage Areas. Visitors to national parks will generally find a high standard of management in evidence, with good information services and lots of walking trails that have been created to encourage people to experience and explore the landscape. Always seek the advice of rangers about local conditions.

It's quite possible you'll meet a stereotypical Australian male while Down Under. You've probably imagined him already: tall, sunburned, probably blond and blue-eyed, short on words but long on ability to sink the stubbies (get drunk) with his mates, unhurried, an enemy of pretentiousness, and unreconstructed in his chauvinism. The stereotype exists, of course, but few Australians can be quite so easily categorized these days.

For many thousands of years, the Aborigines alone inhabited this vast continent. They had possibly arrived during the Ice Age, before Australia became isolated from the rest of Asia by the rising sea levels. Then, in the 1770s, Captain James Cook reached Botany Bay and claimed Australia for the Western world.

14

EARLY IMMIGRANTS The story of Australia's earliest European settlement is bizarre, to say the least. After James Cook's 1770 voyage of discovery, the British government came up

❏ Although rather romantically called 'convicts', most of Australia's earliest immigrants were neither noble political prisoners nor dashing highwaymen. The majority of the First Fleeters were transported for relatively minor offences, such as receiving stolen goods, forgery and petty theft, that ranged from the pathetic (pilfering a packet of snuff) to the tragic (the hunger-driven crime of stealing two hens, worth a total of fourpence). ❏

A classic Aussie 'character'

with an ambitious—many would say outrageous—solution to the 'disposal' of its felons and criminals. In May 1787, 11 ships carrying over 1,400 people, including 759 male and female convicts, set sail from England for the long and arduous journey to the virtually unknown southern continent. On their arrival in Sydney in January 1788, they became Australia's first, albeit unwilling, immigrants.

The 19th- and early 20th-century non-British immigrants to Australia were very conspicuous and often resented, although the pious and hardworking Germans who helped settle South Australia fitted in well enough. Gold rushes brought thousands of Chinese, who were treated with extreme prejudice, and South Sea Islanders known as Kanakas were kidnapped and enslaved to work the sugar plantations of Queensland, until they were repatriated under anti-slavery legislation.

Greek deli in Melbourne

WAR REFUGEES The postwar boom led to a demand for more workers than Britain could supply, and the country opened its gates to a Europe crowded with 'reffos' (refugees) and displaced persons. Australia accepted hundreds of thousands of immigrants from northern and central Europe—Czechoslovakia, Germany, the Netherlands, Scandinavia and the Baltic states.

When this source of workers began to dry up, the emphasis changed to southern Europe, and the next wave of 'New Australians' consisted of Italians, Greeks, Maltese, Croats and Serbs. A tacit 'White Australia' policy was followed; non-Europeans were rarely admitted, excluded sometimes by means of the infamous dictation test that allowed an immigration officer to give the would-be immigrant a test in a language of his (the immigration officer's) choice. An undesirable applicant of Chinese origin could thus have been examined on his knowledge of Gaelic, and, not surprisingly, fail.

A MULTICULTURAL SOCIETY A continuation of this policy became unsustainable with an increasing awareness of Australia's geopolitical position and of its social ties with Asia. A continuing, though fluctuating, demand for workers resulted in a huge influx of Cambodian, Vietnamese, Filipino and other Asian immigrants, a fact that is instantly verifiable on the streets of any of the state capitals.

The total assimilation of the newcomers has been abandoned; today, immigrant culture is preserved. Of the two state-funded television channels, SBS specializes in broadcasts in a variety of different languages. Australia is now one of the most racially diverse countries in the world. More than half of all Australians were either born overseas themselves, or have at least one parent who was born overseas.

In the midst of multiculturalism, the Aborigines, who are, after all, the only Australians who are neither recent settlers nor descended from immigrants, strive to retain their traditions and culture (see pages 24–25). Only in recent times have Australians begun to accept their different way of life.

15

'No worries' seems to sum up much of the average Australian's attitude to life. Work doesn't play the central role here that it does in some societies around the Pacific Rim or even in Europe. Life is to be made the most of, preferably out in the open, enjoying food and drink, watching sports with passionate intensity, or swimming, surfing, bushwalking and simply lazing around in the great outdoors of the 'best country in the world'.

Celebrating at the Melbourne Cup

The founding period of convicts was once a source of shame but is now looked back on with pride. It can be seen as a positive factor contributing to the way Australians are today. Australian 'mateship' has its roots in shared oppression and in the importance of comrades in making a life in a harsh and empty land. The land posed a tough physical challenge, in which the conventional qualities of 'manliness' were directly related to success or even survival. Work was originally performed under duress and for someone else, after which you were free to lead your own life. Authority was exercised by prison wardens and governors, and consequently resented, but there was no old ruling class or complicated code of manners. Strangers were seldom seen, but if they needed help they could be sure of getting it.

EVERYONE IS EQUAL So Australia has long been a land where people feel themselves to be basically equal and as good as the next person. Money and the making of it are admired, but this does not mean that the monied become beings apart. There is an openness about social contacts that is surprising to many visitors. When Australians say 'How are you?' there's a good chance that they actually mean it, and will enjoy hearing your answer (especially if you reveal to them how much you like their country). If you expect to be deferred to, you could be in for an unpleasant surprise; Australians don't like pretension, and will prickle if they detect it.

THE OUTDOOR LIFE Given the character of the country, with its space, climate, the grandeur of its natural landscapes and the fact that the vast majority of the population lives close to a beach, it's hardly surprising that people seem obsessed with outdoor life and sport.

Everyone loves a 'barbie' (a barbecue) and a session on the beach, whether sunbathing or surfing. The great days of lifesaving clubs and parades are certainly not over, and neither is the allure of the beach; surfing is indeed a way of life for quite a number of people.

Gambling is also a national passion, taking place indoors in front of endless ranks of 'pokies', at the casino or

❏ Even though women got the vote at an early date, Australia was always a man's country. The male–female ratio among the transportees brought by the First Fleet was hardly a balanced one, and the scenes that took place when the first cargo of women was discharged were said to be 'indescribable'. 'Sheilas' (women) were 'kept in their place' longer here than in most other countries, both at home and behind the bar, where they filled the glasses while the men on the other side got on with the serious business of drinking. Big changes came during World War II, however, and then later with the growth of feminism, one of the key works of which, *The Female Eunuch*, was by the Australian writer Germaine Greer. ❏

17

Lifeguard at Bondi Beach

outdoors at the racetrack. On the first Tuesday in November, life stops across the nation for the big horse race, the Melbourne Cup.

SPORT Most Australians love sport, to watch if not to play. A passion for cricket is shared with other members of the British Commonwealth, and has been made more exciting by innovations like one-day matches, floodlighting and the move away from traditional cricket whites. Rugby Union and Rugby League are played primarily in NSW and Queensland. The really big ball game, however, and certainly in its Melbourne stronghold, is the one known as Australian Rules Football. It originated on the goldfields, a crude version of Gaelic football (soccer) played by prospectors taking time off from the diggings, and has been described as 'a kind of organized mayhem, remarkable for its lack of obvious rules'. Up to 100,000 spectators gather to watch the grand final at the MCG (Melbourne Cricket Ground) every September. The year 2000, however, placed Australia on the world's sporting map, thanks to Sydney's acclaimed hosting of the XXVII Olympiad.

Australian culture goes back far longer than the 200-odd years of white settlement. Visitors will be fascinated by the evidence of at least 40,000 years of uninterrupted civilization in both the dot and x-ray style rock- and cave-paintings, and in the haunting stories of the creation legends of the Aboriginal Dreamtime.

Australians today have a high regard for culture and talent, and take pride in the international success of Australian artists, filmmakers and writers. Most Aussies cannot resist a good performance, and visitors who demonstrate their enthusiasm will be much appreciated.

LITERATURE AND FILMS Drama has developed from such elegies for lost youth as Ray Lawlor's *Summer of the Seventeenth Doll* to the plays of David Williamson. Les Murray and the late Judith Wright are poets of world status, weaving together the personal and the public, while managing to capture the elusive character of the Australian environment.

Three classic Australian books are Robert Hughes's convict-era history, *The Fatal Shore*, Jill Ker Conway's childhood memoir, *The Road from Coorain*, and Bruce Chatwin's rendering of the Aboriginal relationship with the earth, *The Songlines*. Also

Tongue-in-cheek Crocodile Dundee

look for Barry Hill's *The Rock*, an illustrated multicultural history of Uluru (Ayers Rock).

Aussie novels that comment poignantly, sometimes humorously, on Australian life, history and landscape are Nobel Prize-winner Patrick White's *Voss*, Peter Carey's spirited *Oscar and Lucinda*, David Malouf's *Remembering Babylon* and Thomas Keneally's *The Playmaker*. Elizabeth Jolley sets her novels in her native state, Western Australia.

Since the 1970s, Australian filmmakers have produced an increasing variety of internationally known work. The tragic *Breaker Morant* and Peter Weir's *Gallipoli* and *Picnic at Hanging Rock* are in a class of their own. *My Brilliant Career*, about an aspiring young writer on a sheep station, is another knock-out. *Crocodile Dundee's* bushwhacking swagger has its place in Australian mythology, as does the apocalyptic *Mad Max 2/The Road Warrior*, for different reasons, of course. Other popular Aussie films include *Strictly Ballroom*, *A Cry in the Dark*, *Muriel's Wedding*, the side-splitting *The Adventures of Priscilla, Queen of the Desert*, *Babe*, *The Castle* and *Shine*.

PAINTERS Marvellous light and scenery have contributed to a tradition of outstanding painting. The early dreamy landscapes of McCubbin and the Heidelberg School, lending the Australian scenery a European beauty, gave way to the more distinctively Australian works of painters like Sidney Nolan with his series of pictures depicting the fatal defiance of outlaw Ned Kelly. Arthur Boyd's and Brett Whiteley's enlargements of

18

their own dreams and obsessions sometimes achieve a vast scale, and Fred Williams' wonderful evocations of the arid Australian landscape rival the originality of Aboriginal art, which is now much sought after by collectors all over the world.

Aboriginal paintings are well represented in museums and art galleries, and the outdoor rock art that can be found all over the country is an undeniable cultural achievement.

MUSIC Australia also has much to offer musically. The golden voice of Joan Carden makes her a worthy successor to Dame Nellie Melba and Dame Joan Sutherland ('La Stupenda'). Each state capital boasts an Australian Broadcasting Commission symphony orchestra of world standard, with internationally recognized conductors and repertoires including music by contemporary Australian composers such as Colin Brumby, John Antill and Peter Sculthorpe. Aboriginal music is increasingly entering the mainstream of the country's culture, and the international reputation of Yothu Yindi, the Aboriginal rock band, was recognized by the 1992 'Australian

The Sidney Nolan painting Dog and Duck Hotel

of the Year' award given to its lead singer, Mandawuy Yunupingu. The country is also a hotbed of good jazz (James Morrison), folk (Archie Roach and Ruby Hunter), and country and western (Troy Cassar-Daley and Kasey Chambers).

THE MEDIA In contrast, most Australian newspapers and TV channels are owned by two media moguls —Rupert Murdoch and James Packer. Their content is dominated by personality trivia, sports, 'bushwhacker' pap and investigations into the private lives of public figures, often making the Australian press as sensationalist as any other.

The Australian Broadcasting Commission's radio and television broadcasts, on the other hand, gain many international awards for quality and interest, particularly in the fields of science, environment and religion. Especially outstanding is the current-affairs weekly *Four Corners*, which for over 20 years has exposed big business and government scandals that have been ignored by the commercial media.

The six states that came together on the first day of the 20th century to create the nation of Australia had all developed outwards from the isolated footholds of their port-of-entry capital cities, with very different characteristics and cultures. In contrast with the slow evolution of a national consciousness, the states maintain a vigorous political and economic competition both with each other and with the Federal Government.

20

Since 1940, Commonwealth control of tax revenues and appointment of Supreme Court judges has guaranteed the Federal Government victory in most disputes with individual states. This included the 1983 prohibition of damming of the World Heritage-listed Franklin River in Tasmania and the 1990 exclusion of logging from the unique tropical rain forests of northern Queensland. In these matters, the Commonwealth Government has been influenced by a Green movement that commands a disciplined voting block—generally estimated at between 8 per cent and 15 per cent of the electorate.

THE POLITICAL PARTIES After 13 years in power (an unprecedented six terms of office), Australia's Federal Labor Government was heavily defeated by the right-wing coalition of the Liberal Party (representing the urban middle classes and employers) and National Party (the traditional voice of rural interests) in the March 1996 elections. The current Liberal Party Prime Minister is John Howard, who is best known for his extremely conservative approach.

A large proportion of the population was delighted by this transfer of power after Labor's long, and perhaps increasingly complacent, rule. But many Australians are concerned, for example, about the future of the proposed Australian republic, free of constitutional ties to the reigning British monarch, who is still the official head of the country. There is also an ongoing debate regarding a new and more appropriate flag.

Aboriginal, immigration and arts policies have also changed, with John Howard and his supporters expressing little interest in these issues, and there was strong opposition from many quarters to the government's introduction of a GST (Goods and Services Tax) in 2000. The challenge to the Liberal/National Party coalition in currently being spearheaded by the Leader of the Opposition, Kim Beazley.

ECONOMIC DEVELOPMENT The 'Lucky Country' cannot now find enough markets for its wool, wheat, beef or mineral exports to pay for its insatiable appetite for expensive imports. The tariffs that previously protected small local industries from being swamped by European and Asian manufacturers have been drastically cut in the interests of economic rationalism, and the Australian dollar, although weak, represents very good value for most overseas visitors. However, unemployment has fallen to under 6 per cent and there has been substantial economic growth in recent years, aided by the boom in international tourism.

There is now bipartisan political agreement on the need to develop manufactured goods for export, though the current government policy of reducing tariff barriers has had the opposite result and has caused unemployment. However, there can be no argument about the need to integrate better with the economies of both Europe and Southeast Asia and the Pacific Rim, Australia's closest neighbours.

Australia Was

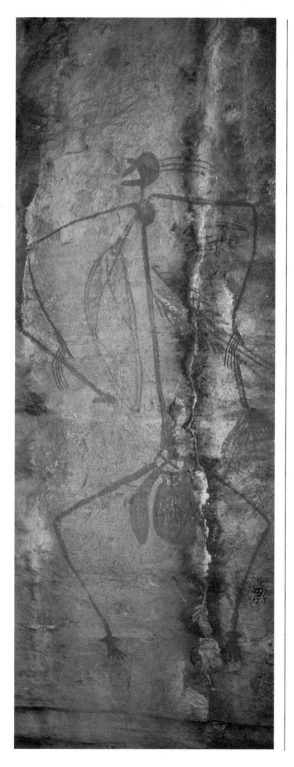

In some parts of the globe, vigorous land-shaping processes are obviously hard at work. Ice and snow attack alpine peaks, glaciers grind through valleys, torrents and waterfalls erode, while elsewhere geysers boil and lava pours from beneath the earth. In contrast, Australia is a quiet continent, much of whose active geological history ended long ago.

22

ANCIENT TECTONICS Some 50 million years ago, Australia was part of Gondwanaland, the great southern supercontinent that slowly split into the separate fragments we know today as Antarctica, South America, Africa and India, as well as Australia and New Zealand. But its geological evolution goes back much further. Precambrian rocks more than 600 million years old are exposed over much of the continent, among them the ancient iron ore deposits of the Pilbara in Western Australia. Subsequently, much of the heart of the continent was periodically submerged beneath the sea, leaving deposits of sands, shells and grits, or the limestone of the Nullarbor Plain. Great coral reefs were also formed, which, when uplifted, became the basis of the extensive cave systems of New South Wales and Queensland,

or the great bastion that today guards the southern rim of the Kimberley. The Great Artesian Basin came into being at this time too, and the water pumped from it continues to support life in much of the Outback.

MORE RECENT CHANGES About 2 million years ago, what is now the arid Red Centre of the continent enjoyed a far higher rainfall and carried a rich vegetation of tropical forest, traces of which can still be seen in the palms and other plants that have found a refuge in the gorges penetrating the area's harsh ranges. In the east, the Great Dividing Range was thrown up as the result of convulsive earth movements; its southern, alpine area, together with the Tasmanian highlands, is the only part of the continent to have been subjected to glaciation in the last Ice Age (10,000 years ago). As the ice melted, the sea

The Great Dividing Range

level rose, creating a wonderful natural harbour for the future city of Sydney. At the same time, the land bridges with Tasmania and New Guinea were cut. Later still (some 5,000 years ago), an outburst of volcanic activity covered the plains of southwestern Victoria with lava, leaving a legacy of cones and crater lakes and of deep fertile soil.

23

Right: Tessellated rock formation on the Tasman Peninsula
Below: Australia in 1848; note the lack of information on the unexplored interior of the continent

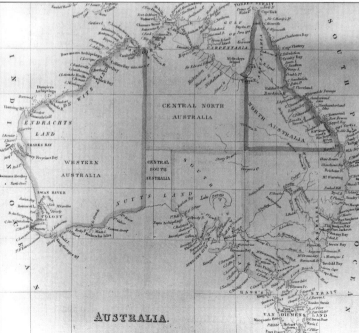

European explorers and educated early settlers tended to romanticize the black people they encountered on the unknown continent. Aborigines were seen by some as typifying the 'Noble Savage' dreamed up by the imaginative powers of 18th-century thinkers. The first Australians, now often referred to as Kooris, were an endlessly fascinating subject for artists and were sometimes depicted in the heroic poses of ancient Greek statuary.

VICTIMS OF THE WHITE MAN The Aborigines failed to correspond to the European stereotypes. In what now seems an entirely appropriate response, albeit one doomed to failure, some groups put up a vigorous resistance to the encroachment of white settlement on the lands that had formed the basis of their lives since time immemorial. Others fell

Ritual and ceremony are central to Aboriginal culture

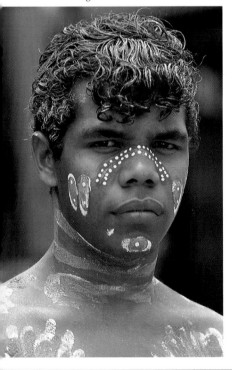

easy victim to the diseases and vices of their conquerors. Only a few decades after the arrival of the First Fleet, the Aborigines of the Sydney region had been decimated by drink and influenza, and before the 19th century had run its course, full-blooded Tasmanians had virtually disappeared. Since then, Aborigines have generally been seen as second-class citizens; it was not until after a referendum in 1967 that they were given the right to vote.

It is only in relatively recent times that white Australians have begun to appreciate the richness and subtlety of the life that their appropriation of the continent all but destroyed, but which sustained the first Australians in material and spiritual harmony with the Australian environment for at least 40,000 years.

DREAMTIME Aboriginals live on the land in a way that is remote from European concepts of ownership and property. Rather than 'own' land, they inhabit it in sacred trust on behalf of ancestral beings who created it during the Dreamtime. The land itself is part of the spiritual realm of the whole of creation, in which all creatures, animals as well as humans and the dead as well as the living, have their being. The landscape is venerated by individuals, large family groups or clans, with certain places—'sacred sites'—having a particularly intense meaning.

A deep understanding of the spiritual significance of the land was passed on by highly refined and diversified traditions of song and

24

Aboriginal rangers are happy to share their knowledge of the land with visitors to the national parks

dance. Never codified in writing, many of these oral traditions tragically have been lost. Ritual gatherings, sometimes known as *corroborees*, took up large amounts of time, with men and women often having strictly separate ceremonies. Visual arts, like cave- or wall-paintings, or designs executed on the ground, had a ceremonial or storytelling role, and were ephemeral or subject to periodic renewal.

LIFESTYLE Virtually all Aboriginal groups were nomads, living a Stone-Age lifestyle of hunting, gathering and fishing based on the seasonal availability of game, seeds and fruits. Controlled burning of the bush took place in order to encourage regrowth and thus attract animals to the area. Material belongings were kept to an absolute minimum, and consisted of baskets and nets, digging sticks, shelters of brushwood, weapons of carved wood and sharpened bone, canoes of bark and boomerangs. Clothes were also minimal, except in the colder, wetter areas of south-eastern Australia, where skins and furs were worn.

Each clan had its own distinct territory, defined orally by song rather than marked out on the ground. For another group to cross such an invisible but nevertheless definite boundary might have involved complex negotiation.

The whole of Australia can now be mapped in terms of these traditional territories, but at the time of European settlement no such map existed, except in the hearts of its inhabitants. This allowed legalistic Europeans to appropriate the land with a more or less clear conscience.

❏ Some 200 Aboriginal languages existed, related to one another but not necessarily mutually intelligible. Most people were multilingual, speaking perhaps five or six tongues. The language of the Aborigines around the future site of Sydney was, of course, unknown to Europeans, and the cry of '*Warra! Warra!*' they were greeted with was not understood. Even if it had been, would they have taken any notice? '*Warra! Warra!*' means 'Go away!' ❏

The first people to explore Australia were the ancestors of today's Aborigines, who may have crossed the still intact land bridge linking the continent to New Guinea well over 40,000 years ago. At first they lived along the coasts and in other areas where food was easily obtainable, and eventually spread all over the country, learning to live even in those regions where survival seemed all but impossible to European explorers.

THE PORTUGUESE AND DUTCH EXPLORERS

The European discovery of the island continent began in a tentative, almost accidental way in the 16th century, as Portuguese mariners looked for routes to the eastern Spice Islands. But the first definite landfall was made in 1606 by the Dutch ship *Duyfken* ('Little Dove') sailing out of the Dutch colony of Batavia (now Jakarta). Her captain, Willem Jansz, was unimpressed by what he saw of the desolate western coast of Cape York and what he called its 'wild, cruel black savages'.

A little later, Dutch skippers on their way to Java found that they could cut weeks off their journey by making use of the Roaring Forties until they made a northward turn well short of the coast of western Australia. Some sailed straight on, like Dirk Hartog in 1616 (who left an inscribed pewter plate nailed to a post on the island that bears his name), and Frederik de Houtman, who landed on the Houtman Abrolhos islands in 1619.

Under the command of a captain whose name is unrecorded, the *Leeuwin* ('Lioness') sighted the southwestern tip of the continent in 1622. Subsequently, more systematic attempts were made by the Dutch East India Company to survey the coastline. The most famous of them was the voyage of Abel Tasman in 1642–1643 in the *Heemskerck* and *Zeehaan*; put ashore on Tasmania's Blackman Bay, his pilot heard voices coming from the bush, but the natives failed to show themselves. Tasman had the flag run up, and named the island after the Governor

W. R. Stott's painting shows William Dampier being attacked by Aborigines when he landed in 1699

of the Dutch East Indies, Van Diemen, a name changed to that of the actual discoverer in 1855.

In the course of a second voyage, Tasman failed (as had all his predecessors) to find the gap between New Guinea and Australia, subsequently called the Torres Strait, but mapped 3,000km (1,865 miles) of the north coast instead. By this time, the coast had been explored by Dutchmen from the tip of Cape York around Western Australia to the archipelago in the Great Australian Bight. Although the Dutch did not take the continent under their control, they named it—New Holland.

26

THE BRITISH ARRIVE The first Englishman to set foot on the shores of New Holland was the adventurer William Dampier, who landed twice on its northwestern coast, first in 1688, then again in 1699. It was Captain Cook, however, who not only found the unknown east coast, but sailed the length of it and identified the spot where British settlement was to take place. He completed his mission in spite of the fact that his ship the *Endeavour* ran aground on the Barrier Reef (see page 214). The name that Captain Cook gave to the land he claimed for the British Crown was New South Wales.

Even after British settlement had been well and truly established around Sydney Harbour (by Captain Phillip in 1788), many uncertainties remained as to whether the three known fragments added up to a continent. Part of the answer was provided by two truly intrepid men, George Bass and Matthew Flinders, who by 1798 had confirmed the existence of a channel between the mainland and Van Diemen's Land. Governor Hunter, impressed by this great discovery, named the channel Bass Strait after the explorer.

Aboard the *Investigator*, Flinders went on to explore the south coast with great thoroughness, meeting the French survey ship *Geographe* in what came to be known as Encounter Bay.

Early settlers: Captain Phillip arriving at Sydney Cove in 1788

The master of the *Geographe*, Nicolas Baudin, behaved impeccably, though Flinders was suspicious of the intentions of a servant of France, a country with which Britain had recently been at war. His suspicions of the French were justified when, later, having sailed around Australia in 1802–1803, he was arrested by the Governor of French Mauritius on his way back to England, unaware that war had broken out again. Held for six years by the French, he returned to England a prematurely aged 40-year-old, barely able to complete his *A Voyage to Terra Australis* before dying in 1814.

❏ Non-Europeans also made contact with Australia. Chinese junks may have sailed to Australia's northern coast as early as the 15th century, and there were exchanges between the Aborigines and the warlike inhabitants of New Guinea. From about 1700 onwards, fishermen from Macassar in the Celebes frequented the north coast in search of trepang (sea-cucumbers), an activity that continues today. ❏

The map of Australia is scattered with surnames attached to natural features or to settlements, honouring governors and other leaders. But there are some, like the Sturt Stony Desert, which commemorate a different kind of fame—that earned by the inland explorers, a breed of men who explored, with varying degrees of success, the new country's uncharted interior.

28

Straightforward curiosity may have impelled some adventures into the interior, but another factor was the hunger for land as the colony grew and needed to be fed. In addition, industrial England developed an insatiable appetite for wool, which the merino crossbreeds so successfully developed by John Macarthur could satisfy only if enough pastures could be found. For many years, the Blue Mountains seemed to bar the way from Sydney to the interior, but in 1813 this obstacle was overcome by William Lawson, William Charles Wentworth and Gregory Blaxland. Governor Macquarie had a road built across the mountains in record time, and settlers rushed into the rich grazing lands beyond.

STURT'S JOURNEY For many years the puzzle of what became of the rivers flowing westward from the

Many lost their lives in the exploration of Australia's interior

mountains perplexed authorities and explorers alike. Did they perhaps feed a great inland sea? A partial answer—no!—was given in 1829–1830, when Charles Sturt hauled a whaling boat over the hills and sailed down the Murrumbidgee to its confluence with the Murray. From there he continued downstream to wide Lake Alexandrina and the river mouth (in South Australia), which had so far been concealed from maritime explorers behind a sand bar. Sturt's return, rowing upstream against a swelling current, was an epic of endurance. It nearly ended in disaster as food for his party ran out and their strength ebbed.

❑ Explorers of several nationalities contributed to the exploration of Australia. In 1839–40, a Polish adventurer, self-styled 'Count' Paul Strzelecki, underwent hardships almost equal to those suffered by Sturt as he traversed the uplands to which he gave the name Gippsland, and from which he was only extracted by the skills of his Aboriginal guide. An impetuous and quarrelsome Prussian, Ludwig Leichhardt, was less lucky, though in 1844 his first journey succeeded in covering 4,800km (2,980 miles) from Brisbane to Arnhem Land. A more ambitious foray that was intended to carry him right across the country from Sydney to Perth failed. Leichhardt and his companions simply disappeared into the void. ❑

Above: Burke and Wills leave Melbourne in August 1860

BURKE'S EXPEDITION Another great failure, but a fully documented one, was the expedition that set out from Melbourne in 1860 under the impatient leadership of Robert O'Hara Burke. The expedition did reach its objective, the mangrove swamps of the Gulf of Carpentaria, but when the party returned to base camp at Cooper Creek, they found that it had been abandoned a mere seven hours previously by their support group. Both Burke and his deputy Wills perished, though another man, John King, was fed roots and fish by the Aborigines and survived to return and tell the tale.

Before successfully crossing the middle of Australia, Stuart had reached Alice Springs

EYRE AND STUART The names of highways spanning the great emptiness of the middle and the west commemorate the epic treks undertaken by two explorers whose persistence was almost legendary. In 1840–41, with the support of his Aboriginal guide Wylie, Edward Eyre reached Albany in Western Australia, having crossed the desert across the top of the Great Australian Bight. In 1862, John McDouall Stuart, almost blind and with hair turned white, finally reached the coast near what was to become Darwin. His previous attempts to cross the country from south to north had been frustrated by spinifex and scurvy, though he had planted the British flag on a hilltop near Alice Springs. His return to Adelaide, where he was mobbed by the ladies of the city, was made partly on a stretcher.

29

In the first half of the 19th century, Australia developed at a steady but unspectacular pace. Free settlers soon outnumbered convicts, and each colony won its right to a separate existence from New South Wales. But the discovery of gold transformed the country, drawing in a mass of enterprising folk who helped lay the foundation of Australia's essentially urban civilization.

GOLD FEVER The news of early gold finds was suppressed by the authorities, who were fearful of the disruption that such an announcement might cause. But there was no stopping Edward Hargraves, a veteran of the Californian gold rush of 1849, who struck gold near Bathurst in NSW in February 1851.

The rush began, draining the cities of population and making Melbourne so fearful for its prosperity that city officials offered a prize to whoever found gold within a certain distance of the city. One James Esmond obliged, and his find at Clunes in July 1851 was followed by others at Castlemaine, Bendigo and

Prospectors in the mid-19th century

Ballarat. Melbourne was emptied of able-bodied men and ships stood crewless in the harbour as sailors hurried inland to make their fortune.

Life in the goldfields was tough, raw and dangerous. Many of the prospectors longed for nothing more than solid respectability. They founded farms and businesses after striking lucky, or returned to seek their fortune among the seemingly limitless opportunities offered by 'Marvellous Melbourne'.

More rebellious spirits took a stand at the Eureka Stockade (see page 110), and even though this revolt failed, their gesture helped create a new democratic atmosphere in which representative government was to thrive. Victoria's population rose in ten years from less than 100,000 to more than half a million, and the whole country received an injection of energy that carried it through a boom lasting until the 1890s.

FORTUNE-SEEKERS Prospectors came flooding in from all over the world, including the gold miners of California and hopeful fortune seekers from Britain. The largest minority were the Chinese, many of whom disembarked in South Australia and walked overland to the Victorian goldfields rather than pay the £10 landing tax at Melbourne. They were much resented by the other settlers for their willingness to work hard, for keeping to themselves and for their sheer numbers. At the time of the Palmer River gold rush in the 1870s in North Queensland, Chinese diggers formed a majority of the male population in the state.

FROM BOOM TOWN TO GHOST TOWN In Victoria, the rip-roaring days were soon over. By the late 1850s, most of the gold that was available on the surface or by shallow diggings had been worked out. Individual miners could not afford the equipment that was needed for the excavation and maintenance of deeper mines, and the initiative passed from the self-sufficient pioneer to companies able to raise the necessary capital. Ballarat ceased being a muddy chaos and turned itself into the most respectable of Victorian cities.

In the second half of the 19th century, gold strikes were made all over Australia, many of them ephemeral and leaving a poignant legacy of ghost towns. The last great rush was to the Eastern Goldfields of Coolgardie and Kalgoorlie-Boulder in Western Australia in 1892–93. This gave a similar boost to the languid economy of the colony, and transformed Perth into a real city. Large-scale operations continue in this area today, based on vast open-cast pits worked by huge machines, in total contrast to the primitive hand tools and hard manual work of the prospectors of early days.

Sovereign Hill at Ballarat in Victoria is a re-creation of gold-rush days

❑ Highway robbery had been practised in the colony for as long as highways had existed, and increased in appeal as the wealth created by the gold rush was moved around. Australia's bushrangers were just as fearsome as the legendary outlaws of the American West, their exploits winning them a heroic status among a population traditionally hostile to the police. The most notorious of them all, and a symbol of Australian defiance, was Edward 'Ned' Kelly, son of an Irish ex-convict. After a series of exploits, which included holding up whole towns, the Kelly gang was cornered in June 1880 at Glenrowan, a small town in northeastern Victoria. Kelly emerged from the pub wearing his famous homemade suit of armour, but was shot in the legs, brought to trial and hanged in Melbourne on 11 November 1880. ❑

31

The Australian landscapes that the early European settlers first cast eyes upon lacked the ordered character of the scenes they had left behind. Much of the European effort in Australia was to impose a rational and productive discipline on this unfamiliar and seemingly chaotic scene. This was sometimes at a cost to habitats and natural beauty that is only now being calculated.

In Europe, the conversion of the forest into farmland began in neolithic times and took some 5,000 years to complete. In the wooded southeastern and western areas of Australia, the same process was virtually complete after only a single century. The replacement of the bush by productive fields was one motive, but in many areas the timber itself was highly valuable and logging quickly developed into a major industry.

The removal of the native forest or its replacement by exotic tree species like radiata pines continued into the 20th century, but a partial halt has now been called. Today, no visitor should miss seeing such glories of the Australian landscape as the tropical rain forest of Queensland, its temperate equivalent in the southeast and in Tasmania, the blue gums that have given their name to the Blue Mountains, or the splendid karri forests of Western Australia.

THE FARMERS MOVE IN Once the bush was cleared, squatters and sheep farmers divided up their land, erecting fences and planting European trees to give the place a more familiar look. They built themselves homesteads with whatever degree of architectural elaboration they could afford. Australian country properties ranged from elegant stone mansions to shacks that were made of corrugated iron.

This attempt to impose order often faltered in the face of the capricious nature of the land. Rainless years ruined many a farmer who had tried to push the frontier of agriculture too far inland. Australia has as many

forgotten farmsteads as it has ghost towns abandoned by prospectors when mineral wealth ran out.

As settlement advanced, native animals retreated, displaced in many cases by flocks of sheep grazing on the imported grass species sown by farmers. Kangaroos and other animals, often shot as pests, sometimes profited by the irrigation of otherwise arid landscapes, and became a greater nuisance than ever.

CONFLICTS OF INTEREST The effect of these and other changes converted a seemingly formless scene into one that made economic and visual sense to the Europeans, and one that could be controlled and managed. It also meant that the landscape became uninhabitable by the Aborigines in any traditional way. Such basic differences of viewpoint probably contributed more than anything else to a conflict between settlers and the Aborigines, in which the latter were the inevitable losers.

❏ Rabbits were imported as game in the 1850s. Within a few years, the population exploded, and they advanced at the rate of 100km (60 miles) a year, destroying much native herbage for ever. Supposedly rabbit-proof fences were built, one running 2,000km (1,240 miles) across Western Australia. But the rabbits found ways round them, and were only curbed when myxomatosis devastated them in the 1950s and by the *calici* virus in the 1990s. ❏

33

How to tackle Australia

The first thing to remember about Australia is that it is a continent. Planning a holiday here is like taking a journey across Europe or the United States—Australia is comparable in size to the US, excluding Alaska, and approximately 24 times as big as the British Isles—you could get an overall idea of the country in one trip, but you need time and money if you want to get to know it really well.

THE EXTENDED VISIT An absolute minimum for an extended trip that takes in all major sights is three months. In this time you could visit all the states, including Tasmania, and cover most of the highlighted attractions of this guide, especially if you were able to do most of your journey, and some of your sightseeing, by plane. If you have more time, so much the better; you could stay in some places and absorb their atmosphere in a relaxed way rather than just hitting the principal sights. Now that you can drive right around the continent on paved roads, many retired Australians are getting to know their own country in a leisurely way, usually by driving an RV or camper van.

THE SHORTER TRIP Most visitors to Australia have only limited time at their disposal, and choices must be made. As well as seeing something of city life, if you want to enjoy what Australia has to offer you will need to get out into the country, drive along the unsurfaced roads of the Outback, leave your car behind and walk through the bush or along the beach, wander around an old goldrush

34

Camper vans are ideal for exploring the country, particularly for those on a tight budget

township, sit at the bar of an Outback pub or sample the excellent diving or snorkelling.

Australians take great pleasure in inviting you to join in: You can take part in all kinds of activities, from riding a camel in the desert to digging for witchetty grubs in the company of an Aboriginal ranger. Not only are there probably more museums per head than anywhere else in the world (ranging from the impeccably professional to the endearingly amateur), but all kinds of industries and enterprises also open their gates to visitors. Wineries without tastings are unheard of, farms make you welcome and there is plenty of accommodation available on country properties that offer the chance to take part in rural activities.

PLANNING AN ITINERARY Within the confines imposed by a conventional holiday of a few weeks, setting definite limits on what you can reasonably undertake is very important. Though vast, nearly all the Australian states are dominated by their respective capital city, each of which has its own character and attractions. This is where colonial life began and where its traces are thickest on the ground. Wild landscapes start just beyond the suburbs; no big city lies out of sight of the hills or mountains of a national park.

One solution would be to choose one city or town as a base and then make excursions, some involving overnight stays, in order to appreciate the extraordinary contrasts between city and rural life that are such a feature of Australia. An overland trip by rental car, train, bus or organized tour beginning at one point and taking your time to reach another is a good way of getting the feel of the country; your round-trip airline ticket can usually be arranged to accommodate this. If you only have a week in Australia, you could just about take in very short visits to Sydney, Cairns, the Barrier Reef, Darwin, Alice Springs and Uluṟu by flying between sites.

The Outback is uniquely rewarding, but before you head off in your rental car or camper van, contemplate the distances involved. Remember that Cairns is 2,680km (1,665 miles) from Sydney, Alice Springs is 2,928km (1,820 miles) distant via Adelaide, Darwin 4,400km (2,735 miles) via Adelaide and Alice Springs and Perth a staggering 4,160km (2,585 miles) from Sydney. You don't have to go all the way out and back overland; if time is short, you can fly to one of the many bases for Outback tours and start from there.

Australia has a varied and well-developed tourist infrastructure, mostly staffed by people who go out of their way to be helpful. Apart from accommodation and restaurants to suit a range of budgets, there are also many tour operators. However, make sure that the tours offered are exactly what you want; the ingredients of a package may have been put together to suit the operator's convenience rather than yours.

AUSTRALIAN ISLANDS
Far out in the Pacific, Lord Howe Island (over 700km/435 miles north-east of Sydney) and Norfolk Island (another 1,000km/620 miles farther on) are popular with Australians in search of something different. Norfolk was a prison island where offenders from Sydney were sent to suffer under a notoriously brutal regime, and the remains of convict-era buildings give it something of the atmosphere of Tasmania's Port Arthur. The climate is subtropical and as well as rain forest, there are stands of the famous Norfolk pines and rolling pasturelands. Lord Howe Island is less than half the size of Norfolk Island and is dominated by mountain peaks, with unique vegetation and birdlife that have led to its designation as a World Heritage Area. There are hardly any cars, and when not snorkelling you will have to get around by bicycle.

35

Drivers: beware of camels!

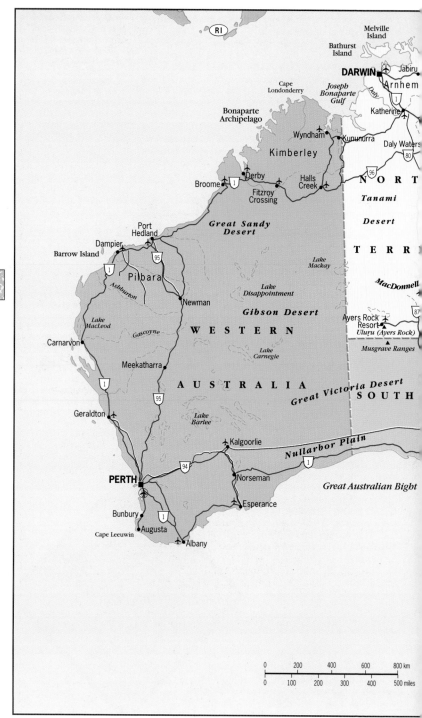

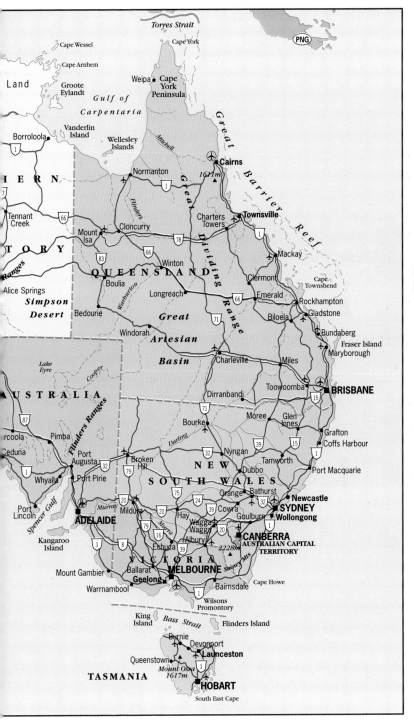

Sydney

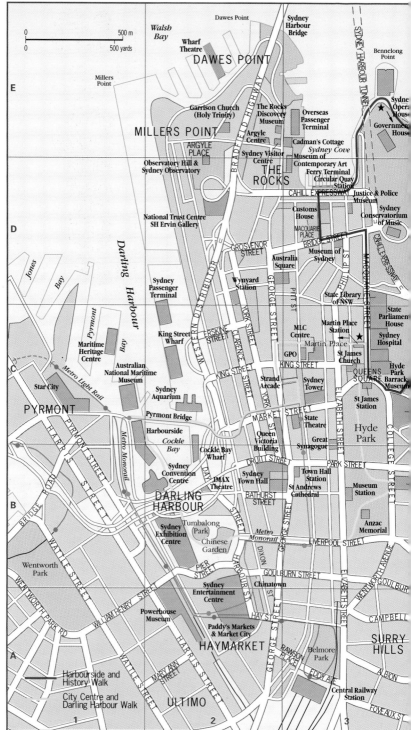

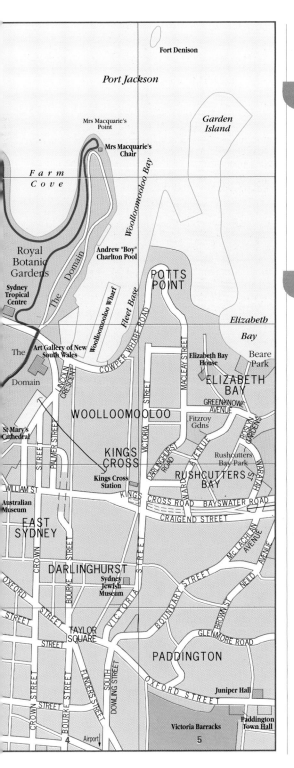

Sydney

Fort Denison

Port Jackson

Garden Island

Mrs Macquarie's Point

Mrs Macquarie's Chair

Farm Cove

Royal Botanic Gardens

Andrew "Boy" Charlton Pool

Woolloomooloo Bay

Sydney Tropical Centre

The Domain

Woolloomooloo Wharf

Fleet Base

POTTS POINT

Elizabeth Bay

Art Gallery of New South Wales

The

Domain

COWPER WHARF ROAD

LINCOLN CRESCENT

WOOLLOOMOOLOO

VICTORIA STREET

MACLEAY STREET

Elizabeth Bay House

Beare Park

ELIZABETH BAY

GREENKNOWE AVENUE

Fitzroy Gdns

GREENKNOWE AVENUE

St Mary's Cathedral

KINGS CROSS

DARLINGHURST ROAD

WARD AVENUE

ROSLYN GARDENS

WARATAH ST

Rushcutters Bay Park

Rushcutters Bay Park

PALMER STREET

STREET

Kings Cross Station

KINGS CROSS ROAD

RUSHCUTTERS BAY

BAYSWATER ROAD

WILLIAM ST

Australian Museum

CRAIGEND STREET

McLACHLAN AVENUE

EAST SYDNEY

CROWN STREET

BOURKE STREET

DARLINGHURST

Sydney Jewish Museum

VICTORIA STREET

NELD AVENUE

BROWN ST

OXFORD STREET

STREET

TAYLOR SQUARE

STREET

SOUTH DOWLING STREET

BOUNDARY STREET

GLENMORE ROAD

PADDINGTON

OXFORD STREET

Juniper Hall

CROWN STREET

BOURKE STREET

STREET

FLINDERS STREET

Victoria Barracks

Paddington Town Hall

Airport

4

5

Sydney

SYDNEY Curling seductively around its harbour, Sydney has a superb setting. It is one of the world's great cities, with over four million people—more than 20 per cent of the population in its metropolitan area, and still seems in the first flush of youth: enthusiastic, welcoming, vibrant and open to growth and change. Two of its famous landmarks, the Harbour Bridge and Opera House, became icons the day they were completed. Seen from across the water, the new glamorous buildings constructed in the city in the last 30 years add further drama and excitement, while all around the 317km (197 miles) of harbour foreshore, waterfront suburbs of dream homes mingle with the remains of wild bushland.

Sydney, then, is beautiful, almost extravagantly so. There is also a fair measure of what has been called 'the Australian ugliness'. The skyscrapers make no attempt to harmonize with their immediate surroundings; close up, much of the city appears chaotic. Beyond the often charming Victorian suburbs sprawls an almost horizonless sea of red-roofed bungalow suburbs. But the monotony of this urban sprawl is compensated for by magnificent natural surroundings: the heaths and forests of **Ku-ring-gai Chase** and **Royal National Parks**, the high wall of the **Blue Mountains** and the string of beaches along many kilometres of Pacific coastline. The climate, despite a fair amount of rain, gives hot summers and bright winter days that enhance your enjoyment.

EARLY DAYS In January 1788, the climate played no part in Captain Phillip's choice of Port Jackson as a landing place for his motley cargo of convicts. The First Fleet had originally anchored in Botany Bay and it was the first site chosen for the colony. Subsequently it

40

THE FIRST SYDNEYSIDERS
The area around Sydney seems to have been inhabited by three main Aboriginal groups, numbering several thousand people, when the 11 ships of Britain's First Fleet sailed in. Large numbers of Aboriginal carvings survive in the sandstone plateaus to the north and south. The Aborigines' response to the invaders was a mixture of indifference, resentment and curiosity, but they were in no position to resist, and by the early 1800s those who remained in the area had been reduced to drunkenness and begging.

was found that the area around today's Circular Quay had fresh water, which Botany Bay did not. And so the British flag was run up. The name given to the landing place, Sydney Cove (after the British Home Secretary of the time), was soon transferred to the disorderly settlement that grew up around its shore.

As the colony became established, free settlers moved in, and the population of the city increased sharply when gold was found to the west of the Blue Mountains in the 1850s. Handsome villas were built on the outskirts, while in the later years of the 19th century, middle- and working-class suburbs like Balmain and Paddington unrolled their streets of humble cottages and superior terraces over the countryside nearby, leaving areas like The Rocks to a life of drink, vice and violence.

By the time the population of the city had reached the million mark in the late 1920s, Sydney was a confident, swaggering sort of place, where a strong trade union movement helped ensure one of the highest living standards in the world for its members.

UP TO DATE World War II brought the city into abrupt contact with a wider world, which came even closer in the postwar period, when Sydney became the recipient of waves of New Australians, first from devastated Europe and later from Lebanon, Vietnam, China, the Philippines and other Asian countries. Once resolutely Anglo-Celtic, it is now a thoroughly multicultural city.

Sydney is a great tourist destination: Its charms are not hidden away, but put boldly on display; its intriguing history is readily accessible; and it has all the museums, galleries, shops, restaurants and entertainment that you would expect in a metropolis.

PENETRATING THE DEFENCES

One of Sydney's earliest fortifications, on Observatory Hill, was built to protect the colony's Establishment against a possible convict uprising; later, it was potential foreign invaders who became the worry, and by the mid-19th century virtually every promontory had been fortified. In World War II, despite a boom across the harbour's mouth, a Japanese midget submarine crept up as far as Garden Island. Here it launched its torpedoes at the cruiser USS *Chicago*; they missed. Depth-charges dealt with the brave and ingenious submariners; their vessel was recovered and is on display in the Australian War Memorial in Canberra.

41

Many consider Sydney to be 'the best address on earth'

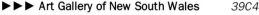

This was the name given to Bondi Beach, and the early days of Australia's exuberant beach culture are celebrated with gusto in the Australian National Maritime Museum. Within living memory, the sands were scoured by inspectors who ensured that no male swimmer went topless. But what emerges from the posters, photos and videos here is the sheer joy Australians have always had in stripping down and letting sea and sun work on their bodies. A serious note is struck by recalling Black Sunday, 6 February 1938, when what was described as an avalanche of waves took five lives in spite of the efforts of 60 lifesavers.

The Australian Museum houses ethnographic displays from all over the world

▶▶▶ Art Gallery of New South Wales 39C4

Art Gallery Road, The Domain (tel: 02-9225 1744 or 02-9225 1790 for recorded information). Open: daily 10–5.
Admission free (varying charges for special exhibitions)
This dignified classical sandstone edifice was opened in 1887 and expanded several times, including major extensions in the 1980s and 2003. Itsgenerous interior houses one of the country's greatest art collection, even though the national collection is at Canberra. It covers the evolution of Australian art up to the present day, and has major sections on Aboriginal, Asian, American and European art; the collection of British 20th-century painting is outstanding. But it is the painters of Australia and their response to the people and places in this strange new land who fascinate; they are all here, from John Glover's Tasmanian landscapes to Grace Cossington Smith's metamorphosis of the Harbour Bridge and Sidney Nolan's interpretation of the Ned Kelly saga.

▶▶▶ Australian Museum 38B3

6 College Street (tel: 02-9320 6000)
Open: daily 9.30–5. Admission: moderate
Australia's largest natural history museum is a lively place, expanded and altered in recent years so that its Victorian architecture almost becomes part of the intriguing displays on earth history, animals, insects and birds, and the life of the sea. Exhibits include human rituals and the evolution of Aboriginal culture over tens of thousands of years. There are also sections on biodiversity, skeletons, birds and Australia's ancient megafauna, as well as the superb Chapman Mineral Collection, showing Australia's extraordinary mineral wealth. There are stuffed animals, shown in context rather than as lifeless specimens, and plenty of 'hands-on' computer displays.

▶▶▶ Australian National
Maritime Museum 38C1

2 Murray Street, Darling Harbour (tel: 02-9298 3777)
Open: daily 9.30–5.
Admission: Galleries free; ships moderate–expensive
Looking more like a ship of the future than a museum, this extraordinary structure has displays of equally extraordinary objects that tell the story of the island continent's intimate relationship with the seas surrounding it.
There are many real vessels in the huge interior of this museum, from Aboriginal canoes to high-tech yachts, but the emphasis is as much on people as on things. There are displays on explorers, convicts, settlers, refugees and other immigrants, on whalers and wharfies who made their living from the sea, on swimmers and surfers who enjoyed it, and on maritime 'neighbours' like the Americans and Japanese. At the dock outside, and at the nearby Maritime Heritage Centre are craft such as the replica of James Cook's *Endeavour*, the 1874 tall ship *James Craig*, a submarine and the destroyer HMAS *Vampire*.

▶ Cadman's Cottage Historic Site 38E3

110 George Street, The Rocks (tel: 02-9247 5033)
Open: Mon–Fri 9.30–4.30, Sat–Sun 10.30–4.30. Admission free
This modest two-floor Georgian house, just 55m (60yd) from the shore, is the city's oldest surviving building, and

is now a museum and the Sydney Harbour National Park information centre. It was erected in 1816, getting its name from the pardoned convict John Cadman who lived in it from 1827 to 1845. A lintel carries the initials GR for King George III in immaculately carved lettering.

▶ Chinatown 38B2

Immigrants from China first arrived as part of the gold rush and took up residence in The Rocks or around Botany Bay. Sydney's Chinese citizens are now scattered around the suburbs, but the city's Chinese heart beats strongest along Dixon Street, behind whose ornamental gateways is an array of exotic goods, food stores and restaurants. A few steps away is the **Chinese Garden of Friendship▶▶**, part of the redevelopment of Darling Harbour. Laid out by landscape architects from Sydney's sister city of Guangzhou in southern China, the gardens are a calm retreat of sensitively designed planting, lakes, bridges and waterfalls, with a traditional tea house overlooking a tranquil lily pond.

▶▶▶ Circular Quay 38D3

Sydney's chief people-watching site is also one of the city's most historic places, since it was here at Sydney Cove that the First Fleet dropped anchor on 26 January 1788. It is still the heart of daily life, with a continuous stream of people pouring out of the railway station, taxis, buses and the busy ferries that bustle in and out of the quays. Trains and traffic roar by overhead, ignored by those with time enough on their hands to stop and listen to the street performers on the broad promenade. Landward are the cliff-like buildings of the city, while towards the water are alluring and ever-changing glimpses of the Harbour Bridge and Opera House. A map on the quayside shows the colony in 1808.

Over 200 years on, Sydney Cove, the First Fleet's landing site, would be unrecognizable to those early pioneers

LOVELY HOMES
Not all Sydney's early houses were as unassuming as Cadman's Cottage, though the first Government House (see page 45) was damp and suffered from inexplicable smells. The aspirations of successful citizens were expressed in such delightful dwellings as Elizabeth Bay House, a splendid 1830s classical mansion in white stucco that turns its back on sleazy nearby Kings Cross (see page 59). Farther to the east is another highly desirable residence, Vaucluse House, whose battlements and verandas were created for the explorer William Charles Wentworth in the 1830s.

DARLING HARBOUR ATTRACTIONS

Apart from the splendid Sydney Aquarium, there are the IMAX Theatre, outdoor entertainments, cruises on the harbour, the many shops of the Harbourside complex, the Cockle Bay Wharf dining precinct, a major convention centre and the Sydney Exhibition Centre, which hosts events like the Motor Show. The vast Saturday and Sunday Paddy's Market is just a step away, as is the King Street Wharf dining strip. The Star City casino complex is also in this region.

UNKNOWN SOLDIER

The Anzac Memorial in Hyde Park was designed by the Sydney architect Bruce Dellit 'to give an impression, not of the glory of war, but of its tragedy and horror'. It is a masterpiece of its kind. The external sculptures depicting the different branches of the services (including nursing) are by British-born Rayner Hoff. Inside, the dramatic central figure of the dead soldier can only be observed properly by bowing one's head. The vault above is pierced by 120,000 stars, each one representing a World War I volunteer.

▶▶▶ Darling Harbour   38D1

The deep inlet on the western side of the city was called Cockle Bay by the early colonists. Like so many docklands of its kind around the world, it eventually lost its commercial functions but is now enjoying a vigorous new lease of life in tourism, with major exhibition and entertainment facilities.

The Harbour is an exciting place, an extraordinary medley of old and new, defined to the east by glittering office towers, with expanses of water and paving framing some of the city's most stimulating new buildings. The parkland at the southern end seems none the worse for its overhead expressways, while the whole area is linked to the heart of Sydney by a controversial monorail that glides over Pyrmont Bridge, the oldest swing bridge of its kind in the world.

For details on attractions in the area other than the Australian National Maritime Museum (covered on page 42), see panel.

▶▶ The Domain   39D4

The Domain extends inland from Mrs. Macquarie's Point to the large green space fringed by fig trees that serves as one of the city's most important parks. This is where orators challenge their audiences along the lines of London's Speaker's Corner, where joggers jog and office workers eat their sandwiches.

Open-air opera and classical music concerts are also held here, particularly during the January Sydney Festival. The Domain has, however, suffered from the incursions of the Cahill Expressway, the Eastern Suburbs Railway and from the construction of an underground parking garage.

▶ Garrison Church   38E2

Millers Point

Hacked through the central ridge of The Rocks area, **Argyle Cut** was one of the colony's early engineering feats. It leads to **Argyle Place**, which has been frequently described as Sydney's sole village green, though not many village greens benefit from such close proximity to a multiple-lane expressway (the Harbour Bridge approach). Nevertheless, it is a pleasant enough place, lined with attractive mid-19th-century cottages. Holy Trinity Church, near the entrance to the Cut, was given the name Garrison Church because of its use by the redcoats manning Dawes Point Battery. Built from the stone quarried from the Cut, its squat appearance isn't helped by its lack of a spire, but it has a spacious interior and some of the city's finest stained-glass windows.

▶ Hyde Park   38C3

Like its London namesake, this fine park once marked the very edge of town, but today it has become one of those central city oases where people retreat from the heat, fumes and noise of the street. Its avenue of majestic Moreton Bay fig trees is particularly fine, and there is a splendid imitation-baroque fountain, but the park's highlight is undoubtedly the **Anzac Memorial**▶▶ (see panel). This solemn but sumptuous essay in art deco forms the focal point of the Anzac Day (25 April) march.

▶▶ Hyde Park Barracks Museum   *38C3*

Queens Square, Macquarie Street (tel: 02-8239 2311)
Open: daily 9.30–5. Admission: inexpensive
This splendid three-floored edifice is one of the city's finest classical buildings. Standing in dignified seclusion behind its grand gates, it was designed for Governor Macquarie by the brilliant ex-convict Francis Greenway, whose architectural skills transformed Sydney. It provided accommodation for up to 1,000 convicts, who until then had had to find their own lodgings. It is now a museum of social history, with excellent displays on the colony's early history and its former inmates' lifestyle.

▶▶ Museum of Contemporary Art   *38D3*

140 George Street, The Rocks (tel: 02-9245 2456.
Open: daily 10–5. Admission free (varying charges for special exhibitions)
This rather forbidding-looking building used to be the offices of the Maritime Services Board. Designed at the end of the art deco period, it is an incongruous setting for the country's major collection of contemporary art.

▶▶ Museum of Sydney   *38D3*

Phillip and Bridge streets (tel: 02-9251 5988)
Open: daily 9.30–5. Admission: inexpensive
Built on the site of the first Government House, this museum offers a portrayal of life in colonial Sydney. Using state-of-the-art technology, the museum takes you on a journey of discovery, from the story of the local Aborigines to the Sydney of the 19th century. One of the museum's highlights is outside in the forecourt. The 'Edge of the Trees' sculpture consists of poles, some of which 'speak', representing Sydney's original inhabitants and the early settlers.

OBSERVATORY HILL AND SYDNEY OBSERVATORY
With commanding views over the harbour, Millers Point was the site of a citadel, a windmill and then an observatory. The latter survives, established in 1858 to survey the hitherto unknown southern skies, and functioned until 1982. With its time-ball tower and domes, the observatory building has now been renovated as a museum of astronomy with plenty of intriguing hands-on features.

Sydney Observatory, a colonial building constructed from the local sandstone

One of the great privileges of life in Sydney is excellent access to the beaches of the Harbour and the Pacific Ocean. Astonishingly, until the beginning of the 20th century, swimming during daylight hours was prohibited by 'decency laws'. Then, finally, the flamboyant editor of a Manly newspaper strolled fully clad into the surf in the middle of the day, defying the prosecution that, in fact, was never made.

CHECK BEFORE YOU SWIM
Few big cities are entirely free of water pollution problems, and some of Sydney's beaches occasionally suffer contamination by storm water. Measures are taken to remedy the situation, and conditions can be checked locally.

THE HARBOUR BEACHES
These hardly compare with those on the ocean, but there are plenty of good spots for picnicking and sunbathing. On the south shore at Vaucluse are Nielsen Park and Parsley Bay; the north shore has beaches around Manly, as well as Mosman's Obelisk and Balmoral.

Surfers and surfboat crews make good use of Sydney's beaches

To the north, **Manly** is the city's shore resort *par excellence*, '7 miles from Sydney, but a thousand miles from care'. Lined with shops, take-away stands, cafés and pubs, a broad concourse called The Corso channels you from the ferry landing to the curving sandy beach with its double line of Norfolk pines facing the ocean. It was here, in 1915, that the art of surfing was born in Australia, and a big surf competition is held here every year. Manly has many other attractions, including the Oceanworld aquarium and the fascinating old Quarantine Station, once used to protect Sydney from contagious diseases, but now open for tours on most days.

World-famous **Bondi**, to the south, has another magnificent beach, stretching between two headlands, though its setting of cafés, pubs and apartment buildings has a tacky look about it. Bondi is suburban and popular, once connected to the city by a famous tramway whose cars would make the final descent to the beach at breakneck speed, giving rise to the expression 'to shoot through like a Bondi tram'.

Eighteen other beaches, equally fine if less famous, stretch north from Manly up the Warringah Peninsula to delightful Palm Beach. Some, like Narrabeen, are urban in character, while others, like Freshwater and Whale beaches, are still largely undeveloped. A string of beaches runs south from Bondi, ending at Cronulla, which is accessible by suburban train.

▶▶▶ Powerhouse Museum   38A2

500 Harris Street, Ultimo (tel: 02-9217 0111 or 02-9217 0444 for recorded information)
Open: daily 10–5. Admission: moderate
The cavernous boiler halls and other generous interior spaces of the old power station and tram depot on the edge of Darling Harbour are now home to the vast collections of Sydney's Museum of Applied Arts and Sciences, one of Australia's largest museums. The array of objects is quite astonishing. The decorative arts are strongly represented, as is social history, with stimulating displays on the life of the local Aborigines, traditional women's work and brewing. There are hands-on exhibits as well as audiovisual presentations, sound effects and holograms.

▶▶ Queen Victoria Building   38C2

George Street
This many-domed, late-Victorian shopping gallery, occupying an entire city block, was completed in 1898; more recently a thorough renovation has restored all of its original features. With its many levels, stained glass and mosaics, it is a cathedral to conspicuous consumption.

▶▶▶ The Rocks   38D2

Named after the sandstone peninsula ending in Dawes Point, this is the site of Australia's first European settlement. For many years, it had a reputation as a place of brawling, hard drinking, whoring and villainy, but this murky past does no harm whatsoever to The Rocks' present status as a tourist mecca (see panel). In fact, the area has long since been tamed, first by wholesale demolition of many of its unsanitary dwellings after the outbreak of bubonic plague in 1900, and then by another swath of destruction preceding construction of the Harbour Bridge.

▶▶▶ Royal Botanic Gardens   39D4

Mrs. Macquaries Road, The Domain (tel: 02-9231 8125 or 02-9231 8111). Open: daily 7–dusk.
Admission: Gardens free, Tropical Centre inexpensive
These luxuriantly planted 30-hectare (74-acre) gardens are the perfect counterpoint to the high-rise buildings and bustle of the city. They benefit enormously from their proximity to the harbour, looking on to the long curving promenade of Farm Cove, which is set between twin promontories, one crowned by the Opera House and the other by Mrs. Macquarie's Point. Once the site of the first government farm, the gardens contain a visitor centre, a restaurant, the National Herbarium (with more than a million plant specimens), a fernery under a slatted steel dome and the **Sydney Tropical Centre▶▶** which shelters tropical plants from many countries.

▶ State Parliament House   38C3

Macquarie Street (tel: 02-9230 3444)
Open: Mon–Fri 9.30–4. Admission free
Like the nearby Mint building, the home of the New South Wales legislature was once part of the 'Rum' Hospital that was built in 1816. The Legislative Council Chamber is a prefabricated iron structure, sent out from England to serve as a goldfields church. State Parliament House is open to the public, even when in session.

The highly entertaining Powerhouse Museum is one of the best places for kids to visit

47

THE ROCKS TODAY
The area is now a place to wander at leisure and enjoy the almost medieval atmosphere, quite absent elsewhere in Australia. You may wish to start your visit at the informative Sydney Visitor Centre, in The Rocks Centre (corner of Argyle and Playfair streets). The Rocks Discovery Museum (Kendall Lane) is also worth a visit.

Sydney

The Sydney Harbour Bridge, completed in 1932, still functions as a major link between north and south

►►► Sydney Harbour Bridge 38E3

Not just a symbol of Sydney but of Australia itself, the Harbour Bridge leaps in a great arch between its granite pylons to span the narrows between Dawes Point and Milsons Point to the north. Opened in 1932, after almost nine years of complicated construction, the bridge carries eight traffic lanes, a double-track railway, a cycleway and a footpath. Its broad deck is the widest in the world and rises 60m (195ft) above water level (the top of the arch is 134m/440ft up). Since the early 1990s the congestion-prone bridge has been supplemented by the Sydney Harbour Tunnel, which passes beneath the harbour.

►►► Sydney Opera House 38E3

Bennelong Point (tel: tours 02-9250 7250, box office 02-9250 7777).
Open: tours daily 9–5, performances most days
Admission: tours moderate–expensive

Once the site of a ramshackle tram terminus, since 1973 Bennelong Point has been crowned by this building, which is the inspired creation of Danish architect Joern Utzon, born in 1918 and educated at the Royal Danish Academy. The construction of this world-famous landmark was plagued by both technical and political problems, leading Utzon to resign from the project before the building's completion. The complex curving shapes of the exterior are spectacular and have been compared to billowing sails, shells or the hoods of nuns' habits. The elegant, soaring roofs are covered in over a million Swedish ceramic tiles. The interior houses the auditorium of the opera and four other performance spaces, including a concert hall and three theatres, plus restaurants, bars, gift shops and a library. Outside are large-scale steps and a promenade around the point. A variety of guided tours of the interior is available on most days.

Harbourside and history

See map on pages 38–39.

This 5km (3-mile) walk from Circular Quay gives magnificent views, leads through the splendid botanic gardens and then returns to Circular Quay past many fine early buildings.

The landward approach to the **Opera House** may lack some of the drama of the waterside approach but is still impressive, past modern apartments, hotels and cafés, then up gigantically scaled flights of steps. The fine trees of the **Royal Botanic Gardens** and Government House sweep down to the path leading around Farm Cove to the promontory of Mrs. Macquarie's Point, a popular harbourside viewpoint. Do not miss the Botanic Gardens Tropical Centre with its 'Arc' and 'Pyramid' greenhouses.

The bridge leading to the **Art Gallery of New South Wales,** over the Cahill Expressway, has good views over the city and east suburbs. Macquarie Street leads northwards, bounded to the west by mostly modern structures, and to the east by a sequence of fine historic buildings. Bridge Street penetrates westward, with modern buildings vying with the old. Macquarie Place makes a green interlude before you reach the **Customs House** (dating from 1885), opposite Circular Quay. This beautifully renovated building is now the home of shops, cafés, bars, a public library and exhibition spaces.

Darling Harbour and the heart of Sydney

See map on pages 38–39.

This walk takes you through built-up streets to the revitalized Darling Harbour and back through Hyde Park.

From Martin Place Station, walk to Martin Place, Strand Arcade and Pitt Street Mall, pedestrian-friendly in their different ways. As you cross Pyrmont Bridge look up to see the monorail—a costly and unpopular initiative—and back to enjoy the city skyline.

An amazing array of new and varied facilities clusters around **Darling Harbour**. A rest in the **Chinese Garden** could precede the final leg of this walk: Cross Dixon Street leading to **Chinatown**, then up into **Hyde Park**, with its splendid avenues of fig trees and the imposing **Anzac Memorial**, from where a visit to the nearby **Australian Museum** is recommended.

The Chinese Garden, designed by landscape architects from China

Sydney

WHERE TO STAY?

In many ways, it's an advantage to be right in the city centre, but Sydney's suburbs offer some excellent alternatives. Kings Cross has a wide range of hotels and price brackets, and is just one train stop from the city. You can stay on the beach at Bondi, Coogee and Manly, and the inner east suburb of Double Bay offers sophisticated surroundings, albeit at a price.

The London Hotel in downtown Balmain

Accommodation

There is a tremendous variety of accommodation in the Sydney area, though the city is not renowned for being cheap, except in the area of backpacker-style lodges. Hotels range from first-rate, like the super Park Hyatt or The Observatory, to modest, and there are also serviced apartments, motels, hostels, campsites and bed-and-breakfast accommodation. An important factor is location, since there are places that are somewhat remote unless you have a car, and others whose distance from the sights is compensated for by good public transportation links. Advance reservation is advisable for peak holiday periods like Christmas and the January school holidays.

Hotels The city has an excellent range of first-class hotels, as do a number of inner suburbs like Manly, Kings Cross and Double Bay. Whatever your price bracket, Manly is worth considering for its vacation atmosphere and its link to the city—by conventional ferry in 30 minutes or in about half that time by JetCat. The heart of town also has medium-priced and budget hotels, with a particular concentration around the Central Railway Station; Kings Cross also has a variety of such places, many of them in streets of relative tranquillity.

Budget Kings Cross is a backpacker's paradise, with many lodges in Victoria Street. The scene here is in constant flux, so it is wise to check at the time whether a particular establishment is for you. Demand is often heavy, and it might be a good idea to start your tour of inspection early in the day. There is another cluster of accommodation at Bondi and Coogee—intriguing temporary addresses! The emphasis here is on affordable lodgings, with plenty of places offering rooms with cooking facilities. Bed-and-breakfast establishments are scattered all over the city, and you can get details from a number of agencies (see also Hotels and Restaurants on pages 268–281). Again, accessibility is a key factor. Camping sites are a long way out of the city.

Food and drink

Eating out Even more so than in the rest of Australia, eating in Sydney has been revolutionized in recent years, largely because of the huge influx of immigrants. *The Sydney Morning Herald's Good Food Guide* covers no fewer than 35 categories of cuisine, beginning with African and ending with Vietnamese. New restaurants continue to open, ingredients are good and chefs are increasingly skilled, particularly in the popular, internationally acclaimed style of cooking known as 'Modern Australian', a fusion of culinary styles and ingredients. Prices are generally reasonable. The better restaurants often offer a fixed-price lunchtime menu at a considerable saving. Prices are kept even lower because of the Bring Your Own phenomenon (this, though primarily a feature of cheaper, unlicensed restaurants, is sometimes available at licensed establishments). Remember that a small corkage charge may be made. The highest prices are reserved for restaurants that offer something extra, like a harbourside setting or a panoramic view.

Ethnic restaurants These are scattered all over the city, though there are concentrations in particular districts that have been settled by different nationalities. Thus **Greek** restaurants cluster around Elizabeth and Liverpool streets, **Chinese** restaurants are found in Chinatown, **Italian** in Leichhardt and Newtown, and **Vietnamese** in the southwestern suburb of Cabramatta. Restaurants of different kinds keep company in certain parts of town, along Darlinghurst's Oxford and Victoria streets, in Kings Cross, or to the west of the city, along Glebe Point Road, in King Street, Newtown, or Darling Street, Balmain. Manly and Bondi have many restaurants, cafés and take-away facilities.

Drink There is no shortage of places to drink in Sydney. The basic 'hotel' or pub is still much in evidence, while others have been renovated and offer a more varied experience, which might well extend to food and entertainment. Further up the scale of sophistication are the many hotel and cocktail bars; the locally famous **Marble Bar** can be found at the Hilton hotel.

Sydney's excellent brasseries and bistros are deservedly popular

EXCLUSIVE EATING
Given Sydney's extensive shoreline, there are plenty of expensive restaurants with harbour-side settings, from The Rocks to Watsons Bay near South Head. The most stunning view is from the two restaurants on top of Sydney Tower.

REFRESHMENTS
Sydney has plenty of cafés offering excellent Italian-style coffee. Visitors may also be pleasantly surprised at the quality of food and refreshments available at the various museums and galleries.

Sydney

Queen Victoria Building: shopping in historic surroundings

THE ROCKS MARKET
A visit to The Rocks on a Saturday or Sunday has the added bonus of the lively market, held in Upper George Street. In addition to the 150 or so stalls that sell jewellery, homewares and unusual gifts, you'll find free entertainment and a carnival atmosphere.

DUTY FREE
Duty- and tax-free merchandise is available to those with an international air ticket, with substantial discounts on electrical goods, jewellery and watches, liquor and perfume. Outlets in the city are sometimes even cheaper than those at the airport.

Shopping

Sydney's CBD (Central Business District) has all the temptations a shopper might reasonably expect in a metropolitan city. There are department stores like **David Jones** and elegant 19th-century galleries like the **Strand Arcade**, or its modern equivalent, the shopping complex inserted into the lower floors of an office block. With its 200 boutiques and cafés on several levels, the immaculately restored **Queen Victoria Building** (see page 47) is a visitor attraction in its own right.

Souvenir hunting Souvenirs are plentiful in places where tourists congregate. Faced with the problem of what to bring home from Australia (apart from the inevitable stuffed koala or kangaroo, often made in China), you might consider a stylish Akubra hat or tough outdoor clothing to go with it, like a bush shirt or an oilskin coat. Sheepskin products, opals or surfing gear are other possibilities. Australians are great readers, and bookstores are well-stocked with a good range of Australiana, albeit quite expensive, while newsagents sell an incredible range of periodicals catering to every taste.

For maps, a visit to the **Travel Bookshop** (175 Liverpool Street) or **Dymocks** (424 George Street) will be helpful. Aboriginal objects of varying quality—paintings, carvings, boomerangs, fabrics and didgeridoos (a large wooden wind instrument)—are widely available, but are better bought from a specialist shop than from a souvenir stall. Try the souvenir shops run by the museums and galleries; the **Australian Museum's** stuffed platypus actually looks like the real thing!

Markets Outside the heart of the city, the more vibrant suburbs such as Paddington and Newtown are good places to browse, while Sydney's markets offer a memorable shopping experience. Usually held on a Saturday or Sunday, they take place in The Rocks, Bondi Beach, Balmain, Glebe, Manly and in Paddington. The famous **Sydney's Paddy's Markets** in the Chinatown area is good for fresh produce, and the vast and lively **Sydney Fish Market** at Pyrmont is a daily spectacle worth watching.

Nightlife

Concerts and theatre With several auditoriums, the **Opera House** is a major site for classical concerts, ballet and drama. Classical music can also be heard at the **Town Hall** and, performed by student musicians, at the **Conservatorium of Music**. Some 20 theatres give you a choice of musicals, mainstream or alternative plays in a variety of locations, some—like the **Wharf Theatre** (near The Rocks) or **Ensemble Theatre** (on the north shore)—in an attractive waterside setting. A visit to the beautifully restored 1928 **Capitol Theatre** in the Haymarket area is highly recommended. The exciting **Sydney Dance Company** and the **Aboriginal and Islander Dance Theatre** appear at various venues.

Film The city's cinemas show the latest blockbusters, and there are a number of houses specializing in second runs and foreign films in Paddington (Palace Academy) as well as in the heart of town (the Dendy and Palace Verona cinemas). The **State Theatre**, with its extravagant decoration, is the home of the city's June Film Festival.

Music Sydney has a lively jazz scene; the best venue is the long-running **Basement**, near Circular Quay. Rock is also well represented, with mammoth concerts held in the **Entertainment Centre**. Discos, cabarets and nightclubs abound, catering to all tastes and pockets. There are probably more gays in Sydney than in the rest of Australia put together, with the bars, clubs and pubs of Darlinghurst's Oxford Street the main focus of the gay scene.

INFORMATION
The wealth of distractions available in this exhilarating city is detailed in the Thursday *Sydney Live Magazine* from the *Daily Telegraph*, and the Friday edition of *The Sydney Morning Herald*, while various free publications also provide comprehensive entertainment listings.

STAR CITY
Sydney's first, temporary, casino opened in the mid-1990s, and has since moved to its permanent site to the west of Darling Harbour. This vast complex includes a hotel and theatre, as well as restaurants, bars, 1,500 poker machines and 200 gaming tables that offer roulette, blackjack, baccarat, Asian games such as pai gow and two-up, a home grown game, which is essentially betting on which way two coins will fall.

The bright lights of Sydney's Star City casino

Sydney

THE SYDNEYPASS

This combined ticket gives unlimited bus (including Sydney Explorer and Bondi Explorer), train and ferry travel for three, five or seven days, and is a bargain well worth thinking about.

TAXIS

Taxis are numerous and can be hailed on the street, picked up at a taxi stand or ordered by telephone. Don't get worried if the driver has to consult his street directory!

SYDNEY METRO LIGHT RAIL

Sydney's newest transportation system re-creates the days of trams. The Light Rail track runs from Central Station to Chinatown, Darling Harbour, the casino and the Sydney Fish Market, then on to the inner west suburbs of Glebe and Leichhardt. At peak times trams run every 10 minutes.

The Metro Monorail

Practical points

Tourist information Contact **Sydney Visitor Centre**, The Rocks Centre, corner Argyle and Playfair streets (tel: 9240 8788; www. sydneyaustralia.com); **Transport Infoline** (tel: 13 1500) for all metropolitan bus, rail and ferry enquiries.

Getting around Probably the best way of familiarizing yourself with the layout of the city is to take a guided bus tour, most of which pick up and drop off at central hotels. Alternatives are the bright red **Sydney Explorer**, which trundles around a 28km (17-mile) circuit of the principal attractions, allowing you to get on and off at will for a set fare, and the blue **Bondi Explorer**, which travels to the harbourside Eastern Suburbs, Bondi, Bronte and Coogee beaches, and Paddington on the same basis.

Buses run a comprehensive scheduled service in both the city and the suburbs. They connect with ferries and trains at Circular Quay and with trains at Wynyard, Town Hall and Central stations. Buses are particularly useful for reaching areas without a rail service, such as the Northern Beaches and Eastern Suburbs.

Ferries travel at frequent intervals between Circular Quay and a number of destinations such as Manly and Taronga Zoo on the north shore, or Balmain and Hunters Hill upriver. There are also daily ferries east to Double Bay, Rose Bay and Watsons Bay, and west to Parramatta.

Double-decker electrified **trains** run on an extensive network of suburban lines (including to the airport) as well as on a City Circle line linking a number of stations in the CBD such as Town Hall, Central Station and Circular Quay. There's a useful spur from Central Station and Town Hall to Kings Cross and Bondi Junction (continue by bus to the beach). The line to North Sydney includes a trip over the Harbour Bridge. A novelty is the overhead **Metro Monorail**, which runs between the southwestern part of central Sydney and Darling Harbour.

What Captain Cook named Port Jackson and Captain Phillip called 'the finest harbour in the world' is still alive with freighters, ferries and pleasure craft. The glorious stretch of water forming the harbour is Sydney, the reason for the city's existence, the source of its distinct identity and special renown.

One of the world's largest harbours Sydney Harbour has a complex outline of inlets, tributary rivers, bays, coves and promontories, so that many city residents have some sight of the water from where they live, though competition is fierce and prices astronomical for those dwellings that enjoy the best views. Much of the 317km (197 miles) of shoreline has been preserved as reserves or national park land. Added interest is given by an array of islands, including Fort Denison, where the skeletons of the executed once swung, and Goat Island with its old shipyards west of the Harbour Bridge.

How to explore Undoubtedly, the best way to explore the harbour would be an unhurried cruise, taking all day, on a friend's yacht! Water taxis would do the same kind of job, albeit expensively. The variety of commercial cruises are a more realistic choice. But perhaps the most authentic way, enjoyed every day by many city commuters, is the ferry. Now that the tramcar has all but vanished from the streets, the ferry is the city's only remaining traditional means of conveyance.

An assortment of vessels plies Sydney Harbour from the central hub of Circular Quay. In a matter of minutes you can slip across the water in the shadow of the Harbour Bridge to Kirribilli, or chug upstream in the afternoon with uniformed schoolchildren returning to their pleasant suburban homes on the promontory of Hunters Hill. Or you could take the 50-minute journey by RiverCat upriver, via Sydney Olympic Park, to the historic city of Parramatta, where you can see some of Australia's very first buildings (see page 61).

The magnificent harbour and its twin symbols of Sydney, and Australia

A STROLL AROUND THE ROCKS
The Museum of Contemporary Art contrasts with Cadman's Cottage of 1816 and the other old buildings in well-restored George Street. Old and new come together around Campbells Cove, while Dawes Point Park, crouching at the feet of the Harbour Bridge, was the first fortified position in Australia. The way back is via the high-level Gloucester Walk and Argyle Street.

Sydney

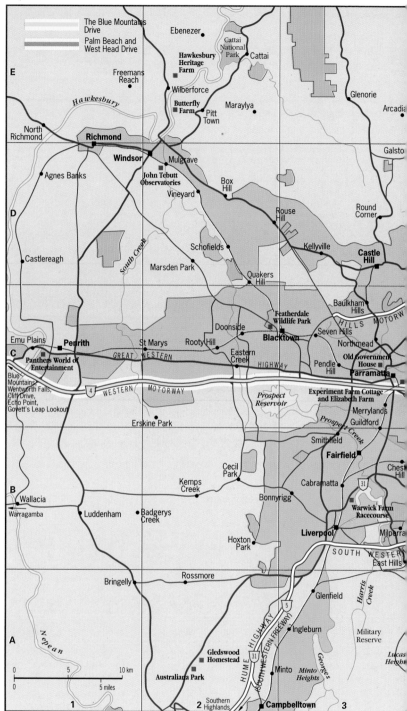

The Blue Mountains Drive
Palm Beach and West Head Drive

Ebenezer

Cattai National Park

Cattai

Hawkesbury Heritage Farm

E

Freemans Reach

Wilberforce

Glenorie

Arcadia

Butterfly Farm

Pitt Town

Maraylya

Hawkesbury

North Richmond

Richmond

Galsto

Windsor

Mulgrave

John Tebutt Observatories

Box Hill

D

Agnes Banks

Vineyard

Rouse Hill

Round Corner

South Creek

Schofields

Kellyville

Castle Hill

Castlereagh

Marsden Park

Quakers Hill

Baulkham Hills

HILLS MOTORW

Doonside

Featherdale Wildlife Park

Seven Hills

Northmead

Emu Plains

Penrith

St Marys

Rooty Hill

Blacktown

Old Government House

Panthers World of Entertainment

GREAT WESTERN

Eastern Creek

HIGHWAY

Pendle Hill

Parramatta

C

Blue Mountains, Wentworth Falls, Cliff Drive, Echo Point, Govett's Leap Lookout

4 WESTERN MOTORWAY

Experiment Farm Cottage and Elizabeth Farm

Merrylands

Guildford

Erskine Park

Prospect Reservoir

Prospect Creek

Smithfield

Cecil Park

Fairfield

Ches Hill

Kemps Creek

Cabramatta

31

B

Wallacia

Bonnyrigg

Warragamba

Luddenham

Badgerys Creek

Warwick Farm Racecourse

Hoxton Park

Liverpool

Milperra

SOUTH WESTER

East Hills

Bringelly

Rossmore

Glenfield

Harris Creek

5

Ingleburn

Military Reserve

A

Nepean

Lucas Heights

Gledswood Homestead

Georges

Minto

Minto Heights

Australiana Park

HUME HIGHWAY

31

(SOUTH WESTERN FREEWAY)

Campbelltown

Southern Highlands

0   5   10 km

0   5 miles

1   2   3

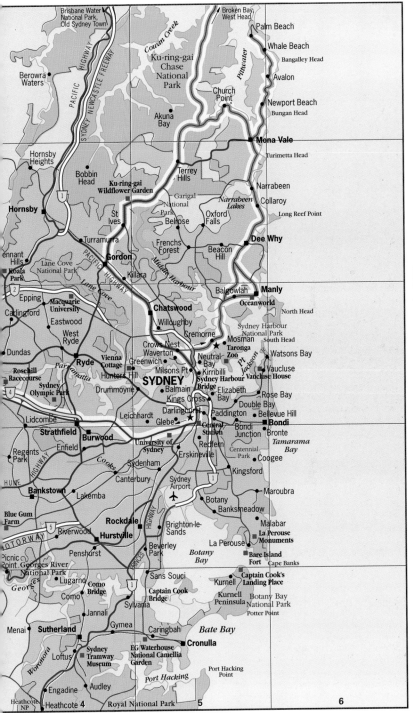

Brisbane Water National Park, Old Sydney Town

Broken Bay, West Head

Palm Beach

Whale Beach

Bangalley Head

Avalon

Cowan Creek

Ku-ring-gai Chase National Park

Church Point

Newport Beach

Bungan Head

Berowra Waters

Mona Vale

Turimetta Head

Hornsby Heights

Bobbin Head

Terrey Hills

Narrabeen

Collaroy

Long Reef Point

Hornsby

Ku-ring-gai Wildflower Garden

St Ives

Garigal National Park

Narrabeen Lakes

Oxford Falls

Belrose

Turramurra

Frenchs Forest

Beacon Hill

Dee Why

Gordon

Killara

Balgowlah

Manly

ennant Hills

Lane Cove National Park

Oceanworld

North Head

Koala Park

Macquarie University

Chatswood

Willoughby

Cremorne

Sydney Harbour National Park

South Head

Epping

Carlingford

Eastwood

West Ryde

Crows Nest

Mosman

Taronga Zoo

Watsons Bay

Dundas

Vienna Cottage

Greenwich

Neutral Bay

Pt Jackson

Vaucluse

Vaucluse House

Ryde

Hunters Hill

Milsons Pt

Kirribilli

Rosehill Racecourse

Sydney Olympic Park

Drummoyne

Balmain

SYDNEY

Sydney Harbour Bridge

Elizabeth Bay

Rose Bay

Double Bay

Bellevue Hill

Lidcombe

Leichhardt

Glebe

Kings Cross

Darlinghurst

Paddington

Strathfield

Burwood

Enfield

University of Sydney

Central Station

Redfern

Bondi Junction

Bondi

Bronte

Regents Park

Sydenham

Erskineville

Centennial Park

Tamarama Bay

Bankstown

Lakemba

Canterbury

Coogee

Sydney Airport

Kingsford

Blue Gum Farm

Rockdale

Botany

Banksmeadow

Maroubra

Riverwood

Hurstville

Brighton-le-Sands

Malabar

Penshurst

Beverley Park

La Perouse

La Perouse Monuments

Bare Island Fort

Cape Banks

Picnic Point Georges River National Park

Lugarno

Como Bridge

Sans Souci

Botany Bay

Kurnell

Captain Cook's Landing Place

Como

Captain Cook Bridge

Sylvania

Kurnell Peninsula

Botany Bay National Park

Potter Point

Jannali

Menai

Sutherland

Gymea

Caringbah

Bate Bay

Cronulla

Loftus

Sydney Tramway Museum

EG Waterhouse National Camellia Garden

Port Hacking Point

Engadine

Audley

Port Hacking

Heathcote NP

Heathcote

Royal National Park

the plain past Penrith to begin the climb up into the mountains, running parallel to the railway. Several places of interest are marked by signs off the freeway; **Wentworth Falls** are probably the grandest waterfalls in the region. Pretty little Leura marks the start of the **Cliff Drive**, which skirts the 300m (985-ft) drop into the valley below. **Echo Point** is, deservedly, the most famous viewpoint in the mountains. Not far from the visitor centre, viewing platforms offer panoramas over cliffs, eucalyptus forest and the Three Sisters sandstone columns. There are designated walks from here, or you can ride the Scenic Railway, Scenic Flyway or Skyway cable car farther along the Cliff Drive.

Stops can be made at **Katoomba**, 'capital' of the Blue Mountains, and northeast of Blackheath at the Blue Mountains Heritage Centre. **Govett's Leap Lookout** offers amazing views of the canyon.

Return on the Western Motorway, via Parramatta and Homebush Bay, where you will see the main venue for the 2000 Olympics—**Sydney Olympic Park**. The International Aquatic Centre and some of the other sporting facilities are open to the public, and informative bus and walking tours of the site and its venues are available.

The famous Three Sisters pillars

The Blue Mountains

See map on pages 56–57.

The spectacular cliffs, canyons and forests of the World Heritage-listed Blue Mountains can be seen in a day.

The fastest exit from Sydney is via Parramatta Road, which connects to the Western Motorway (M4) near Strathfield. The route then crosses

Palm Beach and West Head

This drive goes from Sydney to the splendid Northern Beaches and headlands. *See map on pages 56–57.*

Beyond the Harbour Bridge, Route 10 (Military Road) leads northeastward, crossing Middle Harbour by the Spit Bridge. A detour can be made to **Manly** (better visited by ferry from Circular Quay), or continue northward past the fine beaches of Long Reef, Collaroy, Narrabeen and Whale Beach.

The road narrows and winds as it approaches **Palm Beach**. To the west are fine views over the Pittwater inlet, a contrast to the crashing surf of the ocean beach to the east. On its headland to the north is the **Barrenjoey Lighthouse**. Return to Mona Vale and follow the road around the southern end of Pittwater, turning right through the greenery of the **Ku-ring-gai Chase National Park** to **West Head**.

The head offers a different but equally spectacular view over Pittwater and Broken Bay. There are well-marked trails through this section of the national park, and it is a short walk to see bushland, Aboriginal paintings and, perhaps, wildlife. Return via Mona Vale Road (Route 3) and the Pacific Highway.

The suburbs

There is a great deal to see and do in the various historic inner suburbs of the city.

The red-light district of **Kings Cross**▶ has its fair share of hookers, strip joints and adult bookshops. But there are also lots of places to eat and drink and plenty of shops for the local community. A stroll along Darlinghurst Road between Kings Cross Station and Fitzroy Gardens with its El Alamein Fountain is entertaining day or night. The genteel suburb of Elizabeth Bay next door holds a contrasting attraction—1830s **Elizabeth Bay House**▶. This elegant mansion, built for the NSW Colonial Secretary, is a reminder of the area's 19th-century opulence.

Built in the heady days of the Victorian-era gold rush, then proletarian and now gentrified **Paddington**▶▶, or 'Paddo', has had a varied career as it has passed in and out of popularity. Its glory is its delicious terraced houses with their fine ironwork and their subtle adaptation to the contours of the slopes falling northward towards the harbour. Built between the 1860s and 1890s, most have been carefully restored. Also here are **Juniper Hall** (1824), the **post office** (1885) and **Paddington Town Hall** (1891). Opened to mark Sydney's 100th birthday, **Centennial Park** supports a varied birdlife as well as offering many outdoor activities.

The whole population of **Balmain**▶▶ used to work in its shipyards, but its delightful terraces and little detached timber cottages have been colonized by a middle-class population generally more left-leaning and artistically inclined than Paddington's inhabitants.

Hunters Hill▶ is a tranquil place of expensive, fine stone houses and humbler cottages. Many of the former were built in French style in the 1850s. One of the 19th-century tradesmen's abodes, **Vienna Cottage**, has been restored by the National Trust and houses a local museum.

SYDNEY JEWISH MUSEUM

A short stroll from Kings Cross brings a very different experience. The excellent Sydney Jewish Museum (on the corner of Darlinghurst Road and Burton Street, Darlinghurst) traces Australia's Jewish connections, from the First Fleet convicts to post-World War II arrivals, and serves as a poignant memorial to the millions of Jewish people who perished in the Holocaust.

EASTERN SUBURBS

Sydney's Eastern Suburbs contain the country's most desirable and expensive real estate and at Double Bay it shows, with plenty of designer labels and a discreet lack of price tags in its exclusive shops. There are lots of pleasant cafés too, where shoppers can be seen relaxing after making their choices.

See how the other half lives in exclusive Hunters Hill

UP THE HAWKESBURY

The area around Richmond and Windsor along the upper reaches of the Hawkesbury River was settled within a few years of the arrival of the First Fleet. The winding lower river is best explored in a leisurely way; a unique experience is to board the mail boat at Brooklyn and accompany the letters, packages and much more on their journey to isolated little places along the tranquil river.

THE LOSS OF LA PEROUSE

Jean-François de Galaup, Comte de La Perouse, had brushed with the British before their meeting in Botany Bay with Captain Phillip. He was taken prisoner after the battle of Quiberon Bay in 1759 and later fought in the American wars. His ships *Astrolabe* and *Boussole* had reached Australia after a long search for the elusive Northwest Passage. On quitting Botany Bay, La Perouse disappeared forever, though wreckage assumed to be that of his ships was discovered off the New Hebrides in 1826.

Captain Cook's landing place memorial

Excursions

The easy-to-reach sights from Sydney are covered alphabetically on these two pages.

Broad **Botany Bay▶** (11km/7 miles south of the city), where Captain Cook's *Endeavour* dropped anchor on the 28 April 1770, was given its name in recognition of the array of Antipodean plants collected here by Joseph Banks. Oil installations, industry and the airport now dominate the scene, but to commemorate Cook's historic landing on the Kurnell Peninsula, the national park contains monuments, a visitor centre and a museum. At the northern edge of the bay, La Perouse, named after the commander of the French expedition that arrived just after the First Fleet, is the site of a museum and one of Sydney's principal Aboriginal settlements.

Starting just 75km (46 miles) north of the city, the **Central Coast▶** provides a natural playground for Sydney residents; although so close, this region of surf and uncrowded sandy beaches, bushland and forest, waterways and national parks, is a very different world. There are few man-made attractions here, but the Australian Reptile Park, with its native fauna and fascinating snake venom milking, is well worth a visit.

With splendid coastal and river scenery, Brisbane Water National Park resembles Ku-ring-gai Chase, its sandstone foundation supporting the same spectacular range of flowers and wildlife. There are woodlands of eucalyptus and pockets of rain forest, and Aboriginal carvings can be viewed at the Bulgandry site.

A visit to Parramatta, by road (see page 61) or RiverCat, can easily encompass a tour of **Sydney Olympic Park▶▶** at Homebush Bay (see page 58).

Ku-ring-gai Chase National Park▶▶ (30km/19 miles north of Sydney) remains in its wild state thanks to its designation as a national park as far back as 1894. The rugged sandstone plateau is deeply incised by the deep sheltered waterways of the Hawkesbury River. From West Head there are spectacular views across Broken Bay and the broad expanse of Pittwater. The Ku-ring-gai (Guringai) Aborigines who once lived here traced many carvings in the sandstone. There is a visitor centre at Bobbin Head, with interesting displays on the area's varied animal and bird populations.

At the tip of the Warringah Peninsula, 40km (25 miles) north of the city, lies the exclusive residential area of **Palm Beach▶▶**. To the east, the ocean surf crashes on the beach, and to the west, the tranquil surface of the beautiful **Pittwater▶** inlet is a windsurfer's paradise. The lighthouse on Barrenjoey headland offers a terrific view over Broken Bay and inland up the drowned valley of the Hawkesbury River.

A room inside 1835 Experiment Farm Cottage, Parramatta

Parramatta▶▶ was founded only a matter of months after Sydney itself, because of the fertility of the surrounding area. Now the focal point of the sprawling western suburbs 24km (15 miles) from the city, it has been redeveloped, although traces remain of early days, including some of the nation's very first buildings.

Beyond the mock-Tudor gatehouse to Parramatta Park stands Australia's most venerable public edifice, **Old Government House**, which was built in 1799 though much expanded early in the 19th century. For many years the official Vice-Regal residence, it contains early Australian furniture. **Elizabeth Farm** in Alice Street is even older, begun in 1793 by the agricultural pioneers John and Elizabeth Macarthur. Its veranda is the prototype of countless others that adorn dwellings all over Australia. It too has been refurnished in the style of that period, as has the interior of **Experiment Farm Cottage** in Ruse Street. The land on which this house stands belonged to one of the few convicts with any farming experience; in 1789, James Ruse was the first man in Australia to sow a crop of wheat successfully.

Australia's first national park, proclaimed in 1879, the **Royal National Park**▶▶ consists mostly of a rugged sandstone plateau with a varied vegetation of heathland (which has a brilliant show of wildflowers in spring), fine forests of blue gum and patches of rain forest. Eaten into by the sea, the park has a coastline of spectacular cliffs interspersed with sandy coves. About 35km (22 miles) from Sydney, it has long been popular with serious bushwalkers, and is now *the* place to go for weekend outings of all kinds.

Reached by ferry from Circular Quay, the splendid **Taronga Zoo**▶▶ benefits from its superb site almost directly opposite the city and is worth visiting for the view alone, particularly if you take the cable-car ride. Taronga doesn't limit itself to native animals, but it is the Australian fauna that most visitors want to see.

THE ROAD TO PARRAMATTA
A road was built from Sydney to Parramatta as early as 1794, but for years it was easier to bring people and goods up the river than along the highway. Partly super-seded by an expressway, today's Parramatta Road is neither lovely nor efficient, though a trip along it reveals a cross-section of Australian suburbia. In spite of inter-minable traffic lights and shabby shopping malls, there remains something indefinably romantic - about it, a whiff of the days when it alone pointed to the interior of the unknown continent.

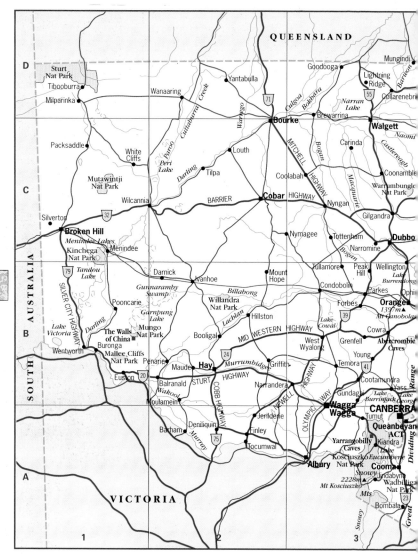

QUEENSLAND

Mungindi

Goodooga
Lightning
Ridge
Yantabulla
Collarenebri
Wanaaring
71
Narran
Lake
Bourke
Brewarrina
Walgett
Sturt
Nat Park
Tibooburra
Milparinka
55
Naomi
Carinda
Castlereagh
Packsaddle
White
Cliffs
Louth
Coolabah
Coonamble
Peri
Lake
Tilpa
Warrumbungle
Nat Park
Mutawintji
Nat Park
Darling
Cobar
HIGHWAY
Nyngan
Gilgandra
Wilcannia
BARRIER
HIGHWAY
Silverton
32
Nymagee
Tottenham
Dubbo
Broken Hill
Narromine
Menindee Lakes
Kinchega
Nat Park
Menindee
Tullamore
Peak
Hill
Wellington
Lake
Burrendong
Darnick
79
Tandou
Lake
Ivanhoe
Mount
Hope
Condobolin
Parkes
Ophi
Gunnaramby
Swamp
Billabong
Willandra
Nat Park
Forbes
Orange
1397 m
Mt Canobolas
Pooncarie
Garnpung
Lake
Lachlan
Hillston
Lake
Cowal
Lake
Victoria
Mungo
Nat Park
MID WESTERN HIGHWAY
West
Wyalong
Grenfell
Cowra
Abercrombie
Caves
The Walls
of China
Booligal
Wentworth
Buronga
Mallee Cliffs
Nat Park
Penarie
24
Young
Temora
41
Maude
Hay
Murrumbidgee
Griffith
Cootamundra
Yass
Euston
20
STURT
HIGHWAY
Narrandera
Lake
Burrinjuck
Lake
George
Balranald
Wakool
Moulamein
COBB HIGHWAY
Gundagai
Wagga
Wagga
CANBERRA
Deniliquin
Jerilderie
Finley
NEWELL
OLYMPIC
WAY
Tumut
Queanbeyan
ACT
Barham
Tocumwal
75
Yarrangobilly
Caves
Kiandra
Lake
Eucumbene
Kosciuszko
Nat Park
Coma
Snowy
Albury
2228 m
Mt Kosciuszko
Jindabyne
Wadbilliga
Nat Park
Snowy
Mts
23
Bombala
Great
Dividing
Range
VICTORIA

Murray

SILVER CITY HIGHWAY
SOUTH AUSTRALIA

MITCHELL HIGHWAY
Bogan
Macquarie
Bogan

Culgoa Bokhara
Warrego
Paroo
Cuttaburra Creek
Bardoon

D
C
B
A
1
2
3

*Sunset on Black
Mountain, Canberra,
capped by the Telstra
Tower*

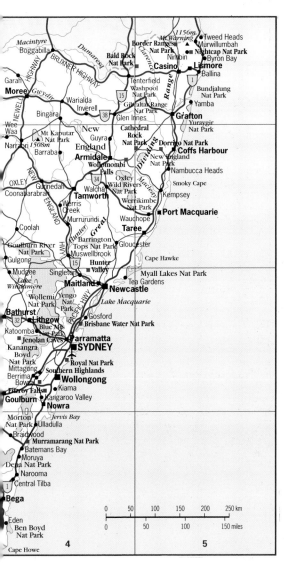

Macintyre
Boggabilla
BRUXNER HIGHWAY
Macintyre
Dumaresq
1156m
Mt Warning ▲ Tweed Heads
Border Ranges Murwillumbah
Nat Park ● ■ Nightcap Nat Park
Nimbin ● Byron Bay
Bald Rock Casino Lismore
Nat Park ● Ballina
Tenterfield
Garah
Moree Gwydir
Warialda
Inverell
Bingara
Washpool
Nat Park 1
Bundjalung
Nat Park
Gibralter Range Yamba
Nat Park
Glen Innes Grafton
Yuraygir
Nat Park
Wee
Waa
Mt Kaputar New Cathedral
Narrabri 1508m Nat Park England Rock
Barraba Nat Park Dorrigo Nat Park
Armidale Coffs Harbour
Wollomombi New England
Falls Nat Park
Oxley Nambucca Heads
OXLEY Wild Rivers
Gunnedah Walcha Nat Park Smoky Cape
Coonabarabran Tamworth Kempsey
Werris Werrikimbe
Creek Nat Park Port Macquarie
Coolah Murrurundi Wauchope
Taree
Barrington
Goulburn River Tops Nat Park Gloucester
Nat Park Muswellbrook Cape Hawke
Gulgong Hunter
Mudgee Singleton Valley Myall Lakes Nat Park
Lake Maitland Tea Gardens
Windamere Newcastle
Wollemi Yengo
Nat Park Nat Lake Macquarie
Bathurst Park
Lithgow Gosford
Katoomba Blue Mts Brisbane Water Nat Park
Jenolan Caves Parramatta
Kanangra SYDNEY
Boyd
Nat Park Royal Nat Park
Mittagong Southern Highlands
Berrima Kiama
Bowral Wollongong
Fitzroy Falls
Goulburn Kangaroo Valley
Nowra
Morton Jervis Bay
Nat Park Ulladulla
Braidwood
Murramarang Nat Park
Batemans Bay
Moruya
Deua Nat Park
Narooma
Central Tilba
Bega

0 50 100 150 200 250 km
0 50 100 150 miles

Eden
Ben Boyd
Nat Park
Cape Howe

4   5

NEW SOUTH WALES This state *was* Australia in the early days of European settlement. Today, with almost 6.8 million citizens, it is still the country's most populous state, and its capital, Sydney, is the country's greatest city. If time is short, some travel planners advise visitors to concentrate on this state alone; a holiday spent entirely within New South Wales' far-flung borders can be very rewarding for both urban pleasures and the delights of wild nature.

THE COASTAL LOWLANDS The 'Premier State' can be divided into four regions, which encompass many facets of the Australian experience. Most of the population lives in the Coastal Lowlands, a fertile strip of country of varying width running some 1,400km (870 miles) from Victoria to Queensland. Apart from glamorous Sydney,

New South Wales and the ACT

▶▶▶ REGION HIGHLIGHTS

**Australian War Memorial,
Canberra** *page 68*

**Blue Mountains National
Park** *page 72*

Kosciuszko National Park
pages 74 and 83

**National Museum of
Australia, Canberra**
page 69

**Parliament House,
Canberra** *page 70*

The Three Sisters
page 73

WHAT'S IN A NAME?
Between 1768 when he
set out for Tahiti, and
1779 when he was killed
on a Hawaiian beach,
Captain Cook probably
named more places than
anyone else in history.
Some recall people (Port
Jackson), some are a
lively evocation of events
(Cape Tribulation, where
Cook's ship was holed by
a reef), some character-
ize a quirk of topography
(Mount Dromedary in
Tasmania has two
humps). Inspiration
seems to have failed him
when confronted with the
task of finding a suitable
name for the whole of the
eastern coast of
Australia, even given the
supposed resemblance of
part of it to the coastline
of southern Wales. But
perhaps New South
Wales, as a name, is one
up on such masterpieces
of inventiveness as South
Australia.

the region is home to the beachside industrial cities of
Newcastle and **Wollongong,** as well as a glorious chain of
little ports and shore settlements like Ulladulla (directly
east of Canberra). White Australia's history began here,
when Captain Cook's charts led the First Fleet to Botany
Bay, and where, after a shaky start, the process of colonization gradually got under way with the founding of
townships and the clearing of the bush for farmland.

The area has also been the focus of much of the country's
modern history, its industrial heartland and stronghold of
the Labor movement that has played an often decisive
role in Australian government and politics. It is here that
the foundation was laid for Australian beach culture, as
love of the sun, surf and sheer physical well-being over-
came the remnants of Victorian prudery in the early
decades of the 20th century, a process that owed much to
the incomparable beaches, which are still one of the state's
main tourist attractions.

THE GREAT DIVIDING RANGE In places, the Great
Dividing Range drops almost directly into the sea. It
provides a constant backdrop to the coast, with its hill
peaks and tablelands also running the length of the state.
Despite their low altitude, the forested hills remained an
impregnable barrier to exploration until 1813, when the
spectacular **Blue Mountains** were successfully crossed for
the first time.

The highlands are as wonderfully varied as the coast: To
the south, in the Snowy Mountains, they include the
country's highest peaks and most extensive snowfields; to
the north lies the high-level plateau of New England,
named after the old country for its misty coolness and
vivid green. In places, as in the **Southern Highlands,** the

ranges are interspersed with broad plains that were converted early on into attractive farmland. Here there is a wealth of old buildings in town and country, as well as a 2,500sq km (965-sq-mile) tract carved out of the state to form the Australian Capital Territory (ACT), the site of the nation's capital, Canberra.

Most of the rivers of southeastern Australia have their source in the uplands, with their relatively abundant rain and snowfall. Some, like the Hawkesbury and Hunter, are quite short, running east to the Pacific; others, much longer, form part of the huge Murray/Darling system, flowing slowly westwards.

THE WESTERN SLOPES Beyond the mountains and tablelands, the Western Slopes fall gradually towards the interior. Settled in the early 1800s, the area today consists mostly of unspectacular wheat and wool country, and there are several substantial towns and even small cities in this region such as Moree, Dubbo, Orange, Wellington, Bathurst and Wagga Wagga. To the south, in the Riverina, the waters of the Murray and Murrumbidgee have been used to create huge irrigated areas that now support a variety of crops.

THE WESTERN PLAINS This area stretches to the borders with South Australia and Queensland. It is the New South Wales Outback, with vastly more sheep than people. Here the township of **Bourke** has given its name ('back of Bourke') to utter remoteness, the Outback beyond the Outback. In the harsh landscape, the city of **Broken Hill** has grown up based on the world's richest lode of silver, lead and zinc; it is a place that attracts many visitors for its sheer strangeness.

CLINGING TO THE COAST
Between them, the cities of Sydney, Newcastle and Wollongong are home to over 5 million people, a very large proportion of the state's 6.78 million. The remainder of the population lives mostly in coastal towns, far from the inhospitable interior.

Attractive Canberra, a modern planned city that is like nowhere else in Australia

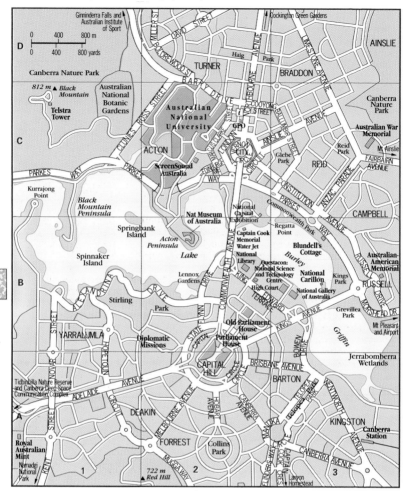

Canberra

The home of foreign embassies

Australia's capital comprises the prestigious buildings that house the nation's central institutions, all in a setting of broad boulevards and intimate districts and framed by glorious mountain scenery. As well as being the country's only major inland city, Canberra is unique in having been planned in every detail from the start.

At the time of Federation, in 1901, the dispute between Sydney and Melbourne about which should become the capital was finally resolved by choosing neither. Instead, the new Constitution stipulated that a site should be found in New South Wales, no closer than 160km (100 miles) to Sydney. After much debate the present location was chosen, and in 1911 some 2,500sq km (965sq miles) of land south of Goulburn Plains became the Australian Capital Territory. Over 130 hopefuls took part in the international competition for the design of the new city, the American landscape architect Walter Burley Griffin, a pupil of Frank Lloyd Wright, emerging as winner.

Griffin had never seen Canberra when he drew up his plans for a new city thousands of kilometres from his Chicago base, but his experience enabled him to interpret maps and diagrams, and to appreciate the potential of the chosen location. His design is very much of his period, a combination of great vistas framing noble buildings, and self-contained residential districts.

The target population for the country's capital was 25,000, but Canberra's growth was painfully slow and this total was only reached in the years following World War II. Growth took off in the 1960s, and today the city is home to over 320,000 people. Around 40 per cent of its workforce consists of public employees, not necessarily a sound basis for a satisfactory social balance. In its infancy and adolescence, the city was seen as a place of exile, populated by bored civil servants longing for the fleshpots of Sydney or Melbourne. Nor is its contemporary image among Australians a particularly happy one; many think of it as a privileged place of parasitic politicians and cosseted bureaucrats. In recent years, though, Canberra's dining, entertainment and nightlife scene has become far more lively than it used to be.

The city of Canberra has been described with some truth as a collection of suburbs in search of a city, but what it lacks in urbanity it more than makes up for with easy access to national parks, wildlife, wineries, sheer spacious beauty and convenience (there are no gridlocks!). It certainly is nothing like any other city in Australia and is well worth visiting for that reason alone, with an array of splendid modern buildings in the immaculately landscaped setting planned for them in the early years of the nation's foundation.

The extraordinary Parliament House (completed in 1988) is rich in national symbolism

67

The 81m (265-ft) flagpole on top of Parliament House and Capital Hill

An Aussie 'digger' (soldier) runs up the flag outside the Australian War Memorial

▶▶ Australian National Botanic Gardens   66C1

Clunies Ross Street, Acton (tel: 02-6250 9540)
Open: daily 8.30–5 (later in Jan–Feb). Admission free

These attractive gardens on the lower slopes of Black Mountain present a wonderful range of native Australian plants—over 7,000 species in all. A network of paths leads through a series of contrasting environments, each with its fully labelled array of trees, shrubs and other plants. This is *the* place to appreciate Australia's flora.

▶▶▶ Australian War Memorial   66C3

Treloar Crescent, Campbell (tel: 02-6243 4211)
Open: daily 10–5. Admission free

The dome of the War Memorial stares somberly from the lower slopes of Mount Ainslie, down Anzac Parade towards Capital Hill on the far shore of Lake Burley Griffin. With its great courtyard containing the Roll of Honour and the Eternal Flame, it was opened in 1941 and redeveloped and expanded in 1998–2001. It is not just a great monument, but a world-class museum that attempts to make some sense of the senselessness of war. Beyond the carefully crafted symbolism of the exterior are extensive galleries and displays evoking the many conflicts in which the country has been involved, from the Maori Wars of the 1860s to 1970s Vietnam. As well as the hardware of war, such as guns and planes, there are superb paintings, photographs, huge dioramas, film and sound recordings, and documents and papers.

▶ Diplomatic Missions   66B2

A fascinating Canberra tour is to the suburb of Yarralumla, where many foreign countries have built their embassies. National self-expression takes a variety of forms: The American embassy is a handsome, Williamsburg-style edifice, Greece's has classical columns, that of Papua New Guinea has an exuberantly gabled longhouse, and Indonesia has a Balinese temple.

▶▶ Lake Burley Griffin   66B2

Burley Griffin included a beautiful lake in his plan for the new city, but it was not until 1964 that the great body of water bearing his name came into being, with an area of more than 704ha (1,740 acres) and a varied shoreline 35km (22 miles) long. A number of islands enliven the scene, which is further enhanced by lakeside landscaping, as in **Commonwealth Park**. The **Captain Cook Memorial Jet▶** waterspout reaches 140m (460ft) in calm weather.

Dating from 1860, **Blundell's Cottage▶** near the lakeshore is one of the few old buildings in Canberra. Rising over the weeping willows on Aspen Island are the crisp white concrete shafts of the **National Carillon**, a gift from Britain to mark Canberra's 50th anniversary in 1963. Its 53 bells play Australian melodies as well as hymns and popular songs. Designed to be the focal point of this city, the lake makes a splendid setting for many of its most prominent buildings; an excursion aboard one of the cruise vessels is a pleasant way to make the most of it.

The slender **Australian-American Memorial**, close to the lake's eastern shore, commemorates the role that American forces played in the defence of Australia during World War II.

▶▶ National Capital Exhibition   66C2

Regatta Point, Commonwealth Park (tel: 02-6257 1068)
Open: daily 9–5 (6 in summer). Admission free
Boasting 'the best view of the national capital', this is the place to appreciate the meticulous and sometimes controversial planning of the city. The exhibition has audiovisual displays, laser map, photographs and objects.

▶▶ National Gallery of Australia   66B3

Parkes Place, Parkes (tel: 02-6240 6502). Open: daily 10–5.
Admission free (varying charges for special exhibitions)
The National Gallery has an excellent array of Australian art, beginning with Aboriginal objects and ending with canvases on which the paint seems hardly dry. There is much else besides, displayed to advantage in well-lit and varied spaces, including a good selection of European and American art as well as works from Asia and the Pacific. Sculpture benefits from the attractive Sculpture Garden, which also serves as a venue for outdoor events.

▶▶▶ National Museum of Australia   66B2

Lawson Crescent, Acton Peninsula (tel: 02-6208 5000). Open:
daily 9–5. Admission free (charges for special exhibitions)
This extensive museum explores the key issues, events and people that have shaped Australia. Focusing on five themes—indigenous peoples, the symbols of Australia, the peopling of the nation, personal stories of ordinary and famous Australians, and the land and its people—the museum uses state-of-the-art technology to express its message. The ultra-modern lakeside building includes cafés, a restaurant and a well-stocked shop.

The National Botanic Gardens are renowned for their splendid collection of Australian native plants

CAPITAL VIEWS
Canberra's ring of uplands provides splendid viewpoints over the carefully planned city in its superb setting. The spike of Telstra Tower rises from the top of Black Mountain (779m/2,555ft), giving panoramic vistas from its viewing galleries. Mount Ainslie (841m/2,760ft) rises through bushland behind the War Memorial and has equally spectacular views, as does Red Hill, which is 2km (1.2 miles) south of Parliament House.

Parliament House, one of Canberra's most popular attractions

CAPITAL COINAGE
As well as a gallery enabling visitors to see the country's money being made, the Royal Australian Mint has a public coining press where you can mint your own coins or tokens.

CAPITAL PUNISHMENT
Justice has moved on in Australia since the early days when the jail was sometimes the most prominent building in town, but modern Australians are second only to Americans in their fondness for litigation. The imposing High Court has an exhibition explaining the workings of the country's legal system.

A SPORTING CAPITAL
Sports fans should not miss a tour of the Australian Institute of Sport (AIS) in the northern suburb of Bruce. The institute, set up in 1980, has top-class facilities and the fascinating Sportex complex with displays and entertaining hands-on exhibits. Tours are conducted by the AIS's élite athletes.

▶▶ Old Parliament House 66B2

King George Terrace, Parkes (tel: 02-6270 8222)
Open: daily 9–5.
Admission: inexpensive
This beautifully renovated 1927 building is now the home of the **National Portrait Gallery**▶, housing a collection of likenesses of famous and lesser-known Australians.

▶▶▶ Parliament House 66B2

Capital Hill (tel: 02-6277 5399).
Open: daily 9–5 (later when Parliament is sitting).
Admission free
Home to the Senate and the House of Representatives, this truly spectacular structure has become a major visitor attraction in its own right, rich in artworks and national symbolism. Over 85,000cu m (3 million cu ft) of soil was removed to make way for the new building, then replaced to form its green roof. This superb viewpoint over the city is topped by an 81m (265-ft) stainless steel flagpole, flying what must be the biggest flag in the world. Inside a complex of beautifully designed internal spaces is adorned with the creations of Australian artists like Arthur Boyd. The 48 marble columns of the foyer recall the country's eucalyptus trees, whose green colour appears again in the chamber of the House of Representatives.

▶▶ Questacon 66B2

King Edward Terrace, Parkes (tel: 02-6270 2800)
Open: daily 9–5.
Admission: moderate
The National Science and Technology Centre has around 200 hands-on displays in six galleries. This informative and interactive centre brings the world of science alive, even to the most non-technical, and is well worth a visit.

▶ ScreenSound Australia 66C2

McCoy Circuit, Acton (tel: 02-6248 2000)
Open: Mon–Fri 9–5, Sat–Sun 10–5. Admission: moderate
Australia was an early leader in the development of the motion picture; exhibits here present an intriguing selection from the nation's contribution to the delights of the silver screen, including a short film of the 1896 Melbourne Cup. Radio, TV and music are also represented.

How to travel

By air A comprehensive network of international and domestic air services operates from Sydney's Kingsford Smith Airport, 11km (7 miles) south of the city. Buses and taxis link the separate domestic and international terminals, as does the Airport Link Railway, which continues to Central Station and several stops in the middle of town. The service takes around 15 minutes to reach the city. There are flights to the NSW Outback and many coastal resorts, to Cooma (for the Snowy Mountains), and to Canberra and all state capitals, including Melbourne, Brisbane and Hobart.

By bus Schedules can be inconvenient to remote townships. On the main routes there is likely to be a choice of operator and times. Many places can be visited by organized bus tours from Sydney. Major cities and some larger towns have a good network of local bus services.

By train NSW has a widespread rail network, and of those towns that have lost their train service, many are connected to a railhead by buses operated by the State Rail Authority (Countrylink). Multiple-unit express trains (XPTs and XPLORERS) ply between many major towns. Interstate trains run to Brisbane and Melbourne, and the legendary *Ghan* now runs from Sydney to Alice Springs and Darwin via Adelaide. Broken Hill is visited by the *Indian Pacific* on its way to and from Western Australia, and has its own weekly XPLORER link to Sydney. The Greater Sydney region is well served by frequent CityRail services, which extend as far as Newcastle and Dungog in the north, the Blue Mountains in the west, Goulburn and the Southern Highlands, and Nowra on the south coast.

By car Driving is not recommended in the Sydney area, unless you are heading out of town to places like Palm Beach or the Royal National Park. Public transport and the taxis are the best option. However, many remote parts of the state are accessible only by car.

SAVE TIME AND FLY
Unless you have plenty of time to spare and are happy to drive, flying to the more distant parts of the state is highly recommended. Regional Express (Rex), along with Qantas and its subsidiaries cover most major NSW destinations.

A LONG WAY BY CAR
New South Wales is crisscrossed by a web of named highways, very helpful in planning an itinerary, though they tend to be of variable quality. Driving the Pacific Highway north along the coast can get tedious, and many prefer the inland and more scenic New England Highway.

71

Renting a 4WD makes sense if you plan to go off road

One of the grand old buildings in the pleasant city of Bathurst

THE WAY TO THE WEST
Just visible from Sydney, the dark escarpment of the Blue Mountains, which rises abruptly (the highest point, near Mount Victoria, is 1,069m/ 3507ft) from the Sydney plains, blocked the way westward to the early colonists. Some convict escapees were convinced that China lay just beyond the mountains as they headed towards what they hoped would be freedom. The puzzle of how to cross the mountains, by keeping to the ridges rather than to the valleys, was solved by Blaxland, Lawson and Wentworth in 1813, and within two years Governor Macquarie had a road built by a convict workforce on the route still followed by the modern road and railway. This marked a great leap forward in the development of the colony, promising an opening up of the immense potential of the then unknown interior.

▶▶ **Armidale**   *63C4*
Unofficial capital of the cool uplands of New England in the northeast of the state, Armidale is the nearest thing Australia has to a university city. There are a number of higher education colleges and several private schools as well as the University of New England in its parkland campus. A couple of cathedrals, plus a number of venerable public buildings and delightful old houses further enhance the refined atmosphere. The modern **New England Regional Art Museum**▶ has a reputation as the best provincial collection of Australian art, and there is a Folk Museum housed in a building dating from 1863.

Armidale is the ideal base for exploring this part of New England (whose Scottish settlers tried and failed to make the name New Caledonia stick); within easy reach are a number of spectacular waterfalls, including the highest in Australia, **Wollomombi Falls**▶ in the World Heritage-listed Oxley Wild Rivers National Park.

▶ **Batemans Bay**   *63A4*
This fishing port and popular tourist resort on the estuary of the Clyde River is the closest ocean beach to Canberra, only 149km (92 miles) away over the mountains. There are fine oysters and lobsters, and a penguin colony on the Tollgate Islands Nature Reserve.

▶▶ **Bathurst**   *63B4*
At the end of the Great Western Highway from Sydney, Bathurst was founded by Governor Macquarie in 1815, making it the country's oldest inland settlement. It was the point of departure for many expeditions farther into the interior, and in 1851 this area was the scene of Australia's first gold rush. Those days are re-created in the open-air museum called **Bathurst Goldfields**▶, and the town itself is full of interest. The scenic drive around Mount Panorama forms part of what is considered to be Australia's finest motor-racing circuit.

▶▶▶ **Blue Mountains National Park**   *63B4*
Sheer cliffs dropping into deep canyons and glorious eucalyptus forests make up some of the most spectacular landscapes to be seen in Australia. The grandeur of this World Heritage-listed natural scene is all the more impressive because of the proximity of the manicured residential and retirement areas clustered along the main road and railway from Sydney, 90 minutes away.

The Blue Mountains are not really mountains, but a vast sandstone tableland, deeply incised by watercourses like the Nepean and Cox's rivers. However, they really are blue; a vaporous emanation from the leaves of the eucalypts hangs in the air as a haze. Since the early part of the 20th century the mountains have attracted serious bushwalkers as well as sightseers, and they offer all kinds of pleasures today, from antique hunting in sophisticated little townships, to real escape into wild country. The following main sights could just about be seen in the course of a day-trip from Sydney, but it would be far better to stay at least a couple of days.

A good place to start is at the excellent **National Parks and Wildlife Service's Heritage Centre**▶▶, 2km (1.2 miles) to the east of the main highway at Blackheath. A

73

Dramatic sandstone cliffs and densely forested valleys around Katoomba in the Blue Mountains

short distance away is one of the most spectacular lookouts in the whole national park, **Govett's Leap**▶▶, with views of the Grose Valley and Bridal Veil Falls. A panoramic walk leads along the clifftop to other vantage points, while a steep track (for experienced hikers) descends into the forest of blue gums far below.

The other great viewpoint in the park is **Echo Point**▶▶, just to the south of **Katoomba**, the 'capital' of the municipality known as City of the Blue Mountains. Here there is another visitor centre whose glass wall looks straight out into the treetops, while projecting platforms give giddy views of the famous sandstone pillars of **The Three Sisters**▶▶▶. A number of popular walks fringe the clifftop or descend into the valley. Just to the west are three exciting forms of transport; the Scenic Railway, an inclined plane dropping steeply into the valley bottom; and the much newer Scenic Flyway and Skyway cable cars.

To the east are the famous **Wentworth Falls**▶, the highest in the area with a drop of 270m (885ft); nearby Faulconbridge is the home of the **Norman Lindsay Gallery and Museum**▶, which commemorates this well-known artist and writer. The charming village of **Leura**▶▶ has historic houses, antiques and craft shops, cafés and the National Trust-listed **Everglades Gardens**▶. Westward are the truly spectacular **Jenolan Caves**▶▶ and the late-Victorian guest house associated with them, while one of the country's great feats of railway engineering, the **Zig Zag Railway**▶ (see panel) can be experienced first-hand at Clarence, near Lithgow.

THE GREAT ZIG ZAG
In 1866, the engineers building the railway line to the west were faced with the problem of how to lower it from the top of the Blue Mountains down the sheer cliff face into Lithgow. Their solution was to construct a line in the form of a letter Z down the cliff face, with reversing stations at two points. This was replaced by the present main line, which takes a long way round but eliminates the need for reversing. The Zig Zag has been restored as a tourist railway, an impressive spectacle as powerful engines haul their coaches up the steep slope.

New South Wales

74

Wentworth Falls lookout in the Blue Mountains

WORLD HERITAGE SITES
Four of the World Heritage sites in Australia lie within New South Wales. The most accessible are the Greater Blue Mountains Area and the lush rain forests of Dorrigo National Park, inland from Coffs Harbour. The others are Lord Howe Island, out in the Pacific, and the Willandra Lakes region, in the state's far southwest.

NOT JUST PARKS
The NSW National Parks and Wildlife Service manages a number of sites whose interest is primarily human, rather than natural. These include places like Mutawintji Historic Site, with its wealth of mysterious Aboriginal relics, and sites of significance in the early European settlement of the country like Captain Cook's Landing Place at Botany Bay. Sydney's oldest dwelling, Cadman's Cottage, is a National Parks and Wildlife Service information centre.

National parks

New South Wales, with its long coastline, mountains and extensive Outback, has wonderful examples of many of the continent's characteristic natural landscapes.

In the far west On the fringes of Australia's Red Centre and well over 1,000km (620 miles) from Sydney are two superb arid wildernesses. In **Sturt National Park** summer temperatures can reach 50°C (122°F) for days on end; grassy plains alternate with claypans and pebbly desert from which rise flat-topped *mesas* (rocky tableland). In the extreme west are the ruddy sand dunes of the Strzelecki Desert. **Kinchega National Park** has vast plains of red sand as well as the strange saucer-shaped overflow lakes of the Darling River. Both areas are home to emus and large red kangaroos.

To the east The land gradually rises through the western slopes of the Great Dividing Range to the range itself, the backbone of the state. On the border with Victoria is one of the world's great national parks, focused on Australia's highest peak, 2,228m (7,310-ft) **Mount Kosciuszko**, after which the park itself is named. Glacial lakes, wild heathlands, alpine flowers and glorious forests of snow gums make a superb setting for summer hiking, while the area is at its most popular in winter, during the ski season, from early June to early October each year. The forested highlands that extend from near Newcastle through New England to the Queensland border have a rich vegetation that includes much undisturbed rain forest; here over 50 separate parks and reserves have been grouped together to form one of Australia's World Heritage areas, the **Central Eastern Rainforest Reserves**. Old volcanoes give rise to dramatic landforms here and at **Warrumbungle National Park** farther inland, a weird world of rocky crags and natural skyscrapers. **Bald Rock National Park**, near the Queensland border in the far north, is another extraordinary landform, a great granite dome rising 200m (655ft) out of the bush.

WHAT TO SEE 'OUT BACK'
From Broken Hill you can travel to many Outback locations. Lying within the relatively small distance of 290km (180 miles) are the opal-mining village of White Cliffs and Mutawintji National Park, Kinchega National Park and the Menindee Lakes, and Wilcannia, a quiet Darling River town with a large Aboriginal population.

75

▶ Bourke   62C2

This Outback town 776km (482 miles) northwest of Sydney seems utterly remote. It is the middle of a vast and semi-arid area supporting large numbers of sheep and cattle as well as some crops on land irrigated with water from the Darling River. Originally a wooden stockade built in 1835 against Aboriginal attack and then a major inland port, Bourke has a number of buildings dating from the latter part of the 19th century. Its main attraction, however, lies in its usefulness as a base for penetrating farther into the New South Wales Outback.

▶▶ Broken Hill   62C1

Founded on a 6.5km (4-mile) lode of silver, lead and zinc, the richest of its kind in the world, the unique 'Silver City' is still a thriving mining town, with metals extracted in large quantities despite low world prices for its products.

BROKEN HILL PROPRIETARY COMPANY
BHP, now known as BHP Billiton since its merger with Billiton, one of the world's leading mining companies, had its roots in Charles Rasp's discovery in 1883 of the immensely rich silver, lead and zinc lode at Broken Hill. It is now Australia's largest company, having long since diversified into iron and coal, gas and oil, and steel-making. Its profits are taken by many as an index of the prosperity of the country as a whole.

Thanks to the water that is piped in from its recreational reservoir at Lake Menindee 108km (67 miles) away, Broken Hill is a surprisingly green and leafy spot in what is one of Australia's harshest environments: bitterly cold in winter, intolerably hot in summer, with a negligible rainfall that is only a tiny fraction of the evaporation rate. Nearly dead from thirst, the explorer Sturt gave the hump-backed ridge its name in 1844, but it was not until the 1880s that a German-born boundary rider, Charles Rasp, founded the Broken Hill Proprietary Company (see panel), which exploited the underground wealth in uneasy partnership with the workforce for many years. A great strike of 1919 ended in a historic compromise; the companies were ensured their profits and the workers granted conditions far in advance of the time, such as a 35-hour week. A confederation of workers unions effectively ran the town, not always on what today would be regarded as progressive lines.

Broken Hill has always been a long way from the government in Sydney, and its ties are closer to South Australia, with smelters at Port Pirie, union beaches at Adelaide, clocks that keep South Australian time—half an hour behind that of Sydney—and a South Australian region telephone prefix code.

Continued on page 78.

Born the son of a farm worker at Marston in Yorkshire in 1728, James Cook became the greatest explorer of his age. He was educated at the expense of his father's generous-minded employer, then learned seamanship aboard a Whitby coal vessel. In 1755, he joined the Royal Navy, where he refined his navigational and other skills in the course of the Seven Years' War. His charts of the St. Lawrence River helped Wolfe in the conquest of Quebec. The achievement for which Cook is best remembered is his voyage of exploration along the previously unknown east coast of Australia in 1770.

76

AHEAD OF HIS TIME
Cook was well in advance of his time in seeing beyond his own culture and background to the deeper harmony of the Aborigines' way of life. He wrote: 'they are...wholy (sic) unacquainted...with the superfluous...Conveniences so much sought after in Europe...the Earth and sea of their own accord furnishes them with all things necessary for life.'

1770: Cook takes possession of NSW for Britain...

As Cook had documented an eclipse of the sun off the coast of Newfoundland, he was a natural choice when the Royal Society wished for an accurate observation to be made from Tahiti of the transit of Venus across the face of the sun. Accompanying him on this mission aboard the barque *Endeavour* was an astronomer, Charles Green, together with two eminent botanists, Daniel Solander and the young Joseph Banks, who was only 25 years of age.

East coast sighting On 3 July 1769, the transit of Venus was duly observed and Cook opened the sealed orders given him by the Admiralty. These instructed him to investigate the existence or otherwise of a great southern continent and to survey and take possession of New Zealand. Having completed a thorough exploration of the New Zealand coast, Cook decided to return via the hypothetical 'East Coast of New Holland'. This was sighted on 19 April 1770, when Cape Everard in Victoria, originally called Point Hicks after Cook's sharp-eyed second in command, came into view.

Sailing northward along the coast, Cook found a convenient harbour where the ship could drop anchor

CAPTAIN COOK'S LANDING PLACE

and he and his men could investigate local conditions. The crew feasted on fresh fish, and the delighted botanists discovered an extraordinary array of plants, birds and animals previously unknown to science. In deference to their serious purpose, Cook altered his original name for the anchorage, Stingray Harbour, to Botany Bay.

Grounded on the Barrier Reef Farther north, Cook noted the existence of what seemed to be a fine natural harbour and named it Port Jackson. The wonderful setting for the future city of Sydney had to await full discovery until the arrival of the First Fleet 18 years later. Feeling his way into 'the labyrinth of coral islands, shoals, rocks and lee shores' of the Barrier Reef, even Cook with his superb seamanship couldn't fend off a grounding, and the *Endeavour* struck a reef.

Although the crew re-floated the vessel at high tide by jettisoning some of its equipment (including a cannon that is now in the Australian National Maritime Museum in Sydney), the barque needed repairs and was beached for a month near today's Cooktown at the base of Cape York. Once more the scientists had a field day, making their first acquaintance with kangaroos and turtles. When the *Endeavour* was seaworthy again, Cook sailed north to the tip of the cape where, on Possession Island, he hoisted the flag and formally declared the whole of eastern Australia to be British, giving it the unremarkable name of New South Wales.

The end of the road Promoted to captain, Cook went on between 1772 and 1775 to become the first to sail within the Antarctic Circle, finally putting paid to the idea of the great southern continent. In the course of an attempt in 1779 to find the elusive northern passage between the Atlantic and Pacific, he landed on Hawaii. As he was mediating in a relatively trivial dispute with the islanders, one of his men stupidly discharged his firearm; enraged, the islanders fell upon Cook, who had turned his back on them to restore order, and he collapsed beneath blows from clubs and daggers.

BANKS THE BOTANIST
Australia's 73 species of *Banksia* commemorate Joseph Banks, the wealthy botanist who sailed with Cook and who has been described as 'the father of Australian botany'. On the voyage out he listed 230 plant species at Madeira, 316 at Rio, 104 at Tierra del Fuego and 400 in New Zealand. Later, Banks was president of the Royal Society for 32 years.

...having made his mark in Botany Bay

Guess what grows at this Coffs Harbour plantation!

SILVER SCREEN SILVERTON

About 25km (15 miles) west of Broken Hill is the ghost town of Silverton, whose population moved to the bigger town when mining became unprofitable in the late 1880s. With its restored buildings seeming to typify the spirit of the Outback, it has taken on a new lease of life as a stage set for a number of films, including *A Town Like Alice* and one in the *Mad Max* series.

OUR BANANA'S THE BIGGEST

The improbably oversized fruit known as the Big Banana dominates the scene on the Pacific Highway just to the north of Coffs Harbour. Made of concrete it marks the entrance to a banana plantation and entertainment complex. Here you can see bananas growing, eat bananas in every imaginable form, buy banana-shaped souvenirs, and find out everything you always wanted to know about bananas but never dared to ask.

Continued from page 75.

Protected from dust storms by extensive tree belts, Broken Hill is laid out on a grid of streets with names like Chloride, Mica and Cobalt. The excellent Visitor Information Centre is close to the old Sulphide Street Station, now a mineral and train museum. **The GeoCentre**▶▶ is an interactive earth sciences museum, but it's more exciting to go down a former mine, like Delprat's Mine or Daydream Mine. The town is also a base for the **Royal Flying Doctor Service**▶ and the **School of the Air**▶, both of which are open to the public. The strange environment of the city and its surroundings seems to have acted as a stimulant to a number of artists, and there is a sculpture reserve and several galleries, of which the best known is that run by Pro Hart.

▶▶ Byron Bay   63D5

Cape Byron is the easternmost point of the Australian mainland, capped with a powerful lighthouse. Byron Bay itself, with wonderful beaches and a gloriously scenic hinterland of forests and mountains, has been a focal point of alternative lifestyles since the late 1960s. A major attraction here is the town's lively dining, shopping and nightlife scene, as well as adventure activities such as sea kayaking and hang-gliding. The beaches on either side of the headland vary in character, from secluded coves to great stretches of sand. Surfing is well established; the first lifesaving club was founded here as early as 1907.

▶ Cobar   62C2

This copper-mining town on the fringe of the Outback straddles the Barrier Highway on its way west to Broken Hill. Founded in the early 1870s as a typical mining city of tents and huts, it soon reached its peak population of some 10,000. Among the buildings that date from the town's early days are the Great Western Hotel with its extraordinarily long veranda and the mining company's office, now the **Cobar Outback Heritage Centre**▶. After a long decline, the place prospered again in the 1960s.

► Cockington Green Gardens, ACT   *off 66D3*

Gold Creek Village, 11 Gold Creek Road, Nicholls
(tel: 1800 627 273 or 02-6230 2273)
Open: daily 9.30–5 (last entry at 4.15). Admission: moderate
The original Cockington in the southwest of England, a
picture-postcard village with thatched cottages, a pub,
a forge and other items of rusticity, is reproduced on the
outskirts of Canberra in miniature form. A new display
has buildings from around the world, including scale
models from South Africa, Ireland and Germany.

►► Coffs Harbour   *63C5*

Roughly halfway between Sydney and Brisbane, this old
timber port is famous for its beaches and banana plantations (see panel on page 78). A string of fine beaches runs
northward from the town's Park Beach, some with good
surf. There is rafting on nearby rivers, while man-made
attractions include the Pet Porpoise Pool, with seals,
sharks and penguins, as well as amiable dolphins. The
harbour is protected by a headland to the south, and by
Muttonbird Island, named after the species of burrowing sea birds that nest there. The town, with its **Historical
Museum►** and **North Coast Regional Botanic
Garden►►**, is some distance inland.

► Dubbo   *62C3*

At the junction of the Newell and Mitchell Highways,
Dubbo is the flourishing hub for a large part of
NSW's Central West area. First settled in the 1840s, it
became a stopping point for those in search of 'better
land, further out'. Overlanders driving their cattle
southward to the markets of SA and Victoria used to
cross the Macquarie River near here. There are a number
of fine old buildings in the town, among them the old
jail, complete with gallows, as well as the impressive
Regional Gallery and Museum complex and the Dubbo
Observatory. But most visitors come here for the
Western Plains Zoo►► which has animals from all
over the world roaming freely across its parkland.

► Eden   *63A4*

The last place of any size on the NSW coast before the border with Victoria, this little port and resort began life as a
whaling station, recalled in the **Killer Whale Museum►**
and the fascinating Davidson Whaling Station Historic
Site on the southern side of Twofold Bay. Also on
Twofold Bay are the remains of Boydtown, begun around
the 1840s by the English entrepreneur Benjamin Boyd and
vaingloriously intended to rival Sydney as the colony's
capital. The region is known for its deep-sea fishing.

► Forbes   *62B3*

Almost deserted after the gold rush of the 1860s, Forbes
survived as the focus for a rich agricultural area. The
Town Hall and other late 19th-century buildings still
grace the wide streets.The bushranger Ben Hall met his
end in Forbes in 1865, an event recalled in some detail at
the Bushranger Hall of Fame Museum in the old music
hall that houses the town's **Historical Society
Museum►**. Other attractions include wineries and a
native bird and wildlife refuge.

WHALE AND CHIPS
The first whaling station
on the Australian
mainland was established
at Eden in 1818, and
whaling continued to be
based here until the
1930s. A revival of Eden's
economy took place in
the late 1960s with the
building of the Harris
Daishowa Chipmill,
designed to turn the
forests of the area (some
of the finest in the state)
into woodchips for the
Japanese paper industry.
The project aroused
the ire of the growing
Australian conservation
movement, whose mem-
bers saw in it the export
of part of the country's
irreplaceable natural
heritage.

Cape Byron's lighthouse
overlooks the beaches of
Byron Bay

WATERING THE WILDERNESS

The explorer John Oxley reckoned no white man would ever want to take up residence in the 'barren and desolate' country he glimpsed from Mount Binya in 1817. But in the early 1900s, the NSW government, enthused by private successes with irrigation experiments, built the Burrinjuck Dam and encouraged settlement in the Murrumbidgee Irrigation Area, in the state's south. Many settlers were out-of-work miners from Broken Hill; later, returned servicemen and Italian immigrants with important agricultural skills moved in, and in spite of many disappointments and technical difficulties, the area produces crops of fruit (including grapes), vegetables, cotton and rice. Together with similar projects in the region, a total of 6,000sq km (2,317sq miles) of near desert has been made to bloom.

All of the 100 or so wineries in the Hunter Valley welcome visitors; most are around Cessnock and Pokolbin

▶ Glen Innes
63D4

This high-altitude town in northern NSW is in the middle of a prosperous farming area, once named the 'Land of the Beardies' after two pioneers. The region is well known for the sapphires and other gemstones that are extracted commercially (amateur fossicking or searching is also possible). The town has Celtic standing stones, an Aboriginal cultural centre, and the **Land of the Beardies History House Museum▶**, one of Australia's most comprehensive small historical museums.

▶ Goulburn
63B4

The second oldest inland town in Australia straddles the Hume Highway some 200km (124 miles) southwest of Sydney and is the focal point of the well-tended farmlands all around, whose speciality is proclaimed by another of those Australian 'big ones'; 15m (50ft) high, the Big Merino sheep guards the town's western approach. Goulburn is a 'real' city, with two cathedrals, a long main street and a number of imposing 19th-century buildings. On the edge of town is Riversdale, a coaching inn dating from the late 1830s, authentically restored and furnished.

▶ Grafton
63D5

The middle of the Clarence River district, Grafton was 'green' before its time. The town council initiated a policy of tree-planting as early as the 1860s, and today's citizens are benefiting from the many jacarandas and other flowering species that grace its broad streets. The bend of the Clarence was only bridged in 1932, by the double-decker structure you see today. Grafton is a good base for tours, with several national parks within easy reach.

▶ Griffith
62B2

Designed by Walter Burley Griffin, the American architect who planned Canberra, this model township was built to act as the urban focus for the Murrumbidgee Irrigation

Area. Its conception can be seen in its radial street pattern. The town is famous for its wine and gourmet food industries and Italian culture

▶ Gundagai
62B3

The name of this township along the Hume Highway is derived from an Aboriginal word meaning 'up-river'; in spite of warnings from the local Aborigines, the first settlers built their houses on the floodplain of the Murrumbidgee, and were duly swept away when the river broke its banks in 1852, causing the country's worst-ever flood disaster. The Murrumbidgee is crossed here by the longest wooden viaduct in Australia.

▶▶ Hunter Valley
63C4

The broad valley of the Hunter River, which ends in the sea at Newcastle, has contrasting landscapes created by mines and wines. The coalfield has been exploited for a century and a half, and has been the making of the city of Newcastle. The vineyards were first planted here in the 1820s and, after periods of decline, are flourishing once more. A day-trip or, better still, one lasting a couple of days is a popular outing for Sydneysiders, not least because of the excellent food offered in the area.

The landscape of the Hunter is one of its attractions, in its framework of wooded hills running down from the Brokenback Range to the southwest of the valley. Grapevines benefit from the rich soil, which has its origin in the outpourings of ancient volcanoes. The wineries range from family-sized concerns to large-scale commercial enterprises. Australia's oldest wine-press is on display at the **Golden Grape Estate**. The Tyrrell's, Wyndham Estate and Tulloch wineries are well worth visiting, while the **McGuigan Cellars▶▶** has a superb cheese shop and the **Hunter Valley Gardens Village** has shops, cafés and a cellar door. Other wineries are in the Upper Hunter Valley, some 90km (56 miles) farther on.

A DOG'S LIFE
As teamsters made their way along the rough roads of early Australia, they were inevitably accompanied by various breeds of dog, one of which seems to have committed an unspeakable act while sitting on his master's tuckerbox (lunch box) by the side of the road. This and other deeds were recorded in the crude ballads of the time, refined somewhat in a version by the poet Jack Moses, and commemorated in a sculpture just outside Gundagai. This is the work of one Frank Rusconi, who was also responsible for the amazing model cathedral of marble on show in the Tourist Information Centre.

81

This part of the Great Dividing Range is the roof of Australia, much of it a highland plateau from which rise a number of peaks more than 1,980m (6,500ft) high. Parts of it have several well-equipped ski resorts. But the mountains are glorious in summer as well as in winter; a carpet of alpine wildflowers unrolls as the snow retreats, and there are superb paths and trails offering some of the most exhilarating hiking in the whole of Australia.

The region is popular with winter sports enthusiasts

THE SNOWY MOUNTAINS SCHEME
This was a visionary project to alter the course of rivers to irrigate the parched agricultural areas farther west and generate hydroelectric power in the process. Many dams were built, of which the largest, at Lake Eucumbene, holds back more water than is contained in Sydney Harbour. There are 80km (50 miles) of aqueducts, 148km (91 miles) of tunnels and seven power stations, the latter providing a good proportion of the electricity consumed in southeast Australia. Some of the impressive installations (like Murray 1 on the Alpine Way, or Tumut 3 at Talbingo) are open to the public.

History Aboriginal interest in the mountains was more recent than in many parts of Australia, dating only from the end of the last Ice Age some 10,000 years ago. This is one of the few Australian landscapes with glacial lakes, cirques and moraines, all the result of the action of the ice sheets that were absent throughout most of the country.

The mountains attracted graziers (sheep farmers) from early on in the days after white settlement, and a few determined bushwalkers between the two world wars, but it was only after the start of the Snowy Mountains Scheme in the late 1940s, when roads were driven through the wilderness and many other facilities created, that the area became accessible and visitors were able to come here in large numbers.

A popular starting point for exploring the mountains, which include the Kosciuszko National Park, is the town of **Cooma** at the junction of the Monaro and Snowy Mountains highways. It was from here that the Snowy Mountains Authority oversaw what was to be one of the greatest 20th-century engineering projects in the world. Two tourist offices provide information on the mountains and the great project that transformed them: the visitor information centre in town, and the Snowy Scheme Information Centre on the Canberra road.

The resort town of **Jindabyne** on its lake provides plenty of lodgings for winter sports enthusiasts and the National Parks and Wildlife Service has a useful visitor centre here, at Kosciuszko Road, before visitors head for the skiing areas in the heart of the mountains.

Popular resorts include the delightful alpine-style village of Thredbo on the southern side of the range, and the mega-resort of Perisher Blue, which encompasses the ski regions of Smiggin Holes, Blue Cow Mountain, Guthega and Perisher Valley—the latter reached by the underground railway known as the Ski Tube.

At the end of the northern road is Charlotte Pass, with superb views of the mountain peaks. This is the starting point for a number of wonderful walks, including the Summit Walk to the top of **Mount Kosciuszko**, at 2,228m (7,310ft) the highest peak in Australia.

Jindabyne is also the terminus of the **Alpine Way**, the splendid scenic highway that leads to the 1,582m (5,190-ft) pass at Dead Horse Gap. From here the partly unsurfaced road descends into the valley of the Murray River and on to Khancoban. This is the starting point for a fair-weather highway leading to **Mount Selwyn**, a winter sports resort on the north side of the peaks, and to the remains of the old gold-mining township of Kiandra.

Farther north are **Yarrangobilly Caves**. Of the dozens of caves so far discovered, six are open to the public.

SKIING
Although the snow isn't always as abundant as resort operators would like, the Snowy Mountains offer ideal conditions for cross-country skiing and some excellent downhill facilities. The main resorts are in the vast Perisher Blue region, which incorporates four ski areas and offers 50 lifts and T-bars, and the smaller and more charming alpine village of Thredbo. The ski season runs from early June to early October.

83

Murray 1 hydroelectric power station

New South Wales

A souvenir of your visit to Kangaroo Valley

THE KIAMA COAST
Kiama's beaches are pleasant enough—and excellent for surfing. Farther south lie Gerroa and Gerringong (which also offer great surfing), and then the spectacular wave-pounded expanse of Seven Mile Beach, part of a national park.

BLACK IS BEAUTIFUL
The Lightning Ridge black opals are not quite unique, but this is the only place in the world where this unusual stone occurs in quantity. It has been described as combining 'the iridescence of the dewdrop with the colour of the rainbow, set in the blackness of night'. The biggest stone ever found was given the name 'Queen of the Earth'.

MUTAWINTJI HISTORIC SITE
Within Mutawintji National Park, this extraordinary site represents one of the state's greatest collections of Aboriginal art and cultural relics. Some of the 20 rock shelters and 15 engraving sites can be visited in the company of an Aboriginal ranger.

► **Kangaroo Valley**   *63B4*

This is a delightful old township tucked away in an upland valley on the beautiful scenic road leading inland from Nowra, 100km (62 miles) south of Sydney. Apart from being the starting point for bushwalks, its main attraction is the **Pioneer Settlement Museum and Park**, a faithful reconstruction of a dairy farm of the 19th century.

► **Kiama**   *63B4*

The most famous feature of this popular and pleasantly situated port and resort on the 'Kiama Coast' south of Wollongong is the **Blowhole**, which gushes a waterspout up to 60m (195ft) into the air. To the west is the **Minnamurra Rainforest Centre►** (part of Budderoo National Park), with palms, fig trees and other rain-forest plants, rare red cedars and exquisite lyrebirds. The reserve can be explored via its two marked and interpreted walking tracks.

►►► **Kosciuszko National Park**   *62A3*

See pages 74 and 83.

►► **Lanyon Homestead, ACT**   *off 66A3*

Tharwa Drive, Tharwa (tel: 02-6235 5677)
Open: Tue–Sun 10–4. Admission: inexpensive
This fine building on the Murrumbidgee River was built in 1859 and extended a few years later. Now in the care of the ACT Government, both buildings and gardens have been sympathetically restored. There is a gallery housing a collection of the works of Australian artist Sir Sidney Nolan.

►► **Lightning Ridge**   *62D3*

Just off the Castlereagh Highway before it quits NSW for Queensland, this far northwestern township is famed for its black opals, mined here since 1902, in recent years by machine rather than by hand. Amateur fossickers (searchers for gold or gemstones) are welcome, provided they don't trespass on professionals' rights, and there are many old mines to visit and cutting demonstrations to watch, as well as artesian baths to relax in.

►► **Mount Warning National Park**   *63D5*

This 1,157m (3,796-ft) peak is the plug of an ancient volcano, given its name by Captain Cook to mark the reefs off Point Danger, on which the *Endeavour* almost came to grief. It is the first place on the Australian mainland to receive the rays of the rising sun, and the view is worth the 750m (2,460-ft) climb from the visitor centre, where you can leave your car. The steep but well-made path rises through splendid woodlands that change from subtropical rain forest to temperate rain forest and finally to open bush.

▶▶ Mutawintji National Park   62C1
Beyond Broken Hill, in NSW's farthest northwest, are the rugged sandstone ranges of this remote national park, which is nevertheless accessible on gravel roads. Arid sandy plains and pebble deserts contrast with pools and watercourses fringed with river red gums and other lush vegetation. Aborigines occupied the area for countless years, leaving a wealth of rock paintings and engravings.

▶▶ Myall Lakes National Park   63B4
These tranquil lakes, 60km (37 miles) north of Newcastle and separated from the Pacific Ocean by windswept sand dunes, are best reached from the township of Tea Gardens by boat up the Myall River. There is little development along the shores, though the fishing village of Seal Rocks on the coast at the eastern end of the park is popular with visitors who want to get away from it all. You can rent everything from canoes to houseboats to explore the magnificent lakes.

▶ Nambucca Heads   63C5
Subtropical crops now grow in this attractive and popular resort, 50km (31 miles) south of Coffs Harbour, where the cedar forests were cleared last century. There are fantastic views from various lookout points, of which Yarrahapini is the most spectacular. You can take tours inland to the rugged ridges and deep forested valleys of the New England and Dorrigo national parks.

MYALL LAKES FLORA AND FAUNA
The Myall Lakes, fringed by splendid forest, that includes rain-forest species such as cabbage palms, make up the largest such lake system in the state. The lakes are also famous for the prawns (shrimp) that breed in them. Waterbirds abound, as well as sea eagles, and the area is rich in other wildlife, too.

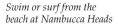

Swim or surf from the beach at Nambucca Heads

Attractive Lake Macquarie, Australia's largest saltwater lake, near Newcastle

AUSTRALIAN COUNTRY
Far inland from Port Macquarie, halfway between Sydney and Brisbane on the New England Highway, is the town of Tamworth. This sizeable place claims fame as the capital of Australian country music. An annual festival, held in January, draws thousands of fans to hundreds of performances; other attractions are the Australian Country Music Foundation Museum and the Hands of Fame Park (handprints).

▶ Newcastle
63B4

Dominated by its docks and the now closed BHP steelworks, industrial Newcastle is the largest city in Australia that is not a state capital. Its fortunes, like those of its namesake in England, were founded on abundant coal reserves that were discovered in the Hunter Valley; Newcastle coal constituted the country's first export.

But there's much more to Newcastle than industry. There are wonderful beaches and the Foreshore Park, Queen's Wharf and Customs House Plaza make a fine setting for festive occasions. **Fort Scratchley▶** is one of the few forts in Australia to have seen active duty—soldiers stationed there in 1942 fired on a Japanese submarine. The old stronghold gives a good panorama over the city in its setting, and houses the **Maritime Museum▶** and **Military Museum**. The city has some imposing 19th-century buildings and more museums and galleries. The 'Bogey Hole' on the city beach below beautiful King Edward Park was built as a saltwater bath in convict days. To the south of the city, **Lake Macquarie▶** offers all kinds of watersports. The country's largest saltwater lake, four times the size of Sydney Harbour, it is also the home of a koala colony and a delightful flora and fauna reserve.

▶ Nimbin
63D5

Set among the natural splendours of northern NSW, Nimbin developed as a hub for artists and bohemians in the early 1970s. Today, its crafts shops and cafés attract the curious as well. It is close to **Nightcap National Park▶▶**, whose 900m (2,953-ft) peaks form part of the outer walls of the huge extinct volcano of which Mount Warning is the core. The park, with its glorious rain forest and diverse wildlife, is now part of NSW's World Heritage Area protecting the temperate and subtropical forests of the north.

▶ Nowra   63B4
Nowra is just upstream from the mouth of the Shoalhaven River. It is an extremely busy tourist resort, largely because of the beaches that extend north and south along the coast, one of them (Hyams Beach on **Jervis Bay▶▶**) boasting the whitest sand in the world.

▶ Orange   62B3
Lava flows from the extinct volcano of Mount Canobolas, the highest point between the Great Dividing Range and the Indian Ocean, have broken down over the millennia into fertile soils that today support great tracts of orchards growing apples, pears, cherries and grapes for wine—but no oranges! The town of Orange has prospered from the fertility of its surroundings and is a busy but pleasant place, leafy with parks and trees. The first goldfield to be exploited in Australia was at nearby **Ophir**, where two prospectors made a sizeable strike in 1851. You can try your luck at searching for gold today in picturesque surroundings along Summer Hill Creek.

▶ Port Macquarie   63C5
At the mouth of the Hastings River, Port Macquarie has turned from trade and commerce to tourism and retirement with considerable success. **St. Thomas' Church** is a reminder of these early days; one of the first churches to be built in Australia (1824–28), it has box pews and a view from its tower. The **Hastings District Historical Museum▶** has good displays on the evolution of the town and its hinterland, and nature is on show at the **Billabong Koala and Wildlife Park▶**, and **Sea Acres Nature Reserve▶▶**, with a boardwalk through the rain forest. Good beaches stretch southward from the town.

▶▶ Southern Highlands   56A2
Easily accessible by train and by the Hume Highway, this is one of the great rural playgrounds of Sydneysiders. The district was opened up early in the colony's history, in the 1820s, and much of it has a pleasant air of maturity, with lush landscapes recalling those of Tasmania. Recreational facilities cater for every possible desire.

Among the towns in the area, **Bowral** is a leafy place with a number of fine old buildings along its main street. **Berrima▶▶** retains even more of its past; founded in the 1830s, it still has many sandstone buildings dating from that period, though the inns have dwindled in number from the original 13. The 1834 Surveyor General Inn claims to be the oldest continuously licensed premises in the country. Popular **Bundanoon▶** acts as the gateway to the Morton National Park, a starting point for energetic bushwalks or casual strolls up Glow Worm Glen.

▶▶ Tidbinbilla, ACT   off 66A1
There are two important visitor attractions at Tidbinbilla, 40km (25 miles) southwest of Canberra. The **Canberra Deep Space Communication Complex▶** is a combined US/Australian deep-space tracking station; it is not open to the public, but the visitor centre has multimedia displays and model spacecraft. Back on earth, **Tidbinbilla Nature Reserve▶▶** is a vast tract of countryside with bushwalks and an array of Australian wildlife.

MORTON NATIONAL PARK
This high sandstone plateau into which rivers have cut deep gorges is one of the most beautiful attractions of the Southern Highlands. Waterfalls pour into the depths from high cliffs, as at Fitzroy Falls, where there is a visitor centre. Scenic highways connect the area to the coast (one of them goes via Kangaroo Valley), making an interesting round trip from Sydney possible.

Rugged Morton National Park is popular with Sydneysiders

The long list of Australian creatures able to cause you harm, in some cases fatal, is particularly impressive. Still, you are much more likely to come to grief at the hands of a local driver or suffer sunburn than you are to fall victim to the wildlife.

CROCODILES

88

SPIDERS AND INSECTS
Spiders can reach an alarming size, and their bite can be unpleasant. Avoid the redback (or black widow), a small black spider with red patches on its back, and the larger funnel-web at all costs—tourist information centres can give further information on how to recognize them. The funnel-web, unlike most of its kind, is aggressive and rears up for the attack. It's also a Sydneysider, so be wary in Sydney gardens and parks. Insects abound in Australia, but flies, wasps, mosquitoes, ticks, ants and even scorpions are more of a nuisance than a real hazard.

Marine hazards Of the 85 species of **sharks** around the coast of Australia, a few are man-eaters. Attacks are rare, and the average number of fatalities per year is just one person. The highest risk occurs in summer when the water temperature is in excess of 22°C (72°F), and during this time it might be advisable to swim only from one of the many beaches protected by systems of netting. More dangerous are **saltwater crocodiles** (salties—see page 183), and on no account should you swim (or stand close to the water's edge) in the northern areas frequented by these formidable creatures. Their numbers have also increased dramatically since they have been given the status of protected species.

Box jellyfish breed in river estuaries and infest the coastal waters of Queensland and the NT from October to May. Practically invisible, they deliver a sting that can be fatal. Stay out of the sea at this time! Some of the beautiful corals can also deliver a mild sting, as can the crown-of-thorns starfish that is attacking the Barrier Reef. Much worse, however, is the **stonefish**, which looks like a rock as its name suggests; wear shoes when walking on a reef, and avoid rockpools. There are also sea snakes, which become active at the same time as the box jellies.

Terrestrial hazards Snakes also inhabit the land, and there are some 170 species, the venomous ones outnumbering the harmless—in Tasmania, for example, *all* snakes are venomous. Rangers and bush folk are fond of detailing their degree of poisonousness in terms of the number of mice a bite could kill; this figure can get into the hundreds of thousands, and is quite enough to fell the strongest human. However, even the most lethal of snakes—like the taipan, tiger snake, death adder or brown snake—will get out of your way if it possibly can.

Steer clear of the deadly taipan

▶ Wauchope   63C5

Among the forests of the Hastings River district, Wauchope has long been a hub of the logging industry, a fact made much of in **Timbertown▶▶**. This ambitious re-creation of a late 19th-century pioneer settlement has a whole range of buildings (shops, houses, a church and sawmill), demonstrations of all the activities associated with logging and processing, as well as rides around the area aboard a cart or a steam train.

Kempsey▶, 25km (16 miles) north of Wauchope, is home to the world-famous Akubra hat. Akubras (believed to be an Aboriginal word for hat) are made from rabbit pelts—as imported rabbits pose a serious environmental threat, many see this as a good use for them.

▶ West Wyalong   62B3

In the harsh countryside at the junction of the Mid-Western and Newell highways, West Wyalong was NSW's busiest goldfield at the turn of the 20th century. Now the heart of an extensive wheat-growing area, it also produces and exports that quintessential Australian fluid, eucalyptus oil. However, visitors may be more interested in the model of a gold mine in the Historical Museum.

▶ White Cliffs   62C1

This old opal-mining settlement more than 1,000km (620 miles) northwest of Sydney is a place to experience life in the Australian Outback. A small, highly individual population of opal miners lives here, some of them underground, where they won't need air-conditioning—elsewhere a must because of the sometimes intolerable climate. There are plenty of opportunities to see opals in their various states, as well as one of Australia's largest solar power stations, which can be toured.

▶ Wollongong   63B4

Industrial Wollongong, NSW's third largest city, is home to the vast **Nan Tien Buddhist Temple▶**, **Australia World▶** and some wonderful beaches. Inland there are splendid hills and forests. Mount Keira and Mount Kembla in the **Illawarra Escarpment State Conservation Area▶** offer fantastic vistas.

Australia's famous Akubra hats are made in Kempsey, near Wauchope

WAGGA WAGGA OR WOGGA WOGGA?
More famous for its name (pronounced Wogga) than for its tourist amenities, Wagga (240km/150 miles south of West Wyalong) is a fair-sized town that has profited from its location on the Murrumbidgee River and Sydney–Melbourne railway line to become the thriving hub of NSW's Riverina district. The region offers wineries, as well as a good museum and art gallery

Victoria

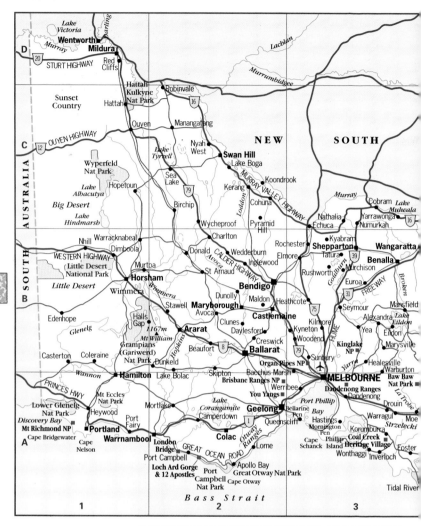

The Dandenong Ranges
are famous for their
profusion of native flora

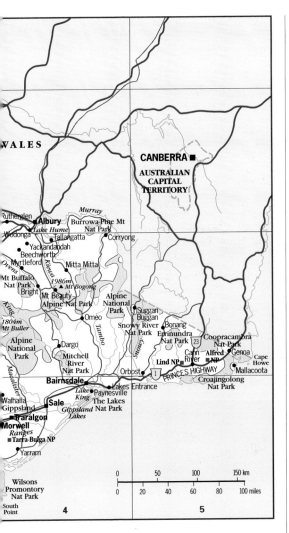

WALES

CANBERRA ■
AUSTRALIAN
CAPITAL
TERRITORY

Murray
Rutherglen • Albury
Wodonga • Lake Hume • Tallangatta
Yackandandah
Beechworth
Myrtleford • Mitta Mitta
Mt Buffalo
Nat Park • 1986m
Bright Mt Beauty ▲ Mt Bogong
Alpine • Alpine Nat Park
1804m
Mt Buller
Alpine
National • Dargo
Park Mitchell
River
Nat Park • Orbost
Bairnsdale •
Walhalla Lake • Paynesville
Gippsland • Sale King The Lakes
Traralgon Gippsland Nat Park
Morwell Lakes
Ranges
■ Tarra-Bulga NP
Yarram

Burrowa-Pine Mt
Nat Park
Corryong

Alpine
National
Park Suggan
Buggan
Snowy River Bonang
Nat Park Errinundra Cooracambra
Nat Park
Cann Alfred • Genoa
Lind NP River ■ NP Cape
Howe
Mallacoota
Lakes Entrance Croajingolong
Nat Park

0   50   100   150 km

0   20   40   60   80   100 miles

Wilsons
Promontory
Nat Park
South
Point   4   5

VICTORIA What used to be known as the Garden State is the smallest of Australia's mainland states. However, it is comparatively densely populated and highly industrialized, with about a quarter of the country's inhabitants living on what amounts to only 3 per cent of its land surface, a substantial proportion of which is agriculturally productive. Out of the state's total of just over 5 million people, 3.6 million live in the metropolitan area of Melbourne, whose area of more than 6,000sq km (2,300sq miles) makes it one of the largest cities in the world.

Beyond the metropolis, Victorians live in a variety of settlements, many of considerable charm and historic interest. There are delightful little ports and several well-established resorts along the 1,200km (745-mile) coastline, a multitude of places founded in the mid-19th-century rush for gold such as charming Bendigo, old river ports along the Murray, and prosperous agricultural areas quietly getting on with their own lives.

91

▶▶▶ REGION HIGHLIGHTS

Ballarat pages 109–110

Melbourne Cricket
Ground, Melbourne
page 99

National Gallery of
Victoria, Melbourne
pages 100–101

Port Campbell National
Park page 119

Royal Botanic Gardens
Melbourne page 103

Sovereign Hill, Ballarat
page 110

The Arts Centre,
Melbourne page 104

Victoria

Old Victorian building in Melbourne

The state's landscapes are diverse; with varied and spectacular coastal scenery, high mountains and extensive forested uplands, rich farmlands and semi-desert, Victoria has been described as a microcosm of Australia, though true Outback lies beyond its border. Agriculture takes many forms. The rolling hills of Gippsland feed dairy cattle, sheep graze on the vast pastures of the plains stretching to the west and fruit grows in profusion along the Goulburn and Murray rivers, thanks to irrigation works carried out on a huge scale at the turn of the 20th century.

For the tourist, the presence of such variety in close proximity to the state capital makes a stay particularly rewarding; few places are more than half a day's drive from Melbourne.

AS IT WAS Victoria belonged to a new phase of European colonization of the continent. The coast had been sighted from aboard the *Endeavour* in the course of Captain Cook's 1770 voyage; in 1803, Lieutenant David Collins attempted to found a settlement on the shores of Port Phillip Bay but gave up and went on to Tasmania instead. For decades, only whalers and sealers landed along the coast. Then, in 1835, one John Batman from Tasmania sailed into the bay again and signed a treaty of dubious legality with the local Aborigines that gave him title to 243,000ha (600,450 acres) of land. In spite of official attempts from Sydney to discourage settlement on the bay, Batman and others persisted; his famous phrase 'This will be the place for a village' marked the founding of Melbourne.

The new settlers wanted nothing to do with the convict system, sending any ships that arrived with prisoners on

BUCKLEY'S CHANCE

One of the members of Lieutenant Collins' party, which tried and failed to establish a settlement at Sorrento on the Mornington Peninsula in 1803, was the British-born convict William Buckley. Taking a chance, he decamped and fled around Port Phillip Bay to the Barwon area, where he lived with the local Aborigines. Decades later, in 1835, some of John Batman's associates were amazed at the emergence of 'a wild white man' at their encampment, hardly able to speak English any more. Buckley earned a pardon, a government pension and a place in the language ('Buckley's chance' means no chance at all).

to Sydney, and petitioning for separation from New South Wales. This was granted in 1851, and the new colony was given the Queen of England's name. It was only weeks after this event that gold was found at Clunes and near Ballarat; other finds followed, the rush was on, and Melbourne and Victoria changed utterly in the process. Handsome new towns arose from the tent cities erected by the prospectors, and Melbourne boomed, fitting itself out with fine new buildings paid for by the profits made from the precious metal.

Melbourne has been eclipsed by Sydney as the financial capital of the nation; Sydney gets more migrants and has a more racially diverse character. But Melbourne is now one of the most cosmopolitan of Australia's major cities, while other places within the state retain a pleasing atmosphere of more stately and sedate times.

OUTDOOR VICTORIANS In spite of (or is it because of?) their unpredictable weather, the people of Victoria embrace the outdoors with enthusiasm, igniting the barbecue or flocking to the beaches at the slightest opportunity. The big event in the racing calendar is the Melbourne Cup, which takes place on the first Tuesday of November, when not only Victoria but the whole country comes to a stop. Australian Rules football is followed with passion by people of all ages and both sexes.

The accessibility of fine scenery brings out bushwalkers in summer, while in winter the roads to the snowfields of the Alps are crowded with the cars of skiers. Skiing began in the 1930s, when the first lift started taking people up to the plateau country beneath Mount Buffalo.

93

SKIING IN VICTORIA
Mount Donna Buang and Mount Baw Baw are accessible to day-trippers from Melbourne. Mount Buller, farther on in the Alps, is one of Australia's most popular winter resorts. The resort at Mount Hotham is the highest in the country, with its own airport and direct flights from Melbourne and Sydney, while Falls Creek in its sheltered bowl in the Alpine National Park has slopes suitable for every kind of skier.

Morning Star Creek, still with one foot in the past

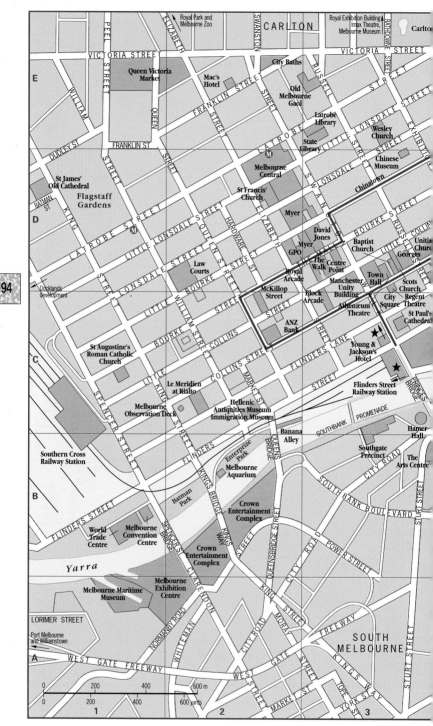

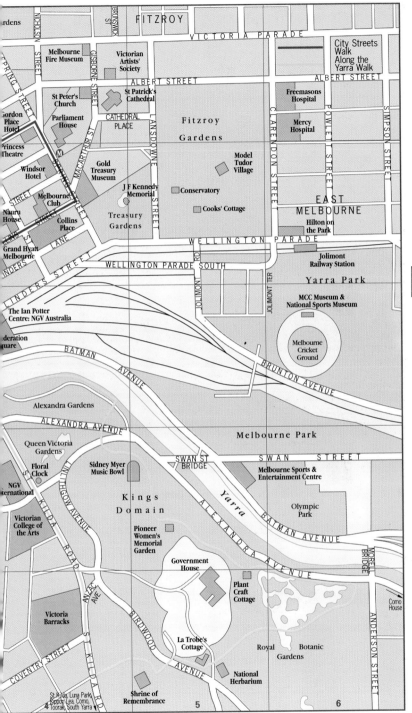

Victoria

*Completed in 1899,
Flinders Street Station is
a popular meeting place*

GOOD FOR A LAUGH
The most popular of the
city's festivals, the hilarious Melbourne
International Comedy
Festival takes place in
March and April each
year. Along with similar
festivals in Edinburgh and
Montréal, this is one of
the world's largest such
events.

BATMAN'S BARGAIN
In exchange for
243,000ha (600,450
acres) of Aboriginal land,
John Batman delivered 40
blankets, 30 tomahawks,
100 knives, 50 pairs of
scissors, 30 mirrors, 200
handkerchiefs, 100
pounds of flour and 6
shirts. The understanding
that a similar quantity of
items would be handed
over annually was soon
consigned to oblivion.

*Outside the 1856
Parliament House*

Melbourne

Australia's second great metropolitan city sprawls
around the head of Port Phillip Bay at the outlet of the
muddy Yarra River. Hardly a generation ago, Melbourne
was almost a synonym for dull respectability of a pecul-
iarly British manner, but since the 1960s, the city and its
population have undergone a startling transformation.
Much of the city has been redeveloped with glittering
office towers, to which the remaining treasures of 19th-
century architecture act as a wonderful foil. Massive
immigration, from southern Europe and Asia, has
enlivened the city's social scene. In addition to countless
galleries, museums, theatres and movie houses, the city
now has a thriving nightlife of bars and discos, cabaret
and comedians, jazz, rock and a casino. Melbourne offers
a multitude of different types of cuisine, from 'Mod Oz' to
Vietnamese. The shopping is a treat, too.

THE EARLY YEARS Once John Batman's illegal treaty of
1835, by which he acquired 243,000ha (600,450 acres) of
land, had been accepted as a *fait accompli* by the authorities in Sydney, his 'village' above the Yarra soon became a
city, laid out on the usual grid pattern by an army surveyor. Within a few years, the wealthy were buying
estates to the southeast of the river where they
could set themselves up as country gentlemen and build elegant houses. Due
to gold and land speculation,
Melbourne boomed for most of the
second half of the 19th century,
leading a roistering kind of life that
was then characterized as
'American' in contrast to Sydney's
staid 'Britishness'. A great slump in
the 1890s ended the era of 'Marvellous
Melbourne', and the city entered the long
period of middle-aged respectability from which its
recent renaissance has so triumphantly rescued it.

ATTRACTIONS TODAY Melbourne is a wonderfully green
metropolis with an abundance of parks and trees, but it is
also renowned for its dining, shopping and excellent
19th-century architecture. The best view of the city—and
probably one of the finest panoramas in Australia—is
from the south bank of the Yarra, particularly from
Alexandra Gardens or the Southgate Precinct.

The Suburbs

The city's inner suburbs have a strong and varied identity that makes them well worth exploring.

Carlton, just north of the city, is home to Italian restaurants, the University of Melbourne and the huge 1870s Royal Exhibition Building. The adjacent Carlton Gardens area includes an **IMAX theatre** and the **Melbourne Museum**, which opened in 2000 (see page 100).

Once regarded as 'rough', **Fitzroy** has now turned Bohemian, its original inhabitants supplemented by students and artists. Brunswick Street is a fascinating mixture of cheap restaurants and alternative bookstores.

East Melbourne is a charming enclave of carefully restored terraced houses within walking distance of the city via Fitzroy Gardens.

The suburb of **St. Kilda** became Melbourne's seaside in the 1880s, when the pier and the substantial villas of the rich were built. These days, St. Kilda is vibrant, and Acland and Fitzroy streets are hard to beat as restaurant strips. The beach that stretches from here to Port Melbourne is still popular, and the bay has been cleaned up in recent years. On Sundays, St. Kilda hosts a big arts and crafts market.

South Melbourne has one of the most attractive of all inner city residential areas; in St. Vincent's Place Square, fine houses in a variety of styles were laid out around central gardens from the 1860s onward.

One of the wealthiest inner suburbs east along the Yarra, **Toorak** is synonymous with trendiness, and nearby South Yarra, where you'll find the historic **Como House**, is famous for its restaurants, shopping and nightlife.

Beyond the Yarra to the west, historic **Williamstown** has a superb view of the city across the water. A stroll along the Strand is well worthwhile, and railway buffs enjoy the Railway Museum. On the way here, at Spotswood on the western side of the Westgate Bridge, is the highly entertaining **Scienceworks**, an annexe of the Melbourne Museum. It has a planetarium and an amazing array of interactive exhibits on the theme of science and technology in the past, present and future.

Melbourne is the only Australian city with an extensive system of tramways

MELBOURNE'S TRAMS
One of the city's emblems, the network of mostly green and yellow trams covers much of the Melbourne metropolitan area. The older trams are classified by the National Trust, while a newer line speeds commuters and workers between the city and Port Melbourne. You can make good use of the free City Circle Tram service, and can even dine aboard a vintage model; the Colonial Tramcar Restaurant.

DOCKLANDS
Immediately west of the city, the vast Docklands development is transforming a former industrial area into a new suburb. When completed it will house waterfront restaurants, shops and entertainment precincts, as well as residential accommodation and office blocks.

COLLINS STREET

This has always been the best address in town, ever since professional men set up here in the late 1840s. The upper, eastern end of the street, tree-planted and close to parklands and government buildings, was more salubrious than the western end, down by the railway tracks of Spencer Street Station. Not quite all the buildings from the era of 'Marvellous Melbourne' have been replaced by developments like twin-towered Collins Place (No. 45) or the harsh precast concrete panels of Nauru House (No. 80); the Melbourne Club, most exclusive of such institutions, still stands (No. 36), as do a number of dignified banks, office buildings, churches and theatres.

The gateway to Chinatown

►► ANZ (Australia and New Zealand) Bank

94C2

380 Collins Street (tel: 03-9558 8522)
Open: Museum Mon–Fri 9.30–4. Admission free

One of the finest examples of Gothic revival architecture in the country, this building is more Venetian than the Doge's Palace in Venice, with a magnificently elaborate interior whose blue, cream and pale green decoration is enhanced by lavish use of gold leaf.

Downstairs, the **ANZ Banking Museum►** has exhibitions on the history of Australian banking.

► Chinatown

94D3

Melbourne's Chinatown, around Little Bourke Street, has existed ever since Chinese prospectors joined the rush to the goldfields in the 1850s. It expanded later in the 19th century as the goldfields contracted and miners drifted back to the big city. Today it still flourishes as a haven for the Chinese community and for diners in search of cheap and excellent food and groceries, and has been fitted out with the usual archways that boldly proclaim its identity.

An interesting addition to the area is the **Chinese Museum►►** in an old warehouse in Cohen Place, just off Little Bourke Street. Its displays bring alive the considerable Chinese contribution to Australian history. Star exhibits include a life-size replica of a warrior-general of the 2nd century BC and Dai Loong, the 100m (328-ft), 100-legged dragon that emerges for the Chinese New Year parade. Guided heritage walks of the Chinatown area depart from the museum.

►► Como House

off 95A6

Corner Williams Road and Lechlade Avenue, South Yarra
(tel: 03-9827 2500). Open: daily 10–5. Admission: moderate

Begun in 1847, this delicious white mansion crowning the rise in the middle of its richly landscaped gardens is a wonderful example of the gracious buildings of

Melbourne's pre-boom period. Behind the mansion's well proportioned façade are a series of furnished rooms evoking the comfortable and very sociable life lived here in the 19th century; the adjacent outbuildings contain the original laundry. Como's unselfconscious elegance was not imitated by the nouveau-riche owners of the next generation of villas to be built in the suburb of Toorak. Most of these pompous residences have not survived, but Como, thankfully, passed into the hands of the National Trust.

▶▶ Fitzroy Gardens   95E5

Just to the east of the city, and a popular place for lunchtime sandwiches and assignations, are the sweeping lawns and splendid trees of these 19th-century gardens, complementing the spires of St. Patrick's Cathedral in the background. Towards the southern end of the park is **Cooks' Cottage▶▶**. A modest stone building of the mid-18th century with a characteristic Yorkshire pantiled roof, this was the home of the great navigator's parents. It was dismantled and brought here in 1934 to mark the centenary of the founding of Melbourne. It is open to the public.

▶▶ Kings Domain   95B5

A splendid tract of parkland sweeps southeast along the Yarra from the city to the Kings Domain and the Royal Botanic Gardens (see page 103). Alexandra Gardens has a fine riverside view of the city. Altogether more functional is the **Sidney Myer Music Bowl**, whose soaring canopy shelters all kinds of open-air musical events. Crowning the higher ground is the great white **Government House**, the fourth to be built on this site (see panel). In contrast to this magnificence is the very first Government House, **La Trobe's Cottage**, a prefabricated, two-floored cottage brought from England.

▶▶ Melbourne Aquarium   94B2

Corner Queenswharf Road and King Street (tel: 03-9620 0999)
Open: Jan, daily 9.30–9; Feb–Dec 9.30–6. Admission: expensive
The Melbourne Aquarium is appropriately set on the north bank of the Yarra. Highlights include the Coral Atoll, an enormous tank containing a floor-to-ceiling coral reef, and the spectacular Deep Sea Oceanarium. The latter is home to sea creatures of many kinds—including turtles, rays and sharks—which are hand fed by divers throughout the day. Visitors can also take a thrilling simulated 'deep-sea shark dive' ride.

▶▶▶ Melbourne Cricket Ground (MCG)   95C6

Yarra Park, Jolimont (tel: 03-9657 8879 for tours)
Open: daily 9.30–4.30, regular tours from 10–3 on non-event days. Admission: museums moderate, tour/museums expensive
To the southeast are sports grounds of all kinds, many of them laid out for the 1956 Olympics. The central site for the games and the 2006 Commonwealth Games was the great MCG—a vast stadium with a capacity up to 100,000, just as much associated with football ('Aussie Rules') as with cricket. Here, too, are the Melbourne Cricket Club Museum (visited on the tours), as well as the National Sports Museum (opening late 2007 and including the former Olympic Museum and Aussie Rules section). A guided tour of this complex is very worthwhile.

GOVERNMENT HOUSE
Built by government architect William Wardell in the 1870s, the present Government House was based on Queen Victoria's Osborne House on England's Isle of Wight. That monarch is supposed to have been rather miffed that Government House's ballroom was twice as big as the one in Buckingham Palace.

FEDERATION SQUARE
Melbourne's most controversial architecture can be found at the Federation Square precinct, opposite Flinders Street Station. The futuristic buildings here house the Ian Potter Centre (a branch of the National Gallery of Victoria; see page 100), the Australian Racing Museum (horse-racing) and the Australian Centre for the Moving Image, as well as the Melbourne Visitor Centre, bars, restaurants and shops.

99

One of the world's greatest stadiums, the Melbourne Cricket Ground at Jolimont creates an incredible atmosphere

Victoria

*The carefully restored
barque* Polly Woodside
at the Maritime Museum

*The National Gallery of
Victoria is also the site
for international
touring exhibitions*

►► Melbourne Maritime Museum   94A1
South Wharf Road, Southbank (tel: 03 8341 7777)
Closed until 2008
Due to the redevelopment of a large section of Melbourne's
southern riverbank to create a new convention centre, a
hotel and other major buildings, the Melbourne Maritime
Museum will be closed until late 2008. Visitors can, however, still admire (but not board) the museum's
highlight—the *Polly Woodside*—a beautifully restored sailing barque build in Belfast, Northern Ireland in 1885.

►► Melbourne Museum   *off 94E3*
11 Nicholson Street, Carlton Gardens (tel: 03 8341 7777)
Open: daily 10–5
Admission: inexpensive
This ultramodern establishment is Australia's largest
museum. The vast building contains several themed galleries—the Australia Gallery has icons such as the famous
1930s racehorse, Phar Lap; Australian fauna is presented
imaginatively in the Science and Life Gallery; and the
Aboriginal section—Bunjilaka—is particularly good. The
complex also includes an IMAX theatre, the Children's
Museum and tours of the nearby World Heritage listed
Royal Exhibition Building depart from here.

►► Melbourne Observation Deck   94C2
525 Collins Street (tel: 03-9629 8222)
Open: daily 10am–late. Admission: moderate
From this viewing area on the 55th floor of Melbourne's
highest building the views of the city, Port Phillip Bay and
many of the city's outlying regions are stupendous.

►► Melbourne Zoo   *off 94E2*
Elliott Avenue, Parkville (tel: 03-9285 9300)
Open: daily 9–5. Admission: expensive
This vast zoo, with its progressive approach, is in Royal

Park, the city's largest tract of open space. Visitors move easily through large enclosures that simulate the native habitat of the creatures within, including an African rain forest, an elephant village and a butterfly house. A wide range of Australian fauna is also on show.

▶▶▶ National Gallery of Victoria   94B3/94C3

Ian Potter Centre, Federation Square (tel: 03-8620 2222)
Open: Tue–Sun 10–5. Admission free (charge for exhibitions)
NGV International, 180 St. Kilda Road (tel: 03-8620 2222)
Open: daily 10–5. Admission free (charge for special exhibitions)
Victoria's premier art gallery owns some of the finest artwork in Australia. The extensive collection of Australian art, in the new **Ian Potter Centre: NGV Australia**, Federation Square, includes Aboriginal, Colonial and contemporary works in 20 galleries on four levels

The international collection is in the original but redeveloped and expanded premises at St. Kilda Road, now known as the **NGV International**. Exhibits here range from European Old Masters to photography, and Asian and pre-Columbian to contemporary art.

▶▶ Old Melbourne Gaol   94E3

Russell Street (tel: 03-9663 7228)
Open: daily 9.30–5. Admission: moderate
Of all the countless jails that are such a feature of Australian townscapes, this grim bluestone building with its chilling interior seems to sum up the harshness of 19th-century concepts of justice and punishment. Here you can see the death mask of Ned Kelly, made in 1880. The most notorious and defiant of Australia's bushrangers looks peaceful enough, his wayward spirit expressed perhaps more strongly by the homemade suit of armour that is displayed alongside.

▶ Parliament House   95E4

Spring Street (tel: 03-9651 8568). Open: Mon–Fri, tours depart from 10–3.45 when Parliament is not sitting.
Admission free
Begun in 1856, this great neo-Grecian building was planned on such an ambitious scale that it has never been completed. The state government was moved from its home here in 1901 to make way for the newly established Federal Parliament, which sat in Melbourne until finally persuaded to make the move to Canberra in 1927.

There are guided tours of the splendid interior when parliament is not in session; the Legislative Council Chamber was described by poet and connoisseur of Victorian architecture John Betjeman (1906–84), as 'the best Corinthian room in the world'.

▶▶ Queen Victoria Market   94E1

Corner of Queen and Therry streets (tel: 03-9320 5822)
Open: Tue and Thu 6–2, Fri 6–6, Sat 6–3, Sun 9–4.
Closed 1st Tue in Nov. Admission free
Melbourne's sole surviving 19th-century market, exuberantly multicultural, is an exciting place to shop or just wander. Trading has been carried on here since 1859, and more than a thousand stalls sell everything imaginable at affordable prices.

DREAM ON ELM STREET
Some of the prestige of the top end of Collins Street in early days was due to the fact that it was one of the few places to have any street trees. Early photographs of Melbourne show the young city, once the bush had been cleared to build it, was a virtually treeless town. Today the city enjoys the benefit of the countless trees, now fully mature, that were planted towards the end of the 19th century. Scorning the rich array of native trees, city fathers planted to remind themselves of 'home', and as a result, streets and parks are graced with wonderful specimens of oaks, elms and poplars.

101

The Botanic Gardens: a fine example of 19th-century English landscaping

Early European Australia was not distinguished by its architecture. No architect sailed with the First Fleet, and the very first structures were primitive affairs of sticks, mud, thatch, bark or any materials that came quickly and easily to hand. Some prefabricated structures were shipped out from England and reassembled on site, sometimes by guesswork.

The first proper edifice in Sydney was Government House, a two-floor brick dwelling that amazed the Aborigines when they found people walking around above their heads. A sense of restraint and emphasis on good proportion contributed towards simple but effective structures like Elizabeth Farm at Parramatta, built in 1793. Its veranda, destined to become a persistent motif in Australian building, was derived from British practice in India. But architecture capable of making some kind of civic statement had to await the rule of Governor Macquarie and his forger-turned-architect, Francis Greenway. Thanks to buildings like **Hyde Park Barracks** and **St. James' Church,** Sydney began to take on the airs of a real city for the first time.

The development of the terrace Gold was the making of Melbourne, and of many architects, too. Melbourne is still one of the world's great 19th-century cities in terms of building, with grand self-confident edifices in a variety of revived styles—Gothic for churches, Romanesque and Venetian for offices and banks, and Classical for public buildings. This was the period when terraced houses reached a high point of development, their elegance and cast-iron decoration helping to make the inner suburbs of both Melbourne and Sydney some of the most liveable of their kind in the world.

AUSTRALIA'S OWN
What has been described as the most original local contribution to Australian architecture is the tropical house of Queensland. Raised above ground for ventilation, it is liberally provided with verandas and with a roof of corrugated iron—handsome, cheap and durable.

An Aussie style The terraced house was replaced after the turn of the 20th century by the detached villa, built for a decade or so in a wealth of varied forms and with features like terracotta kangaroos on the roof line and eucalyptus leaves in the barge boards.

The 20th-century suburbs are undistinguished. The interwar California bungalow has given way to brick veneer dwellings and bizarre neo-Grecian palaces. Similarly, the redeveloped cities do not seem to have embraced Australian style either.

Right: Renovated Victorian building in downtown Melbourne

▶▶ Rippon Lea Estate   off 95A4

192 Hotham Street, Elsternwick (tel: 03-9523 6095)
Open: daily 10–5. Admission: moderate
Begun in 1868 by the London-born Frederick Thomas
Sargood, this two-tone brick house is perhaps the most
splendid surviving late-Victorian mansion in Melbourne's
suburbs. The gardens are both opulent and extensive.

▶▶▶ Royal Botanic Gardens Melbourne   95A6

Birdwood Avenue, South Yarra (tel: 03-9252 2300)
Open: Nov–Mar daily, 7.30–8.30; Apr–Oct 7.30–5.30. Guided
walks Sun–Fri 11, 2. Admission free, walks inexpensive
These superb, lush and beautifully landscaped gardens
rank among the finest in the world. The site was chosen as
early as 1845, and the gardens were laid out and stocked
with an incredible range of plants by successive directors.
Ferdinand von Mueller (director, 1852–73) preferred a
formal layout, while his successor, William Guilfoyle, re-
designed the gardens in a more romantic, English style
with sweeping lawns, informal lakes and curving paths.

Plants from all over the world thrive in Melbourne's
climate. There are more than 6,000 tree species, ranging
from cool temperate regions through to subtropical areas.
English elms and oaks contrast with grass trees and river
red gums. The Australian Lawn is planted with eucalypts
from all over the country, and there is also the Australian
Rainforest Walk, a rose garden, herb and succulent gardens and a fern gully. There are a number of buildings in
the garden, which complement the plantings, including
the classical Temple of the Winds and the restored Old
Melbourne Observatory. A good way to familiarize yourself with these wonderful gardens is to take one of the
guided walks from the modern visitor centre.

▶ St. Patrick's Cathedral   95E4

Cathedral Place, East Melbourne
Less hemmed in by modern buildings than the Anglican
Cathedral (see page 104), the 103m (338-ft) central spire of
this great Roman Catholic cathedral (see panel) features
in many city views. It was designed by William Wardell,
who also built the ANZ Bank.

*One of the inhabitants
of the highly acclaimed
Melbourne Zoo (page
100)*

THE SEPARATION TREE
This is the name given to
one of the fine river red
gums in the Royal
Botanic Gardens, since it
was beneath its branches
that the grand public
celebration took place
in 1851 to mark the inde-
pendence of Victoria from
New South Wales.

INSIDE ST. PATRICK'S
St. Patrick's has a
splendidly soaring
interior, with magnificent
stained-glass windows.
Long regarded as an
Irish stronghold, it also
has a statue of Daniel
O'Connell—the great
19th-century Irish
patriot known as 'the
Liberator'—in the
churchyard.

On guard at the impressive Shrine of Remembrance

ARTS TOUR
The Arts Centre complex is adorned inside and out with numerous works of art, many of them specially commissioned. The Centre's guided tours are an excellent way of getting to grips with them all.

MELBOURNE'S MIGRANTS
Melbourne's fascinating Immigration Museum is well worth a visit. Housed in the beautifully renovated 1876 Old Customs House at 400 Flinders Street, the exhibits portray the departures, arrivals and impacts of Victoria's settlers during the last two centuries. Particularly interesting are the personal and often very moving stories of refugees and other migrants from many cultural backgrounds.

▶ **St. Paul's Cathedral**   *94C3*

Corner of Swanston and Flinders streets
No longer the dominant element in the cityscape, this fine Gothic Revival-style church still has a commanding presence. Standing on the site where the first official church service in Melbourne took place in 1836, the cathedral was built between 1880–1891 to a design by the British architect William Butterfield, also responsible for the Chapter House and Diocesan Offices in the cathedral complex.

▶▶ **Shrine of Remembrance**   *95A5*

St. Kilda Road (tel: 03-9654 8415)
Open: daily 10–5. Admission: donation
Based on the Parthenon, this shrine to the Victorian war dead sits massively on top of a rise in the ground in Kings Domain. It was completed in 1934 in memory of the 114,000 Victorians who served in World War I, of whom 19,000 died. The Stone of Remembrance in the central chamber is illuminated by a shaft of light at 11AM every 11 November. Below is the crypt, displaying regimental flags, and above is a gallery with fine views over the city and environs. The grounds have been laid out to commemorate those who fell in other wars.

▶▶▶ **The Arts Centre**   *94B3*

100 St. Kilda Road (tel: 03-9281 8000). Open: daily, tours Mon–Sat noon, 2.30, Sun 12.15 (backstage tour). Admission: Museum free, tours moderate
Not a cultural ghetto, but a vibrant part of city life, the modern arts centre, completed in 1984, comprises a complex of exciting buildings on the south bank of the Yarra.

Next to the National Gallery is the **Theatres** building, topped by a 115m (377-ft) high spire, one of Melbourne's cultural landmarks. The three theatres themselves are below ground: the State Theatre is the home of the Australian Ballet; the Melbourne Theatre Company performs in the Playhouse; and the third is a highly adaptable studio space. The spectacular interior of the **Hamer Hall** is done in mineral shades that reflect the geology of the Australian continent. The centre also embraces two restaurants, the Arts Centre shop, a Sunday market, the entertaining Performing Arts Museum and, in Kings Domain, the Sidney Myer Music Bowl.

Melbourne's city streets

See map on pages 94–95.

From the traditional meeting place of Melburnians—'under the clocks' at Flinders Street station—to grandiose Parliament House, this walk (about 2km/1.2 miles) covers civic and commercial aspects of Melbourne.

The station steps open on to the bustling heart of the city. Across the road is the new **Federation Square** development, where you'll find the Ian Potter Centre (see page 101), then Swanson Street and the Gothic grandeur of **St. Paul's Cathedral**. Modern City Square marks the junction with Collins Street, dominated by the splendid Town Hall. Commercial dynamism has taken many shapes along this prestigious artery, from American deco of the 1930s to Victorian Gothic.

In Queen Street, the elaborate Safe Deposit Building (No. 90) is dwarfed by the soaring **ANZ Tower**. Trams and shoppers throng Bourke Street Mall, off which runs the city's oldest shopping gallery, Royal Arcade. Traditional archways signal the entry to Chinatown. The grid of city streets ends where Little Bourke Street emerges into Spring Street, overlooked by the imposing colonnade of Victoria's **Parliament House**, and the Windsor Hotel of 1883. Nearby stands the **Old Treasury Building**, completed in 1862, which contains the Gold Treasury Museum, dealing with Melbourne's history, architecture and comtemporary life.

Return to Flinders Street station via the eastern end of Collins Street.

Along the Yarra

See map on pages 94–95.

A 5km (3-mile) walk along Melbourne's River Yarra into Kings Domain and the Botanic Gardens.

Downstream from Princes Bridge, the Yarra is crossed by a footbridge. Avoiding the tempting riverside cafés of the Southgate Precinct, you are rewarded with a stunning view of the city skyline from Southbank Promenade on the far side of Princes Bridge.

Negotiate the crossing of Alexandra Avenue with care and enjoy the calm of **Kings Domain**, with its various focal points like the Sidney Myer Music Bowl and the Pioneer Women's Memorial Garden. The far bank of the lake in the **Royal Botanic Gardens** marks the outermost point of the walk, excuse enough for a pause at the lakeside café.

Beyond the Herbarium and Visitor Centre is the **Shrine of Remembrance**, whose outside gallery gives a wonderful vista back towards the centre of Melbourne.

The return to Flinders Street station can be made on foot or by tram along St. Kilda Road.

At leisure on the Yarra River

Victoria

THE BIRDS OF WYPERFELD

Much of this national park is alive with great flocks of birds: white and pink cockatoos, galahs and regent parrots. The most curious bird, though, is the mallee-fowl, builder of underground nests in which its young are hatched in meticulously controlled incubation conditions.

PEAKS AND BEACHES

Although Victoria cannot lay claim to any of Australia's World Heritage regions, this small state encompasses an extra-ordinary variety of national parks and wilderness areas. Apart from the alpine regions, Victoria's most popular park is probably the superb coastal region of Wilsons Promontory (see page 121).

At Point Nepean on the Mornington Peninsula—the entrance to Port Phillip Bay

National parks

From high alps to rolling downlands, from luxuriant rain forests to desert scrub, and from the spreading floodplains of the Murray River in the north to some of the country's most dramatic coastline in the south, Victoria's landscape is as varied as its climate. A high rainfall over much of the state contributes to the luxuriance of the forest cover as well as to the productivity of grasslands and other farmed areas; by contrast, the far northwest is extremely arid.

Victorian Alps The dominating physical feature of the state is its mountain backbone, a southern stretch of Australia's Great Dividing Range. Majestic alpine summits rise to almost 2,000m (6,560ft), while foothills and lower ranges stretch southward and westward to form a hilly backdrop to the metropolitan area of Melbourne. Many of the highest and most spectacular parts of the Victorian Alps are protected as national parks; they include **Mount Buffalo** (1,720m/5,643ft), whose characteristic hump-backed shape was first seen by the explorers Hume and Hovell in 1824. Beneath the summit, stretches a vast upland plateau bounded by cliffs falling abruptly to the plains below. Used for skiing in winter, the plateau is embroidered with wildflowers in spring.

The vegetation cover varies with altitude, the dense wet forest of the valleys becoming more open farther up the slope, with peppermint gums giving way to alpine ash and finally to snow gums. In the early days of white settlement, cattlemen drove their beasts high into the uplands to feed off the summer pastures, building stone huts for shelter. Many of the huts remain, but grazing has been forbidden because of erosion. A number of physically separate national parks—Bogong, Cobberas-Tingaringy and Wonnangatta-Moroka parks—have since been grouped together to form the exhilarating **Alpine National Park**, Victoria's largest at 646,000ha (1,596,000 acres).

Southeastern Victoria Along the border with New South Wales lies some of the most unspoiled scenery in the state. Inland are a number of national parks. **Errinundra National Park** encompasses a large tract of cool, temperate woodland, and there are other pockets of rain forest at **Lind** and **Alfred national parks**. The splendid gorges along the course of the **Snowy River** offer exciting whitewater canoeing; this park is also the habitat of the rare brush-tailed rock wallaby. Running from Sydenham Inlet to the NSW boundary is one of the country's finest coastal reserves, the **Croajingolong National Park**, with savage cliffs and headlands protecting pristine beaches and tranquil inlets. In complete contrast is **The Lakes National Park** to the west, where the seemingly infinite Ninety Mile Beach is backed by lagoons and waterways.

As well as the Dandenongs (see page 114), day-trips from Melbourne can take in Point Nepean at the tip of **Mornington Peninsula National Park**, the **Brisbane Ranges**, the forests and fern gullies of **Kinglake National Park** to the northeast and the basalt columns of **Organ Pipes National Park** to the northwest. The **Grampians (Gariwerd) National Park** in the west is one of Victoria's highlights. With its Aboriginal sites, stunning scenery and abundant wildlife—more than 900 wildflower species, 40 species of native mammals and 200 species of birds—the reserve is reachable in a day, but merits a longer stay.

Victoria's southwestern coastline The best can be seen in two contrasting parks: Between Lorne and Cape Otway, the high ranges of the **Great Otway National Park**, still covered in glorious rain forest, rise steeply from the sea; farther west, the breakers are constantly resculpting the cliffs of the **Port Campbell National Park**, creating spectacular coastal scenery. Inland, at **Mount Eccles** volcanic activity has given rise to fertile farmland interspersed with crater lakes and worn-down volcanic cones. Far from the coast and wooded uplands is **Wyperfeld National Park**, a complex system of normally dry lakes and lagoons, with mallee (see panel) stretching to the horizon.

The basalt columns of the aptly named Organ Pipes National Park

MASTERING THE MALLEE
Much of northwestern Victoria was once covered in mallee, 'a blue and level sea stretching to the horizon'. Mallee is an Aboriginal word describing the fire-resistant scrub composed of 20 or so species of low-growing eucalyptus. The mallee burns fiercely, but quickly regenerates from the surviving roots, making it difficult for farmers to clear. Its demise came about with the invention of mullenization; a heavy roller was dragged through the scrub by oxen, followed by an ingenious 'stump-jump' plough. Years of burning and cropping finally eradicated the troublesome mallee, except in areas like Wyperfeld, itself threatened with clearance as late as the 1960s.

Getting around Melbourne is easy using the city's trams

THE GREAT OCEAN ROAD

One of Australia's most famous drives, the Great Ocean Road stretches 300km (186 miles) from south of Geelong towards the South Australian border, and takes in beaches, charming ports and villages, forested hillsides and, around the town of Port Campbell, dramatically eroded coastline (see page 119).

THE UNPREDICTABLE STATE

The weather in Victoria can be very changeable; desert influences may be felt one moment, with searing dry winds and high temperatures, giving way suddenly to cold and wet air from the ocean to the south. If you don't like our weather, say Melburnians, just wait a minute—it's bound to change!

How to travel

By air Melbourne Airport is 22km (13.5 miles) northwest of the city and is connected to many overseas destinations as well as to all major cities in Australia. Domestic and international flights share the same terminal. Frequent Skybus services link the airport to Southern Cross (formerly Spencer Street) station downtown, from where a shuttle transports passengers to the city's hotels.

By bus Express buses travel to major destinations in Australia and within Victoria. Because of the (relatively!) small size of the state, public transport is a reasonable proposition for most journeys. Many places in Victoria are accessible in a day's outing from Melbourne. There is the usual excellent range of organized bus tours; shop around for the one that suits your requirements.

By train Greater Melbourne's comprehensive public transportation network is marketed under the name of **Metlink**. Electric suburban railways that travel as far afield as the Dandenong Ranges and Mornington Peninsula are supplemented by systems of tramways and by urban buses. Through-ticketing is based on a zoning system, and there are a number of special deals like day tickets or weekly passes that are worth considering. The principal station is Flinders Street, and most trains travel around the underground loop that circles the city, with useful stops at Southern Cross, Flagstaff, Melbourne Central, Parliament and Flinders Street. There is also a free City Circle Tram, which runs every 10 minutes.

Quite a number of towns in Victoria can be reached by **V-Line train** (sometimes supplemented by a V-Line bus). There are interstate services to Adelaide and Sydney as well as to Perth (changing at Adelaide or Port Pirie), and Alice Springs and Darwin on the famous *Ghan* (see pages 134 and 189).

By car Road conditions in Victoria are generally good. Melbourne has an excellent freeway system and the traffic flows much more freely than in Sydney. To visit the more inaccessible national parks renting a car is recommended.

►► Apollo Bay 90A2

This little fishing port about 185km (115 miles) to the west of Port Phillip Bay has magnificent beaches and makes an excellent base for exploring the superb forests of the **Otway Ranges►►**. The hills reach the sea at Cape Otway, the 'fearful coastline' described by the explorer Matthew Flinders, with a lighthouse rising from high cliffs.

► Ararat 90B2

This town (200km/125 miles northwest of Melbourne) owes its foundation to the gold strike of 1857, when 85,000g (3,000 ounces) of alluvial gold were found in the space of three weeks. Ararat was the only town in Australia founded by the Chinese—one of the town's highlights is the Gum San Chinese Heritage Centre. To the north is the world-famous **Seppelt Great Western Winery►**, where the sparkling wine is stored in underground galleries originally dug out by the gold miners.

► Avoca 90B2

On the Pyrenees Highway between Ararat and Castlemaine, Avoca was once a gold town and is now the hub of an agricultural area. Since the 1960s, vineyards have been replanted on the north-facing slopes of the foothills, making this one of the state's newer wine districts. The solid Court House complex with bluestone jail, powder magazine and police residence dates from the mid-19th century.

►►► Ballarat 90B2

No bigger since its gold-rush heyday, Ballarat has preserved much of its 19th-century townscape and the atmosphere of those heady times. Gold was found in 1851, and within a few months thousands of ill-assorted diggers were frantically prospecting in spite of mud, cold and often bitter disappointment. Surface deposits were soon exhausted, and individual miners were succeeded by companies with the clout to dig deep mines and run them. Gold may have made Melbourne, but it made Ballarat too; profits were not gambled or drunk away, but invested in bricks and mortar, giving the town as splendid an array of fine 19th-century building as anywhere in the country. Banks, churches, a synagogue, clubs, a mining exchange, a splendid town hall and an art gallery show how quickly the raw life of the diggings was transmuted into civic respectability.

BALLARAT'S BOTANICS By the side of beautiful Lake Wendouree, the Botanic Gardens in Ballarat are a perfect example of High Victorian taste, with white marble statuary among the pretty pavilions and bedding plants. On plinths beneath the trees stand the busts of former prime ministers, some, like notorious protagonists Gough Whitlam and Malcolm Fraser, none too comfortable at seeing each other in such close proximity again.

109

The gold-rush town of Ballarat contains many grand buildings that date from the 19th century

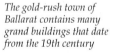

Victoria

EUREKA!
By 1854, passions were running high in Ballarat's goldfields. Grim working and living conditions and encroachment by bigger mining companies were compounded by high licence fees, extracted from resentful diggers by heavy-handed and much hated special police. Eventually, a band of Irish-led miners staged the only major revolt by whites in Australian history. Licences were burned in a joyous conflagration, and the rebels, armed with pikes, assembled in the Eureka Stockade under the banner of the Southern Cross. But they were swiftly overcome by government soldiers, who left 30 dead. Australia's 'Civil War' lasted 15 minutes; it is convincingly re-created, using advanced *son et lumière* techniques, at Sovereign Hill. The imaginative multimedia Eureka Centre is also well worth a visit.

A statue of Queen Victoria presides over formal gardens in Bendigo

BRED IN BALLARAT
Ballarat Wildlife Park has a wonderful selection of mostly Antipodean animals in its park-like setting. It is one of the few places where Tasmanian Devils are successfully bred; if you are so inclined, you can see these thugs of the animal world being fed their daily ration of white mice.

Sovereign Hill►►► is a superb re-creation of life and work on the goldfields in the 1850s. Visitors can pan for gold, ride Cobb & Co.'s stagecoach, shop in the emporiums of Main Street, enjoy the unique world of the Chinese Village or even spend the night in 1850s-style accommodation at the Sovereign Hill Lodge. Other highlights include the Quartz Mine, with 600m (1,970ft) of underground workings, and the Gold Museum, which has displays showing the history of the precious metal.

►► Beechworth   91B4
This exceptionally well-preserved gold town in the foothills of the Australian Alps, 268km (167 miles) northeast of Melbourne, has a old gold-mining sites and a fine array of old buildings, many of warm, honey-tinged stone. Over 30 of these structures are National Trust-listed and contained within the excellent **Beechworth Historic and Cultural Precinct►►**. As well as the post office, with its imposing tower, there is also the **Burke Museum►►**. Named after the ill-fated explorer, the museum is packed with memorabilia, including mementoes of Ned Kelly who spent a night in the cell beneath the town hall.

►► Bellarine Peninsula   90A3
Stretching eastward into Port Phillip Bay, this broad peninsula, with its fine surf beaches and popular resorts like Ocean Grove and Barwon Heads, has become a popular summer desination with the inhabitants of Geelong. One of the peninsula's greatest attractions is the charming resort town of Queenscliff (see page 119), known for its fort, lighthouse and grand old hotels.

▶▶ Bendigo   90B2

Like Ballarat, Bendigo began as a gold-rush town, expanding rapidly from 1851 onwards to become one of the state's largest inland towns. Many of its fine late 19th-century buildings, erected with the wealth won from the ground, remain in peak condition. These include the vast Shamrock Hotel, a number of imposing churches and a fine group of public buildings. The work that paid for all this architectural glory is celebrated in the completely preserved **Central Deborah Goldmine▶▶**, with its impressive underground galleries, while the special contribution of Chinese miners is recalled in the Golden Dragon Museum and the delightful **Joss House▶▶** at Emu Point. The best way to get acquainted is to take the 'Talking Tram', which runs along an 8km (5-mile) route and gives a full commentary on all the sights.

▶ Brisbane Ranges National Park   90A2

This extensive block of slate and sandstone has been eroded in places to form deep defiles like Anakie Gorge, a popular spot for not-too-demanding bush walks. Gold was once mined in quantity at the ghost town of Steiglitz, now a historic park.

▶ Camperdown   90A2

This township is on the sweeping plains formed from lava and ash that ran from the South Australian border to Port Phillip Bay and have long been the basis of a prosperous grazing industry. Now silent, the volcanic cones responsible for all this fertility are scattered over the area. Mount Leura and Mount Sugarloaf are to the southeast, while to the west stand two examples of crater lakes—Lake Bullen Merri (brackish water) and Lake Gnotuk (salt water).

▶▶ Castlemaine   90B2

Once gold had been discovered here in Specimen Gully by a shepherd, 25,000 diggers joined the rush, although Castlemaine declined fairly quickly because of the lack of reef gold. Today it is an attractive township, popular with Melbourne folk and full of interesting old buildings. Most striking is the classical market hall, an almost exact reproduction of a Greek temple which now contains the local visitor centre. Castlemaine is also home to an excellent art gallery and historical museum, some fine botanic gardens and the mansion known as Buda, begun in 1857.

The **Victorian Goldfields Railway▶▶** is a steam train ride that is very popular with children. It is based at Maldon station, 17.5km (11 miles) northwest along Highway 122 (see also page 117).

▶▶ Coal Creek Heritage Village,
   Korumburra   90A3

The railways of Victoria used to run on Korumburra coal, and after the last mine had been closed down in the late 1950s it was decided that the days of coal and steam should be re-created at Coal Creek Mine just outside town (about 120km/75 miles southeast of Melbourne). As well as the gallery of the mine, the popular site has a railway station and tramway rides, tradesmen plying their crafts, old stores and settlers' cottages.

THE GIPPSLAND WHOPPER
Of the 100 or so species of Australian worms, *Megascolides australis* is easily the biggest, measuring up to 3.5m (11.5ft) long and 2.5cm (1in) thick. This extraordinary creature has its own worm-shaped museum at Wildlife Wonderland at Bass, near the turn-off for Phillip Island on the Bass Highway.

111

Castlemaine is a former mining town about 40km (25 miles) north of Daylesford

For much of its length, the Murray forms the boundary between Victoria and New South Wales. The longest river in Australia rises in the Great Dividing Range near Mount Kosciuszko, flowing past red gums and irrigating the land around Mildura before entering the sea at Encounter Bay in South Australia.

BARMAH FOREST

Spreading for 30,000ha (74,130 acres) over the floodplain of the Murray upstream from Echuca is this magnificent forest of river red gum trees, some of them 500 years old. Australia was largely built on the timber milled from these majestic trees, which was used for railway construction, bridges, mines, fences and wharves. When the river spills over its banks during exceptionally rainy spells, the forest comes alive with the calls of more than 200 species of migrating birds.

A journey to the past aboard a paddle steamer...

For thousands of years, the rich wildlife of the Murray and its tributaries gave sustenance to the Aborigines who lived along its banks. It was discovered by Hume and Hovell in 1824, and explored more thoroughly by Charles Sturt in the course of his expedition of 1829–30. As settlers arrived, in the beginning strongly opposed by the Aborigines, the river took on great importance as a transport route. A spirited contest took place in 1853 between the *Mary Ann* and the *Lady Augusta*, to see which would be the first steamboat to make it up the Murray as far as Swan Hill. With the prize money of £4,000, the master of the winning steamboat founded the Murray River Navigation Co., whose sternwheelers dominated river traffic for many years until the coming of the railway rendered them obsolete.

The greatest handicap to navigation was the irregularity of the Murray's flow; for many months of the year there would not be enough water to float a boat of any size, and the risk of running aground was constant. Today, a number of proud vessels survive to carry cargoes of nostalgic tourists rather than the bales of wool that filled the holds in their 19th-century heyday.

Attractions Upstream from the twin towns of Albury (NSW) and Wodonga (Victoria) is **Lake Hume**, several times the size of Sydney Harbour. Built to regulate river flow, it is now an ideal place for watersports. Downstream are the wineries around **Rutherglen**, while **Yarrawonga**, thanks to Lake Mulwala, has become a major inland water recreation area. Around **Cobram** are dozens of fine sandy beaches.

Echuca was once Australia's busiest inland port, with a truly magnificent wharf more than 1.5km (1 mile) long built from the timber of red gums. The people of the town are very proud of its heritage, and have taken pains to preserve it for the pleasure of visitors. The **Port of Echuca** has been fully restored and has a whole series of visitor attractions, including the Cargo Shed with life-like dioramas. The Bridge Hotel is

...stopping at Echuca, Swan Hill, Mildura and other places along the Murray

THE CHAFFEYS
Canadians George and William Chaffey pioneered artificially irrigated settlements in California before being invited to bring their expertise to the Murray. They both succeeded and failed; from the 1880s on, thousands of new settlers flocked to the newly irrigated areas around Mildura, and the town itself prospered, but there were floods, problems with leaching and salinity, and the great slump of the 1890s. By 1896 George had had enough and borrowed his fare home, but William stayed on, helping to put the area's economy on a firmer footing once the railway arrived in 1903. The water pumps that George had designed continued to work into the 1950s.

full of period furniture, and the old Customs House has been put to use as the information centre. It is rare to see so many steamboats, under restoration or in action.

To the northwest of the Kerang Lakes is another river port, **Swan Hill**, named by explorer Thomas Mitchell who was kept awake at night by the swans on a nearby lagoon. In addition to paddle-steamer cruises, the town's outstanding attraction is the **Swan Hill Pioneer Settlement**, a painstaking riverside re-creation, put together using original buildings as well as accurate replicas, and brought alive by the presence of craftspeople practicing traditional trades. The Pioneer Settlement also has a sound and light show, which concentrates on the early pioneers. A strong sense of the past can also be experienced in two fine old properties, the **Tyntyndyer Homestead** to the north, and **Murray Downs** to the east, the latter designed to repel attack by Aborigines.

Red to green At the heart of the irrigated area, **Mildura** was originally laid out on the American pattern, with streets given numbers rather than names. In the language of the Kulkyne Aborigines, Mildura meant 'dry red earth', but here red has turned to green—the Chaffey brothers, who arrived in 1885 from Canada, brought advanced irrigation techniques (see panel). Avocados, melons, oranges and grapes, both for the table and for wine-making, are all grown here, as is a whole range of fruit for drying. Some establishments are happy to share their production secrets with you, among them **Orange World** and the **Lindemans Karadoc** and **Stanley wineries**. Alternatively, you could take a trip upriver aboard one of the paddle steamers that operate from here.

The lovely National Rhododendron Gardens at Olinda in the Dandenong Ranges

A FEATHERED PHILANDERER
The forests and gullies of the Dandenongs provide a habitat for *Menura novae-hollandiae*, the superb lyrebird, a wonderful singer and mimic of the calls of other birds. The rather ordinary-looking male of the species comes into his own in winter, when he senses that female lyrebirds are ready to respond to his advances. Having built a series of mounds through-out his territory, the male mounts one and undergoes an extra-ordinary transformation, fanning out his lyre-shaped tail-feathers so that his body disappears in a froth of plumage, at the same time pouring forth a cascade of song. The more impressive the display, the greater the bird's chances of winning his way with a succession of females.

▶ Colac   90A2
Colac is the market town for the agricultural wealth of the surrounding basalt plains. This southwestern area incorporates a lake district of some 50 to 60 water bodies. Those that have formed in deep craters contain fresh water, while the shallower lakes contain salty water because the rate of evaporation from them exceeds the rate of replenishment; Lake Corangamite is a saline lake, and is also Victoria's largest. There are superb views of the lake and surrounding plains from Red Rock Lookout.

▶▶ The Dandenong Ranges   90A3
Melbourne is fortunate to have these magnificently wooded hills, part of a national park, on the eastern edge of the metropolitan area; a wonderful destination for a day's outing. The highest point is **Mount Dandenong**▶▶ (633m/2,077ft), with fantastic views over the sprawling city to the west and the hills farther to the east.
   Because of their accessibility, the Dandenongs have long been a popular residential area, and there are pretty townships and many fine mansions, some converted into hotels and restaurants. There are lush gardens, too, like the **National Rhododendron Gardens**▶ at Olinda, whose exotic shrubs contrast with the native vegetation of towering mountain ash trees, massive tree ferns and rampant creepers. At Belgrave is the terminus of **'Puffing Billy'**▶▶, the vintage narrow-gauge steam locomotive that pulls trainloads of tourists on a scenic trip through the forest.

▶▶ Daylesford   90B2
Between them, Daylesford (109km/67 miles northwest of Melbourne) and Hepburn Springs contain half of Australia's mineral springs. The supposedly therapeutic waters were discovered in the course of gold mining in the 1850s and 1860s, and by the turn of the 20th century the place had taken on the character of the spa resorts so common in Europe, perhaps because many of the early

inhabitants were originally immigrants from the Swiss canton of Ticino. At the **Hepburn Spa►►**, the old spa building is still intact; you can buy bottled water, take various treatments and enjoy relaxing walks. The excellent **Daylesford Historical Museum►** is housed in the old School of Mines, and there are attractive botanical gardens. To the north is the old volcanic cone of Mount Franklin with a fine view from its summit.

► Dunolly   90B2

The area around Dunolly, 173km (107 miles) northwest of Melbourne, yielded more nuggets than any other Australian goldfield, including the Welcome Stranger, weighing 71kg (2,505 ounces). Reproductions of this and other mega-nuggets are in the town's **Goldfields Historical and Arts Museum►**.

► Geelong   90A2

This industrial port city, Victoria's second largest, once saw itself as a rival to Melbourne, but has long since given up the struggle, though its harbour still exports the rich produce of its agricultural hinterland. In spite of much redevelopment, including a lively waterfront dining strip, there is plenty of evidence of 19th-century grandeur; imposing public buildings adorn the city and prosperity is reflected in the many elegant properties, such as Barwon Grange overlooking the Barwon River. Corio Villa above Eastern Beach was prefabricated in Scotland and assembled here by guesswork after the plans had been destroyed. One of the fine old bluestone woolstores has been restored to house the **National Wool Museum►►**. Come here if you want to understand how Australia 'rode to prosperity on the sheep's back'.

►► Gippsland   91A4

Named in the 1840s by Polish explorer Count Strzelecki after the Governor of NSW, Gippsland is the loosely defined region comprising most of southeastern Victoria between the highlands of the Great Dividing Range and the coastline of Bass Strait. The superb temperate rainforest that once blanketed the area has mostly been cut down to yield rich dairying and fruit-growing land, though fine tracts of woodland remain in the state forests and national parks along the NSW border in the far east. This is one of the areas where protest action by conservationists has focused public attention on the fact that the glories of Australia's natural heritage are not inexhaustible. The La Trobe Valley in the heart of Gippsland has one of the world's biggest deposits of brown coal, burned here in power stations to provide something like 90 per cent of the state's electric power, while oil and gas is extracted in quantity from offshore wells in Bass Strait.

The scale of contemporary opencast mining can be appreciated in the course of tours of the **PowerWorks►** visitor centre and lookouts at East Morwell, while more traditional activities can be contemplated in the **Gippsland Heritage Park►** at Moe, with its collection of old buildings from many parts of Gippsland. Inland is some of Victoria's most attractive countryside, running up into the alpine foothills of the Great Dividing Range, while the Gippsland Lakes (see panel) lie landward of Ninety Mile Beach.

GIPPSLAND LAKES
Sometimes described as 'the best example of a coastal lagoon in the world', and with a near-Mediterranean climate, this area has unrivalled opportunites for sailing, cruising, fishing or just taking it easy. Both beach and lakes are protected as national parks.

115

Rich dairy lands make for fine Gippsland cheeses

Victoria

116

▶ **Goulburn Valley** 90B3

The Goulburn River runs northwest from artificial Lake Eildon in the foothills of the Victorian Alps through a rich fruit- and vine-growing area to join the Murray River near Echuca. With an indented shoreline more than 480km (300 miles) long, Lake Eildon is an immensely popular place for watersports of all kinds. There is also some good walking in this area. The lake is fringed by **Lake Eildon National Park**▶, a forested environment that is also rich in wildlife. To the west of the river, Rushworth is a fine example of a gold-rush town of the 1850s.

▶▶ **Grampians (Gariwerd) National Park** 90B1

The Aborigines, who left many traces of their rock art here, knew the Grampians as Gariwerd. Forming one of the largest national parks in Victoria, the region consists of a succession of sandstone ridges sloping gently to the west, ending in sheer cliffs and jagged rock formations to the east. The area is rich in wildlife and is carpeted with wildflowers in summer.

The park has an excellent network of trails and paths, and can also be appreciated by car, thanks to a series of scenic roads. There are any number of spectacular viewpoints; **Boroka Lookout**▶▶ gives a fine panorama over the town of Halls Gap, where there is a visitor centre and **Brambuk–the National Park and Cultural Centre**▶, which brings the history and culture of local Aborigines to life. To the west are two of the most spectacular sights of the ranges; the rock formation known as the **Balconies** and the grandiose water staircase of the **Mackenzie Falls**.

▶ **Hamilton** 90A1

Focal point of much of the prosperous agricultural plains of central western Victoria, Hamilton likes to style itself the 'Wool Capital of the World'. Its outstanding attraction is the **Hamilton Art Gallery**▶, with a large and varied

The huge overhanging rocks in the Grampians National Park known as the Balconies

collection including examples of the applied arts of many countries, plus a splendid array of the watercolours and etchings by the British topographical artist Paul Sandby.

117

Maldon's wide main street, sloping gently downhill has some typically Australian country architecture

▶▶ Healesville   90B3
Nestling among its green hills in the Yarra Valley, this attractive township is a good place for walks and picnics, but it is mostly visited now for the **Healesville Sanctuary ▶ ▶**. A visit to this wildlife park is an excellent way to appreciate the strange and wonderful fauna of the Antipodes, in a range of cleverly re-created habitats and walk-through enclosures. Other local attractions include an Aboriginal cultural centre, galleries, antique shops and the wineries of the Yarra Valley (see panel opposite).

▶▶ Lorne   90A2
Protected from the north by the steep forested slopes of the Otways, this charming little village, facing on to the curving beach of Loutit Bay, has enjoyed a high reputation as a Great Ocean Road beach resort for over a century. There are also delightful walks in the forest park.

▶▶ Maldon   90B2
Among the many old gold-rush townships of central Victoria, Maldon is outstanding, 'the best preserved town in Australia of the gold-mining era' according to the National Trust. It is certainly full of charm; the scale of the place is modest and the tone is set by delightful cottages, many of them with pretty gardens.

▶ Marysville   90B3
In the foothills of the Victorian Alps, the township of Marysville has long been popular with weekending Melburnians. In summer, there is wonderful bushwalking to the Steavenson Falls, some of the highest in Victoria, or to the Cumberland Valley where the state's tallest trees grow, while in winter there is good cross-country skiing, particularly on the popular snowfields of Lake Mountain.

DUCKBILLED DENIZEN
The normally bashful platypus can be observed going about its daily life at the Healesville Sanctuary. The sanctuary has the distinction of being the first place to successfully breed this reclusive egg-laying mammal in captivity.

Victoria

PENGUINS ON PARADE
The endearing little fairy penguins that live along the coasts of southern Australia are the smallest of the species in the world, being only about 35–40cm (less than a foot) in length. At Phillip Island they spend their days feeding at sea, then as evening falls they gather in groups to waddle to their burrows at the back of Summerland Beach. They maintain this routine with apparent indifference to the floodlighting and to the countless tourists huddled in the stands watching them.

►► Mornington Peninsula   90A3

Melbourne's best-loved weekend and holiday area embraces Port Phillip Bay in a great curve of sheltered beaches before ending at Point Nepean, overlooking the dangerous currents of the narrow entrance to the bay known as The Rip. Much of the peninsula is suburban in character, with dwellings crowding along the main road and spreading out from the residential and resort towns like Frankston and Mornington, but there are over 100 wineries to visit. In the season, the foreshore is crowded with campers and motor-homes.

Towards the tip, refined Sorrento and exclusive Portsea have retained the feeling of early days, when paddle steamers plied across the bay from Melbourne. Once off limits as a naval base, Point Nepean is now part of the **Mornington Peninsula National Park**, reached from the visitor centre by shuttle. The 'front' beaches facing the bay tend to be calm but busy, while the 'back' beaches looking out on to the Bass Strait are rough—no place for inexperienced swimmers. Former Australian Prime Minister Harold Holt disappeared here in 1967, and was presumed drowned.

The peninsula's importance in Victoria's history is recalled by the graves of the 'early settlers' at **Sorrento►**, and by the 1844 **McCrae Homestead►**, the home of the first permanent settler family. The best overall view is from 305m (1,000-ft) high **Arthur's Seat►►**.

►► Phillip Island   90A3

Bounded to the west by the Mornington Peninsula, the great tidal estuary of Westernport Bay is broken up by a number of islands. French Island and little Churchill Island—the latter is part of the Phillip Island Nature Park—

Mount Martin Beach at Port Phillip Bay on Mornington Peninsula

are rich in wildlife, but the most famous is Phillip Island, whose irresistible **Penguin Parade▶▶▶** (see panel opposite) pulls in hundreds of thousands of onlookers. Reached by bridge and about 130km (80 miles) from Melbourne, Phillip Island has a varied coastline that includes rugged cliffs and long surf beaches. Muttonbirds nest on **Cape Woolamai**, the island's highest point; the **Koala Conservation Centre▶▶** has a large koala colony; and Seal Rocks is home to the world's largest Australian fur seal colony. **Cowes** is the main resort, with restaurants, shops, a good range of accommodation and boat trips to see the seals and French Island.

▶▶▶ Port Campbell National Park   90A2

Backed by the Great Ocean Road running west from Geelong, this park comprises 30km (19 miles) of some of the world's most spectacular coastal scenery, a succession of high cliffs, headlands and strange rock formations standing out to sea. Biscuit-like beds of limestone, sand, mud and seashells formed beneath the sea and then uplifted 25 million years ago are now being eaten away by the breakers rolling in from the Southern Ocean. Because the rock varies in strength and texture, the sea advances more rapidly in some places than others, leaving behind isolated features that have been given evocative names like the **Twelve Apostles** (at Port Campbell). In a dramatic demonstration of the rate of erosion, the arch of 'London Bridge' collapsed into the surf in 1990, stranding the walkers who had ventured on to it. Quickly rescued, they were luckier than the many passengers and crewmen who perished along what was named the 'Shipwreck Coast' in the days of sail (see pages 242–243).

▶▶ Port Fairy   90A1

This delightful little Great Ocean Road fishing port and beach resort at the mouth of the Moyne River is one of the oldest settlements in Victoria, having been home to sealers and whalers in the early years of the 19th century. There are 50 buildings classified as historic by the National Trust, including Mott's Cottage and a wooden house erected by a whaling skipper in the 1830s.

▶ Portland   90A1

Founded in 1834, this busy deep-water port is the oldest permanent settlement in Victoria. To the southwest are the spectacular seascapes of Cape Nelson and the blowholes and petrified forest of Cape Bridgewater.

▶▶ Queenscliff   90A3

Separated from Point Nepean on the Mornington Peninsula by the treacherous waters of The Rip, Queenscliff is an old-fashioned place, with a harbour, a fort (1882), grand hotels and the Black Lighthouse, prefabricated in Scotland and shipped here in 1863.

▶▶ Strzelecki Ranges   91A3

The best way to see these forested ridges is to follow the Grand Ridge Road from Nyora, southeast of Melbourne, to Carrajung (about 128km/80 miles), passing through some of Victoria's finest upland scenery and numerous pretty towns and villages.

Queenscliff on the Bellarine Peninsula— where Melburnians come to get away from it all

119

COUNT THE CONSONANTS
The Polish explorer Paul Edmund de Strzelecki styled himself 'Count', a claim with little apparent substance. Although it was Angus McMillan who had first blazed a trail through the almost impenetrable rain forest jungle of southeast Victoria, it was not his name for the area ('New South Caledonia') that was adopted, but Strzelecki's 'Gippsland'. Strzelecki's own venture into Gippsland was only saved from disaster by the skill of his Aboriginal guide, Tarra, after whom the Tarra-Bulga National Park has been named.

Gum trees or, to give them their more correct name, eucalypts, are the trees most closely identified with Australia. They comprise more than 500 different species, and grow in most parts of the country; some three-quarters of all Australian trees are eucalypts, many of them with wonderfully descriptive names like peppermint, iron-bark, bloodwood or blackbutt.

EUCALYPTUS LEAVES
All eucalyptus leaves contain a fragrant oil that is used for various medicinal purposes. Their indigestible look doesn't deter the koala either, which in fact depends entirely on a single eucalyptus species for its food source.

120

WORLD-BEATER
The confusingly named mountain ash (*Eucalyptus regnans*) is the tallest flowering plant in the world, reaching an extraordinary height of up to 100m (328ft) in the forests of Victoria and Tasmania.

The great river red gum forest at Yarrawonga

Early settlers didn't much like the look of the unfamiliar eucalypts, with their pale greyish-green or peeling, untidy bark hanging in strips and tatters and the unseasonal failure of their dull grey leaves to fall at the proper time of year. Many farmers and sheep graziers brought cuttings of other trees from home, and trees such as elm, oak, willow and poplar are now considered environmentally inappropriate in their Australian context. The same was true of townsfolk, who preferred the more orderly European trees for their parks.

Forests and felling But eucalypts have their own distinct allure, individually or in mass, forming magnificent forests or growing with other trees, shrubs and grasses to create the surprisingly park-like landscapes of many parts of the interior. Over the millennia, eucalypts have also learned to live with fire, regenerating almost miraculously after the all-too-common bushfires from buds concealed within their bark. Many species, like jarrah and messmate, yield first-rate wood, and in consequence were felled ruthlessly until recently. Others are logged, somewhat demeaningly, to be turned into woodchip for foreign pulp mills.

Varieties There are many types of eucalypts, from the Tasmanian blue gum that provided the wood for railway ties, to the river red gum of semi-arid areas, the ghost gum of deserts and the hardy, cold-resistant snow gum, symbol of the Australian Alps.

▶ Walhalla 91A4

Tucked away in the deep wooded valleys north of Moe, isolated Walhalla boomed in the late 19th century when more gold was extracted here than from any other area in Victoria. By the time the railway reached here in 1910, via a series of spectacular tunnels and trestle bridges, the gold had more or less run out. A stroll along the crooked main street recalls some of the atmosphere of former days, and you can visit the **Long Tunnel Extended Gold Mine**▶. You can also ride on the restored **Walhalla Goldfields Railway**▶ through this magnificent upland scenery.

▶ Wangaratta 90B3

The Hume Highway is the main route north between Melbourne and Sydney. About 240km (150 miles) from Melbourne is Wangaratta, a service hub for the surrounding agricultural area. The body of the notorious bushranger Daniel 'Mad Dog' Morgan is buried here minus his head, the latter having been sent to Melbourne in order to establish whether he really was mad, or just plain bad. The town's major attraction is the annual Festival of Jazz and Blues (November).

▶ Warrnambool 90A1

The biggest town on Victoria's southwest coast, Warrnambool has superb beaches. Founded by whalers in the 1840s, it is still frequented by southern right whales, which come here in winter to calve (see panel). **Flagstaff Hill Museum**▶▶ is a conscientiously re-created port village with several historic vessels, a sound and light show and other fascinating displays.

▶▶ Wilsons Promontory National Park 91A4

The southernmost point of mainland Australia, this wild and mountainous granite peninsula protruding into Bass Strait is perhaps Victoria's best-loved national park. Many of its rocky headlands, splendid beaches and dense forests are only accessible on foot, and in spite of its popularity it is always possible to find whatever degree of isolation you want (except for kangaroos, of course). The only settlement is at Tidal River, where the road ends and a network of wonderful hiking trails begins.

Southern right whales playing off Warrnambool

THE WARRNAMBOOL WHALES
Between May and August, southern right whales gather off Logan's Beach to bear their young. A special viewing platform has been built from which you can observe these magnificent creatures, once hunted to near-extinction, as they dive and play, making spectacular fountains from their blowholes or leaping bodily from the waves.

'THE PROM'
Discovered by maritime explorer George Bass in 1798 and named after a friend of Bass's colleague Matthew Flinders, Wilsons Promontory attracts all kinds of nature-lovers. In summer, the area is great for scuba diving and snorkelling; there are wonderful walks; and the hundreds of species of plants make the park a botanist's dream.

The Dandenong Ranges

Less than an hour from Melbourne, the 'Blue Dandenongs' are a popular recreation area and summer retreat for the inhabitants of the city.

Canterbury Road (Route 32) leads to Montrose at the northern end of the Dandenong Tourist Road. If you have time, continue 30km (19 miles) to **Healesville Sanctuary** in the Yarra

Valley, one of the best places to see Australian wildlife at close quarters.

Mount Dandenong, at 633m (2,077ft) the highest point of the range, and the sculptures of the **William Ricketts Sanctuary** are accessible from the Tourist Road. The route to the village of Kallista passes the Alfred Nicholas Gardens and the Sherbrooke Forest section of the **Dandenong Ranges National Park**, where you can see the tree ferns and the magnificent mountain ash trees for which the area is famous.

Belgrave is the terminus for the irresistible *Puffing Billy*, a restored steam train that hauls delighted passengers through the forest along its narrow-gauge track.

Mornington Peninsula

The 100km (62-mile) drive to Point Nepean at the tip of the Mornington Peninsula passes through resorts and residential areas with access to the beaches of Port Phillip Bay. Frankston

marks the end of the commuter railway line from Melbourne. Beyond **Dromana** with its excellent Tourist Information Centre the coast is lined with holiday homes and campsites, while above the town **Arthur's Seat** rises 305m (1,000ft) to give a fine panorama over bay and ocean. On its northern slope is the little **McCrae Homestead**, built in 1844 and still evocative of pioneer days despite its proximity to nearby suburbia.

With its broad main street, **Sorrento** has a charm all of its own, while posh **Portsea** does its best to maintain its exclusivity. On the outer rim of the peninsula, the 'back beaches' face the ocean surf of Bass Strait. For a long time off limits as defence land, the **Point Nepean** section of the **Mornington Peninsula National Park** can now be visited. With 40km (25 miles) of rugged coastline, this park and its adjacent marine reserve encompass excellent surfing beaches, diving spots and wildlife, including dolphins from November to March.

Other attractions on the Mornington Peninsula include wineries, golf courses and a reputation for boutique guest houses and dining. From Frankston, the Mornington Peninsula Freeway and Monash Freeway can be used to speed your return to Melbourne.

Port Phillip Bay begins at the tip of the Mornington Peninsula (right)

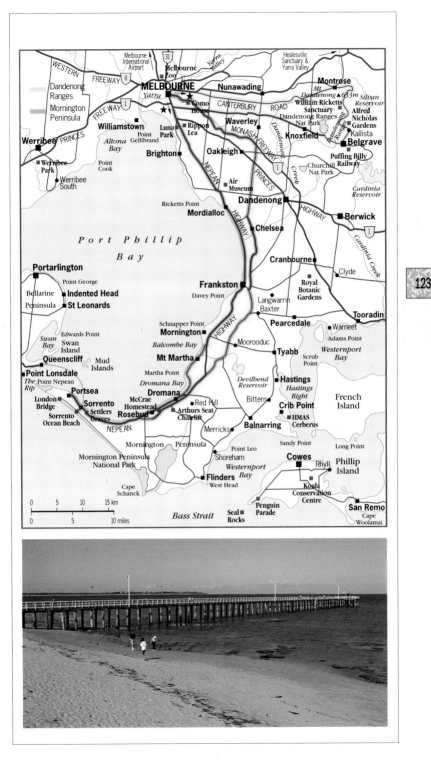

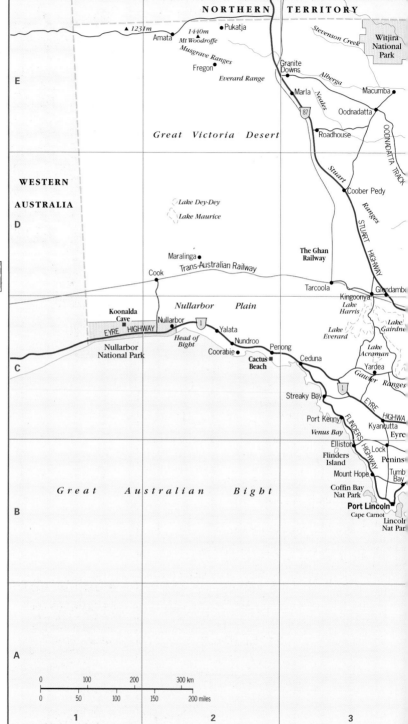

124

NORTHERN TERRITORY

▲ 1231m
Amata
1440m
Mt Woodroffe
● Pukatja
Musgrave Ranges
Fregon ●
Everard Range

Stevenson Creek
Witjira
National
Park

Granite
Downs
Alberga
Marla ●
Macumba ●
Needles
87
Oodnadatta
Roadhouse ●
OODNADATTA TRACK

Great Victoria Desert

WESTERN

AUSTRALIA

D

Stuart
Coober Pedy ●

Lake Dey-Dey
Lake Maurice

Maralinga ●
Trans-Australian Railway
Cook ●

The Ghan
Railway

Ranges

STUART HIGHWAY

Tarcoola ●
Kingoonya
Glendambo

Nullarbor Plain
Lake
Harris
Lake
Gairdner

Koonalda
Cave
Nullarbor ●
1
Yalata ●
Nundroo ●

Lake
Everard

Lake
Acraman

EYRE HIGHWAY
Head of
Bight
Coorabie ●
Cactus ▪
Beach
Penong ●
Ceduna ●

Yardea ●
Gawler Ranges

Nullarbor
National Park

Streaky Bay ●
1
EYRE HIGHWAY

Port Kenny ●
Kyancutta ●
Venus Bay
Eyre

Elliston ●
FLINDERS HIGHWAY
Lock ●
Penins

Flinders
Island
Mount Hope ●
Tumb
Bay

Great Australian Bight

Coffin Bay
Nat Park
Port Lincoln ▪
Cape Carnot ●
Lincoln
Nat Par

B

A

0   100   200   300 km
0   50   100   150   200 miles

1   2   3

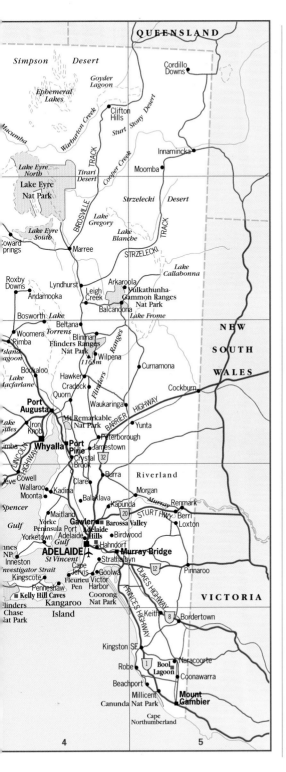

QUEENSLAND

Simpson *Desert*

Ephemeral
Lakes

Goyder
Lagoon

Cordillo
Downs

Macumba

Warburton Creek

Clifton
Hills

Sturt Stony Desert

Cooper Creek

Innamincka

Moomba

Lake Eyre
North

Tirari
Desert

Lake Eyre
Nat Park

BIRDSVILLE TRACK

Strzelecki *Desert*

Lake Eyre
South

*oward
prings*

Marree

Lake
Gregory

Lake
Blanche

STRZELECKI TRACK

Lake
Callabonna

Roxby
Downs

Lyndhurst

Arkaroola

NEW

Andamooka

Leigh
Creek

Vulkathunha-
Gammon Ranges
Nat Park

SOUTH

Bosworth *Lake*

Balcanoona

Lake Frome

WALES

Woomera

Beltana

Torrens

Blinman

Rimba

Flinders Ranges
Nat Park

Wilpena
1165m

*sland
agoon*

Lake
acfarlane

Bookaloo

Flinders Ranges

Hawker

Curnamona

Cradock

Quorn

Port
Augusta

Waukaringa

BARRIER HIGHWAY

Cockburn

*Lake
illes*

Iron
Knob

Mt Remarkable
Nat Park

Yunta

imba

Whyalla

Port
Pirie

Jamestown

Peterborough

Crystal 32
Brook

eve Cowell

Clare

Burra

Riverland

Wallaroo

Kadina

Moonta

Balaklava

Morgan

Spencer

Kapunda

Murray Renmark

STURT HWY

Maitland

20

Gulf

Yorke
Peninsula

Gawler

Barossa Valley

Berri

Loxton

Yorketown

Port

Adelaide
Hills

Birdwood

Adelaide
Gulf

Hahndorf

*nnes
NP*

ADELAIDE

St Vincent

Murray Bridge

Inneston

Strathalbyn

12

nvestigator Strait

Cape
Jervis

Goolwa

Pinnaroo

Kingscote

Fleurieu
Pen

Victor
Harbor

VICTORIA

Penneshaw

Coorong
Nat Park

Kelly Hill Caves

Kangaroo

Nat Park

Keith 8 Bordertown

*linders
Chase
Nat Park*

Island

Kingston SE

PRINCES HIGHWAY

DUKES HIGHWAY

Robe 1

Bool
Lagoon

Naracoorte

Coonawarra

Beachport

Millicent

Canunda Nat Park

Mount
Gambier

Cape
Northumberland

LINCOLN HIGHWAY

4

5

South
Australia

125

South Australia

DRY DOCK

Australia's driest state covers an eighth of the continent's total area, but has a population of just 1.5 million. South Australia also has the distinction of being the only state established without the aid of convict workers, a fact of which it is particularly proud.

126

WOWSERS NO MORE

A wowser originally meant someone who didn't know how to enjoy himself. The epithet was maliciously applied to the good citizens of Adelaide because of their supposed piety and apparent aversion to letting their hair down. The visitor to South Australia is unlikely to see much trace of this today, least of all in Adelaide. It may still be a city of churches, but it is now also a city of restaurants, watered by the products of its wineries. And it was in South Australia that the country's first nudist beach, Maslin, was opened, on the coast south of Adelaide.

SOUTH AUSTRALIA Virtually all the inhabitants of Australia's third largest state live along the fertile coasts of its gulf lands and southeastern plains, three-quarters of them in Greater Adelaide. Northward from this tamed littoral with its almost Mediterranean climate stretches an immense and arid area of Outback and desert, some of it bearing the traces of failed European settlement, and huge tracts of it returned to the Aborigines. This is a land of sharp differences, with a capital that is the most elegant and obviously cultured of all Australian cities.

IN THE BEGINNING South Australia was not a prison colony but a 'province', settled by free people (mostly from the south of England, but also many from Germany) under the auspices of the South Australia Company. The first group landed from the *Buffalo* in 1836, but the true founding father was Colonel William Light, a brilliant and unorthodox character whose visionary plan for Adelaide has shaped the city to the present day. The development of the colony was erratic. Within a few years of its foundation it was only saved from economic collapse by the discovery of copper at Kapunda and Burra. Attempts to push the frontier of agriculture north were defeated by long years of drought, although the peninsula's corn lands flourished.

For many years Adelaide remained simply the middle of a vast agricultural and mining area, its affairs conducted by merchants who lived sober lives ('wowsers' to other Australians, see panel). Much of the tone of South Australian life was indeed set by the seriousness with which its Nonconformist (British) or Lutheran (German) citizens took their religion; not for nothing was Adelaide known as the city of churches.

The vulnerability of what was an almost entirely rural economy became apparent in the years of the great Depression, and following World War II the state underwent an industrial transformation, with shipyards at Whyalla and car factories at Adelaide's satellite town of Elizabeth. In the 1970s, these activities showed themselves to be vulnerable in their turn, and South Australia, along with much of the rest of the country, has had its share of economic and financial troubles.

Given the state's range of landscapes, it is not surprising that tourism is of increasing importance. Adelaide attracts visitors with its biennial Festival of arts (even-numbered years), as well as with the elegance of its townscape and its reputation for good living. A newer attraction is the Womadelaide Festival—a biennial celebration of world music (odd-numbered years). An immensely long coastline offers endless opportunites for water-based activities of all kinds at unspoiled towns such as **Robe**, south of the spectacular Coorong National Park. Coastal landscapes vary from the wild isolation of rugged headlands to delightful little fishing ports and resorts. Offshore islands invite those with a taste for escapism; the biggest of them, **Kangaroo Island**, offers sea lions, koalas, kangaroos, pelicans, sea eagles and fairy penguins in their native environment. The state is also becoming increasingly famous for its excellent wines, gourmet foods and fine dining opportunities.

South Australia is the starting point for many of the country's great tourist itineraries. Outback Tarcoola is the junction for two trains of almost legendary reputation—the *Ghan*, on its way north to Alice Springs and Darwin, and the *Indian Pacific*, pausing here on its transcontinental run westwards across the Nullarbor.

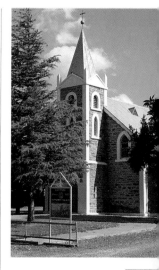

Bethany's Lutheran church and hall in the Barossa Valley

127

DASHING DON'S DERRING-DO
South Australia's Premier from 1967 to 1968 and again from 1970 to 1979, Don Dunstan not only cultivated a progressive and dynamic image, but was also instrumental in dragging his state into the late 20th century. Under his leadership, South Australia passed legislation outlawing racial and sexual discrimination. Pastor Sir Douglas Nicholls, a distinguished Aborigine, became Governor, while a police chief who refused to reveal who had instructed him to keep secret files on MPs and other potential subversives was dismissed. Sadly, the popular ex-premier died in 1999.

It is possible to tour some of the World Heritage-listed Naracoorte Caves

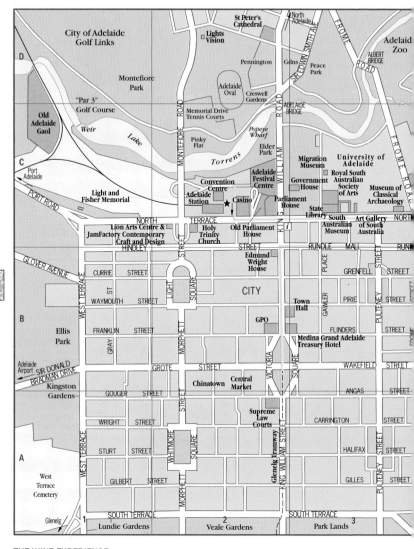

Adelaide

Australia's fifth largest city, with a population of 1.1 million, likes to be known for its biennial Festival of arts and its generally high cultural tone. Many of its early citizens were religious dissenters escaping from persecution in their home countries; they pursued both work and recreation with what seemed a kind of earnest dullness, in rationally planned surroundings of dignified elegance.

These surroundings were the vision of one man, Colonel William Light, who, as South Australia's Surveyor-General, drew up a brilliant plan in 1836, to which the city has adhered ever since. Having found a suitable site on the banks of the little River Torrens, he set out a square-mile grid of streets on the south bank. The central thoroughfare was impressively wide, and the whole was

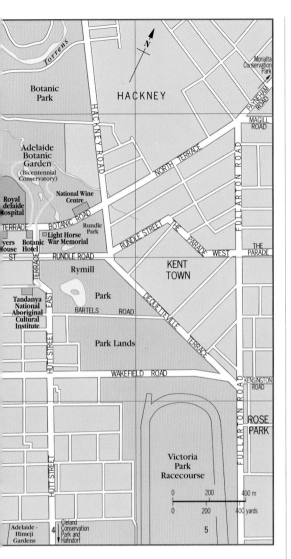

SHOP 'TIL YOU DROP
Adelaide offers a good range of shopping opportunities. The Central Markets are excellent for food and produce, the JamFactory Contemporary Craft and Design Centre sells fine art and crafts, North Adelaide and King William Road (south of the city) are the perfect places for designer clothing, while Unley and Port Adelaide are known for their antiques.

SON OF A GUN!
Most Australian cities developed in a totally chaotic way. It was left to an army officer, illegitimate offspring of the English founder of Penang in Malaysia and a Eurasian woman, to conceive and implement the ambitious plan for Adelaide. William Light had served as an intelligence officer with the Duke of Wellington, gaining his rank of colonel on a temporary posting in Spain; he revelled in the commission to survey and plan not only the site of Adelaide but much of the rest of the new province. Married to the daughter (also illegitimate) of the Duke of Richmond, he left his wife at home in England, and when he died (probably from overwork) in 1839, was refused the last rites because he had been 'living in sin' with another lady.

enlivened with a series of squares. A green belt around the city was to remain parkland in perpetuity, a fit setting for public buildings such as Government House; on the far bank of the river was the fine suburb of North Adelaide. In spite of opposition at the time, in spite of the building boom of the 1970s and 1980s, and in spite of the automobile, all these elements are in place today, helping make Adelaide a delightful city.

It is rare in a metropolis to be able to live in a Victorian villa looking on to splendid parkland, walk or cycle to work in the city, spend the evening at the theatre, then walk home again, but here the residents can do exactly that. The majority of people, however, live in the pleasant, uncrowded suburbs that have spread across the coastal plain between the magnificent beaches along the gulf and the Adelaide Hills to the east.

Sailing is a popular pursuit at Port Adelaide, the city's harbour town

FESTIVE SEASON
They say in Adelaide that the Adelaide Festival Centre cost less to build than it did to carpet Sydney's Opera House. The centre is busy all year round, with three theatres and two outdoor performance areas. Its plaza, designed by the German environmental sculptor Otto Hajek, has been described as Australia's biggest outdoor art work.

The Adelaide Festival is held in even-numbered years for three weeks in February/March. Warm days and mild nights help create the right atmosphere for a wonderful choice of events—opera, ballet, concerts, theatre, exhibitions, children's activities, the Fringe Festival and a literary festival—all of which are within walking distance of each other.

►► Adelaide Botanic Garden 129C4
North Terrace (tel: 08-8222 9311). Gardens: Mon–Fri 7.15–dusk, Sat–Sun 9–dusk; Bicentennial Conservatory: daily 10–4 (5 in summer).
Admission: Gardens free, Conservatory inexpensive
Founded in 1855, these 20ha (49 acres) of trees, shrubs, lawns and lakes glitter with an array of heritage buildings. As well as the Museum of Economic Botany, there is the 1868 Victoria House with its giant waterlily, and the wonderful Palm House, brought from Germany in the 1870s. But most extraordinary is the 1988 **Bicentennial Conservatory►►**, a soaring environmental capsule, within whose high-tech skin flourish plants from the rain forests of North Australia and its neighbours.

►►► Art Gallery of South Australia 128C3
North Terrace (tel: 08-8207 7000). Open: daily 10–5
Admission free (varying charges for special exhibitions)
Behind this classical portico is one of the country's most important collections of Australian, European and Asian art. Some of the paintings by Australian artists are familiar, seeming to encapsulate key aspects of the country's character, like the stampeding sheep in Tom Roberts' *The Breakaway* of 1891 or the subtle beach flirtation depicted in Charles Conder's *Holiday at Mentone* (1888). The Aboriginal section is particularly good, and the gallery also has a large collection of Rodin's works.

► Glenelg off 128A1
One of Adelaide's most popular seaside districts, with splendid sandy beaches stretching far in either direction, suburban Glenelg still has plenty of charm, epitomized by the 1920s trams that link it to the city's Victoria Square (a 30-minute trip). It was here that Governor Hindmarsh and the first band of settlers landed in 1836.

►► Migration Museum 128C3
82 Kintore Avenue (tel: 08-8207 7580)
Open: Mon–Fri 10–5, Sat–Sun 1–5. Admission: donation
Housed in the city's old Destitute Asylum, this innovative institution presents the story of the immigrant groups who have populated South Australia. The museum tells stories of the successful adaptation to life in a new country, as well as those of disappointment and difficulty.

▶▶ North Adelaide   *off 128D3*

Adelaide's classiest and oldest suburb has many fine houses. Melbourne Street has shops, restaurants and boutiques, while O'Connell Street is famous for its restaurants. St. Peter's Cathedral boasts the heaviest bells in the southern hemisphere, and at Light's Vision lookout, overlooking the historic Adelaide Oval, a statue of the good colonel surveys the city he created.

▶▶ Port Adelaide   *off 128C1*

Some 14km (8.5 miles) northwest of the landlocked city, Adelaide's harbour town has been deserted by most of its maritime traffic, leaving it free to concentrate on its fascinating past; it has South Australia's largest collection of distinguished 19th-century buildings. Among the long quayside sheds is the bright red 1869 lighthouse; river and ocean cruises are available from the nearby wharf. A short distance inland on Lipson Street are a couple of first-rate museums, each well worth the bus or train trip out from the city. The main building of the fascinating **South Australian Maritime Museum▶▶** is an old bond store, while the **National Railway Museum▶▶**, with steam train rides and many locomotives, is the biggest of its kind in the country.

▶▶▶ South Australian Museum   *128C3*

North Terrace (tel: 08-8207 7500)
Open: daily 10–5. Admission free

The state's museum of natural history has geological and zoological displays on six floors, but its main attraction is its outstanding Australian Aboriginal Cultures Gallery. All its exhibits are presented in an imaginative and accessible fashion, making the museum perhaps the best place to study the past of the original Australians.

▶▶ Tandanya National Aboriginal Cultural Institute   *129B4*

253 Grenfell Street (tel: 08-8224 3200)
Open: daily 10–5. Admission: inexpensive (tours: moderate)

This exciting addition to Adelaide's vibrant East End offers the opportunity to learn about contemporary Aboriginal culture. There are dance and theatre performances, meetings, talks, celebrations, constantly changing exhibitions, tours and demonstrations and sales of arts and crafts.

OTHER ADELAIDE SIGHTS
The 19th-century Ayers House with its curving bays is perhaps the most elegant structure in North Terrace. Seven times premier of South Australia, Sir Henry Ayers (after whom Ayers Rock was named) used his home for state functions; the hub of city life, its ballroom was washed down with milk to give it a smooth and fast surface.

The Adelaide Zoo, next to the Botanic Garden, is worth a visit, and a cruise on the tranquil Torrens offers a different perspective of the city.

NGURUNDERI'S DREAMING
An extensive display in the South Australian Museum tells the story of Ngurunderi, one of the great ancestral dreaming figures of the Ngarrindjeri people. His travels from high up the Murray River to Kangaroo Island in pursuit of his miscreant wives are said to explain many of the features of the river and coastal landscape. The bends of the Murray were made by the giant cod Ponde sweeping his tail, while Long Island near Murray Bridge is Ngurunderi's spear, which missed its target. Another spear thrust created the islands off Victor Harbor, while his abandoned club became The Bluff. As his wives fled west along the causeway that then connected Kangaroo Island to the mainland, Ngurunderi caused the waters to rise and drown them. They turned into the rocky Pages Islands, while Ngurunderi rose to become a star in the Milky Way.

Impressive Ayers House is open to the public

The Tandanya National Aboriginal Cultural Institute in Adelaide's East End

132

Walk

Green spaces and old buildings

See map on pages 128–129.

Linking some of Adelaide's splendid green spaces with North Terrace, the city's boulevard, this walk passes through the central shopping mall before ending in Victoria Square, the geographical heart of the city.

A walkway leads to North Terrace from the **Adelaide Festival Centre** complex overlooking parkland along the River Torrens. Stay on the north side of North Terrace to admire the sequence of historic buildings and monuments revealed as you walk eastwards. The postmodern forecourt of the Hyatt Regency hotel contrasts with the grandiose railway station now housing the city's casino. The **Old Parliament House** of 1855 seems modest compared with the ultra-conservative design of its successor,

completed in 1939. **Government House** behind its garden wall gives way to the State Library (1884), the **South Australian Museum** (1898) and the **Art Gallery of South Australia** (opened in 1881). The south side of the Terrace has imposing edifices and modern buildings, ending with the fine colonial **Ayers House** and the Botanic Hotel with tiers of verandas.

A detour to **Adelaide Botanic Garden** should take in the remarkable Bicentennial Conservatory and National Wine Centre (see page 128). Rundle Street is the heart of Adelaide's lively East End region. Here you will find plenty of shops, historic pubs and dozens of great cafés and restaurants. Take a short detour to the excellent **Tandanya National Aboriginal Cultural Institute** in Grenfell Street just to the south.

Rundle Mall is a cheerful pedestrian precinct, the main focus of city shopping. It leads into King William Street, Adelaide's main north–south route. The General Post Office and Town Hall stand at the northern end of Victoria Square, where the city's last surviving original tramway waits to take its passengers down to the sea at **Glenelg**.

National parks

Dry as dust The interminable flatness of the interior is broken only by two mountain ranges. Part of the vast Pitjantjatjara Aboriginal Lands, the Musgrave Ranges in the far northwest parallel the other ridges of the Red Centre just over the boundary with the Northern Territory. The ancient Flinders Ranges run some 480km (300 miles) from near the head of Spencer Gulf toward Lake Eyre, their most spectacular single feature being the magnificent natural fortress of **Wilpena Pound**, a 77sq km (30-sq-mile) natural amphitheatre. Northwards are the interminable sand ridges of the **Simpson Desert**, laid down by winds that ceased to blow in prehistoric times. In the rare bouts of rain, its sparse cover of spinifex is supplemented by a sudden tapestry of wildflowers, while its inhabitants include unique creatures like hopping mice and marsupial moles. The Sturt Stony Desert is a virtually impassable plain of wind-polished stones known as gibbers, while, much farther south, **Mount Remarkable** has deep gorges.

The wildlife-rich south Towards the sea, the near-total aridity of South Australia's interior gives way to a Mediterranean-type climate, whose hot summers are relieved by relatively cool and moist winters. More than a century and a half of settlement has converted much of the area into productive farmland. There is still plenty of wilderness left, along the coast from **Coffin Bay** and **Lincoln national parks** at the tip of the Eyre Peninsula in the west to **Coorong National Park** in the far southeast. In between are the dunes and cliffs of **Innes National Park** on the toe of Yorke Peninsula and the scenic and wildlife wonders of **Kangaroo Island**. The extraordinary Coorong begins at the mouth of the Murray where the great river reaches the sea. A 144km (90-mile) beach stretches southeastwards, backed by sand dunes and a long, shallow lagoon. This is one of the best places for observing the pelican.

AUSTRALIA'S DEAD SEA
Much of the huge expanse of Lake Eyre is below sea level. When filled with water, an event that has only occurred four times in living memory, the lake becomes alive with birds. On the map it appears to be fed by rivers over 960km (600 miles) long, but their waters usually run dry long before they reach the lake. Its salty surface, flat and featureless, made it ideal for Donald Campbell's successful attempt on the world land-speed record in 1964.

133

The Remarkable Rocks on Kangaroo Island are famous for their strangely weathered granite shapes

South Australia

THE *GHAN*
One of Australia's most famous railway lines runs from Adelaide to Alice Springs and Darwin in the Northern Territory. The route is named after the Afghan (and other) camel drivers that the railway superseded in the late 19th century. (See also page 189.)

BY CAR
Roads in the relatively densely populated coastal area are good and the main interstate highways are all paved, including the Stuart Highway north to Alice Springs. In the Outback, roads are of variable quality and you must check conditions first and take adequate provisions (see page 143).

BY WATER
You can take the car andpassenger ferry to Kangaroo Island from Cape Jervis at the tip of the Fleurieu Peninsula.

A diesel commuter bus on Adelaide's 'O-Bahn' line

How to travel

By air Only 6km (4 miles) from the city, Adelaide's airport is served by both international and domestic flights, linking it to all important destinations in Australia and many overseas. The size of South Australia makes flights within the state an attractive proposition. There are frequent flights between Adelaide and places on the Eyre Peninsula such as Port Lincoln, or to Kangaroo Island and Mount Gambier. Other flights serve Port Augusta and Broken Hill in NSW, though many tourists heading into the Outback get there by road.

By bus Adelaide has a comprehensive metropolitan transport system with integrated ticketing, mostly based on buses, but also including suburban trains. The free City Loop and Bee Line buses run frequently between the main railway station and the Glenelg tram terminus in Victoria Square. The Adelaide Metro InfoCentre in King William Street is helpful in planning tours around Greater Adelaide. The Glenelg Tram (a vintage 1929 model) and the replica Adelaide Explorer tram, which tours the principal attractions on a 2.75-hour circuit, are an excellent introduction to the sights.

Long-distance buses operate express services to all major destinations, and even quite remote places in the Outback may have a bus service of some kind, albeit an infrequent one. If you have a little time to spare, a fun way to travel between Adelaide and Melbourne or Alice Springs and take in many of the good things en route is by the very reasonably priced **Wayward Bus** (three days to Melbourne and three to eight to Alice).

By train Long-distance trains leave Keswick terminus in the city for Perth, Alice Springs, Darwin, Melbourne, Broken Hill and Sydney. There are also services to the Barossa Valley, Port Pirie and Mount Gambier. Adelaide's suburban network based at the main station on North Terrace is quite extensive, with services to places of interest like Port Adelaide.

*Visitors and cuddly
residents at Cleland
Wildlife Park*

▶▶ Adelaide Hills 125B4

Sprawling over the coastal plain, Greater Adelaide is
defined to the east by the gorges and steep slopes of these
beautiful hills. With scenic drives and hiking trails through
wild bushland, this is an area of richly varied landscapes—
vineyards, avenues of tall conifers, towns of rough-hewn
stone, with some of the oldest settlements in South
Australia. The forest has regrown since 'Black Sunday'
(2 January 1955), when an uncontrollable bush fire raged
for days. As well as vineyards, orchards and gardens there
are many other attractions. These include the **Cleland
Wildlife Park▶▶** on the slopes of Mount Lofty, 20km
(12.5 miles) southeast of Adelaide; the views from the
summit of Mount Lofty; and the **Warrawong Wildlife
Sanctuary▶▶** at Mylor.

▶▶ Arkaroola Wilderness Sanctuary 125D4

Formerly a vast sheep station, the Outback resort and
wildlife sanctuary of Arkaroola is now a great base for
exploring the northern parts of the spectacular Flinders
Ranges. The rugged ridges of the **Vulkathunha-Gammon
Ranges National Park▶▶** glint and glitter with quartz,
fluorspar and other minerals. There are hot springs, a vast
salt lake, an observatory and an abundance of wildlife.

▶▶▶ Barossa Valley

See page 144.

▶ Birdwood 125B4

The **National Motor Museum** is a good excuse for a
leisurely drive through the Adelaide Hills. Australia's
biggest collection of vintage, veteran and classic cars is
grouped around the stone-built Birdwood Mill of 1852.

▶▶ Burra 125B4

In the 1840s, the discovery of rich copper deposits in
Kapunda and Burra rescued the ailing South Australian
economy. Miners flocked to Burra, 154km (96 miles) north
of Adelaide, and within 10 years had created the Monster
Mine, 13km (8 miles) long and 6km (3.75 miles) across.
Today, an 11km (7-mile) heritage trail includes a museum,
a mine captain's cottage and the extraordinary riverbed
dugouts in which as many as 2,000 miners once lived.

**DEUTSCHLAND DOWN
UNDER**
Germans sailed into
Sydney Harbour with the
First Fleet, and many
thousands have come
since. South Australia
was the destination in
the 1830s and 1840s for
whole communities from
Brandenburg and Silesia
suffering religious intoler-
ance at the hands of the
Prussian authorities.
The first settlements
were Klemzig, now over-
whelmed by Adelaide's
suburbia, Hahndorf and
Lobethal in the Adelaide
Hills, then in the
Barossa Valley, originally
called Neuschlesien
(New Silesia).

135

HOLDEN'S HEROES
Australia became one of
the world's major car-
owning nations from early
on; by the beginning of
the 1960s there was one
car per family. Sir Edward
Holden's car body firm
merged with General
Motors in 1931, initially
assembling British and
American vehicles.
'Australia's Own Car'
rolled off the Holden
production line in 1948,
the millionth in 1962.
With the advent of the
inexpensive and reliable
Japanese cars Holden
faltered, but has made
a comeback.

The lives of the first 'opal gougers' on display at Coober Pedy's Old Timer's Mine and Museum

THE AUSSIE WAVE
When you're watching an Australian game of cricket on TV, why do the spectators always seem to be waving casual greetings to unseen friends? It's not friends, but the persistent flies—as noted by Dutch Commander Pelsaert in 1629: 'Such a host of flies came to sit in the mouth and eyes that they could not be beaten off.' This early observation would seem to disprove the theory that the plague is due to the dung dropped in quantity by all those cattle in the Outback. Australians protect themselves from this nuisance with door and window screens at home and, outside, with insect repellent and as nonchalant a wave as possible, since frantic swatting seems only to encourage the fly. No one (except in jest) wears a hat with dangling corks to keep the flies away.

▶▶ **Coober Pedy**   *124D3*

The search for opals has created a landscape of mounds and holes in the ground that greets you on the Stuart Highway, some 858km (535 miles) northwest of Adelaide. The name Coober Pedy comes from the Aboriginal *kupa piti* meaning something like 'white fellow's burrow'. Ever since opals were first discovered here in 1915, enterprising folk from all over the world have been hacking away in the hope of making their fortune, living underground in order to escape the sweltering conditions on the surface. As well as comfortable troglodyte homes, there are underground shops, restaurants, hotels and even a couple of churches. Several old, non-working mines in the area can be visited.

▶ **Eyre Peninsula**   *124B3*

This vast triangle faces the breakers of the Great Australian Bight to the west and the sheltered waters of the Spencer Gulf to the east. The northern base of the triangle is formed by the uninhabited Gawler Ranges, while its southern apex is near the deep-water harbour of Port Lincoln. The sandy soils of the peninsula support wheat and sheep, while the subsoil yields iron ore, converted into steel at Whyalla, South Australia's second city.

The Eyre Highway runs from Port Augusta at the head of the Gulf toward the Western Australian border. The journey south on the Lincoln Highway reveals a magnificent coastline of cliffs and white sandy beaches, dotted with fishing towns and holiday resorts. There are seals and dolphins around **Tumby Bay▶**, while **Port Lincoln▶** is home to Dangerous Reef, sea lions and white pointer sharks. To the south, **Lincoln National Park▶** is famous for its beaches and scenic drives. Beyond here the unspoiled coastline stretches northwestwards to remote **Ceduna▶**, from where migrating whales can be seen between June and October.

▶▶ **Fleurieu Peninsula**   *125B4*

Rolling countryside, vineyards and a superb coastline of wild cliffs and fine beaches provide a wonderful holiday region right on Adelaide's doorstep. Within half an hour's drive south of the city is the **McLaren Vale wine district▶▶**, focused on the township of McLaren Vale amid delightful hills. Farther south, around Willunga, the crop changes to almonds, with a froth of blossom in July. Studded with sandy beaches, including the country's first official nudist one, Maslin, the coast runs southwestwards along the gulf to terminate in rugged terrain around Cape Jervis. The far shore of Backstairs Passage belongs to Kangaroo Island, reached from here by ferry.

Around the corner of the Cape the scenery is no less spectacular, particularly at **Deep Creek Conservation Park▶** where the land falls sheer into the ocean. **Victor Harbor▶▶** (see page 142) is a pleasant resort, guarded by the massive lump of rock known as Rosetta Head. From here the vintage Cockle Train chuffs eastwards past the breakers crashing on the beaches of Port Elliot to the charming town of **Goolwa▶** near the mouth of the Murray River (see page 138). The story of the Murray, including its current problems, is told at the impressive interpretative centre at Signal Point (see page 138).

▶▶▶ Flinders Ranges 125C4

These ranges are made up of some of the world's most ancient rocks, marking the landscape northeast of Port Augusta with steep ridges and rugged gorges. These peaks have been cracked, folded and sculpted by millions of years of rain and sun. Of no great height, the ranges owe their popularity to their vivid mineral tones, dramatic landforms and fascinating plant and animal life.

One of the gateways to the main part of the ranges is the township of Quorn, once an important railway junction, but now a small town of 1,500 or so people; here is the terminus of the **Pichi Richi Steam Railway▶**, part of the old *Ghan* line. Beyond Quorn, the road to Hawker passes close to the ruins of the old **Kanyaka Homestead▶**, which was constructed in the 1850s but has long since been abandoned, as well as the **Yourambulla Caves▶▶** with their Aboriginal rock-paintings.

The road to one of the country's great geological curiosities, the mighty natural stronghold of **Wilpena Pound▶▶▶**, turns off at Hawker. The Pound is a great oval, 20km (12.5 miles) long by about 8km (5 miles) wide, protected from the outside world by sheer 1,000m (3,280-foot) high walls, sloping steeply to a park-like interior where the flat floor is rich in sugar gums and, in spring, wildflowers. Like any great fortress, the Pound has only one way in, a narrow gorge cut by the Wilpena Creek, sometimes a torrent but usually just a trickle. A number of marked trails of varying difficulty lead from the visitor centre near this entrance; anyone capable of walking 20km (12.5 miles) lengthwise and 500m (1,640ft) vertically should consider the trek across the Pound and up to its highest point, St. Marys Peak. The stunning panorama includes the dazzling white surface of salty Lake Torrens.

Beyond Wilpena on unpaved roads is the main part of the Flinders Ranges National Park. Its wildlife includes hosts of birds and two types of kangaroo, as well as the rare yellow-footed rock wallaby.

REPTILIAN RAMPARTS
Like so many features of the Aboriginal landscape, the walls of Wilpena Pound are perceived to be the petrified forms of the animal ancestors who assisted at their creation. Two giant serpents were lying in wait here for those who gathered to celebrate the very first ceremony of initiation of a young man into adulthood by circumcision. The serpents devoured them all, save for Wala the wild turkey, Yulu the kingfisher and the young man himself, who all escaped and founded new tribes. The serpents expired, their bodies curling round to enclose the Pound for ever.

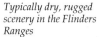

Typically dry, rugged scenery in the Flinders Ranges

South Australia

The Germanic town of Hahndorf was home to Sir Hans Heysen

SIR HANS HEYSEN

Young Hans came to South Australia from Germany in 1884 at the age of seven. He is one of the best-loved painters of the Australian landscape, whose natural features, particularly its trees and the play of light on them, he studied with great meticulousness. His charming works grace many an Australian gallery, and can also be seen at his Hahndorf home, The Cedars (and its adjacent studio), where he lived from 1912 until his death in 1968. Sir Hans is remembered by having the long-distance walking trail from the Fleurieu Peninsula to the Flinders Ranges, as well as part of the ranges themselves, named after him.

AUSTRALIAN SEALS

Of the three species of seal that inhabit Australian waters, two live around Kangaroo Island: the New Zealand fur seal and the Australian sea lion. The former were almost hunted to extinction in the 19th century; now protected, their numbers are recovering. Sea lions had an easier time, largely because they lack the warm coat of the fur seal.

▶ Goolwa   *125B4*

This little riverport on the lower reaches of the mighty Murray River is the terminus for two enjoyable trips: the old-timer Cockle Train that runs along the coast, and cruises to the mouth of the Murray. The **Signal Point River Murray Centre▶** has comprehensive displays on the theme of the Murray River yesterday and today.

▶▶ Hahndorf   *125B4*

South Australia's second-oldest German settlement (dating from 1839) can be found in a pretty spot in the Adelaide Hills. Conveniently close to the South Eastern Freeway, Hahndorf is full of Teutonic tradition, with German-style architecture and cafés serving traditional foods. Other attractions are the fine artworks of the Hahndorf Academy and **The Cedars▶▶** (see panel). You can still see how the first settlers laid out their homes in orderly fashion along the main street.

▶▶▶ Kangaroo Island   *125B4*

Separated from the Fleurieu Peninsula by the deep straits known as Backstairs Passage, this is Australia's third largest island, a paradise for lovers of nature, with wild coastal landscapes and a particularly rich animal life. The island was named by the redoubtable Matthew Flinders; when the *Investigator* called here in 1802, his crew shot a few of the locals, members of the subspecies of grey kangaroo still present in large numbers.

Most visitors arrive by ferry from the mainland at the little fishing port of Penneshaw on the Dudley Peninsula at the eastern end of the island. Fairy penguins frequent Christmas Cove just to the west of the harbour. On Nepean Bay, Kingscote preserves some traces of its past in its oldest building, Hope Cottage of 1859. A paved main road heads past the airport into the interior, but the island's unique sights lie on the south coast.

Seal Bay Conservation Park▶▶ is home to Australia's largest colony of sea lions, seemingly indifferent to their many human visitors. Farther west is the spectacular underground world of **Kelly Hill Caves▶**, discovered by a horse of that name that disappeared forever into their still unexplored depths (Kelly's rider was saved).

The surging waters around Cape du Couedic at the southwestern tip of the island are often visited by another marine mammal, the New Zealand fur seal. At the cape itself is awesome **Admirals Arch▶**, a natural bridge hollowed out in the limestone cliffs, while to the east are the aptly named **Remarkable Rocks▶▶**. Crowning a smoothly planed promontory, great blocks of granite have been eroded into strange shapes as if by the chisel of an abstract sculptor at his most imaginative.

These dramatic natural features are part of **Flinders Chase National Park▶▶**, much of which is a wilderness of low-growing eucalyptus and shrubs. The headquarters of the park is at Rocky River, where friendly kangaroos, wallabies and emus are likely to pester you for your sandwiches. Koalas can be seen in the trees nearby, and platypuses sometimes reveal themselves to the patient observer. The northwestern tip of the island is marked by the isolated lighthouse at Cape Borda. To the east, accessible by a rough road, stretches a spectacular coastline of cliffs, some rising to over 200m (650ft), and sandy bays.

▶ Mount Gambier   125A5

The most important town in the southeast of South Australia had a turbulent volcanic past that only came to an end in relatively recent times. This has left a legacy of cones and craters, with one water-filled hole right in the middle of town. Blue Lake, just outside town, mysteriously changes its hue according to the season.

▶ Murray River   125B5

The sluggish Murray (see pages 112–113) meanders into South Australia near Renmark. From here to where it meets the sea at Lake Alexandrina, the river is popular with holidaymakers. A great way to experience the river is to stay on a houseboat—they can be rented at Renmark, Berri, Loxton, Murray Bridge and several other towns.

ALONG THE MIGHTY MURRAY
Massive irrigation projects have transformed the area into a vast orchard and vineyard, producing oranges, apples, pears and some 40 per cent of the state's grape harvest. Loxton Historical Village re-creates life as it was in the difficult early days of settlement. Many of the places along the river have a poignant feel about them, now that the great days of river trade have gone. There is another evocation of bygone times at the Old Tailem Town Pioneer Village, and the old paddle steamer *Marion* moored at Mannum has been fully restored as a working boat that cruises the river.

139

A trip up the broad Murray River is a wonderfully relaxing way to travel and view the striking scenery

Vine cuttings were among the plants imported with the First Fleet, though the very first attempts to produce an Australian wine met with failure. However, persistence has paid off, and today Australian wines enjoy a high reputation at home and abroad.

AMBER FLUID IN ICE-COLD TUBES

Despite the rise in wine consumption, Australians remain some of the most committed beer drinkers in the world. A century ago, most beers tended to be top-fermented on the model of British ales and stouts, but these have steadily been displaced by bottom-fermented, lager types. These were first brewed by Melbourne Germans as well as by the Foster brothers, originally from New York, who gave their name to Foster's Lager. Visitors used to six-packs may be surprised at the standard-sized 'slab' (a 24-pack).

A winery at Nuriootpa in the Barossa Valley

In the early days, the colonists preferred rum; later it was the country's beer that was rated highly, in contrast to its wines, which foreigners wrote off as crude imitations utterly failing to fulfil the promise of their labels.

Since the 1960s things have changed as a result of increased prosperity and greater sophistication. A visit to a well-stocked wine merchant reveals a whole world of home-grown wine; like other great wine countries, Australia has no real need to import. In fact exports of wine are now reaching AU$2 billion.

New South Wales This state has the most venerable vineyards, in the reputed Hunter Valley only a short way north of Sydney. Wine has been produced in this area since the 1830s, and the valley's 100 or so wineries include some of Australia's best. Quality is the keynote here, whereas far to the southwest, in the irrigated valley of the Murrumbidgee River, producers concentrate on making as great a quantity as possible for the wine casks that are Australia's '*vin ordinaire*'.

Victoria Here there were once as many vineyards as NSW and SA had put together, but most were wiped out by *phylloxera* in the 19th century and later replaced by

phylloxera-resistant American root stock. Victorian wines could now be described as up and coming; there are many 'boutique' wines, some of the best from the **Yarra Valley** near Melbourne. The Great Western area is famous for sparkling wine.

Western Australia This state has its old vineyards too, planted along the Swan Valley in the early days of settlement. Exciting (and expensive) wines come from the **Margaret River** area.

Tasmania Lying closer to the South Pole, Tasmania is benefiting from a fashion for growing vines over a long ripening period in a cool climate, and there is an increasing number of vineyards (mostly around Hobart and Launceston) producing wines of fine quality.

South Australia This is the heartland of Australian wine, contributing over half of the country's total production. Most of the original vineyards of the Adelaide Plains have disappeared, and the huge quantities of grapes grown along the Murray are the basis of Australia's bulk wine trade, but other districts make wines of the highest reputation. Far-off **Coonawarra** in the southeast produces wonderful reds on a tiny band of volcanic soil, while **Adelaide Hills** is the most successful of the newer, cool climate regions. The boutique wines made among the rolling hills of the **McLaren Vale wine district** are much in vogue and the **Clare Valley's** cool-climate vintages are excellent, but perhaps the best of all wine districts is the **Barossa Valley**, north of Adelaide. The combination of suitable soils, summer sun and reliable winter rain makes for an excellent product, grown amid a delightful landscape of old-established towns and well-ordered countryside.

Tastings Vintners welcome visitors to their wineries. Tastings have become a popular pastime, though choosing can be difficult. The name of a reputable vineyard is generally considered a good starting point.

A RUM CORPS
Historical records show that in the early days of NSW coinage was short; in its absence Bengal rum took over many of the functions of currency. Its sale was controlled by the officers of the New South Wales Corps, perhaps the least prestigious of the British regiments of the time. With little to occupy them in the way of genuine military activity, these gentlemen devoted their time to enriching themselves by all possible means, only stirring into martial action when their monopoly on rum was threatened by Governor Bligh. Their march on Government House on 26 January 1808, and arrest of the governor has become known as the 'Rum Rebellion'.

Mount Pleasant in the Hunter Valley, New South Wales

Petrel Cove at Victor Harbor

STRANGE MEETING
Two centuries ago, Britain and France competed in the race for colonization of the Pacific, and Australia was one of the prizes. In the early 19th century, an expedition under the command of Nicolas Baudin made an extensive exploration of the southern coast and of Tasmania, leaving a sprinkling of Gallic names, like Tasmania's Freycinet Peninsula. On 8 April 1802, Baudin's ship the *Geographe* was sighted coming westwards along the South Australian coast by Matthew Flinders, in the course of his circumnavigation of the whole continent. Eventually convinced of her peaceful intentions, Flinders went aboard the French ship. This meeting of two great navigators is marked by the name given to the broad body of water where they met off Victor Harbor—Encounter Bay.

▶ Naracoorte   *125A5*

This southeastern town celebrates the prosperity of its pastoral surroundings in the excellent Sheep's Back wool museum. But most visitors come to marvel at the beauty of the World Heritage-listed **Naracoorte Caves▶**. Only a few of the 25 or so known caves are accessible; there are guided tours into the Blanche, Alexandra and Victoria Fossil caves. In 1969, the bones of hitherto unknown marsupials, giant kangaroos and wombats were found in Victoria Cave. To the south, Bool Lagoon forms an important wetland region that attracts thousands of waterbirds and other wildlife.

▶ Strathalbyn   *125B4*

Strathalbyn, at the neck of the Fleurieu Peninsula, has something of Scotland in its dignified public buildings and neat public gardens on the banks of the Angas River. The town's past has been tidily gathered up and is presented by the National Trust in two buildings, the 1858 police station and the 1867 court house.

▶▶ Victor Harbor   *125B4*

Victor Harbor's setting on Encounter Bay is superb, protected as it is from the ocean by both Rosetta Head ('The Bluff') and Granite Island, the latter reached across a causeway by horse-drawn tram. The island's colony of fairy penguins generally puts in an appearance in the evening, and whale watching is a popular winter activity.

▶ Yorke Peninsula   *125B4*

This boot-shaped peninsula projects southwards, bounded by Spencer Gulf on the west and Gulf St. Vincent to the east. South Australians come here for quiet vacations, fishing, boating and all kinds of water activities. Towards the tip of the peninsula, around **Innes National Park▶**, the coastline becomes more rugged, though there are still splendid beaches. Copper was once mined around Moonta in the north, and this area, known as 'Little Cornwall', offers evidence of this rich mining history, particularly in the **Moonta Mines State Heritage Area▶▶**.

Strangely compelling, South Australia's Outback includes some of the least hospitable parts of the earth's surface. Distances are vast, water is sparse and summer temperatures are almost unbearable. Human life is spread thinly over cattle stations the size of small European states and 'towns' no bigger than hamlets. But the Outback has its own fascination; its arid beauty is liable to sudden and miraculous change when rain falls, as salt lakes fill with water and wildflowers carpet the land.

The great vastness of the South Australian Outback is penetrated by a small number of roads, tying together the isolated stations and settlements. Some are paved throughout, while others are still rightly referred to as 'tracks' and set a challenge for the more adventurous.

The Oodnadatta Track This track is part of a route from Adelaide to Alice Springs, an alternative to the Stuart Highway. Beginning at Marree near the southern end of Lake Eyre, it follows the route taken by the explorer John McDouall Stuart and subsequently by the Overland Telegraph and the original *Ghan* railway line. Before the line was completed to The Alice, Oodnadatta was the railhead, goods being carried on from here on the backs of camels. The old station, now a museum, still stands.

The Strzelecki Track Named for the Polish explorer Count Paul Strzelecki, this track runs northeast from Lyndhurst towards the Queensland border, following the trail used by the notorious Captain Starlight to drive stolen cattle down to southern markets in 1871. The track fringes the northern Flinders Ranges before crossing the interminable sandhills of the Strzelecki Desert and ending at Innamincka where the unfortunate explorers Burke and Wills finally expired.

The Birdsville Track Also a cattle-driving route, this was traced out by stockmen possibly more law-abiding than Captain Starlight but equally tough. Like the Oodnadatta Track it begins at Marree, but this track ends up in Queensland's Birdsville some 512km (320 miles) later.

Above: William Creek, on the Oodnadatta Track

143

BIRDSVILLE TRACK SIGHTS
Along the track's course are hot springs, deserted homesteads, 10m (30-ft) high sandhills and the wind-polished pebbles of the Sturt Stony Desert stretching to the horizon. The old frontier post of Birdsville, with its famous pub, comes alive when its annual horse races are held—an event that can yield up to 50,000 empty beer cans!

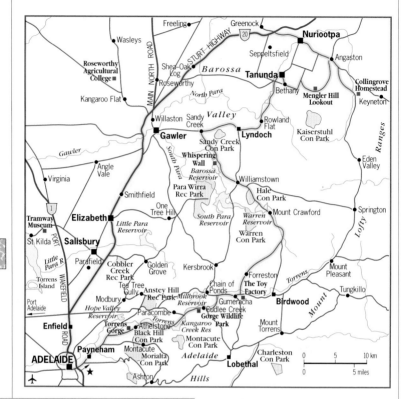

144

Barossa Valley

The world-famous wine-growing district of the Barossa Valley can be reached by this indirect but rewarding route through the varied countryside of the northern Adelaide Hills.

Adelaide's Payneham Road, then Gorge Road lead to the rocky defile followed by the River Torrens, and so into the orchard and vineyard country around **Gumeracha**. Among the many dams built to take advantage of the relatively high rainfall of these uplands, the **Barossa Reservoir** is a popular stopping point because of the curious sound effects produced by its

'Whispering Wall'. The little town of Lyndoch is the gateway to the Barossa Valley, while **Tanunda**, with its informative Barossa Wine & Visitor Centre and charming main street, is the cultural hub of what was Australia's major German-settled area. All around are inviting wineries. **Bethany**, founded in 1842, the valley's oldest village, sits beneath Mengler Hill Lookout, with its splendid panorama over the neatly ordered countryside. It is worth taking a detour to Angaston's 1850s **Collingrove Homestead**, now managed by the National Trust but once the heart of the huge estate belonging to the Angas family, early pioneers of South Australia.

The route back to Adelaide passes through **Nuriootpa**, the commercial heart of the Barossa, the prosperous agricultural centre of **Gawler** and the satellite town of **Elizabeth**, home to many British immigrants in the post-war years.

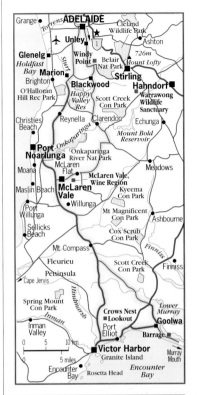

Bird-attracting banksias

McLaren Vale wine region and Fleurieu Peninsula

This drive leads through the vine-growing countryside of the McLaren Vale wine region, across the rolling farmland of the Fleurieu Peninsula to the mouth of the Murray River and the dramatic ocean setting of Victor Harbor.

From Adelaide, Unley Road soon reaches the surrounding hills and climbs to the **Windy Point Lookout**, from where there is a fine panorama of city and suburbs sprawling over the coastal plain. The uplands are a popular residential area for the city's more affluent commuters, but the suburban

housing soon gives way to farmland and forest, and to the vineyards and welcoming wineries around **McLaren Flat** and **McLaren Vale.**

A beautifully engineered highway speeds you towards the coast through the broad 'waist' of the **Fleurieu Peninsula** to the small town of Goolwa. Here the excellent **Signal Point River Murray Centre** tells all you could want to know about the longest river in Australia, the Murray, which flows through the bird-thronged barrage to the east of the town. You can take cruises from here to the mouth of the Murray and the Coorong rivers.

A short drive along the shore of Encounter Bay leads to **Victor Harbor** with its causeway linking the resort to Granite Island. The view of town and ocean is worth the 100m (330-ft) climb up **The Bluff**, to the west of town. Return to Adelaide by the direct route to complete a 200km (125-mile) drive.

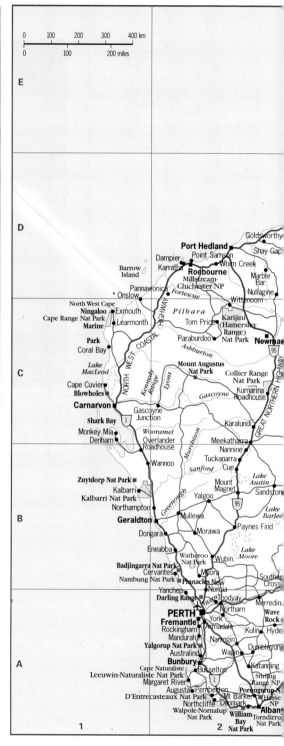

Perth's Swan River was named after the black swans that live here

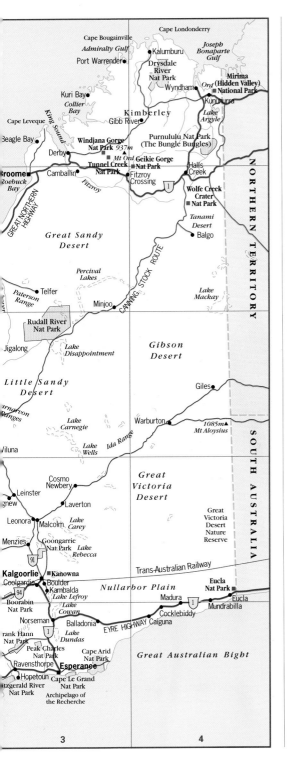

Cape Londonderry

Cape Bougainville

Admiralty Gulf

Kalumburu

*Joseph
Bonaparte
Gulf*

Port Warrender

Drysdale
River
Nat Park

**Mirima
(Hidden Valley)
National Park**

Wyndham

Ord

Kuri Bay

*Collier
Bay*

Kununurra

Kimberley

Gibb River

*Lake
Argyle*

Cape Leveque

King Sound

Beagle Bay

**Windjana Gorge
Nat Park** *937m*

Purnululu Nat Park
(The Bungle Bungles)

Derby

▲ *Mt Ord*

**Tunnel Creek
Nat Park**

**Geikie Gorge
Nat Park**

Halls
Creek

roome

*Roebuck
Bay*

Camballin

Fitzroy
Crossing

Fitzroy

GREAT NORTHERN
HIGHWAY

**Wolfe Creek
Crater
Nat Park**

N
O
R
T
H
E
R
N

T
E
R
R
I
T
O
R
Y

*Tanami
Desert*

Balgo

*Great Sandy
Desert*

*Percival
Lakes*

CANNING STOCK ROUTE

*Paterson
Range*

Telfer

Minjoo

*Lake
Mackay*

Rudall River
Nat Park

Jigalong

*Lake
Disappointment*

*Gibson
Desert*

*Little Sandy
Desert*

Giles

*arnarvon
anges*

*Lake
Carnegie*

Warburton

1085m ▲
Mt Aloysius

Ida Range

Viluna

*Lake
Wells*

S
O
U
T
H

A
U
S
T
R
A
L
I
A

Cosmo
Newbery

*Great
Victoria
Desert*

Leinster

Laverton

gnew

Leonora

Malcolm

*Lake
Carey*

Great
Victoria
Desert
Nature
Reserve

Menzies

Goongarrie
Nat Park

*Lake
Rebecca*

Trans-Australian Railway

91

Kalgoorlie

■ Kanowna

Coolgardie

Boulder

94

Kambalda

Lake Lefroy

Nullarbor Plain

Eucla
Nat Park ■

Boorabin
Nat Park

*Lake
Cowan*

Madura

1

Eucla

Mundrabilla

Norseman

Balladonia

Cocklebiddy

Caiguna

EYRE HIGHWAY

1

rank Hann
Nat Park

*Lake
Dundas*

Peak Charles
Nat Park

Cape Arid
Nat Park

Great Australian Bight

Ravensthorpe

Hopetoun

tzgerald River
Nat Park

Cape Le Grand
Nat Park

Esperance

Archipelago of
the Recherche

3

4

Western Australia

Virgin karri forests at Warren National Park, southwest of Pemberton

ON TOP OF THE STATE
The Stirling Range is the highest mountain range in southwestern Australia, and is carpeted by wildflowers during the spring (September to October). The area has numerous hiking trails, but don't forget your rain gear, because sudden storms are common.

TROPICAL NORTH
Parts of the Kimberley are subject to monsoonal rainfall; rivers that may have been reduced to a few pools in the Dry quickly fill and spill over the surrounding plains. In the far north are habitats of such biological value that their national park status, far from opening them up to the public, has led to the banning of all access.

WESTERN AUSTRALIA Devotees of this state, Australia's largest, are fond of producing maps showing how much of Europe or the USA might be fitted into its 2,500,000sq km (965,000sq miles). Western Australia is undoubtedly *big*—larger than Alaska and Texas combined. With a population of just over 2 million it is also very empty, much of it consisting of variations on the theme of desert—voids of various kinds extend from the desert beaches of the Indian Ocean in the far northwest to the cliffs of the Nullarbor being eaten away by the Southern Ocean. A further factor is its isolation. Perth is generally reckoned to be the most remote city on earth; its nearest large neighbour, Adelaide, is over 2,700km (1,678 miles) away and Sydney is 4,176km (2,595 miles) away. For all this, the West has some of Australia's great holiday destinations.

Friendly, sunny **Perth** is every Australian's second best-loved city, next to Sydney; until recently, this was the place other Australians migrated to in search of the good life at an affordable price. It certainly ranks high in the hierarchy of Australian cities, not least because of its stunning site on the beautiful Swan River, just inland from its port of **Fremantle**, one of the country's most atmospheric historic towns.

Perth and its metropolitan region dominate the coastal plain spreading westwards from the **Darling Range**, Western Australia's modest equivalent of the Great Dividing Range. With a Mediterranean climate, an often spectacularly rugged coastline, fine forests and the lion's share of fertile farmland, this is the most densely inhabited part of the state. Inland stretches the Wheat Belt, its yields of grain dependent on a variable rainfall, gradually merging into the scrublands that herald the desert itself. Straggling along the desert rim is a line of gold-rush towns, some defunct, some, like **Kalgoorlie–Boulder**, still with plenty of kick in them.

In the rest of the state, people are thinly spread. Towns, none of them of any size, are widely spaced along the immensely long coast. The old pearling base of **Broome** is enjoying a revival as a tourist attraction, while **Port Hedland** deals efficiently with the iron ore being extracted in huge quantities from its Pilbara hinterland. Here are strange new settlements of prefabricated buildings, erected quickly to create air-conditioned shelter from the fierce temperatures for miners and prospectors.

The grandeur of Western Australia's natural landscapes is more attractive to its visitors than the urban amenities. The paving of the highways to the north and the northwest of the state has encouraged visitors to explore areas previously considered to be well off the beaten track. Even more than the harsh, vast **Hamersley Range** in the Pilbara, the far-off tropical **Kimberley** is attracting tourists to its wealth of natural wonders, sometimes as part of a trip to the adjoining Northern Territory.

HISTORY New Holland was the unlikely name bestowed in the early 1600s on the western rim of the unknown continent by Dutch seamen on their way to their country's possessions in the East Indies. They would race eastwards across the Indian Ocean, then sail along the Australian coast towards Java. Sometimes they were sailing too fast, and Western Australia's earliest European history is studded with the names of famous ships such as the *Zeewijk* and *Batavia* wrecked on the reefs and shoals of its treacherous coastline.

The first British impressions were not good either; William Dampier's reports in 1688–89 on the barren northwest were distinctly discouraging. It was a (largely imaginary) French threat in the 1820s that impelled the British to add the west of the continent to the Empire; the port of Albany was founded on the south coast in 1826, and in 1829 Lieutenant-Governor Stirling and his band of free settlers established the Swan River colony where Perth now stands. Progress was fitful, and the colony was only saved by a massive infusion of convict workers in the 1850s and 1860s, then in the 1880s and 1890s by the opening up of the Eastern Goldfields, where the combined city of Kalgoorlie–Boulder still thrives on mining today.

In the early 20th century, Western Australia's adherence to the Federation was only secured by a promise to link it to the rest of the country by the construction of the Transcontinental Railway. Even as late as the 1930s, a referendum revealed a majority wanted secession. Today, in spite of extraordinary financial mismanagement on the part of politicians and unscrupulous entrepreneurs, the west's position seems to be secure, based on massive postwar immigration and seemingly unlimited mineral wealth.

A LAND APART
Despite modern transportation and communications facilities, Western Australia is still very much a land apart. Anything east of the South Australian border—be it Adelaide, Melbourne or Sydney—is often referred to under the blanket term 'Eastern States', and West Australians are more likely to vacation in Bali or Singapore than on the Great Barrier Reef.

149

The Stirling Range National Park near Albany in the southwest

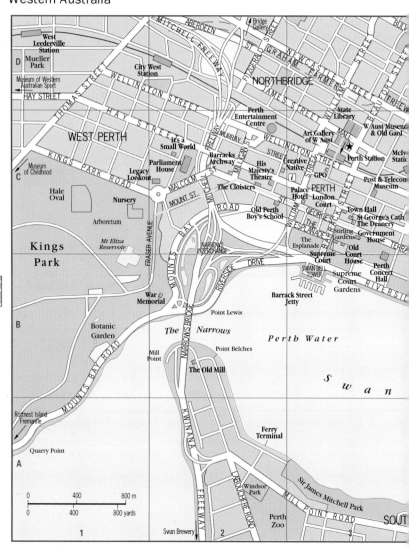

Perth

Perth, like Sydney, is an inspired fusion of fine buildings in a splendid natural setting. The view eastwards from **Kings Park** reveals one of the world's great urban panoramas—to the left are the office towers of the city, glittering in the constant bright sunlight; to the right lies the glorious stretch of Perth Water alive with pleasure craft.

The city seems to offer its citizens most of the ingredients of the good life: a Californian-style climate unspoiled by smog; attractive homes in every price category in suburbs that range from the merely pleasant to the opulent; and every kind of outdoor playground, from the sweeps of the Swan River and superb ocean beaches, to lavish parklands that bring the bush almost into the heart of the city.

SUBURBS

The plush succession of waterside suburbs you pass if you take the ferry to South Perth (see panel opposite) may tempt you to sell up and move here without further ado. This is where the millionaires of the 'Golden West' choose to live, with easy access to their yachts at the marina or yacht club.

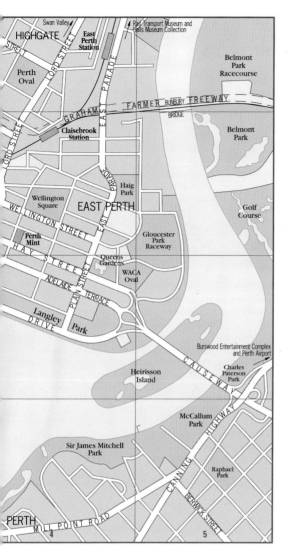

Covering a large area of bushland and parks, Kings Park in the middle of Perth is an ideal place to relax

RIVERSIDE PERTH
True Perth is a synthesis of city and river, and you should make sure that you enjoy this not only from Kings Park but from the river itself. At the very least, take the ferry across to South Perth (and back again!), but better still travel by ferry to Rottnest Island or Fremantle. For much of the latter part of the journey, your eye will return again and again to the unforgettable image of the city's clustering towers rising over the functionally elegant Narrows Bridge.

CITY OF PLENTY Perth used to be known for its dullness. True or false then, this is no longer the case. Contrasting with the historic restored **His Majesty's Theatre**, the home of Western Australian opera and dance, the **Perth Concert Hall** is a major addition to the city's cultural life. Another modern landmark is the white tower of the **Burswood Entertainment Complex**, containing one of the biggest casinos in the southern hemisphere.

Other buildings of high cultural significance (the Art Gallery and State Museum) have been grouped together to form an urban focal point in Northbridge. The city is compact. A network of futuristic walkways straddles streets and tunnels through buildings, linking transportation terminals, shopping arcades, pedestrian precincts and civic plazas. Spectacular sights may be few, but there are a host of urban pleasures.

Perth, viewed from the Kings Park area—a most attractive city

SUN, SAND AND SURF
Perth's suburban beaches are the finest in Australia. The white sands and clear blue Indian Ocean waters of Cottesloe, Scarborough, Swanbourne and many other beaches are far superior to those of more famous Bondi, Sydney's most popular strip of sand.

SIGHTSEE BY WATER
Ferries connect the jetty at Barrack Square in Perth with South Perth, Fremantle and Rottnest Island, and there are trips upstream, too, visiting the early colonial landscapes and wineries of the upper reaches of the Swan River. Cruise ships still occasionally call at Fremantle.

►► Art Gallery of Western Australia 150C3
Perth Cultural Centre, James Street Mall (tel: 08-9492 6600 or 08-9492 6622—recorded information). Open: daily 10–5 Admission free (varying charges for special exhibitions)
This gallery, housed in a modern building and the old Police Courts, has a fine collection of mostly Australian art, including an acclaimed array of Aboriginal art. There are also collections of traditional and contemporary crafts, ceramics, textiles, jewellery, woodwork and glass. The museum extends its influence with sculpture gracing the plaza linking the city to Northbridge.

►► Kings Park 150C1
Few cities in the world enjoy anything like this great swath of natural landscape on the edge of the city. From the founding of the colony in 1829, it was always intended that this area, known as Mount Eliza, should be an open space. About two-thirds of the park is bushland, glorious with wildflowers in the spring, and accessible by scenic drive as well as on foot. Fraser Avenue, with its monuments, memorials and lines of lemon gums, gives an unequalled panorama of Perth in its Swan River setting, while the **Botanic Garden** encapsulates the incomparable floral wealth of Western Australia in a series of gardens.

►► Perth Mint 151C4
310 Hay Street, East Perth (tel: 08-9421 7223). Open: Mon–Fri 9–4, Sat–Sun 9–1 (except 25 Apr). Admission: moderate
Established as a branch of London's Royal Mint in 1899, the Perth Mint still operates as a gold refining and coining facility. This is one of the city's most popular attractions, where visitors can see molten gold being poured, view a collection of nuggets and mint their own medallion.

► Perth Zoo 150A2
20 Labouchere Road, South Perth (tel: 08-9474 0444 or 08-9474 3551—recorded information)
Open: daily 9–5. Admission: moderate
An excellent reason for taking the ferry to South Perth, the

city's zoo has a fine collection of exotic animals as well as native Australian creatures such as emus, koalas and kangaroos, all of which you can meet in the Australian Walkabout. The zoo is famous for its research and breeding of endangered species, and one resident of Western Australia now on the endangered list, the little termite-eating numbat, a small marsupial, is provided with its own quarters.

Perth Zoo is constantly developing innovative features such as the Reptile Encounter, a Nocturnal House and the African Savannah, a complete reconstruction of an African ecosystem.

▶▶▶ Western Australian Museum   *150C3*

Perth Cultural Centre, James Street Mall (tel: 08-9427 2700)
Open: daily 9.30–5. Admission: donation

This museum complex comprises a cluster of buildings of many different dates and styles contributing in their various ways to the attractive ambience of Perth's Cultural Centre. Half a day spent here is no substitute for a month spent exploring the natural wonders and human heritage of Western Australia, but it will go a long way towards it.

As well as a variety of buildings, the complex contains many different galleries and displays. One of the highlights is the Katta Dijnoong Aboriginal gallery, a magnificent attempt to review in a comprehensive and sympathetic way the art, religion and culture of the first Australians. Other displays highlight the history of the state's land and people, natural history and marine habitats. The history of white settlement of the west is evoked in the cool spaces of the stone-built **Old Gaol**, Perth's original prison complex, which dates from the 1850s.

ALL THAT GLITTERS
Perth is home to several shops that sell precious and semiprecious stones. You can buy pearls from Broome, opals from Coober Pedy and, not least, pink diamonds from the state's own Argyle Diamond Mine.

SUBURBAN ATTRACTIONS
In the southern suburb of Canning Vale you can tour the famous Swan Brewery, while the northern coast offers the AQWA (Aquarium of Western Australia) at Sorrento and Hillary's Boat Harbour at Hillarys. The historic port of Fremantle lies downstream, and a cruise to the Swan Valley wineries is highly recommended.

The mock-Tudor London Court, built in 1937, runs between the Hay Street Mall and St. George's Terrace

Walk

Through the heart of Perth

See map on page 150.

This walk of about 4km (2.5 miles) takes in many of the contrasts of old and new that make Perth such a stimulating capital city.

North of Perth's City Railway Station are the buildings and plazas of the **Cultural Centre** including the Western Australian Museum and Art Gallery of Western Australia. The pedestrian mall south of the station is dominated by the sandstone **General Post Office** (1925). The junction of Hay Street Mall with Barrack Street is overlooked by the tower of the **Town Hall**, behind which is **St. George's Cathedral** and the cottage-style **Deanery** (1859) facing on to **St. George's Terrace**.

Government House was built in the mid-19th century and enclosed in luxuriant gardens. Towards the Swan River are **Stirling Gardens** and **Supreme Court Gardens**. Next to the Supreme Court itself is the city's oldest surviving building, the **Old Court House** (1837). Beyond here is Barrack Square and the dramatic Swan Bell Tower, containing the bells of St. Martin-in-the-Fields, one of London's most famous churches.

The mock-Tudor arcade known as **London Court** links St. George's Terrace with Hay Street Mall. Despite its ecclesiastical Gothic appearance, 139 St. George's Terrace is not a church but the National Trust-listed **Old Perth Boy's School**. Farther west is **The Cloisters**, founded in 1858 as Perth's first secondary school and now tastefully converted to offices.

Complete your walk here, or carry on on foot or by free Central Area Transit (CAT) bus past **Barracks Archway** to the viewpoints in **Kings Park**. If on foot, take a look at **Parliament House** (which can be toured on weekdays) beyond the archway.

Drive

The southwest

This day's outing from Perth follows the coastline south of Fremantle toward the state's southwestern tip, an area rich in forests and vineyards.

Beyond the resort of **Mandurah**, the Old Coast Road passes close to the lakes, swamps and woodland of **Yalgorup National Park**. **Bunbury** has fine beaches; between here and **Busselton** on Geographe Bay the highway runs through fine stands of tuart trees, some of the few remaining after the uncontrolled felling that took place in colonial days. The coastline of the **Leeuwin-Naturaliste National Park** stretches for about 120km (75 miles) between Cape Naturaliste in the north and Augusta in the south.

The back-bone of the area is formed by a granite ridge capped by limestone; water erosion has created hundreds of caves (some are open).

There are 70 or so wineries in the region—mostly around the little township of **Margaret River**. To the south are the karri trees of the **Boranup Forest**, best seen from the forest drive and the **Boranup Lookout**. There are fine coastal views at Prevelly Park at the mouth of the Margaret River.

If time permits, the tour can be extended to **Augusta** and to **Cape Leeuwin**. The return to Perth is faster via the South Western Highway beyond Bunbury.

Drive

Mundaring Weir

This short excursion enters the heavily wooded Darling Range.

The Great Eastern Highway leaves the city behind as it winds up the Darling scarp. The **John Forrest National Park** is a recreation area, with streams, waterfalls and a pool, while the dam and reservoir of **Mundaring Weir** have an attractive bushland setting. Make your return journey via Lesmurdie Falls and Kalamunda.

155

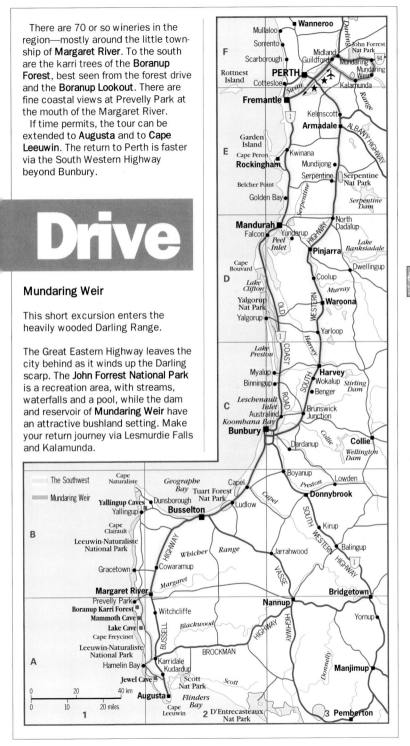

The eerie landscape of The Pinnacles, 243km (151 miles) north of Perth, within Nambung National Park

GRASS-TREES
Among the oddest of Australian plants are the grass-trees. They used to be known as blackboys, from their supposed resemblance to an Aborigine brandishing a spear, but this term has been discarded, at least officially. Resin exudes from the blackened, stubby trunk above which flares a skirt of grass-like leaves and a spectacular flower spike (the 'spear'). Grass-trees depend on fire for their growth, reaching a maximum height of about 5m (16ft).

National parks

The immense spaces of Western Australia include great swaths of unvarying country of little obvious interest, but there are also any number of landscapes well deserving of their national-park or special-interest designation. The state contains two of Australia's 14 World Heritage Sites—spectacular Shark Bay and Purnululu National Park.

The southwest Facing the meeting point of the Southern and Indian oceans, the southwest of the state enjoys a reasonably high rainfall that encourages the growth of magnificent forests, notably of the karri tree. Its numbers much reduced by the 19th century's insatiable appetite for wood, this forest giant nevertheless survives in substantial patches in a number of national parks. In the southwest, these include the Stirling and Porongurup Ranges, the Boranup Forest in the Margaret River area, and the **Walpole-Nornalup National Park**, a coastal park beautifully sited around the Nornalup Inlet, where deep rivers wind seaward through heath-covered dunes.

Battered by breakers, these southwestern coasts have a rugged quality, well exemplified in the wild cliffs and rocky shoreline of the **Leeuwin-Naturaliste National Park**. On the shoreline farther north, resorts mix with wildlife-rich lagoons and lakes, as at **Yalgorup National Park**. The backdrop to the coastal plain is formed by the escarpment of the Darling Range, covered with jarrah woods and bushland. The jarrah (a eucalyptus) is one of the characteristic trees of the southwest, much logged in the past and sawed up for railway ties. The range is accessible at any number of points along its length, from the **John Forrest National Park** east of Perth, or **Lane-Poole Reserve** on the Murray River, to Marrinup and Pinjarra.

One of the privileges of life in Perth is easy access to unspoiled nature. Only 40km (25 miles) out of the city to the northeast is **Walyunga National Park**, an area of wild bushland where the Swan and Avon rivers have cut through the Darling Range. Equally near the city, but due north, is **Yanchep National Park** where the bush is home to honey possums, kangaroos and bandicoots; a lake and limestone caves can be explored. Few sights are as compelling as the countless limestone pillars known as **The Pinnacles** in the Nambung National Park.

The northwest A great contrast of natural landscapes is found in the vast northwest. Some of the most stunning scenery is on the coast. Among the inlets and peninsulas of the World Heritage-listed **Shark Bay** is unique and dazzlingly white Shell Beach, 60km (37 miles) long and built up to a 10m (33-ft) depth of crushed and compacted shells. The North West Cape has twin parks of outstanding interest. To the east are the parched plateau and deep rocky gorges of the **Cape Range National Park**, descending to the west through fossil reefs and sand dunes to Australia's 'other' barrier reef, the **Ningaloo Marine Park**, 260km (160 miles) of coral reef, sheltering a shallow lagoon. Running inland from the tidal flats and mangrove swamps of the coast is the **Pilbara**, a spectacular upland deeply incised by river valleys and culminating in the vivid gorges of the **Karijini (Hamersley Range) National Park**.

Between the Pilbara and the Kimberley, the Great Sandy Desert claims part of the coastline. Where it merges with the Little Sandy Desert, far inland, are the salt lakes of the **Rudall River National Park**, an extremely remote area which offers no facilities whatsoever.

The Kimberley Beyond the desert, dramatic landforms include **Geikie Gorge**, **Windjana Gorge**, the world's second largest meteorite crater at **Wolfe Creek**, and the strange beehive rock formations of the **Bungle Bungles** (see page 160). Plant life ranges from sparse spinifex to scenes of great luxuriance in spots with a guaranteed water supply.

A possum—part of the myriad wildlife of the state

A RARE BIRD
In 1894 Windjana Gorge in the Kimberley was the scene of a gun battle between heavily armed police and a band of Aborigines led by Jundumurra, known to his adversaries as Pigeon. A skilful horseman and tracker, Pigeon had been compelled to work for the police against his own people. Eventually turning against his masters, he shot a constable, set prisoners free, and for years waged a minor guerilla war. He was finally hunted down and killed at Tunnel Creek on 1 April 1897.

The fragile silica and sandstone forms of the Bungle Bungles are best seen between April and October

The rugged wilderness of Kalbarri National Park can be appreciated by helicopter

EYRE TRAVEL
The 1,195km (742 miles) of the Eyre Highway between Ceduna (SA) and Norseman are less of an obstacle than might be supposed. Plenty of Australians refuse to be deterred by such distances and plan their driving accordingly, settling down to a steady pace and accepting the discipline of distance. At holiday periods it's wise to reserve ahead if you plan to stay in any of the motels along the route. Your vehicle should be absolutely roadworthy before setting out, since repair facilities are limited. Two hazards to remember: The sign 'Road Train' identifies a truck with up to three trailers— make sure the road is clear before attempting to overtake a road train; and when journeying west, you will have the setting sun to reckon with for long and disagreeable periods. One solution (reserve well in advance!) is to put the car on the train for the westward journey and drive back to the east.

How to travel

By air The remoteness and sheer size of Western Australia mean that air travel is often used for journeying between major cities, to reach faraway places of interest and for day and half-day trips. Perth has direct connections to numerous overseas destinations, as well as daily flights to all state capitals and a number of other Australian cities.

By bus Express buses link Perth to the rest of the state, and to other Australian cities (given time!). The metropolitan area of Perth has a comprehensive network of buses, some of them operating out of the futuristic terminal near The Narrows. The capital also enjoys free services in the central area: Central Area Transit (CAT) buses circle the city each day at regular intervals, a great boon once you've got the hang of their routes.

By train Perth has a four-pronged suburban rail service, connecting City Station with Midland, Armadale, Joondalup and Fremantle. Fares are reasonable, and the service is efficient. Most of the state's long-distance railways now carry freight only, though there are passenger trains from Perth to Bunbury in the south (the *Australind*) and west to Kalgoorlie (the *Prospector*). One of the world's great trains runs from Perth Terminal Station, the twice-weekly *Indian Pacific* to Sydney via Adelaide. Linking west and east across the Nullarbor Plain, this train is the railway experience of a lifetime—the journey to Adelaide takes 38 hours, and it is a three-night trip to Sydney.

By car The alternative routes north from Perth to Port Hedland, the **North West Coastal Highway** and the **Great Northern Highway**, are both paved, as is their continuation onwards to the Kimberley and the Northern Territory. It's a long way, though. The road network around Perth and much of the southwest is well developed, but many places can only be reached on unpaved roads, in varying states of upkeep. Some popular routes, like the rough but very scenic **Gibb River Road** through the Kimberley, can definitely only be negotiated by 4WD, and this road is often closed during the December–April wet season.

▶▶ Albany 146A2

Albany was the first European settlement in Western Australia, founded in 1826 by Major Edmund Lockyer to preempt any possible French interest in this quarter of the continent. It became an important base for whalers, then a coaling station for ships on the India–Sydney run; it is now a popular holiday town. The 19th-century buildings include the **Old Gaol;** the **Patrick Taylor Cottage▶** of 1832, constructed from wattle and daub and now a folk museum; the **Old Post Office▶**, now occupied by the University of WA; and the excellent **Albany Residency ▶**, part of the Western Australia Museum. Nearby is the *Amity* **Replica**, a full-size reproduction of Major Lockyer's brig, which was built from local timber in 1975.

The town nestles between Mount Clarence and Mount Melville, the summits of which give terrific views over coast and countryside. Farther inland are the granite domes and karri forests of Porongurup National Park, and farther still the high Stirling Range. To east and west lies one of Australia's finest stretches of coastline, and protecting the sound to the south is the rugged peninsula of **Torndirrup National Park▶▶**, with spectacular features like the **Blowholes▶**, **The Gap▶**, and **Natural Bridge▶**, a huge granite bridge-like suspension. The old whaling station on Frenchman Bay is now **Whaleworld▶**, which claims to be the world's largest whaling museum.

▶ Augusta 146A2

Augusta is one of Western Australia's oldest settlements, founded in 1830. This popular holiday resort overlooks the mouth of the Blackwood River and has some delightful beaches, plenty of good fishing spots and offers river cruises. This region is perhaps best known for its remarkable series of caves, particularly the spectacular **Jewel Cave▶**, with its strange rock formations that include an enormous straw stalactite and an underground river. In town, the Augusta Historical Museum is worth a visit, and there are panoramic views from lighthouse-capped **Cape Leeuwin▶**, 8km (5 miles) to the south.

DIGGERS ON HORSEBACK
Australia's Desert Mounted Corps distinguished itself in the Middle East in the course of World War I. Albany was the port of embarkation for many of its troops, and they and their mounts are commemorated by the dramatic statue on top of Mount Clarence. This is a recast of the bronze erected on the banks of the Suez Canal in 1932, which came to a sorry end during the Suez crisis of 1956. The original of the horse's head was recovered, and is on view in the Residency Museum.

A LADY LION
The map of Australia reveals a number of names of Dutch origin. Perhaps the most famous of these is Cape Leeuwin, with its lighthouse overlooking the meeting point of the Indian and Southern oceans. Its name recalls the Dutch vessel that first put it on the map, the *Leeuwin*, or lioness, which passed this way in 1622.

The town of Albany viewed from the water

Western Australia

A STAIRWAY TO THE SKY
Another effect of Broome's exceptional tidal range is the optical illusion known as 'The Staircase to the Moon', visible only at certain times of the year when the rays of the moon are reflected off the exposed bed of the ocean.

The pleasant town of Bunbury is a major seaport and the heart of the southwest

▶▶ Broome   147D3

The tourist's southwestern gateway to the Kimberley, Broome makes the most of its lively past, when divers from all over Asia braved the bends and fierce rivalry to harvest precious mother-of-pearl from the sea bed (see page 161). Although only a few luggers still sail today, cultured pearls are farmed in the vicinity.

The past can best be enjoyed in the **Broome Historical Society Museum▶**, at the facinating **Pearl Luggers▶** displays or in the **cemetery**, its graves a grim record of the dangers of life as a diver. The Japanese section is particularly impressive. The town overlooks the mud flats and mangroves of Roebuck Bay, a rich haven for birdlife.

The tidal range at Broome is exceptional, up to 10m (33ft), and at very low tide the footprints of dinosaurs can be seen at **Gantheaume Point▶▶** to the south of the town. From here the splendid white sands of **Cable Beach▶▶** stretch north for 22km (14 miles).

▶ Bunbury   146A2

Bunbury's population of over 53,000 inhabitants makes it one of Western Australia's largest settlements. The viewpoint known as Boulter's Heights provides a panorama over the town and its surroundings. As well as a port, Bunbury is a popular resort, with good fishing, a fine string of beaches along Ocean Drive and, a relatively recent phenomenon, a friendly school of dolphins that enjoy the company of visitors to Koombana Beach.

▶▶ Purnululu National Park
(The Bungle Bungles)   147E4

The soft sandstone of this part of the East Kimberley has been eroded into strange rock formations resembling domes, turrets and beehives. Access to the national park, World Heritage listed in 2003, is by 4WD only and there are no facilities: the region is closed from January to March during the wet season. Most visitors prefer to see the park by plane or helicopter; the aerial perspective reveals nature's weird beauty and striking hues. The park also has numerous examples of the art of the indigenous people who lived here, plus a number of burial sites.

Pearl oysters thrive in the tropical seas from Cape York in northern Queensland right round to Shark Bay in the west of Western Australia, a distance of some 3,000km (1,865 miles). There is a particularly large concentration of them between Derby and Cossack in the northwest. From early on, the pearls themselves were a bonus, the mainstay of the industry being mother-of-pearl shell, used for jewellery and, above all, for humble buttons.

Commercial exploitation This began in the 1880s, when Aborigines were more or less forced by pearling masters into diving for the shell on the sea bed, an often lethal task; even if they could avoid the danger of drowning, there were shark attacks, and many boats and their crews were lost in the frequent cyclones. With the expansion of the trade and the introduction of diving suits later in the century, there was an influx of Chinese, Filipinos, Malays, Koepangers from Timor and the most expert of all pearlers, the Japanese. In the 1920s Broome, one of the world hubs of pearling, had a population of about 3,000, some 1,200 of Japanese descent. A typical pearling lugger might have had a European master, a pair of Japanese divers and a crew from Timor. The different races lived in sometimes uneasy proximity in Broome, with occasional outbreaks of violence. Each September during the famous Shinju Matsuri (Pearl Festival), Broome remembers its golden days.

Pearling today By the 1930s, the shell beds had been seriously depleted and, later, mother-of-pearl was displaced by plastic in the manufacture of buttons. Today, a few luggers still set off for the oyster beds some 6.5km (4 miles) off the coast, but most of Broome's current output comes from cultured pearls, raised in 'farms'. Pearling's history is explained in the **Broome Historical Society Museum**, while old pearling luggers can be seen at Broome's **Pearl Luggers** display and at the **Maritime Museum** in Fremantle. A real curiosity connected with the trade is the Catholic mission at Beagle Bay, 128km (80 miles) north of Broome, its altar shimmering with mother-of-pearl.

THE PEARL FARMER'S YEAR
From December to March there is little to do, for this is the region's wet season; from April to August the young oysters are seeded so that they produce pearls; during the remainder of the year the large oysters are removed and their shells used for mother-of-pearl.

Until recently, Broome relied on pearling for its livelihood

WESTERN ROCK
Mount Augustus, 450km (280 miles) inland from Carnarvon, may lack the unique beauty of Uluru but beats it hands-down for size. This is the world's largest monocline, created—according to the Aborigines—when a man called Burringurrah was speared by his enemies in the Dreamtime. From a viewpoint southeast of the rock, his form can still be made out, with the stump of the spear in his leg.

162

WATERING THE GOLDFIELDS
Extracting gold from the fields of Western Australia posed fewer difficulties than finding water in this utterly arid area. The Irish-born engineer Charles Yelverton O'Connor solved the problem. Already responsible for the construction of Fremantle Harbour and the building of much of the state's railway system, this late-Victorian genius built one of the wonders of the age, known as the Goldfields and Agricultural Water Supply Scheme. Beginning at the splendid dam at Mundaring Weir near Perth, O'Connor's great pipe sucked water 558km (347 miles) eastward in sufficient quantities to quench the miners' thirst and leave some over to irrigate the farms of the Wheat Belt. Attacked by landed interests and ridiculed by critics, O'Connor lost heart and committed suicide a year before completion of the project.

Coolgardie—model of Ned Kelly

▶ Busselton   146A2
Busselton is a pleasant family resort with good beaches, facing north across Geographe Bay and sheltered from the west. The 2km (1.2-mile) long Busselton Jetty is a major attraction, with an interpretative centre, train rides and the **Underwater Observatory▶**, which has viewing windows that look out on to coral and a profuse array of marine life.

The approach to the town from the north passes through a splendid forest of tuarts, a tree unique to Western Australia. Just off the highway is the long and low tin-roofed 1830s colonial mansion known as **Wonnerup House▶**, furnished in period style and open to the public.

▶ Carnarvon   146C1
Only about 144km (90 miles) south of the Tropic of Capricorn, Carnarvon wears a tropical air, with palm trees lining its fascine promenade, and hibiscus and bougainvillaea blooming in its elegantly broad main street. Famous for its fishing industries (you can visit the prawn (shrimp) and scallop processing plant), it is also the heart of a prosperous fruit (particularly bananas) and vegetable growing area, the Gascoyne district. The **Bibbawarra Bore▶**, 16km (10 miles) north of town, produces a constant gush of water at 65°C (149°F). At **The Blowholes▶**, 69km (43 miles) north, jets of water spout 20m (65ft) into the air.

▶ Coolgardie   147B3
A classic boom-and-bust town 557km (346 miles) east of Perth and 39km (24 miles) from Kalgoorlie–Boulder, Coolgardie was the focus of Australia's most frantic gold rush, with a peak population in the 1890s of 15,000. The then residents' needs were catered for by two stock exchanges, three breweries and a couple of dozen hotels. The population is now only a tenth of its former size.

Looking like an exceptionally grand railway terminus, the old Government Buildings are now the home of the **Goldfields Exhibition Museum▶**, with extensive displays including a model of the town at its height. Opposite is the weird **Ben Prior's Park**, its scrapped machinery and statues of Australian heroes standing out surrealistically in the implacable sun. More abandoned machinery, rolling stock and a locomotive have been preserved in Coolgardie's **Railway Museum**, which is in the 1896 railway terminal.

▶ Darling Range   146A2
The unbroken line of this wooded escarpment stretches far to the north and to the south of Perth, rising to a height of about 580m (1,902ft) and defining the boundary of the coastal plain. Not far from the

city are several popular recreation areas, like the bush-land and streams of the John Forrest National Park or Mundaring Weir. The reservoir here was built between 1898 and 1902 to supply the far-off Eastern Goldfields with water; attractively landscaped, it is a popular picnic spot. The Number 1 Pump Station Museum► at the reservoir commemorates C.Y. O'Connor who oversaw this vast project and tells the story of its construction (see panel).

► Denmark   146A2
Rugged coastal scenery contrasting with the tranquil Denmark River and attractive farmlands makes the small town of Denmark in the extreme southwest a popular place for family holidays. Wilson Inlet offers fine fishing, boating and other aquatic pleasures. To the west, **William Bay National Park►** has sand dunes and pristine beaches, as well as heathland and karri forest, while nearby is the Valley of the Giants Treetop Walk above the forest floor.

► Derby   147E3
On the shores of King Sound to the north of the mouth of the Fitzroy River, and within striking distance of the West Kimberley, Derby likes to describe itself as the 'Gateway to the Gorges'; indeed, Windjana Gorge is only about 139km (86 miles) east of the town. Nearer at hand (8km/5 miles away) is a famous boab tree, popularly supposed to have served as a lock-up for a small part of its 1,000-year life.

► Esperance   147A3
This deep-water port on the south coast flourished and declined in parallel to the boom and bust in the goldfields to its north. Now tourism has discovered Esperance, not least because of the magnificent beaches and the islands of the Recherche Archipelago. A scenic drive takes in part of the fine coastline and leads to **Pink Lake►**, an extraordinary salt lake that is genuinely pink. Some of the best coastal scenery is some 48km (30 miles) to the east; here is the **Cape Le Grand National Park►**, with stunning bays of blue water and white sand set between rocky headlands.

►►► Fremantle   146A2
Now part of the built-up area of Greater Perth, the old harbour town of Fremantle continues to serve as Western Australia's principal port. Founded in 1829, Fremantle owes some of its attractive appearance to the convict crafts-men shipped in to save the colony's faltering fortunes in the gold-rush building boom of the 1890s. These were Fremantle's great days, when the harbour was improved by the great engineer O'Connor (see panel opposite).

The heart of town is compact, its venerable townscape best enjoyed on foot. A good place to get your bearings is the **Round House►**, erected in 1831 as the new colony's prison. The highlight here is the **Western Australian Maritime Museum►►**, housed in two buildings—the original museum that concentrates on shipwrecks, and a modern structure at Victoria Quay, with various galleries and a 1960s submarine, HMAS *Ovens*. Other museums include the **Fremantle Prison►**, with displays and a fasci-nating convict database, and the **Fremantle Motor Museum►**. There is also Fisherman's Wharf, a lively café strip and the famous **Fremantle Markets**.

The fine port and city of Fremantle lies southwest of Perth, where the Swan River meets the Indian Ocean

163

HOW FREMANTLE GOT ITS NAME
Fremantle is named after the commander of the British naval force sent here to claim the west before anyone else. Captain Charles Howe Fremantle planted the Union Jack here on 2 May 1829, a month before the first settlers arrived to found the Swan River colony. An optimist, he believed that the colony would become 'in time, a place of consequence', in spite of 'its sandy and uncompromising appearance'.

164

Crumbling sandstone has created rugged cliffs around the resort of Kalbarri

►► Geikie Gorge National Park   *147D4*

The tiny settlement at **Fitzroy Crossing** has grown up around the point where the Northern Highway traverses the 640km (400-mile) long Fitzroy River that drains much of the Kimberley. Reduced to a series of pools in the Dry, the Fitzroy rises 16m (52ft) in the Wet (between December and March, when the park is generally closed), flooding vast areas. The effects of this phenomenal difference in water level can be observed by taking a boat trip up nearby Geikie Gorge, where the lower parts of the sheer cliffs have been dramatically scoured by the annual floodwaters. The gorge is home to tropical aquatic life forms, including stingrays and freshwater crocodiles, and is fringed by reeds and dense forest supporting a rich range of birdlife.

► Geraldton   *146B2*

This prosperous harbour town to the north of Perth, noted for its export of locally caught lobsters, is popular with visitors year round but particularly in winter because of its excellent sunshine record. Some 60km (37 miles) off shore is the archipelago named the Houtman Abrolhos (derived from the Portuguese for 'Keep your eyes open!') Islands, notorious as a death trap for ships. Relics from famous wrecks are the mainstay of the **Western Australian Museum Geraldton►**, while the **HMAS** *Sydney* **Memorial►** commemorates the 645 men who lost their lives in 1941 while engaged in battle with the German ship *Kormoran*.

► Halls Creek   *147D4*

Halfway through the Kimberley on the Great Northern Highway, Halls Creek seems the archetypal Outback town, the middle of a vast area thinly populated by cattle-men and mineral prospectors. A short distance away is Old Halls Creek, with its evocative remains of an 1880s gold rush. Between the two settlements is a natural curiosity, a vein of white quartz standing clear of its surroundings and named the **China Wall►**. A 130km (80-mile) drive south brings you to the **Wolfe Creek Crater National Park►**.

Instead of horses, cars now stand in front of Kalgoorlie's often elaborate hotels

► Kalbarri 146B1

The gorges in the **Kalbarri National Park►►** are up to 80km (50 miles) long and 170m (558ft) deep, cut into the vivid red tumblagooda sandstone. A number of easily accessible viewpoints, like Hawk's Head Lookout, overlook this landscape in its setting of sandy plains. The coastal scenery has its drama, too, with high red cliffs dropping sheer into the ocean. The national park is also famous for its spring wildflowers, which bloom in a great diversity of species.

►►► Kalgoorlie–Boulder 147B3

The classic gold-rush towns of Kalgoorlie and Boulder were amalgamated in 1989. Gold was first found at nearby Coolgardie; not long after, on 10 June 1893, Patrick (Paddy) Hannan and two mates made the greatest find of all—known for ever after as Hannan's Reward—and within a year, tens of thousands of eager prospectors had swarmed to the 'Golden Mile'. In under a decade, both places had been transformed from ragged settlements to solid-seeming municipalities.

Hannan's slightly bemused statue sits outside the massive 1908 Town Hall on the pavement of the street named after him. This gently sloping roadway is of boulevard dimensions, wide enough to turn a camel train. On either side are monuments to the town's great days: grand public buildings, canopied shopfronts and several elaborate 19th-century hotels. Other attractions include the Royal Flying Doctor Service base and a range of mining-related museums (see panel page 167).

►►► The Kimberley 147E4

See page 173.

► Kununurra 147E4

This town in the East Kimberley was created in the 1960s to act as an urban focus for the Ord River Irrigation Scheme (see panel). A solitary relic of the past, the **Argyle Downs Homestead** was rescued when the land on which it stood was flooded, and is now a pioneer museum. Outside town at **Mirima (Hidden Valley) National Park►**, 300 million years of erosion have created spectacular patterns in the red sandstone.

THE WILD WEST
Kalgoorlie always was a rip-roaring kind of place. In 1926, gold thieves hacked to death the detectives sent after them, and ten years later anti-immigrant riots raged for two days before a train-load of police could be brought up from Perth. Many of today's misdeeds seem to be the result of enthusiastic weekend drinking getting out of hand rather than anything more serious.

165

OUT OF ORDER
Frustrated at seeing the floodwaters of the Ord River in the Kimberley running uselessly into the sea while for the rest of the year the land lay scorched and thirsty, the goverment spent huge sums on the Ord River Irrigation Scheme. Completed in 1972, its dams held back the muddy tide and distributed it among thousands of acres of irrigated cropland. But the desert, on the whole, failed to bloom. The cotton crop was killed by caterpillars, and other crops have been only partially successful, while DDT-resistant insects seem to enjoy life in the 984sq km (380sq miles) of the project's main water body, Lake Argyle.

'We can make this country a quarry to serve the whole world,' enthused Henry Bolte, the Premier of Victoria (1955–72). The prosperity of Australia's states and territories rests largely with the abundant mineral resources locked up in their ancient rocks.

Visitors can pan for real gold at the Sovereign Hill historical park in Victoria

A wealth of minerals Western Australia really came alive with the discovery of gold in unprecedented abundance in the Eastern Goldfields at the end of the 19th century, but the state also has (or had) reserves of antimony, bismuth, asbestos, coal, tin, copper, iron and nickel, as well as such rarities as tungsten, tantalite and beryl. Exploration and prospecting are very much a matter of the present as well as of history. The world's biggest iron mountain was discovered by accident in the Pilbara in the 1950s (see panel); while the incredibly productive Argyle Diamond Mine near Kununurra, which produces exquisite white, champagne and pink stones, and is the world's largest producing diamond mine, only came on stream in the 1980s.

The first rush But it is the lure of gold that still catches the imagination most. Gold rushes, here as everywhere, were epic events, with their extraordinary mixture of greed, determination and endurance amounting to heroism. The first rush in Western Australia was to Halls Creek in the Kimberley, in 1885, when Charlie Hall's Christmas present to himself was a 800g (28-ounce) nugget. Conditions in this utterly remote and harsh area were perhaps the worst anywhere; one devoted mate, Russian Jack, carted a sick friend 320km (200 miles) in a wheel-barrow in search of a doctor.

Halls Creek failed to live up to its promise, and the prospectors soon abandoned the Kimberley for the greater pickings to be found in the Eastern Goldfields. In 1892 Arthur Bayley rode into Southern Cross with the gold that he and his partner, Bill Ford, had found at Fly Flat, 200km (125 miles) to the east; bars emptied as the news got around, and within hours the greatest rush in the colony's history had begun. Fly Flat was renamed

IRONING OUT THE LANDSCAPE
Long suspected, the existence of unbelievably rich deposits of iron ore in the Pilbara were confirmed almost by accident in the 1950s. Forced by poor weather to fly low over one of the area's many gorges, Lang Hancock noticed that its walls gave off a metallic sheen. Subsequent investigation revealed what proved to be the world's greatest concentration of iron ore. The topography of whole tracts of land has been transformed by its removal, for example at the BHP Billiton Mount Whaleback Mine near Newman, the biggest opencast iron ore pit in the world, which can be toured.

Coolgardie; within six months thousands were living in a city of tents, having trekked through the waterless waste on foot or horseback, while supplies were brought up by dray or camel train. A year later, the biggest find of all was made at Boulder. The rush greatly increased Western Australia's population and was a stimulus to the colony's development. Terrible conditions endured for a while, with plagues of flies, outbreaks of typhoid and water that sometimes cost as much as champagne. Before the completion of O'Connor's pipeline from Perth in 1903 (see panel on page 162), traders in water often became richer than prospectors.

Companies move in Within the space of a few years, individual prospectors had scarred most of the Eastern Goldfields area with their shallow diggings ('specking') and extracted most of the alluvial gold. From now on it became necessary to mine more deeply, requiring the use of sophisticated machinery and the outlay of capital. Companies took over from rugged individuals.

Contemporary opencast methods of gold extraction and the amazing landscape they create can be observed from the viewing platform overlooking Kalgoorlie's **Super Pit**, which stretches for 3km (2 miles) and will eventually reach a depth of 600m (1,970ft).

KALGOORLIE–BOULDER
The Australian Prospectors & Miners Hall of Fame tells the story of the past, present and future of the region's, and Australia's, mining history. Based at the Hannans North Mine complex, the hall of fame, a faithful reconstruction of a mine and its surroundings, has displays dedicated to prospecting and minerals. The site also offers underground mine tours and gold panning.

Other Kalgoorlie–Boulder mining-related attractions include the WA Museum Kalgoorlie–Boulder, with exhibits, hands-on activities and outdoor displays, and the School of Mines Rocks and Minerals Museum.

Pilbara: Giant trucks transport the iron ore

The golden sandy beaches around the resort of Mandurah are always popular

RAILS THROUGH THE FOREST
In the early part of the 20th century, the jarrah forests inland from Mandurah echoed to the hiss of steam and the toot of whistles as narrow-gauge locomotives hauled timber to the mills. One of these forestry railways, the Hotham Valley Tourist Railway, running between Pinjarra and Dwellingup, has been kept alive by enthusiasts, and historic steam and diesel trains meet passengers off the modern *Australind* train from Perth. The enthusiasm is such that an additional line, the Etmilyn Forest Tramway, was opened in 1986, leading deep into the heart of the atmospheric jarrah woodlands.

▶ **Mandurah**   *146A2*

Less than an hour's drive south of Perth, Mandurah is deservedly popular with city weekenders. Vast areas of sheltered water along the Murray and Serpentine rivers and the Peel Inlet, 40km (25 miles) of beaches, and shady picnic spots help distribute the crowds and keep at least some of the town's tranquil atmosphere.

▶▶ **Margaret River**   *146A2*

The township of Margaret River is at the heart of the attractive district named after it, where the manicured landscape of prestige wineries contrasts with the savagery of surf pounding a rugged coastline and with a mysterious underground world of limestone caves. Arts, crafts and gourmet foodstuffs abound in the town, while once a year music of the highest calibre is performed in the delightful grounds of the Leeuwin Estate winery.

Among the more sheltered places along the coast, most of which forms part of the Leeuwin-Naturaliste National Park, is **Prevelly Park▶**. This is one of Australia's premier surfing spots, and the Margaret River Pro surf competition is held in the area each March. Only a few of the hundreds of caves are accessible, among them **Mammoth Cave▶** (named for its size) and **Lake Cave▶**. The **Boranup Karri Forest▶** in Leeuwin-Naturaliste National Park is a good place to see the massed ranks of karri trees.

▶▶ **Monkey Mia**   *146C1*

Some of the several hundred bottlenose dolphins living in Shark Bay mix with humans and accept fresh fish. To stand in the water of Monkey Mia beach and be nuzzled by a dolphin is an experience that few can resist, but the rangers at the Dolphin Information Centre ask that you check with them first. (See also page 174.)

▶ **New Norcia**   *146B2*

The Benedictines came to Western Australia in 1846, leaving the imprint of Mediterranean Catholicism here in the bush 128km (80 miles) north of Perth, where they established a mission for the Aborigines. As well as National Trust-listed buildings such as the Abbey Church and Monastery, there is a fine museum and art gallery.

The 'strangeness' of Australian plants, including eucalypts, wattles and banksias, fascinates visitors from abroad. Australia's native vegetation provides a constant reminder that you're not in the northern hemisphere anymore.

Early settlers tackled the isolation of this unfamiliar land by manipulating its appearance to recall the landscapes left behind. Planted in uncountable numbers, oaks, elms, willow and poplars transformed whole tracts of countryside —particularly in Tasmania – into a version of lowland England; the occasional eucalyptus looked like an intruder.

A great variety One of the joys of springtime is the abundance of wildflowers, particularly in Western Australia. Here a twofold isolation, not only from the rest of the world but from the rest of the continent, has resulted in flora of extraordinary variety. The state has some 8,000 named species, plus a further 2,000 that are still anonymous, three-quarters of them unique to the area though not necessarily unrelated to plants elsewhere in Australia. Some of Western Australia's most famous plants are the kangaroo paw, with its strangely shaped red or green flowers; a range of banksias, including the scarlet and acorn varieties; and the 60 species of tooth-leafed dryandras.

Below: Trailing orchid in bloom

169

Wildflowers in coastal Western Australia

Springtime spectacular Wildflowers pattern the ground from north to south as springtime advances. At the **Kalbarri National Park**, 600km (370 miles) north of Perth, flowers begin to bloom in July. Some of the most spectacular displays occur in the heathlands of the southwest, where there are more species of plants than in the rain forest. In places like the **Stirling** and **Porongurup ranges** spring arrives later, with November being the most rewarding month. **Kings Park** in Perth has large areas of natural bushland and a special section devoted to Australian trees, shrubs and wildflowers.

HAROLD HEIGHTS
Named after former Prime Minister Harold E. Holt, the joint US/Australian Naval Communication Station keeps in touch with what is going on around the oceans with an extraordinary cluster of tall towers, the central one of which, at 388m (1,273ft), is taller than the Empire State Building. American accents can be heard in the streets of Exmouth, founded in 1964 as the support town for the base, but visitors come here mostly for the excellent fishing; North West Cape is the nearest point in Australia to the teeming marine life of the continental shelf.

The lesser-known rival of the Great Barrier Reef, Ningaloo Reef is home to over 500 varieties of fish

▶▶ Ningaloo Marine Park and Exmouth area   *146C1*

A long detour leads off the North West Coastal Highway to far-off North West Cape, whose backbone is formed by the rugged **Cape Range**▶. This national park is made up of a high limestone plateau cut into by gorges and ravines, some containing deep pools. To the west stretch rarely visited dunes and beaches, protected from the ocean rollers by a barrier reef, 260km (160 miles) long and extending some 16km (10 miles) from the coast. The reef of Ningaloo Marine Park, with its 220 species of coral, whale sharks (the world's biggest fish) and more, is as yet hardly exploited; there is fishing, camping, diving and swimming, and glass-bottomed boats operate from Coral Bay and **Exmouth**. The best place to begin your exploration of these natural wonders around Exmouth is at the innovative Milyering Visitor Centre in the Cape Range National Park.

▶ Northam   *146A2*

An important road and rail junction and depot for the Goldfields Water Scheme, this Wheat Belt town is the regional focus for much of the attractive Avon Valley. The railway from Perth, 96km (60 miles) away, used to terminate here, so Northam was the point at which prospectors would begin their thirsty trek to the Goldfields 450km (280 miles) east. Nowadays, visitors can catch the modern AvonLink rail service from Perth.

▶ Northcliffe   *146A2*

This tiny place, lost among the magnificent karri forests of the extreme southwest, began as one of the townships of the ill-fated Group Settlement Scheme of the 1920s, whose hopes and failures are documented in the excellent **Pioneer Museum**▶. A good base for viewing the karris (some of the tallest of them grow in the nearby Forest Park), Northcliffe is also the starting point for a 27km (17-mile) road leading to Windy Harbour, the only readily accessible beach between Augusta and Walpole.

A forest of karris,
the tallest of the
eucalypts, which can
reach a height of 85m
(280ft) or more

THE GLOUCESTER TREE
It was difficult to build
fire-watch towers of sufficient height to rise above
the canopy of the giant
karris. The answer was to
wind a peg ladder around
the trunk of a suitable
tree and make a lookout
cabin at the top. Planes
perform the lookout func-
tion nowadays, but the
Gloucester Tree in
Gloucester National Park,
near Pemberton, has
been kept for fearless
tourists to climb its 153
rungs and be rewarded
with a stupendous view
over the treetops. It's the
loftiest fire lookout tree
in the world, but at
around 60m (195ft),
it is by no means the
tallest karri.

▶ **Nullarbor Plain** *147B4*

Renowned for its utter desolation, the world's largest flat surface stretches interminably eastwards into South Australia, covering an area of more than 200,000sq km (77,000sq miles). Few plants (other than saltbush) and fewer animals flourish in this unyielding environment—the name Nullarbor means 'no trees'.

The explorer Edward John Eyre survived his terrible journey across the plain from east to west between 1840 and 1841 by keeping close to the coast, where brackish water could occasionally be found beneath patches of sand dunes. The highway named after him also follows a southern route, while the transcontinental railway strikes off boldly from the goldfields far inland. The landscape along the highway, which is coated entirely in asphalt, is not entirely without incident, since only a relatively short section traverses the Nullarbor proper, but the 144km (90-mile) continuous straight between Balladonia and Caiguna tests any driver's ability to stay alert.

▶▶ **Pemberton** *146A2*

Steeped in logging lore, the township of Pemberton in the southwest corner of the state is the best place to experience the magic of the magnificent karri forest. Its wonders can be appreciated in a variety of ways—by car, on foot, or aboard a steam train or 1907 replica tramcar of the Pemberton Tramway or at the Karri Forest Discovery Centre. The **Gloucester Tree▶** (see panel) can be climbed, and the area is renowned for its trout fishing. You can visit a restored 1865 sawpit, take a guided tour around a huge modern sawmill, or trace the area's history in the nearby **Manjimup Timber Park▶**. The beauty of the forest is enhanced by clear streams, pretty cascades and a wealth of wildflowers in the spring.

**RAILS ACROSS
THE DESERT**
Passengers on the Trans
Australia Railway have
the dubious distinction of
taking part in one of the
world's few railway jour-
neys where the view from
your sleeping berth in the
morning is identical to
the one on which you
closed the curtain the
night before! Imposing-
sounding stations turn
out to be nothing more
than a marker planted in
the wilderness, or at the
very most a huddle of railway paraphernalia with a
section of loop allowing
trains to pass. The
478km (297-mile) 'Long
Straight' between Ooldea
and Watson tests the
patience of the most dis-
ciplined driver of the big
diesel hauling its train of
stainless steel cars.

There are several high peaks in Porongurup National Park in the Albany hinterland

KARRIED TO EXTREMES
One of the tallest of all eucalypts is the karri (*Eucalyptus diversicolor*), a magnificent tree reaching a height of 85m (280ft), and with a lifespan of up to 1,000 years. Growing together in the forest, the soaring stems of the karris create the stately atmosphere of a Gothic church. The finest tracts of karri forest are found in the well-watered south, inland from the coast between Augusta and Albany; much of it was cleared after both world wars to make smallholdings for returned soldiers. Most of these settlements failed, since the deep loamy soil preferred by the karris was good for trees but not for crops.

▶ Pilbara 147C2

Until the 1960s, a few cattlemen were the only inhabitants of this remote port of the northwest. The accidental discovery in the 1950s of what proved to be the world's largest deposit of iron ore (see page 166) was the stimulus for the construction of mining cities like Tom Price and Newman and the growth of deep-water harbours like Dampier and Port Hedland. Trains 2,000m (6,560ft) long haul the ore from huge opencast pits down the tracks to the sea. Much of this exported raw material is later returned to Australia in the form of Japanese cars.

Tourists come this way for winter sun and for the stunning landscapes of the **Karijini (Hamersley Range) National Park▶▶**. The vivid rocks of this ancient plateau have been bitten into deeply by the action of rivers, forming splendid gorges where intensely cold water gathers in pools and where a surprisingly lush vegetation flourishes. Even more luxuriant plants are a feature of the **Millstream-Chichester National Park▶**, to the north, where there is a large colony of fruit bats and permanently flowing water, nourishing the palm trees of a relict rain forest.

▶▶ The Pinnacles (Nambung National Park) 146B2

The thousands of limestone monoliths scattered around the sandy plain south of the coastal township of Cervantes were mistaken by Dutch sailors for the remains of an ancient city. Varying in size from 6m (19-ft) giants to finger-thick pieces of piping, they may well be the fossilized roots of long-dead trees and shrubs. Whatever their origin, they remain compelling in their desert setting. The Cervantes area boasts several beautiful beaches, popular with sailboarders and boaters.

▶ Porongurup National Park 146A2

The ancient granites of this range of hills in the Albany hinterland have been eroded into domes and formations like Balancing Rock. Castle Rock (570m/1,870ft) gives stunning views over karri forest and the country beyond. In spring, the forest floor is brilliant with wildflowers.

This remote land in the far north of Western Australia was explored in 1879 by Alexander Forrest, who thought that it might sustain grazing animals. Huge stations still graze their stock on the sparse vegetation. There is diamond mining in the East Kimberley, and tourists pass through on around-Australia trips or make the Kimberley their prime destination, drawn by the lure of a 'last frontier'.

East Kimberley The modern township of Kununurra is the gateway to the East Kimberley, a region of ancient volcanic rocks and sandstone ranges. Tropical rainfall fills the rivers in the Wet, supporting a rich pattern of vegetation and wildlife, while mangrove swamps clothe the margins of estuaries. The Ord River Irrigation Scheme has attempted to harness the river's summer flow to irrigate vast areas of cropland, with only limited success; remote **Wyndham**, the state's northernmost harbour and a port town since the 1880s, exports cattle as well as whatever crops the project produces. Persistence will lead the determined visitor to natural wonders like the **Mitchell Falls**, or even (with a permit) along the Kalumburu Road to the far off Aboriginal Reserve near the mouth of the King Edward River. Some areas, like the Drysdale River National Park, of unresearched biological value, may not be visited at all.

West Kimberley Entered via Broome and Derby, the west has spectacular inland gorges, cut through the limestones of an ancient barrier reef, long since hoisted high above sea level. The river through **Windjana Gorge**, composed of rocks that are part of a 350-million-year-old limestone shelf, is reduced to a series of pools in the dry season, while the mighty Fitzroy River manages to maintain an all-year flow through the longer **Geikie Gorge**.

HOW TO GET THERE
Most traffic takes the long way round from Derby to Kununurra via the main highway. This gives access to Wolfe Creek Crater National Park as well as the magical Purnululu National Park (or The Bungle Bungles), though both of these extraordinary natural phenomena are better seen from the air. The shorter route is the Gibb River Road, rougher but more rewarding, with well-vegetated creeks, gorges and waterholes.

173

The Argyle Diamond Mine in the East Kimberley produces high-quality stones

Rottnest Island, meaning rats' nest island, was named in 1696 by Dutchman Willem de Vlamingh who found the place infested with what he took to be large rodents. The rats were in fact the hare-sized marsupials known as quokkas, a kind of small wallaby, found here on 'Rotto' and on parts of the mainland.

MARINE WONDERLAND
Shark Bay's UNESCO World Heritage status was bestowed for its remarkable natural beauty and significance. The Monkey Mia dolphins are the region's best-known attraction, but the bay also contains stromatolites—fossilized layers of blue-green algae, and the oldest form of life on earth—at Hamelin Pool, and one of the last-surviving herds of dugongs, or sea-cows.

Some of the hundreds of dolphins that inhabit the warm waters of Shark Bay

174

▶ Rottnest Island   155E2

Perth's weekend paradise, 19km (12 miles) off the coast and reached by air or ferry from Perth and Fremantle measures a mere 11km (7 miles) long by a maximum of 4.8km (3 miles) across. It has a special charm, enormously enhanced by the lack of cars; bicycles are the main mode for exploring the delightful bays and white beaches along the rugged coastline. The extraordinarily clear turquoise waters are ideal for diving and snorkelling.

▶▶ Shark Bay   146C1

Divided into a series of inlets by peninsulas and islands, and with 1,500km (930 miles) of coastline, Shark Bay was named in 1699 by the adventurer William Dampier. The waters of the bay provide excellent swimming, fishing and other watersports, and there are spectacular dunes of red sand, high limestone cliffs and extraordinary beaches as well. Shell Beach, 60km (37 miles) long, is made up of countless shells to a depth of 10m (33ft); naturally compacted at this depth, this strange material can be cut into blocks and used in buildings. The little resort of **Denham** is the westernmost town in Australia; on the opposite side of the Peron Peninsula are the famous dolphins of Monkey Mia (see page 168).

▶ Southern Cross   146B2

The streets of Southern Cross, founded by gold prospectors in 1888, are still wide enough to turn a camel train. There are mementoes of the old days in the 1891 court-house, now a local history museum.

▶ Stirling Range National Park   146A2

A scenic highway threads through this range, 100km (62 miles) north of Albany, whose peaks rise 1,000m (3,280ft) above the surrounding country. As well as being southwestern Australia's highest mountains, with occasional snowfall, they are a botanical reserve of importance and great beauty, with over 1,200 wildflower species.

► ► **Wave Rock**   *146A2*

Wave Rock is a surfer's dream turned to stone. More than 100m (325ft) long and 15m (50ft) high, the petrified breaker's resemblance to the real thing is emphasized by the vertical streaking, the result of natural chemicals in the granite reacting with rainwater.

Other curiosities near the little Wheat Belt town of **Hyden** (337km/210 miles inland from Perth) include further odd rock formations with names like the Humps and the Hippo's Yawn. In Mulka's Cave the visitor can view Aboriginal wall paintings.

► **Yanchep**   *146A2*

Days out from Perth often take in the coastline to the north of the city with its fine beaches, sand dunes and chain of lakes just inland. Yanchep itself is a resort, but around it stretches the **Yanchep National Park►**, with limestone caves, a lake, eucalyptus woods, koalas and a wealth of wildflowers in the spring.

► **York**   *146A2*

With Northam (see page 170) and Toodyay, York is one of a trio of much-visited towns in the picturesque Avon Valley, 96km (60 miles) northeast of Perth. Western Australia's most historic inland town, York was founded in 1831, and many of its lovely old sandstone buildings have survived the ravages of time, including an earthquake in 1968.

The **Residency Museum►** evokes the early days of life in Western Australia, as does the **Avondale Discovery Farm►** at nearby Beverley, which also has a flora and fauna reserve and farm animals. More than 200 vintage cars, motorcycles and even some horse-drawn vehicles are on display in the **York Motor Museum►►**.

175

Wave Rock: another ancient geological curiosity

RIVER OF THE BLACK SWANS
The Avon is a tributary of the Swan River, named for the black swans that make it their home. Both rivers formed a corridor for early settlement, and the area around Guildford includes many historic buildings like Woodbridge House at nearby Midland, built in 1885 and now restored and authentically furnished (open to the public). The Swan Valley is famous for its wine. A tour of the wineries is always a popular excursion.

Hotel sign in the small, respectable town of York

Northern Territory

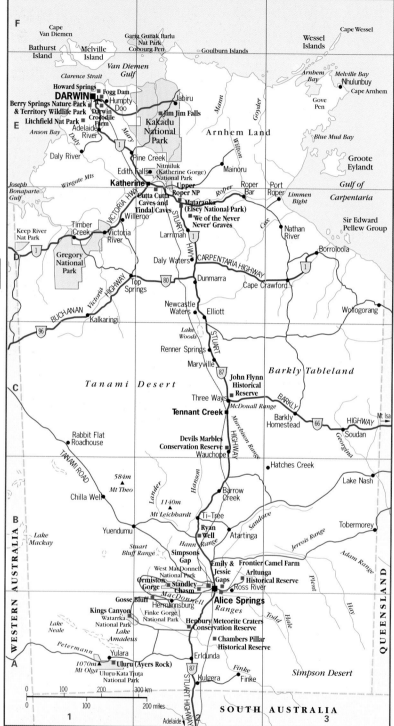

THE NORTHERN TERRITORY With the thin bitumen ribbon of the Stuart Highway as its backbone, the third largest territorial area in Australia stretches from the country's desert heart, the 'Red Centre', to the coast and islands of the tropical north, the 'Top End'.

The cattle industry, once the basis of the Territory's economy, has been overtaken by mining (bauxite, manganese, uranium) and by tourism; more and more visitors are drawn here, not only to the mysterious landforms of the desert, of which **Uluru (Ayers Rock)** is just one, but to Darwin; to the natural riches of the north; and, above all, to the incomparable World Heritage wilderness of **Kakadu National Park**.

A ghost gum, recognizable by its white trunk

FIRST SETTLEMENT The first European sighting of the coast of the Northern Territory seems to have been made in 1623 by the Dutchman Jan Carstenzoon on board the *Arnhem*. However, the process of colonization did not actually begin until the 1820s.

The first attempts to found settlements came to grief; Port Essington (1824) on the Cobourg Peninsula had no fresh water, Fort Dundas (1824–29) on Melville Island suffered from attacks by hostile Aborigines, and Raffles Bay (1827), also on the Cobourg Peninsula, was abandoned after only two years. Victoria (on an inlet of Port Essington) was established in 1838, and despite cyclones and earthquakes, managed to last until 1849, when it too was given up.

The splendid natural harbour of Port Darwin was given its name in 1839 by Captain J. C. Wickham of the *Beagle* in memory of Charles Darwin, a member of an earlier voyage. However, it was not until three decades later, in 1869, that the site of the present capital of the Territory was surveyed and a start was made on building houses. The choice turned out to be a propitious one, and Darwin, which was originally named Palmerston, has survived and prospered in spite of numerous cyclones and Japanese air raids during World War II.

▶▶▶ REGION HIGHLIGHTS

CONQUERING THE INTERIOR The interminable and arid spaces of the Centre resisted attempts to cross them until 1862 when, undeterred by five heroic failures, John McDouall Stuart finally blazed a trail from south to north; Stuart's route is followed by the highway named after him. Before the road was built, the famous Overland Telegraph, spanning the unmapped wilderness between Port Augusta on the coast of South Australia and Darwin, had been completed in less than two years. Linked at Darwin to the submarine cable from Java in 1872, Australia was connected with the 'grand electric chain that unites the nations of the earth'. The repeater stations, constructed along its 2,897km (1,800-mile) length at Alice Springs, Tennant Creek and other places, became focal points for travellers and townships later developed around these isolated outposts. Pastoralists then moved into the territory, and it became part of South Australia in 1863. The telegraph station at Alice Springs still stands, though the town itself has moved south.

INTO THE 20TH CENTURY In 1911, the Northern Territory, a drain on the meagre resources of South Australia, became the responsibility of the Commonwealth. Though self-governing since 1978, it has still not acquired full statehood, and some of its affairs (Aboriginal matters and uranium mining) continue to be handled by Canberra. For many years it stayed a backwater; few drivers braved the horrible surface of its unpaved roads and there were very few tourists. However, World War II changed all that. In a series of heavy raids, Japanese aircraft inflicted severe damage not only on Darwin but on the Australian psyche. Acutely aware of the country's vulnerability via the empty and remote north, government and armed forces paved the road from the railhead at Alice Springs to the coast, and built a chain of depots, bases and airfields, remains of which can be seen along the highway. The Northern Territory was hauled bodily into the life of the nation by these events.

ROAD TRAINS

The first car to cross the desert Centre took 51 days on its arduous trip from Adelaide to Darwin, and signalled the beginning of the end for the horses, camels and buffalo-drawn carts that had served the Northern Territory's needs until then. In the 1930s, a cumbersome A. E. C. diesel and trailer formed what was called the Government Road Train, hauling supplies to isolated communities. After World War II, Kurt Johannsen used an old army tank transporter to pull no less than eight cattle trailers. Today's road trains are limited to a maximum of three 'dogs' or trailers, a formidable sight as they roar along the highways of the Northern Territory, Queensland and Western Australia.

178

One of the lovely gorges cut by the Katherine River

National parks

Journeying along the Stuart Highway between the arid Red Centre and tropical Top End you experience some of the most dramatic contrasts nature has to offer.

THE RED CENTRE Geological processes have shaped the red rocks of the Centre, creating an almost abstract world of crater and boulder, jagged ridge and lonely monolith, starkly defined against a background of sandy plain or pebbly desert. Etched into this awesome pattern are the winding beds of watercourses, filled only when rare rainstorms rage. Ancestors of the present rivers were fed more generously, and they carved chasm, gorge and canyon niches in this hostile world for a surprisingly rich and varied wildlife. The rugged **MacDonnell Ranges** to the west and east of Alice Springs are breached by many a gap filled with ferns, palms and other exotic plants, some of them descendants of the flora that flourished on the shore of the vast sea that once covered much of central Australia. Waterholes persist here long after rivers have dried up, creating a refuge for both animals and humans.

Experiencing the desert is not difficult. Parks Australia (Kakadu and Uluṟu–Kata Tjuṯa) and the Parks and Wildlife Service NT (other parks) are improving facilities while preserving the landscapes entrusted to them. Their management of Uluṟu is a model of its kind.

THE MORE VERDANT NORTH Towards the northern rim of the Centre, permanently flowing rivers are a reminder of a more abundant, monsoon rainfall (up to 160cm/63in a year compared with around 12cm/4.75in in the south). Many rivers have their source on the high plateau of Arnhem Land; the Katherine River has cut a series of spectacular gorges in **Nitmiluk National Park**, while **Kakadu National Park** teems with wildlife. The Top End has some of Australia's remotest places, while Darwin has a super-abundance of natural areas in its hinterland.

DARWIN'S TERRITORIAL WATERS

At Doctors Gully at the end of the Esplanade, thousands of fish, and no small number of tourists, come together at Aquascene during every high tide—the former to be fed and the latter to do the feeding.

179

RAIN FOREST AND RIVERS

An easy day's outing from Darwin, Berry Springs has both a nature park with natural swimming pools and the splendid Territory Wildlife Park. This tract of bushland and the aquarium is aimed at introducing visitors to the NT's varied wildlife.

Well off the beaten track down the Daly River Road, the Douglas River/Daly River Esplanade Conservation Area is a popular spot for barramundi fishing and boating, although the large number of salties (saltwater crocodiles) precludes swimming.

The remote Gregory National Park has a spectacular gorge and escaprments, and there are boat trips along the Victoria River.

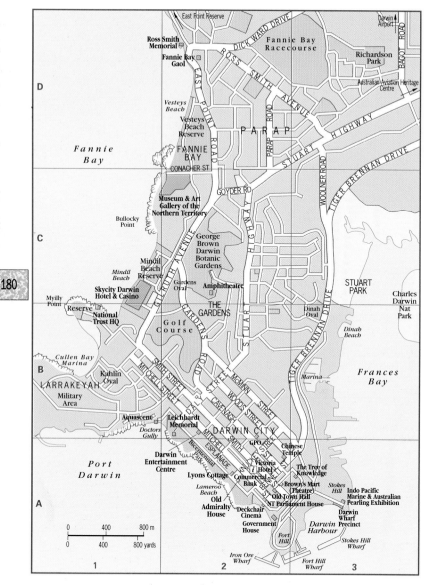

Darwin

The capital of the Northern Territory clings precariously to the peninsula protruding into Port Darwin, a superb natural anchorage that is approximately twice the size of Sydney Harbour.

Darwin has almost disappeared from the map four times. Cyclones flattened the place in 1897, 1937 and again in 1974. In between, the aviators of the Imperial Japanese forces did their best to imitate nature at her most furious in the course of no less than 60 air raids. But Darwin's resilience is legendary; after each disaster, the evacuated population has returned to rebuild. In 1974, Cyclone Tracy

GETTING AROUND
The best way to orientate yourself is to take a trip on the Tour Tub, an open circulating minibus that allows you to get on and off at any point along its route.

destroyed nearly all the town's old buildings, including elegant old stilt houses; their replacements, although not as picturesque, still give Darwin a tropical feeling.

DIVERSE COMMUNITY Advertised as Australia's front door, Darwin has looked for much of its life more like the country's backyard. Its appeal is that it is on the edge, a place in touch with other places. Founded in 1869, it became a base for 'fabulous old-timers—pearlers, buffalo hunters, trepangers, prospectors, cattlemen and overlanders'. The city's population of around 109,000 is extraordinarily mixed; the number of ethnic groups varies between 49 and 61 depending on who is doing the counting. Many are Asians, and of all Australian cities, Darwin is the most conscious of the lands just to the north; Singapore is no farther away than Sydney, and Jakarta is closer.

Many visitors who pass through Darwin have other destinations in mind, either abroad or in the Northern Territory, many of whose attractions are within easy reach. However, they should beware the place's allure, based on a very relaxed, tropical lifestyle.

CITY SIGHTS AND ORIENTATION Small enough to walk around, the heart of the city has a number of surviving (or reconstructed) buildings from early days. Some of these face the parkland of the west-facing Esplanade; here is **Government House** (1883) as well as **Old Admiralty House**, a fine example of a tropical building on stilts dating from the 1920s. Among the grid of streets farther inland is the much rebuilt **Victoria Hotel**, the **Chinese Temple** or Joss House and, in the courtyard of the Civic Centre, an ancient banyan, the **'Tree of Knowledge'**, one of Darwin's most resilient landmarks. These venerable structures contrast strongly with the modern Northern Territory Parliament House, which can be toured. Other sights lie farther afield, many of them overlooking beautiful Fannie Bay to the north. Here is the Skycity Darwin hotel and casino, close to Mindil Beach where a famous sunset market is held from May to October.

1883 tropical-style Government House, Darwin's oldest building

181

SHIP OF BREWS
Darwin's famous Beer Can Regatta, held each July or August at Mindil Beach, is one of Australia's most unusual festivals. This charity event, which attracts thousands of spectators, consists of beach and water races, involving craft made from soft drink cans. Beer cans were formerly used, but these days it's deemed more responsible to use the containers of non-alcoholic beverages.

Meet the awesome crocodile, Sweetheart, at the Museum & Art Gallery

A FAST LADY
Darwin lies in the path of cyclones, none of which have raged as fiercely as Cyclone Tracy on Christmas Day 1974. In the space of four hours, two-thirds of the city's buildings were destroyed and most of the rest severely damaged. The death toll was put at 66. No one knows exactly how much puff Tracy had in her—the windspeed indicator at the airport broke showing 217kph (135mph)—but the peak velocity has been estimated at around 299kph (186mph). The disaster wasn't totally regretted. Pre-1974 Darwin was no showpiece of urban planning; rebuilding has been carried out along more orderly lines, with the provision of a satellite town, Palmerston, 19km (12 miles) to the southeast.

▶▶ George Brown Darwin Botanic Gardens
180C2

Gardens Road, The Gardens (tel: 08-8981 1958). Open: daily 7–7 Admission free

Plants grow rapidly in Darwin's climate, and damage done to these fine gardens in 1974 (see panel) has been made good. The opportunity was taken to add new features, including collections of orchids, figs and ferns, and an exceptional array of around 450 tropical palms and cycads.

▶ Fannie Bay Gaol
180D2

East Point Road, Fannie Bay (tel: 08-8999 8290)
Open: daily 10–4.30. Admission free

Although it has no history of convict settlement, Darwin nevertheless has an old prison, built in 1883 and in use until 1979. The museum has a gallows, used for the Territory's last execution in 1952.

▶▶ Indo Pacific Marine
180A3

Darwin Wharf Precinct (tel: 08-8981 1294)
Open: Apr–Oct daily 9–4; Nov–Mar 9–1. Admission: moderate

One of the city's most popular attractions, this marine display in the lively Darwin Wharf Precinct focuses on a re-created coral reef. The informative **Australian Pearling Exhibition** is nearby.

▶▶▶ Museum & Art Gallery of the Northern Territory
180C2

Conacher Street, Bullocky Point (tel: 08-8999 8201)
Open: Mon–Fri 9–5, Sat–Sun 10–5. Admission free

This modern complex emphasizes the unique geographical position of the Territory and its capital. In addition to an excellent collection of Aboriginal art and other items, there is a wealth of objects from southeast Asia and the southwest Pacific. The complex includes a maritime section with original seagoing vessels, among them sinister war canoes, dugouts, outriggers, a *lipa-lipa*, *proas* and the last of Darwin's pearling luggers, the *Vivienne*. However, pride of place goes to Sweetheart, a monster crocodile, which is now stuffed and harmless.

Crocodiles are compelling because many of us can't resist our morbid fascination with the havoc they can wreak. The crocodiles of the Northern Territory, Western Australia and Queensland have loomed large in the public mind not only because of the movie Crocodile Dundee, *but also because of their increasing numbers (a result of effective conservation measures), the opening-up of their habitat to wilderness tourism and the readiness of the media to dramatize any crocodile attack.*

Two kinds of crocodile live in Australia. Harmless to humans, the relatively small freshwater crocodile frequents rivers and billabongs between the Gulf of Carpentaria and Broome in Western Australia. Double its size (6m/20-ft specimens are not uncommon), and distinguished by a broader snout, the saltwater or estuarine crocodile prefers the brackish waters of tidal rivers, though it is quite capable of penetrating far inland as well as out into the ocean. It occurs from India to the western Pacific, and in Australia from the central Queensland coast around Rockhampton to the Broome area.

Salties prey on fish and animals of all sizes, including human beings. Many victims are taken unawares at the water's edge; the crocodile makes its approach underwater, then uses the massive muscle of its tail to propel itself from the deep like a Polaris missile. The prey is dragged underwater and drowned rather than immediately torn apart; the croc can stay below the surface for up to an hour. Male crocodiles lord it over a territory they defend from other males. Much of their time is spent lying log-like in the shallows, conserving energy that is expended in violent display needed to secure dinner.

Look before you dive Darwin's swimming pools and ornamental waters have to be checked before they are opened to the public. Swimming or paddling in areas frequented by crocodiles could well be fatal. Remember, too, that crocodiles are amphibians, capable of reaching high speeds on land. Always obey the signs forbidding swimming (though people sometimes take them for souvenirs!) and seek local advice if in doubt. The best way to see these intimidating creatures is to take a conducted tour in a steel-bottomed boat (one legendary beast—long since dealt with—developed a taste for the more chewy kind of outboard motor, so don't trail your hand in the water!). Craft of this kind ply Yellow Water in Kakadu and, nearer Darwin, the Adelaide River.

CROCODILES
The Darwin Crocodile Farm, 40km (25 miles) south of the city, is home to thousands of crocodiles reared for their skins. Closer to town, you can view crocs and other wildlife at Crocodylus Park in the suburb of Berrimah.

WARNING
Crocodiles respect neither man nor beast, so take no chances. Just because you can't see them, it doesn't mean they're not there.

Northern Territory

ALBERT NAMATJIRA

Born at Hermannsburg Mission in 1902, this member of the Aranda tribe became a talented watercolourist in the European tradition, his subject the stunning landscapes of his native MacDonnell Ranges. He and his work were acclaimed; he was presented to the Queen during a royal visit, and in 1957 he was given the extraordinary privilege (for the time) of full citizenship. But Namatjira was destroyed by the tension between white and Aboriginal society and by alcohol; imprisoned for supplying drink to a fellow Aborigine, his morale collapsed and he died in 1959 at the age of 57. His wonderfully fresh paintings can be seen in many Australian galleries. His representational, European style of painting has since been generally abandoned by contemporary Aboriginal artists in preference to a more abstract, traditional form of expression, typified by so-called 'dot' paintings.

Alice Springs has a number of memorials to...

►►► Alice Springs   *176B2*

Smack in the middle of the continent, The Alice (as it is widely known) has transformed itself from a dusty outpost to an indispensable stop on the tourist itinerary. Equipped with all modern amenities, this pleasant town makes an excellent base for exploring the Red Centre.

The township began in 1871 as a convenient place for a repeater station on the Overland Telegraph between Adelaide and Darwin—it was named for local waterholes, and after the wife (Alice) of Sir Charles Todd, the Postmaster General of South Australia. Development was slow until the arrival of the railway from Adelaide in 1929, the famous but rickety *Ghan*. In World War II, the railhead acquired strategic value, particularly after the Stuart Highway leading on up to Darwin had been given its first coat of asphalt. But it was the advent of mass tourism from the 1970s onward that persuaded the town to provide comfortable hotels, sophisticated restaurants and even a tastefully landscaped shopping mall. All this came as something of a surprise to the old-timers, who not so long ago would ride in for an evening's drinking and hitch their horse to the rail in the main street.

The best place to get an overall impression of The Alice in its desert setting is to climb (or drive up) **Anzac Hill►** with its obelisk memorial. The town stretches out on the west bank of the bed of the Todd River. The fact that it rarely contains any water has not stopped the hilarious Henley-on-Todd Regatta becoming a major annual event, with legs rather than oars supplying the motive power for the bottomless craft. To the south are the town, attractions like the Royal Flying Doctor Service base, the golf course and the long ridges of the MacDonnell Ranges, pierced by the Heavitree Gap, through which run road and railway. Beyond is the airport, and then the US/Australian Pine Gap communications base.

Although visitors come to Alice Springs more because of where it is than for what it is, there are a fair number

of attractions in the town and its immediate vicinity. A few older buildings recall its beginnings; the **Old Stuart Town Gaol** is the most venerable of these, a jail dating all the way back to 1907. **Adelaide House** was built between 1920 and 1926 to serve as a hospital; it now houses memorabilia related to the early days of the Royal Flying Doctor Service. With settlements and homesteads hundreds of kilometres apart, doctors need aircraft to make house calls. For a short time in the 1920s the administration of the NT was split between Darwin and Alice Springs. The **Residency▶** dates from this period, and now houses a small but well-presented museum of local history. The town's main museum is the **Museum of Central Australia▶** at the Alice Springs Cultural Precinct; it has extensive exhibits on the art and natural history of central Australia. Also at this precinct is the **Central Australian Aviation Museum▶**, which celebrates early flight in the Outback.

Transportation and communications are one theme of Alice Springs, if not *the* theme. The place's *raison d'être* was the **Old Telegraph Station▶▶**, and its plain but evocative stone buildings still stand just north of the town. Both the **School of the Air** and the **Royal Flying Doctor Service▶▶** have bases in town that are open to the public, while off the Stuart Highway beyond the Heavitree Gap is the **National Road Transport Hall of Fame▶**. In pioneering days, the arid interior relied on camel trains for supplies; at the **Frontier Camel Farm▶▶** you can ride one and find out about them and their Afghan masters.

Alice Springs is one of the places where visitors can become better acquainted with the Aboriginal presence. Part of the town's living comes from money spent by Aborigines, even more from the merchandising of Aboriginal souvenirs, though you are unlikely to be able to buy a painting by Albert Namatjira (see panel opposite). At the **Aboriginal Art & Culture Centre▶** you can learn to play the didgeridoo, sample bush tucker and try your hand at spear throwing, or just absorb the culture through music, performance and visual arts. Another major attraction is the award-winning **Alice Springs Desert Park▶▶** with its native animals, walking tracks and Aboriginal presentations.

...and reminders of the Royal Flying Doctor Service

185

They both feed and entertain you in The Alice

Northern Territory

THE STUART HIGHWAY

This 2,700km (1,678-mile) road unrolls its thin band of bitumen through the vast and deserted spaces of Central Australia between Port Augusta and Darwin. Known to all as 'The Track', it follows the route first traced in 1862 by the tough Scotsman John McDouall Stuart. For many years it was a notorious axle-breaker, but nothing was done until Australia's war situation became desperate in 1942 when, with US Forces' help, the road was speedily asphalted from the railhead at Alice Springs to Darwin. Several decades passed before the southern half of the highway was completely paved, and the adventure of gravel, rock and bulldust replaced by the relative predictability of bitumen.

186

One of the huge road trains that travel across the continent's north and Outback

How to travel

By air Darwin's international airport acquired a bright new terminal in 1991. From here there are connections to many overseas destinations, including direct flights to Singapore, Indonesia, Brunei and to all major Australian cities. Alice Springs also has a modern airport, again linked to a variety of Australian destinations. Connellan Airport, serving Uluru and its resort, has a more limited range of connections. If you are in a hurry, a light aircraft will take you virtually anywhere you want to go in the Territory; day tours are also available. The desert looks at its most dramatic from the air; try a hot-air balloon ride at Alice Springs.

By bus Long-distance buses link Darwin, Alice Springs, Uluru and other points in the Territory with major Australian cities. Tour operators offer any number of trips. Some day-trips, like Darwin–Kakadu–Darwin and Alice Springs–Uluru–Alice Springs, are not recommended for the faint-hearted—it is often better to arrange an overnight stop. Only Darwin has a public bus service.

By train The rebuilt line north from Tarcoola in South Australia carries the revived *Ghan* (see page 189), a luxury train connecting Sydney, Melbourne, Adelaide, Alice Springs and Darwin; this is the only railway within the Northern Territory. There are bus and air connections from various towns to the railhead at Mount Isa, terminus for the *Inlander* train from Townsville, almost 1,000km (620 miles) away on the Queensland coast.

By car From Darwin, the **Stuart Highway** runs south through Alice Springs to Port Augusta and Adelaide (3,050km/1,895 miles); at Three Ways the **Barkly Highway** leaves the Stuart for Mount Isa and on to Townsville (2,556km/1,588 miles); at Katherine, the **Victoria Highway** branches off towards the Kimberley and thence to Perth (4,081km/2,536 miles). Paved roads reach Uluru and Jabiru in Kakadu National Park, and all-weather roads will take you to most major tourist destinations.

▶ Arnhem Land   176E2

East of Kakadu, a rugged sandstone escarpment seems to bar the way to this mysterious and inaccessible area. Given the name of the Dutch ship whose crew were the first Europeans to sight it, Arnhem Land stretches spectacularly eastwards to form the western coastline of the Gulf of Carpentaria. Now in the hands of its Aboriginal owners, most of it can only be entered by permit, though a limited number of guided tours do take place from Darwin, Kakadu and Katherine, and you can also fly into the remote resort of Seven Spirit Bay on the nearby Cobourg Peninsula.

▶▶▶ Uluru (Ayers Rock) and
Kata Tjuta (The Olgas)   176A1

Reproduced a million times on film, tape and glossy brochures, the great red monolith of Uluru has become one of the world's greatest tourist clichés, yet it still retains the power to stir the spirits of all those who visit it. Not surprisingly, Uluru, the Aboriginal name for Ayers Rock, has a unique spiritual significance for the Aboriginal people of the region, whose ancestors may have frequented the area for at least 20,000 years. A number of sacred sites around the base are protected, and they must not be entered or photographed.

The first European to sight the rock was the explorer Ernest Giles in 1872. In 1985 the land, which includes the World Heritage-listed **Uluru-Kata Tjuta National Park**, was ceremonially handed back to an Aboriginal trust on behalf of the traditional owners, then immediately leased for 99 years to the federal government. Hotels and other visitor facilities are at **Ayers Rock Resort▶**, 18km (11 miles) away from Uluru itself.

The sediments that make up Uluru and the neighbouring Kata Tjuta were laid down some 500–600 million years ago and they were then tilted almost vertically by earth movements. Uluru rises 348m (1,142ft) above the plain and Mount Olga rises 546m (1,790ft), but their foundations go far deeper into the earth.

Continued on page 190.

The domes of Kata Tjuta, just waiting to be explored

187

ABORIGINAL PLACE-NAMES
While many Australian place-names were borrowed from the 'old country', the early settlers also used Aboriginal names. Parramatta was the first town to be designated in this way, and others can be seen all over the map, often sounding more appropriate than names recalling the villages, suburbs or shire towns of faraway England. Who could resist Woolloomooloo? Nowadays, many of these foreign names are being replaced with Aboriginal ones; The Olgas (named after a 19th-century queen of Spain) are now officially called Kata Tjuta ('many heads') and Ayers Rock is known as Uluru.

Great Southern]

In such a vast country, the battle to overcome the tyranny of distance was a long and difficult one, and the role of the railway in shaping the country, helping it both to grow economically and to grow together politically, was of outstanding importance.

A LONG SHORT CUT
Once the Transcontinental Railway had linked west to east, those journeying from Europe who were in a hurry to get to Melbourne or Sydney would leave their ship at Fremantle and continue their journey by rail. In spite of having to change trains each time there was a break of gauge (at Kalgoorlie, Port Augusta and again at Albury in NSW), the advantage was that a day or two would be saved. The fare, just as on the ocean liner, included all meals—as it still does—but today you no longer need to change trains as the standard gauge stretches right across the continent from Perth to Sydney.

A train crossing Sydney Harbour Bridge

Gauging success The first iron road in Australia was a short line in Adelaide for horse-drawn traffic. The earliest steam railways were those linking Melbourne to its port (September 1854) and Sydney to Parramatta (a year later). But already there was trouble. What track gauge should be adopted?

The colonies initially agreed among themselves that the gauge should be George Stephenson's standard of 143.5cm (56.5in), but then a broader gap between the rails of 160cm (63in), as used in Ireland, was introduced. In the end each colony went its own way, Victoria and South Australia adopting the broad gauge and New South Wales adopting the standard gauge. Queensland and Western Australia came up with a different idea altogether, that of systems built entirely on the narrow gauge of 106.7cm (42in). Tasmania began with standard gauge, then converted to narrow gauge.

This was fine as long as each system remained self-contained, but eventually the tracks reached out to connect (or rather not connect) with those of other networks. Through-passengers had to disembark, goods had to be unloaded and re-loaded, and the most hated three words in all Australia at the time were supposed to have been 'All change! Albury!' the name of the station on the border between New South Wales and Victoria. In 1897, Mark Twain was more than vexed to have to change trains here, because it involved a tedious walk along a lengthy track.

Natural hazards Railways were often difficult and expensive to build in Australia, because of the distances that had to be covered, the variety of natural obstacles that had to be overcome and the high cost of importing rails and other materials. The capricious nature of the landscape didn't help, and flooding often occurred in places where no rain had fallen for years, washing the track away. To keep costs down, many countryside lines were built to a low standard, resulting in irksome speed restrictions. Bridges remained unbuilt; the train ferry that for years carried the coaches and wagons of Sydney–Brisbane trains over the Clarence River was replaced by a bridge only in 1932. Secondary lines were built not only to the 106.7cm (42-in) gauge but to an even narrower 76.2cm (30-in) standard, virtually a miniature railway of the kind that still chuffs between Belgrave and Gembrook in the Victorian Dandenongs today (the famous *Puffing Billy*). Narrower still—a mere 61cm (24in)—are the sugarcane railways that wander through the plantations of Queensland.

THE GHAN

From time to time some parts of Australia have toyed with the idea of going their own way. Such a stance was taken up by Western Australia at the end of the 19th century, when it only joined the Federation on condition that it was physically linked to the rest of the country by a transcontinental railway (paid for by the Federation). It took years to lay the rails across the 480km (298 miles) of the waterless Nullarbor Plain, but the line was ready for traffic in 1917 and is now traversed by the world-famous *Indian Pacific*.

The *Ghan* A fascinating railway project was the South Australia–Northern Territory link. Shakily built narrow-gauge tracks snaked out from Port Augusta in the south and from Darwin in the north. The southern section was called the *Ghan* because it replaced the Afghan camel trains that had hitherto been the most effective means of transportation along the route. Reaching Oodnadatta in 1890, it took another 39 years to get as far as Alice Springs, and the top section only went as far as Birdum, 500km (310 miles) south of Darwin. Both lines were ripped up in the 1970s.

After decades of debate and delay the 1,420km (882-mile) northern section from Alice Springs has finally been completed, while the southern section was rebuilt many years earlier along a less flood-prone alignment. A luxury train, also called the *Ghan*, now provides one of the world's classic train journeys along this line, all the way to Darwin.

AFGHAN NIGHTS
An early passenger on the *Ghan*, Wilfred Thomas, settled down to try to get some sleep, but was amazed when his fellow-passengers—a tough-looking bunch of miners and stockmen—cleared the seats away brusquely, brought out the drink and some bagpipes, and then danced the night away together.

The Puffing Billy *steam train passes over a wooden trestle bridge across Monbulk Creek Belgrave in the Dandenong Ranges National Park*

The Mala Walk starts from the Mala Walk sign at the base of Uluru; it is led by a Ranger, or you can do it by yourself if you buy a brochure at the Cultural Centre

AN OUTBACK DRAGON
The fearsome-looking thorny devil is one of the most astonishing denizens of the desert, well deserving its zoological name *Moloch horridus*. In spite of its bulbous spine-covered body and blotchy skin, it is an inoffensive creature, relying on its unappetizing appearance to deter any predator.

Continued from page 187.

Much is made of the mysterious responsiveness of both Uluru and Kata Tjuta to lighting conditions, and few visitors will want to miss the changes produced by dawn and sunset; the basic red is due to the presence of iron.

Most visitors rush to climb **Uluru**, but the expedition should not be undertaken lightly, least of all by the elderly or by those with a medical condition. Take the advice of Rangers and tour guides concerning timing, water supplies and the route (the only one) that must be followed. You might even respect the expressed wish of the local Anangu people (the Traditional Owners of Uluru and Kata Tjuta and the surrounding land) that Uluru should not be climbed, but experienced by a circular walk or tour around its 9.4km (5.8-mile) base. This reveals a wealth of fascinating detail, such as the strange, almost biscuit-like texture of the stone, and the way in which the almost vertical lower slopes have been eroded into deep furrows.

Of geologically related origin, the 36 domes of **Kata Tjuta** offer a quite different but no less fascinating experience, not least because of the rich vegetation and wildlife that flourish in the sheltered gorges between the individual summits. All those able to undertake one of the somewhat stony walks through the area should certainly do so, though perhaps the most spectacular way to view these sleeping dinosaurs (as they have been called) is aboard a light plane on one of the short flights that also takes in Uluru. As well as the isolated table mountain known as Mount Connor, which is perfectly aligned with Uluru and Kata Tjuta, this aerial perspective reveals the layout of the Ayers Rock Resort (see panel opposite). Its architecture and landscaping represent a remarkably sensitive response to its desert environment.

The visitor to Uluru will find an array of tours available, ranging from bus trips to a personalized commentary given while riding pillion on a Harley-Davidson. Aboriginal-led tours aim to bring small groups of participants into more intimate contact with the plants and animals of the desert, as well as with Anangu life and their Tjukurpa (Law). A visit to the **Uluru–Kata Tjuta Cultural Centre▶**, with its dynamic displays, artworks and video presentations, is a must.

▶ Bathurst and Melville islands   *176E1*

Lying off the coast to the north of Darwin, and separated from each other by the narrow Apsley Strait, these two large islands are the home of the Tiwi people. Lacking contact with the Aborigines of the mainland, they developed their own distinct culture, including the making of the extraordinary and highly decorated Pukamani burial poles. The British settlement at Fort Dundas, the first on the north Australian coast (1824–29), was a failure. A Catholic mission was set up in the early 1900s, but the islands have now been returned to their traditional owners and can only be visited on an organized tour.

▶ Chambers Pillar   *176A2*

This 50m (164-ft) high red and yellow sandstone monolith rises abruptly from its spreading foundation to make one of the desert's most striking landmarks. On the fringes of the arid Simpson Desert, the pillar, protected in a historical reserve, was long used as a navigational aid by intrepid explorers, some of whom left their inscriptions in the soft rock.

▶ Cutta Cutta Caves Nature Park   *176D2*

South of Katherine on the Stuart Highway, these ancient limestone chambers linked by narrow passages are the home of the rare orange horseshoe bat, which was once believed to be extinct. Near by are the Tindal Caves, which have unusual sponge formations. The caves may be closed from December to April because of flooding.

GREEN ON RED

Deserts are fragile environments, whose ecological balance and visual appeal can easily be degraded when visitors arrive in large numbers. The collection of motels and other facilities that had accumulated at the base of Uluru was no triumph of design. Its replacement, the Ayers Rock Resort, is distinguished both architecturally and ecologically. Sited 18km (11 miles) away from Uluru, its visual impact on its unique surroundings is minimal, partly because of skilful landscaping using the characteristic landforms and plants of the desert. The hotel and other buildings of the resort have thick masonry walls for insulation, while shady verandas and eaves shield windows and walkways from the sun. The huge shade sails rising over the main hotel have become the emblem of the place, but they too play a role in energy conservation.

BARRAMUNDI

This fine tropical fish is Australia's most popular catch, making an excellent meal as well as providing good sport. Barramundi can grow to huge sizes; specimens 1.3m (4.2ft) long weighing up to 10kg (22 pounds) are not uncommon. They live in most northern aquatic environments, making their way to river estuaries to breed. The barramundi also has a feisty reputation as a fighting fish. Barramundi are still plentiful but catches are restricted.

Looking for the rare orange horseshoe bat in the Cutta Cutta Caves

191

The rounded granite forms of the Devils Marbles, around 100km (62 miles) south of Tennant Creek

CASTLES OF CLAY
In a land of minimal moisture, there are no earthworms to turn the soil. This role is taken over in the Northern Territory and other arid lands by termites, which pattern whole landscapes with their extraordinary mounds (see below). Sometimes rising to a height of 3m (10ft), these insect fortresses are built from a mixture of soil, spit and dung. However hostile conditions outside may be, behind the rock-hard walls the interior of the mound is a climate-controlled environment of 100 per cent humidity and a constant temperature of 50°C (122°F).

▶▶ Devils Marbles Conservation Reserve 176C2
Hundreds of granite boulders lie scattered across the plain beside the Stuart Highway just north of the township of Wauchope—some huge, some tiny and some perched in impossible positions. To the geologist, they are all that remains of the ancient mountains that once rose here, but to the Aborigines they are the eggs of the Rainbow Serpent, Wanambi. They are best seen in the early morning.

▶▶ Finke Gorge National Park 176A2
Access to the famous gorge in the West MacDonnell Ranges known as **Palm Valley** is along the rocky bed of the Finke River, normally dry but impassable after rain. In contrast to the desert is the lush vegetation thriving in the protected environment of the gorge. The 46,000ha (113,650-acre) national park's 3,000 or so cabbage palms are unique to the area, the descendants of prehistoric trees that grew on the shore of what was then a tropical sea. A walk to Kalaranga Lookout affords a great view of the rugged sandstone gorge, while the Mpaara Walk introduces the mythology of the local Aboriginal culture.

▶▶ Garig Gunak Barlu National Park 176F2
Now returned to its traditional Aboriginal owners, this national park covers the whole of the remote Cobourg Peninsula, protruding westwards from Arnhem Land, and its surrounding waters. There is splendid sailing and fishing, as well as the experience of utter isolation, since the number of visitor permits issued is strictly limited (contact the Parks and Wildlife Service NT for details). The superb natural harbour of **Port Essington** was the site of Victoria, one of the early British settlements.

▶ Henbury Meteorites Conservation Reserve 176A2
At the end of a dirt road off the Stuart Highway south of Alice Springs is a curiosity: A swarm of craters formed about 5,000 years ago when a big meteorite split into pieces on entering the earth's atmosphere. The largest crater is 180m (590ft) across and 15m (50ft) deep.

►►► Kakadu National Park 176E2

Some 250km (155 miles) east of Darwin, Australia's largest national park joined UNESCO's World Heritage Area list in 1987 on account of the Aboriginal art sites it contains and its almost unbelievably rich and varied wildlife.

Kakadu extends over a number of distinct landscapes. The tidal zone along the shore of Van Diemen's Gulf is pierced by the estuaries of four great rivers, the East, West and South Alligator rivers and the Wildman River. Here the grey of tidal mudflats contrasts with the bright green of mangrove swamps, breeding grounds for the well-known barramundi (see panel on page 191). The floodplains of the rivers become a vast freshwater sea in the Wet (November to April), teeming with migratory birds and other waterfowl, including egrets, brolgas, pelicans and jabiru. Salt and freshwater crocodiles lurk in creek and billabong. As the land rises southward, eucalyptus woodland develops, interspersed with termite mounds or dramatically interrupted by massive rock outcrops, fragments of the formidable sandstone escarpment marking the western edge of Arnhem Land. This rugged north–south barrier runs for 500km (310 miles), broken by gorges cut by the streams draining the vast interior, the scene of spectacular waterfalls in the wet season. Two of the best known of these are **Jim Jim Falls►** and **Twin Falls►**, in the south of the park, both with abundant tropical wildlife.

Natural galleries in the escarpment sandstone contain some of the country's choicest examples of early Aboriginal art. The most visited are those at **Ubirr►►**, where there are 'X-ray' paintings as well as other styles, and at **Nourlangie Rock►**. The **Bowali Visitor Centre**, located near the main town of Jabiru and the excellent **Warradjan Aboriginal Cultural Centre** provide more insight into the area's indigenous history and culture. It is just possible to get some idea of Kakadu in the course of a day visit by air from Darwin (there are bus trips too, in spite of the distance).

ART OF THE OUTBACK

Aboriginal art is traditionally connected to ritual and ceremony rather than self-expression, and is ephemeral or renewable. Much of the art of Central Australia is abstract and symbolic. The artist's canvas could be a rock wall or the ground itself, with sand paintings executed in earth, pebbles, feathers and so on. The wall paintings at Kakadu National Park are representational. Some of them, depicting hunting scenes, are incredibly old, dating from the pre-estuarine period up to 23,000 years ago. The X-ray style, showing the internal organs and bone structure of fish and animals, dates from the estuarine period, which followed a rise in sea level some 7,000 to 9,000 years ago. More recent depictions of Europeans and their accoutrements belong to the so-called contact period.

193

Dawn over Kakadu—a sight to remember

In the early part of the 20th century, it seemed as if Australia's indigenous people were doomed as a race. Their numbers had diminished drastically—from an estimated population of half a million at the onset of European colonization to perhaps 60,000 in the 1920s; and many of these were of mixed blood.

GOOD GRUB
While Aboriginal men hunted game with boomerang and fire, women and children foraged for smaller animals, lizards, insects, seeds and fruit. A particular delicacy is the witchetty grub, which is usually seared briefly in hot ashes before being eaten. Initiation into the delights of 'bush tucker' can be a fascinating experience.

194

Christian missions established in the Outback destroyed the Aborigines' ancient spiritual links with the land, government 'Protectors' moved them around at will, and Aboriginal children were removed from their parents and brought up in homes or by foster parents. Devastated by alcoholism, exploited by ranchers as a cheap work-force and consistently denied rights and privileges available to other Australians, it seemed to some as if it would only be a matter of time before mainland Aborigines suffered the fate of the Tasmanians (see page 241).

A genius not extinguished Today, the situation is more hopeful. A voice has been found, one moreover that is listened to and sometimes acted on by those in positions of power. The Aboriginal plight has been noticed by the white majority, thanks to protests like the 'tent embassy' in front of the Canberra Parliament, or the march of 30,000 people through the streets of Sydney, part of a boycott of the 1988 Bicentennial (or 'Invasion') celebrations, and the tens of thousands of people who took part in reconciliation marches in 2000. On a small scale, Aboriginal voices are heard over the air on Aboriginal-owned radio and television stations.

In the realm of politics, reforms have been carried out. The incredible situation in which Aborigines were not

These children live near a school; for those too far away there is always the radio-transmitted School of the Air

classed as citizens or even counted in the official census of population was rectified by the 1967 referendum that gave the Federal Government overall responsibility for Aboriginal affairs. One outcome was the drafting and passing of the *Aboriginal Land Rights Act* of 1976 that enabled Crown lands to be handed back to the 'traditional owners'. A dramatic illustration of the effect of this took place in 1985, when the **Uluṟu-Kata Tjuṯa National Park** formally became the property of the Uluṟu-Kata Tjuṯa Land Trust on behalf of the traditional owners. Entry to such lands is now only possible by means of a permit. Inspired by the success of the 1992 landmark native title claim by Eddie Mabo in the Torres Strait Islands, and the passing of the Native Title Act in 1993, Aboriginal people have since made successful claims for ownership of former Crown Land around the continent.

As seen by others White attitudes have undergone change, even transformation. In an age of environmental devastation and loss of spiritual direction, the way in which Aborigines lived for tens of thousands of years in material and religious harmony with their surroundings has earned respect. Aboriginal art, both traditional and contemporary, is widely admired. There is a widespread wish, expressed by many, to make restitution for over 200 years of injustice. But problems remain, even if they no longer seem quite so insurmountable.

While some younger people of Aboriginal descent try to combine old ways of living with some of the benefits of European civilization, others fail to find a place any-where and continue to live on the margins of society. Aborigines are far more likely to face a court for minor offences than other Australians; a shameful number of young blacks have died while in police custody.

It may be that Aborigines need to stand back from white values and return as far as possible to their tradi-tional customs before the races can come together again in harmony, and the right of refusal of entry to Aboriginal lands should be seen in this light, rather than denounced as incipient apartheid. In any case, many Aborigines wish to share their heritage with their fellow Australians and with visitors. Contemporary Aboriginal art is widely available, while traditional rock paintings are best experienced with an Aboriginal ranger. Music, dance and ritual are performed in many places, but the high point of many people's experience of Australia is a visit to an Aboriginal community (information is avail-able from Tourism Australia—see page 266).

A RIGHT TO LAND
Since 1976, Northern Territory Aborigines have owned the land in what were formerly reserves and have been able to lay claim to vacant Crown Land. Many claims have been opposed, and even when successful do not necessarily inhibit mining and quarrying. But royal-ties have to be paid to the owners, and quite a few communities in areas like Arnhem Land now derive some income from this exploitation of resources.

Some communities are willing to share and explain their traditions

The total number of sheep in Australia today amounts to over 100 million, over three-quarters of them the resilient merino with a fleece of up to 2kg (4.5 pounds) in weight. Australia accounts for a substantial portion of the world's wool and is the biggest exporter of lamb and mutton. In some places the sheep/people ratio begs belief: At one time one million sheep roamed Kangaroo Island, for example, compared with only 4,000 humans.

196

RECORD SHEARING

Traditionally working in teams that moved from station to station during the shearing season, shearers honed their skills to an almost incredible pitch; in 1892 a Queensland man, Jackie Howe, set the record for hand-shearing, having shorn 321 sheep in 7 hours 40 minutes. Even with electric clippers, today's shearers find this difficult to match.

Will this be a new sheep-shearing record?

A tough breed One of the animals most closely identified with Australia, sheep were among the passengers of the first fleet, though 59 of Governor Phillip's 90 beasts soon perished. A certain Captain John Macarthur had better luck; he cannily bred Bengal ewes with English rams, then crossed them with Spanish merinos. This mixed breed flourished in the new environment, yielding a fleece of fine quality and good weight—making Macarthur a rich man and providing the foundation of the wool industry, an important contributor to the national economy even today. In the 19th century, it was sheep as much as people that colonized the vast spaces of the new country; by 1900 there were nearly 100 million of them.

Sheep shearers Watching sheep shearers at their highly skilled work is quite a spectacle. The sheep are driven into the shearing shed, thrown to the ground by the shearer, and held fast between their legs. The electric clippers, which long ago replaced the more laborious hand shears, are run swiftly through the fleece, which is removed in one piece if possible. The heaps of wool are sorted according to quality and are then dispatched in huge bales.

▶▶▶ Kata Tju̠ta (The Olgas)   *176A1*

See pages 187 and 190–191.

▶ Katherine   *176E2*

This township is the middle of the vast and remote territory described by Jeannie Gunn in her classic 1908 novel of the Outback *We of the Never Never*. The area derives its name from the saying that those who live there can 'never never' leave. You can visit the Northern Territory's oldest surviving homestead, Springvale, but most of the town's 250,000 annual visitors come for the spectacular Katherine Gorge at **Nitmiluk (Katherine Gorge) National Park▶▶**, about 29km (18 miles) east. Rising in Arnhem Land, the Katherine River has cut a series of stunning gorges through the sandstone plateau, providing a refuge for a surprising variety of flora and fauna. The first two gorges can be seen aboard tourist boats, the defiles farther upstream in your own canoe. There are a number of walks from the information centre to points along the gorge.

▶▶ Kings Canyon   *176A1*

One of the most spectacular natural landscapes of Central Australia, this deep canyon (in **Watarrka National Park**, some 330km/205 miles southwest from The Alice), with its rugged sandstone cliffs rising over 200m (650ft) above the dry river bed, is becoming increasingly popular with visitors. A short walk leads up the floor of the canyon to a lookout point, but anyone with proper walking shoes who is reasonably fit should not miss the more challenging 6km (4-mile) walk up on to the plateau and around the rim of the canyon. Steep to start with, it gives panoramic views over the canyon and a distant glimpse of Ulu̠ru.

▶▶ Litchfield National Park   *176E1*

This tract of sandstone plateau and lush rain forest is becoming increasingly popular with both tourists and locals, not least because of the excellent swimming in the clear pools at the foot of its numerous waterfalls. The park also has many tall termite mounds and the free-standing sandstone pillars of the 'Lost City'. Access is via

---

Kings Canyon, rugged, but good walking country

A LIVING TRADITION
As a result of both increasing interest in indigenous Australian history and culture, and the initiative of Aboriginal people, several cultural centres have sprung up in the Territory. There is an excellent establishment in Kakadu (see page 193), as well as the Ulu̠ru-Kata Tju̠ta Cultural Centre, near the base of Ulu̠ru with traditional dance, art and craft demonstrations.

SPINIFEX
Early explorers cursed the spiky tussocks of spinifex as its spear-like blades impeded their progress through the desert. Spinifex grasses are often the only plants able to withstand the extreme heat and aridity of the cen-tre, thanks to a deep tap root that manages to extract moisture from far below the surface. Growing outwards into hollow clumps, the plants provide a habitat for other forms of desert life, such as insects, lizards, skinks and even a species of pigeon.

the pleasant tree-shaded township of Batchelor, a couple of hours drive from Darwin.

▶▶▶ MacDonnell Ranges   *176A2*

These parallel ridges of red quartzite and sandstone extend their corrugations hundreds of kilometres across Central Australia, an impressive panorama of rugged natural grandeur when seen from the air. But this was home to the Aranda people until well after the arrival of the white man, and in the gorges cut long ago by the now infrequently flowing rivers there flourishes a lush vegetation of palms and ferns, descendants of the flora that grew on the shore of an ancient tropical sea.

Some of the most spectacular landscapes of the **West MacDonnell National Park** are easily accessible from Alice Springs via Namatjira Drive. Overlooking The Alice itself from a height of 940m (3,084 ft) is the distinctive peak of Mount Gillen. Only a little farther out at 18km (11 miles) from Alice Springs is **Simpsons Gap▶▶**, where the steep-sided gorge, pale sands and fine specimens of river red gums and ghost gums make an excellent introduction to the landscape of the ranges. The reserve is accessible by vehicle but, as always, the best way to explore is on foot, using one of several marked hiking tracks; there is also a special cycle path. Among the wildlife of the gorge is a colony of black-footed rock wallabies.

In dramatic contrast to the impressively wide gorge at Simpsons Gap is **Standley Chasm▶▶**, an incredibly narrow cleft between 100m (330ft) quartzite cliffs. For a short period around midday the sun fills the red walls of the gorge with vibrant light, a popular spectacle for visitors who have walked the kilometre (0.5 mile) or so along the bed of the creek. At **Ellery Creek Big Hole▶▶**, high red cliffs frame the water-filled gorge, which is a popular spot for swimming and fishing. **Serpentine Gorge▶** consists of a narrow winding defile with semi-permanent waterholes

198

THE LARAPINTA TRAIL
This long-distance trail leads from the old Alice Springs Telegraph Station right into the West MacDonnells. Hikers can either walk its entire 223km (138-mile) length or undertake shorter sections with an overnight camp. Full details can be obtained from the NT's Parks and Wildlife Service.

The blue lagoon of the Glen Helen Gorge

A noble face, first imported but now native

and ghost gums, and has been left deliberately undeveloped. **Ormiston Gorge and Pound**▶ ▶ is the largest of the reserves in West MacDonnell National Park, and has permanent waterholes and magical ghost gums, while **Glen Helen Gorge**▶ ▶ has rugged reddish-tinged cliffs contrasting with the blue water that forms a deep lagoon in the bed of the Finke River. Farther west is **Redbank Gorge**▶ with its chilly rockpools. Farther on still, Tylers Pass leads to Gosse Bluff, then back towards Alice Springs via the old Hermannsburg Mission; a possible detour is to spectacular **Palm Valley**▶ ▶ (see page 192).

In the MacDonnells east of Alice Springs, **Emily and Jessie Gaps Nature Park**▶ has semi-permanent waterholes and Aboriginal paintings, while in **Trephina Gorge Nature Park**▶ ▶ the pale stems of splendid ghost gums stand out starkly against the rugged cliffs. High above **John Hayes Rockhole**▶ is a vista of spectacular scenery and Aboriginal rock art. Beyond here, it is possible to explore further—to **Arltunga Historical Reserve** (gold mining) and **Ruby Gap Nature Park**, for example.

▶ Mataranka (Elsey National Park) *176D2*

Just off the Stuart Highway, 97km (60 miles) southeast of Katherine, is the Mataranka Homestead and the thermal pool, a popular stop-off point. Every minute, 20,450 litres (4,500 gallons) of water at a temperature of 34°C (93°F) gush into a crystal-clear waterhole fringed by palm trees.

▶ Pine Creek *176E1*

Ah Toy's store in this tiny Stuart Highway township is a reminder of the gold-rush days of the 1870s, when the Chinese population outnumbered Europeans 15 to 1. The old times are recalled in the **Pine Creek Miners' Park**.

▶ Tennant Creek *176C2*

Legend has it that Tennant Creek came into existence in the 1930s when the axle broke on a wagon carting beer and building materials for a hotel farther north. Moving on seemed too much bother, so once the beer had been drunk the building was put up here. Then gold was found and Tennant Creek became one of the roughest places along the track. Relatively calm now, the town has plenty of amenities. The **Battery Hill Mining Centre**▶ offers tours of a mine and the Gold Stamp Battery, as well as gold panning and a Minerals Museum. The 1874 Overland Telegraph Station is also open to the public.

NOT A MIRAGE
Right up to the 1930s, camels played an indispensable part in opening up the middle of the continent. Explorers, surveyors, miners and pastoralists all used camel trains to transport food, equipment, building materials, barbed wire and metal ores. Their equally tough attendants all acquired the epithet 'Afghan', though many of them were from India. Turned loose when trucks, jeeps and planes took over their work, the camels adapted easily to the wild and today are numbered in the thousands. In captivity, they are successfully bred for export to Arabia, as well as giving many visitors the thrill of a humpback ride. The Frontier Camel Farm 6km (3.5 miles) south of Alice Springs is one of the best known of such establishments.

200

Idyllic Green Island

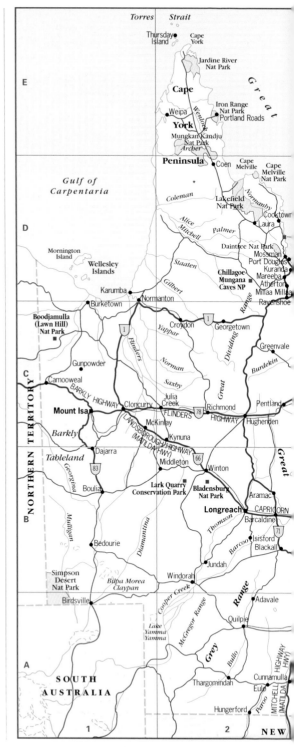

Torres   Strait

Thursday • Island   Cape York

Jardine River Nat Park

G r e a t

E   **Cape**

Weipa   Iron Range Nat Park • Portland Roads

Wenlock

York   Mungkan Kandju Nat Park
Archer

Peninsula   Coen   Cape Melville   Cape Melville Nat Park

Gulf of Carpentaria   *Coleman*   *Normanby*

Lakefield Nat Park   Cooktown

Alice   *Palmer*   Laura

Mitchell   Daintree Nat Park
Mossman
Port Douglas
Kuranda

D   Mornington Island   **Wellesley Islands**   *Staaten*   **Chillagoe-Mungana Caves NP**   Mareeba Atherton
Milaa Milaa

Gilbert   Ravenshoe

Karumba   Normanton

Burketown   Croydon   Georgetown

Boodjamulla (Lawn Hill) Nat Park   *Yappar*   *Dividing*   Greenvale

Flinders   *Norman*   *Burdekin*

Gunpowder   *Saxby*

C   Camooweal   *Great*   Pentland

BARKLY HIGHWAY   Cloncurry   Julia Creek   Richmond   Hughenden
FLINDERS   HIGHWAY

Mount Isa   McKinlay   78

Barkly   LANDSBOROUGH HIGHWAY (MATILDA) HWY   Kynuna

Tableland   Dajarra   Middleton   66   Winton

83   Boulia   **Lark Quarry Conservation Park**   **Bladensburg Nat Park**   Aramac

Georgina   *Diamantina*   **Longreach**   CAPRICORN

B   *Mulligan*   *Thomson*   Barcaldine

Bedourie   *Barcoo*   Isisford   Blackall   71

Jundah

NORTHERN TERRITORY

Simpson Desert Nat Park   Windorah   *Cooper Creek*   Adavale

Birdsville   *Bilpa Morea Claypan*   *McGregor Range*   Quilpie

Lake Yamma Yamma   *Grey*   *Range*

A   *Bullo*   Cunnamulla   HIGHWAY HWY

SOUTH AUSTRALIA   Thargomindah   Eulo

Hungerford   *Paroo*   MITCHELL (MATILDA)

1   2   **N E W**

Queensland

(PNG)

| 0 | 100 | 200 | 300 | 400 km |

| 0 | 100 | 200 miles |

Daintree Nat Park
(Cape Tribulation)

Cairns
Babinda
512m
Innisfail
Mission Beach
Tully
Hinchinbrook Island
Ingham
Mt Spec Nat Park
Townsville
Ayr
1234m Cape Upstart Nat Park
Charters Towers Bowen Airlie Beach
Proserpine Conway Nat Park
Collinsville Whitsunday Group
Cape Hillsborough Nat Park
Eungella Nat Park **Mackay**
Sarina
Moranbah
Clermont Dysart
Capella
Emerald
HIGHWAY Lake Maraboon Blackwater
Alpha Springsure
Carnarvon Moura Biloela
Tambo Gorge Nat Park Monto
Carnarvon Expedition **Bundaberg**
Gorge Nat Park Taroom Hervey Great Sandy
Bay Nat Park
Augathella Dawson Childers Fraser Island
Charleville Mitchell Roma Taroom Burnett **Maryborough**
Miles Kingaroy Cooloola Nat Park
Bunya Mts Gympie
Wyandra Surat Nat Park Noosa Heads
Condamine Dalby Glass Sunshine Coast
House Mts Nambour
39 Moreton
Darling **Toowoomba** Island NP
Bollon St George Cunningham's Blue Lake NP
Downs Gap **BRISBANE**
Dirranbandi Warwick Tamborine Mt NP
Goondiwindi Stanthorpe Gold Coast
Mungindi Lamington Surfers
Nat Park Paradise
SOUTH 3 WALES

Barrier

Coral

Sea

Reef

Belyando *Denham Range* *BRUCE*

Dividing *Drummond Range* *HIGHWAY*

Range *Dawson* *Auburn*

Warrego *Maranoa* *Condamine* *Moonie*

CARNARVON *HIGHWAY*

Range

NEXT
20 km

SUGARCANE
One of the spectacles of
Queensland is the fires
that rage through the
cane plantations in win-
ter near towns such as
Mossman (75km/46
miles from Cairns), when
the dry stalks are burned
off to get rid of debris,
snakes and insects. At
other times the tall green
crop presents a peaceful
sight, often combined on
the coastal plain with
tropical fruits like pineapples, mangoes, paw-paws
and guavas. Sugar
production goes back to
the mid-19th
century, when South Sea
Islanders were brought in
in large numbers as
indentured workers
(called 'Kanakas'). Many
of Queensland's sugar
mills can now be visited.

QUEENSLAND Second only to Western Australia in area,
the Sunshine State straddles the Tropic of Capricorn
between the New South Wales border and the Torres
Strait separating Australia from Papua New Guinea. The
immensely long and fertile coastline, with its beaches and
island paradises, is mostly within sight of the hills and
mountains of the **Great Dividing Range**. To the east, across
the transparent waters of the Coral Sea, is the **Great
Barrier Reef**, the largest structure in the world to have
been built by living creatures. To the west, the subtropical
rain forest covering the seaward slopes of the mountains
gives way to plateau farmlands of gradually diminishing
quality; here, where cattle stations sometimes provide the
only names on the map, is some of the country's most
authentic Outback, merging in the end with the sands,
stones and spinifex of true desert. In the far north, the
Cape York Peninsula remains one of the continent's
strangest and most remote places.

Almost over-endowed with natural beauty and a
benign climate, Queensland has become a popular destination with visitors from abroad as well as with
Australians on vacation or in retirement. Together with a
superabundance of mineral wealth, mined in such areas
as **Mount Isa** (the world's largest city in terms of area),
the growth of tourism has helped Queensland prosper
when the economy of other states has languished.
Agriculture maintains its importance; along the coastal
plain it has created richly textured landscapes of tropical
crops including sugarcane, which is delivered to mills by
a network of narrow-gauge agricultural railways.

CONVICT ROOTS Queensland's recent history began with
the establishment of a convict settlement at Moreton Bay
in 1824. This dumping ground for particularly recalcitrant
offenders was soon transferred to an upriver site near by,
which was named Brisbane after the Governor of New
South Wales at the time. In 1859, independence from
New South Wales was granted, and the new colony was
named for Queen Victoria.

The population increased and settlement spread; timber
workers took the best trees from the rain forest, leaving
farmers to clear the resulting scrub. Gold and other
mineral finds helped open up the country; Queensland's
richest goldfield was the remote, disease-ridden Palmer
River, scene of a rush in the 1870s. Immigrant workers
played a minor role in Queensland's history, but at one
point the gold-digging Chinese on the Palmer outnumbered the rest of the Far North's population. Another
immigrant group were the Kanaka—many thousands
were abducted from their islands in the South Pacific and
New Guinea to work in the canefields (see panel).

A high proportion of Australia's Aborigines lived in
Queensland, perhaps more than 200,000 at the time of
white settlement. Of a fiercer and more warlike disposition
than their fellows elsewhere, they put up a spirited resistance to their dispossession. All their efforts were to little
avail, however; by the turn of the 20th century the white
settlers had reduced the number of these Aborigines to no
more than 15,000.

Queensland has contributed much to Australian history—the state was the birthplace of both the Royal Flying

Doctor Service and Qantas, as well as the trade union movement and, eventually, the Australian Labor Party.

POLITICS AND PEOPLE For a generation, Queensland was governed by the ultra-conservative National Party, who were formerly known as the Country Party and represented rural interests. This organization was led from 1968 by the robust peanut farmer Sir Joh Bjelke-Petersen, a sworn opponent of moral permissiveness, conservation or anything that stood in the way of 'development'. Under his authoritarian rule, demonstrations were banned, books were censored and protected buildings demolished. Building speculators prospered and foreign capital was encouraged to share in the state's wealth, with few strings attached or questions asked. Sir Joh's demise was accompanied by numerous revelations of police misconduct and corruption.

The typical Queenslander is popularly supposed to be the most Australian of Australians. A macho frontier mentality lasted longer here than in the southern states, and until fairly recently, Brisbane took a positive pride in its decidedly provincial character. The state has changed dramatically, however, since the early 1990s and Brisbane is now a modern, vibrant city.

View from the world-famous Cairns–Kuranda train

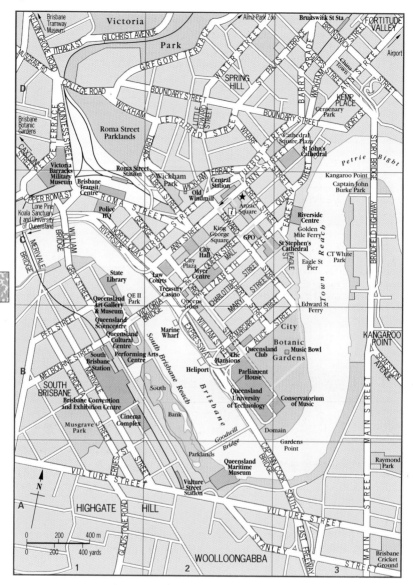

Brisbane

Australia's third largest city, with a population of almost 1.8 million, stands on the banks of the winding Brisbane River just inland from Moreton Bay. It used to be regarded as a provincial backwater and as recently as 1961 still had hundreds of kilometres of unpaved streets. Perhaps in order to combat this image, since the mid-1980s Brisbane has embraced the idea of progress with an enthusiasm that has transformed the city into a vibrant modern metropolis.

OLD-TOWN SIGHTS Not all traces of an older charm have been erased in the pursuit of modernity, however, and enough older buildings remain to tantalize the visitor with thoughts of the stylish tropical metropolis Brisbane might well have become. One such example is the corner of George and Alice streets where the **City Botanic Gardens** help frame the white stuccoed fronts of the **Queensland Club** and **Parliament House.**

A more positive face of modernization than the high-rise parliamentary annexe is across the river at South Bank. **Expo 88** was held here, leaving behind a legacy of parkland as well as an entertainment precinct and a number of cultural buildings of the very highest standard.

SUBURBAN SPLENDOUR The suburbs are among the best places in which to experience the city's special quality. Spread over a vast and largely hilly area, they consist almost entirely of single-family houses, and in areas like Red Hill, Paddington and Bardon, the Queensland stilt house can be studied in all its variety.

CITY ORIENTATION The heart of Brisbane's small city is easily explored on foot, although a nice idea is to take the free Loop bus, or the City Sights bus, which wanders around most of the sights, allowing you to jump on and off for a flat fare. A boat cruise to **Lone Pine** (see page 206) or historic **Newstead House** (see page 207) makes a pleasant excursion, too, while ferries link a number of destinations along the river bank.

The handsome 1868 Parliament House has been carefully restored

Brisbane's buildings and City Botanic Gardens

See map opposite.

Allow a half-day to explore the peninsula on which Brisbane is built.

Extending almost an entire block, the **Central Railway Station** of 1901 faces **Anzac Square** with its **Shrine of Remembrance**. At the corner of Ann and Edward streets stands the extraordinary **People's Palace** (now a backpacker hostel) with its verandas and cast-iron balustrades. The **General Post Office** is an imposing building; its arcade leads to Elizabeth Street, to **Old St. Stephen's Church** and to **St. Stephen's Cathedral** near the waterfront.

The riverside walk extends beyond the Edward Street gates of the **City Botanic Gardens**, flanked by the **Queensland University of Technology**. An intimation of the tropical paradise Brisbane might once have been is given by the lovely 1880s **Queensland Club** in its garden setting.

Opposite are **The Mansions**, striking terraced houses, now home to shops and restaurants. Just off Queens Gardens in William Street are the 1829 **Commissariat Stores**, one of only two convict-era buildings remaining intact in the city. On George Street, the Lands Building and old Treasury have been restored to become the Conrad Treasury hotel and Treasury Casino respectively.

Across the river, reached via Victoria Bridge or the pedestrian Goodwill Bridge, are the **Queensland Cultural Centre** and **South Bank**. A visit here could easily last a whole day; a quicker tour can be made using the Brisbane Transport ferry to return to the heart of the city.

Queen Street Mall is more commercial, though there are some fine older buildings. The walk ends in **King George Square**, which is dominated by the tall tower of **City Hall**.

Home of the Queensland State Parliament

SOUTH OF THE RIVER
South Brisbane's 17ha (42-acre) Parklands have a man-made beach and many other attractions (see opposite), while the nearby Queensland Maritime Museum is also worth visiting. Also in this area is the vast modern Convention and Exhibition Centre.

PARKS AND GARDENS
Brisbane has a number of green spaces in its heart and immediate environs. The **Brisbane Forest Park** is 28,500ha (70,400 acres) of forests, hills and reservoirs, while the **City Botanic Gardens** occupy the tip of the peninsula formed by the great bend in the Brisbane River. There is a riverside walk, and the gardens form an ideal setting for the buildings of the Queensland University of Technology, among them the 1860 Old Government House. At the foot of **Mount Coot-tha** (244m/800ft), about 6.5km (4 miles) from the city are the splendid **Brisbane Botanic Gardens**, with stunning tropical greenhouses and planetarium.

▶▶▶ Brisbane River　　　204B2
There are many ways to experience this meandering river: ferry rides and cruises; the South Bank; the RiverWalk pathway that winds its way around the city centre and beyond. Maps are available, and bikes, rollerblades and kayaks can be rented from an adventure centre below the Kangaroo Point cliffs.

▶ City Hall　　　204C2
King George Square (tel: 07-3403 8888)
Open: Museum daily 10–5. Admission free
In the late 1920s, a determined attempt was made to overcome Brisbane's provincial image by the erection of this colossal edifice. Inside, there is a museum, with plenty of exhibits celebrating the city's importance. Guided tours are available and Brisbane's Heritage Trail starts here, taking in the most important historic sites and buildings.

▶▶▶ Lone Pine Koala Sanctuary　　　off 204C1
Jesmond Road, Fig Tree Pocket (tel: 07-3378 1366)
Open: daily 8.30–5. Admission and cruise: expensive
This wildlife sanctuary offers an array of wildlife—wombats, Tasmanian devils, kangaroos—and the chance to cuddle a koala. The most enjoyable way to arrive is via a 90-minute cruise upstream from the city.

▶ Parliament House　　　204B2
George and Alice streets (tel: 07-3406 7562 for tours)
Open: daily; Mon–Fri tours from 10.30 on sitting days, from 9 on other days, Sat–Sun tours from 10. Admission free
Opened in 1868, this fine French Renaissance-style building is still the home of the Queensland State Parliament. Tours are available at various times throughout the day.

▶▶ Queensland Cultural Centre　　　204B1
Melbourne and Grey streets, South Brisbane
Art Gallery: tel: 07-3840 7303. Open: Mon–Fri 10–5,
Sat–Sun 9–5. Museum: tel: 07-3840 7555. Open: daily
9.30–5. Admission free (charges for special exhibitions)

9.30–5. Admission free (charges for special exhibitions)
Brisbane's cultural heart is on the river's south bank. Completed in 1985, this complex includes the Queensland Art Gallery, Queensland Museum, State Library and Performing Arts Centre, the latter with a 2,000-seat theatre and an equally large concert hall. Further development of the area will see the construction of the new Queensland Gallery of Modern Art and expansion of the State Library. The **Queensland Art Gallery**▶▶ has a good selection of Australian and Aboriginal art, and a small collection of European painting, some of it arranged by theme rather than by artist or country. The contemporary Asian art collection is particularly good. Exhibits in the **Queensland Museum**▶▶ include dinosaurs, kangaroos and sections on endangered species and the history and geography of Queensland, plus a major display on the history, art and culture of the Aborigines and Torres Strait islanders.

▶▶ Queensland Sciencentre   204B2
Queensland Museum, Melbourne and Grey streets, South Brisbane (tel: 07-3840 7555).
Open: daily 9.30–5. Admission: moderate
This interactive science and technology centre is one of Brisbane's most entertaining attractions. With around 100 hands-on exhibits in three themed galleries—Body Zone, Earth Space and Action Stations, even non-scientific visitors will be captivated.

▶▶ South Bank   204B2
South Brisbane (tel: 07-3867 2051)
Once the crowds have gone, Expo sites can become forlorn places, but many of the pavilions and facilities erected for Brisbane's 1988 bonanza are still here, bringing life to this area of parkland. The attractions include a state-of-the-art cinema complex, a kilometre-long (half-mile) floral canopied walkway (the Grand Arbour), Friday night and weekend art and craft markets, shops,

Modern Brisbane is Australia's third largest city

Glass House Mountains scenery

Drive

The Sunshine Coast and hinterland

A full day's drive along Queensland's Sunshine Coast that also goes into the hinterland of farming and hill country west of the Bruce Highway.

About 60km (37 miles) north of Brisbane, the **Glass House Mountains** interrupt the monotony of the coastal plain. These old volcanic hills are best viewed from the old main road north of Caboolture as well as from the Mary Cairncross Scenic Reserve near Maleny. The **Blackall Range** panoramic drive gives access to this upland country of undulating hills and verdant valleys, tea rooms and craft studios. Just north of the little highland resort of Montville is the **Kondalilla National Park**, where splendid waterfalls crash down through the rain forest. Equally spectacular falls can be experienced at **Mapleton Falls National Park**.
  In **Nambour**, an area of tropical fruit production, a narrow-gauge sugarcane train trundles through the streets. A sequence of splendid beaches unravels along the Sunshine Coast north of Coolum to the highly fashionable

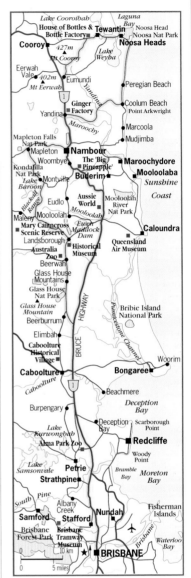

community of **Noosa Heads**, while **Tewantin** boasts a couple of curiosities—a house built of bottles and the Big Shell. Back inland, the charming village of **Eumundi** makes a good stopping place, though it is packed on market days (Sat and Wed). The Bruce Highway is the best route for a swift return to Brisbane.

National parks

As may be expected in a state of its vast size, Queensland has an extraordinary variety of landscapes, many protected by designation as national or environmental parks.

Tropical coastline to desert heartlands Most visitors will become familiar with the reef and rain-forest parks of the tropical and subtropical coastline, but the spectacular and often unique parks of the interior demand attention too. More than 1,200km (745 miles) to the west of the coast are the monotonous sandhills of the **Simpson Desert National Park**, 'stretching interminably like waves of the sea' according to the explorer Charles Sturt, who gave up his attempt to conquer them. First crossed on foot in 1973, they still offer a challenge to anyone venturing into them today.

Farther east, the sparse vegetation of the desert gives way to grasslands, wattle scrub, eucalyptus woodland or scattered individuals of the strange Queensland bottle tree. Among the spinifex and rugged hills of the **Lark Quarry Conservation Park**, the footprints of dinosaurs that perished in a stampede 100 million years ago are preserved in mud that has long since turned to rock.

Farther east still, a broad belt of sandstone gives rise to spectacular scenery. This is where many of Queensland's major rivers have their origin; their erosive action has formed deep gorges in which a rich flora thrives, including the cabbage palms of **Carnarvon Gorge National Park**, also well known for its strange rock formations. As the land rises and rainfall increases, the blue-green of eucalypts gives way to the dark green of tropical rain forest, with its incredible species including ferns, climbers and other epiphytes. In parts of north Queensland, the World Heritage-listed rain forest descends to the beaches fringing the Great Barrier Reef, whose cays and islands are preserved as part of the **Great Barrier Reef Marine Park**.

Wild north to friendly south Cape York has some of the finest but least accessible of Queensland's national parks, where nature displays herself in all her savage unpredictability. In the wet season, rivers fill with fierce-flowing, silt-rich water, closing fords and cutting off communications for weeks on end, only to dry up into a series of isolated pools when the rain has finally stopped. Strange termite mounds stud the inland landscape, while mangrove swamps grow from the mud of the coastal plain. Brisbane must be one of the world's best endowed capital cities when one thinks in terms of grand scenery that is within easy reach of the town. A crescent of gloriously wooded highlands extends from close to the city boundary south to **Lamington National Park** on the border that lies between Queensland and New South Wales.

Brisbane's Lone Pine Koala Sanctuary is the state's best-known animal park, where kangaroos, Tasmanian devils and other creatures can also be seen

209

IN THE SOUTH
Near Warwick, at Cunningham's Gap in the Main Range National Park, there are fine views and a number of trails through rain forest and eucalyptus woodland.

Keep an eye out for the beautiful crimson rosella

Queensland

The Pacific Highway to the south of Brisbane runs through eucalyptus country

A QUEENSLAND HIGHLAND LINE
Although there is now an alternative form of transportation (see page 220), half a million people travel the Cairns–Kuranda railway line every year. Few are disappointed by the spectacular 33km (20-mile) ride from coast to mountain rain forest. The line climbs from sea level to a summit at 328m (1,076ft) via a series of tunnels and sharp bends, stopping for a breather at the spectacularly tall Barron Falls. The railway was built between 1886 and 1891 to link the agricultural Atherton Tableland with the port at Cairns; it immediately put an end to Port Douglas as a harbour of any significance. The terminus at Kuranda, planted with palms and shady with ferns, would win any international award for the best-kept station.

How to travel

By air Queensland is unique among Australian states because it has three international airports—Brisbane, the Gold Coast and Cairns—with regular connections to many overseas airports. A variety of airlines links cities elsewhere in Australia with many places in Queensland, for example with the airports serving the Gold Coast (Coolangatta) and Sunshine Coast (Maroochydore). Given the large size of the state, internal travel by air is well developed, and may sometimes be the only way of reaching remote northern destinations during the wet season. Smaller aircraft, including helicopters and sea-planes, spin a web of services spanning mainland and islands; some islands can only be reached in this way.

By water Visitors are bound to find themselves afloat at some point in their Queensland holiday, even if it is only for a day-trip to part of the Great Barrier Reef aboard a high-speed wave piercer or a more humble craft rented locally. Most, but not all, of the islands are accessible by ferry or launch, which also carry vehicles to Fraser Island and a few of the Brisbane region isles. The best way of getting the feel of reef and islands might be to cruise; there are any number of operators competing for your business, some with sleek modern vessels calling at luxury resorts, others offering a more adventurous experience involving camping on uninhabited islands. Do not forget to take a cruise or ferry trip up the Brisbane River.

By bus Bus services link Brisbane with other Australian cities as well as major destinations within Queensland. Local services are variable, though well developed in Brisbane and on the Gold Coast.

By train Queensland has the longest rail network in the country. Services include two Brisbane–Cairns options: the twice-weekly *Sunlander* (which incorporates luxury *Queenslander*-class sleeper carriages), and the fast, comfortable *Tilt Train*, which travels via Rockhampton, Mackay and Townsville several times a week. Other services include the *Inlander* (Townsville–Mount Isa); the *Spirit of the Outback* (Brisbane–Longreach via Rockhampton); and the *Westlander* (Brisbane–Charleville). There are two rail curiosities to attract the adventurous: the weekly run from Cairns to Forsayth, via Kuranda, in the deep interior on the *Savannahlander*, and the *Gulflander* running on an isolated section of line near the Gulf of Carpentaria. The only interstate rail link is with Sydney.

By car The road system in the densely populated coastal strip is well developed, and reaches east–west across Queensland and into the Northern Territory via Mount Isa. Many places in the state are only accessible on unpaved roads. Cape York and other far northern places may be cut off in the wet season when fords become impassable and roads are swept away. Your own car, preferably a 4WD, will be an almost indispensable asset if you want to visit many national parks, though some sort of guided tour can be found for almost any destination.

► Atherton Tableland 200D2

From Cairns south for over 145km (90 miles) to near Innisfail, high tablelands rise steeply from the coastal plain. There are remnants of the once dense rain forest, preserved in several national parks and reserves, but the area's rich volcanic soils now mostly support sugar and exotic fruits. Southeast of Atherton on the Gillies Highway is **Yungaburra►►**, with extinct volcanoes and crater lakes.

►►► Cairns 201D3

Cairns is closer to Papua New Guinea than to most of Australia. The city, the key to far north Queensland, breathes in the balmy air of Trinity Bay. It helped open up the goldfields and tin mines of the interior, then became a major outlet for the booming agriculture of the area, particularly sugarcane. But tomorrow seems to promise even more expansive times; because of the proximity of the Barrier Reef, superb beaches to the north and south, and the rivers and forests of the Daintree and the Atherton Tableland, tourism flourishes. Cairns International Airport, only opened in the mid-1980s, is now high on the list of ports of entry in the amount of traffic it handles.

The town's founders laid out a generous grid of streets, whose width and relative absence of traffic contribute to the relaxed atmosphere. The waterfront complex housing boutiques, shops, the Reef Hotel Casino, cruise boat wharves and a luxury hotel add a sophisticated note, as do the ocean-going vessels of the super-rich in the adjacent marina.

Cairns Museum and nearby **Cairns Regional Gallery►** give an insight into a past populated by Aborigines, railway workers, goldminers and Chinese workers. For a different experience, journey just outside town to the **Flecker Botanic Gardens►**, with more than 200 varieties of palm trees and the tranquil Centenary Lakes. Also on the edge of town is the excellent **Tjapukai Aboriginal Cultural Park►►**, which offers a re-created Aboriginal camp, traditional dance performances and much more.

BUNDABERG
The name of this substantial town about 370km (230 miles) north of Brisbane is synonymous with its principal product—rum, distilled from the canefields of the coastal plain. Bundaberg is also the main gateway to the southern Barrier Reef. Mon Repos Conservation Park, a beach to the north, is a spot popular with turtles during their egg-laying season (November–February).

BIRDS AND BEACHES
Although Cairns lacks a decent beach, swimmers and sun-worshippers can head for the string of beaches stretching along the 26km (16-mile) 'Marlin Coast', a 10-minute drive to the north, each of them more paradisical than the last. From October to May, swimming is permitted only on netted beaches because of the presence of box jellyfish (see page 212).

211

The Esplanade and pier at sunny tropical Cairns

Drive

The Daintree and Cape Tribulation

If you can resist the temptation of the glorious beaches along the way, this full day's return drive from Cairns will take you over the Daintree River to tropical rain forest and coral reef.

The **Captain Cook Highway** is without doubt one of the world's finest coastal roads. Rarely overburdened with traffic, it runs inland at first from Cairns, rejoining the shore north of the exclusive resort town of Palm Cove. **Port Douglas**, the coastline's northernmost resort of any consequence, is home to the **Rainforest Habitat Wildlife Sanctuary**, an ambitious re-creation of the tropical rain-forest environment.

The canefields around **Mossman** feed the town's sugar mill via a stretch of narrow-gauge railway. A short detour leads to the rain forest of the Mossman Gorge in **Daintree National Park**, with its graded walking track, rapids and delightful swimming holes. At the turn leading to the ferry over the Daintree River the tarmac comes to a (temporary) end; non-4WD vehicles should pro-

The goanna, or monitor lizard

ceed with caution or not at all in the wet season. The wide river is lined with mangrove swamp and is home to crocodiles.

Beyond the ferry begins the ecological wonderland of the **Cape Tribulation** section of the **Daintree National Park**, a remnant of the forests in which flowering plants first appeared on earth. The road lurches through the forest and across dry river beds, pale dust from vehicles coating the luxuriant vegetation with a thin film.

The **Heights of Alexandra Lookout** gives a superb view over the forest tumbling down to the sea. The best initiation into the complex ecology and beauty of the World Heritage Area is at the **Daintree Discovery Centre** with its boardwalk leading deep into this mysterious realm.

Even if the presence of highly toxic box jellyfish inhibits swimming in the sea, you should at least walk along one of the incomparable beaches of **Cape Tribulation**, several of which are easily accessible from the road. Beyond the cape itself, the 32km (20-mile) Bloomfield Track begins; it is only negotiable by 4WD.

212

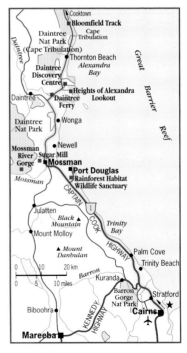

The bottlebrush is native to Queensland

213

ANCIENT HOME
Mount Moffat in Carnarvon Gorge National Park has strange sandstone formations as well as Kenniff Cave, lived in by Aboriginal people nearly 20,000 years ago and containing Aboriginal rock paintings.

▶▶ Cape York Peninsula   *200E2*

Often described as one of the world's last wildernesses, this great peninsula tapers northward for hundreds of kilometres to its tip at Cape York itself, overlooking the island-studded Torres Strait. A total of perhaps 10,000 people are thinly distributed over this vast area, most of them Torres Strait Islanders and Aborigines, whose ancestors left a legacy of remarkable rock painting that is best seen around **Laura**. This little township straddles the lower end of the Peninsula Developmental Road, a less developed highway than its name implies, especially in the Wet when river crossings become impassable even for the most rugged of 4WDs.

In the Dry, the Cape becomes a fascinating destination for the more adventurous tourist. The rain forest along the Pacific coast gives way to savannah-like country farther inland, punctuated by the surreal turrets of termite mounds, some of them reaching an extraordinary 3m (10ft). The peninsula possesses some remarkable national parks—including **Lakefield**, coastal **Cape Melville** and the remote crocodile habitat of **Mungkan Kandju National Park**. The future of the peninsula probably lies in wilderness tourism; civilization's other activities, apart from bauxite mining at Weipa, have left little mark on the land.

UPLAND ARCHITECTURE
Following the discovery of gold in 1872 at Charters Towers, the town fitted itself out with some fine buildings. Some of these can still be seen today, including banks, the stock exchange, the School of Mines, the city hall and the courthouse.

▶▶ Carnarvon Gorge National Park   *201B3*

Much of this spectacular park is difficult to get to (and access is restricted during wet weather), but the extraordinary gorges cut by the Carnarvon Creek and its tributaries into the soft sandstone of the plateau can be reached from the Carnarvon Highway between Roma and Rolleston. Here 200m(650-ft) high cliffs tower over cabbage palms, ferns, mosses and orchids. A number of caves shelter Aboriginal rock paintings. A footpath leads up the gorge from the ranger station, with side tracks leading to all the park's delights.

▶ Charters Towers   *201C3*

In contrast to the tropical environment of Townsville, 135km (84 miles) away, this upland town enjoys an invigorating climate. It has some of the best early Australian architecture to be seen anywhere (see panel).

▶ Chillagoe–Mungana Caves National Park 200D2

Around the old mining village of Chillagoe, west of Atherton Tableland, are extensive, spectacular caves eroded in the limestone by the headwaters of the Mitchell River. Not all are accessible, but the Donna and Trezkinn caves are artificially lit to enhance the drama and strangeness of the limestone formations. On the surface, the same rock has been weathered into equally peculiar shapes—turrets, pinnacles and forms resembling animals.

▶ Cloncurry 200C1

Once a bustling gold and copper town, Cloncurry sits astride the main road and railway line from Mount Isa to the coast, earning its living nowadays from sheep and cattle grazing. It was here in 1928 that the Royal Flying Doctor Service began operating (see panel).

▶ Cooktown 200D2

A late 19th-century boomtown in the days of gold strikes on the Palmer River, Cooktown was named for Captain James Cook. His ship, *Endeavour,* was beached here after she had been holed on the Barrier Reef. Though the peak population of 30,000 has shrunk to around 1,000, enough traces of the past remain to make Cooktown an attractive tourist destination. The Captain's enforced stay is recalled in the Victorian villa housing the **James Cook Museum▶**, as well as by his statue and by the annual reenactment in June of his landing. Other attractions include the Botanic Gardens, home to Nature's PowerHouse—an environmental interpretative centre. Cooktown is reached from Cairns by the inland road or, more picturesquely, by the partly unpaved Cape Tribulation coast road.

▶▶▶ Daintree National Park 200D2

The outstanding international significance of the Queensland rain forest has been recognized by the designation of the Daintree and Cape Tribulation region as a World Heritage Area (part of the Wet Tropics of Queensland). A relic of Cretaceous times over 100 million years ago, the jungle of far north Queensland escaped the volcanic eruptions that destroyed other primitive forests in the region, and consequently has a unique ecological value. The tiny settlement of Daintree is on the banks of the Daintree River, famous for its mangroves and crocodiles. The rain forest can be visited on guided or self-guided bushwalks via river cruises or you can simply appreciate its wonders at the **Daintree Discovery Centre▶▶**.

▶▶ Fraser Island 201B4

This is the largest sand island in the world, stretching 121km (75 miles) beside the south Queensland coast. With wonderful beaches, dunes rising to an extraordinary heathland, rain forest, mangroves and dozens of freshwater lakes, this World Heritage island attracts many visitors, though access is only by 4WD (there are no roads). A drive along the east coast takes you past the wreck of the *Maheno* and cliffs of multihued sandstone to the resort villages of Eurong Beach and Happy Valley. There are two other resorts on the island, as well as campsites and cottages.

IF DOCTORS COULD FLY
Set up in 1927–28 by the Rev. John Flynn, the Royal Flying Doctor Service (RFDS) began operations in Cloncurry with a plane supplied by the Queensland and Northern Territory Aerial Service (Qantas). The event is recalled in a memorial to Flynn, its missionary founder, and in the John Flynn Place Museum in Cloncurry.

214

SAVING THE WILDERNESS
Destruction of the Daintree by volcanic explosions and lava flows may have been avoided in the remote geological past; more recent threats have involved the dividing of the rain forest into handy packages for 'development' and the construction of the controversial Bloomfield Track. World Heritage designation has now rescued this irreplaceable tract of wild nature.

The island is easily reached by ferry from the mainland (Inskip Point, Hervey Bay and River Heads), or by air.

▶ Glass House Mountains   *201A4*

Inland from the Bruce Highway north of Brisbane rises a group of steep and strangely shaped peaks, the cores of old volcanoes. Given their enigmatic name by Captain Cook, they are popular with climbers; the inexperienced can best view them from the Old Gympie Road or from Mary Cairncross Scenic Reserve near Maleny.

▶▶▶ Gold Coast   *201A4*

Between Tweed Heads on the New South Wales border and Paradise Point in the north stretches a 71km (44-mile) chain of 35 glorious sandy beaches blessed by regular rolling surf and basking in regular sunshine. Everyone is catered for here: Swimming, surfing and sunbathing all have their place, but so do many other activities—golf and adventure sports like parasailing. There are any number of theme parks and similar establishments, among them the incredibly successful **Sea World**▶▶▶ at Main Beach, smoothly entertaining its tidal wave of visitors, and the popular Warner Bros. Movie World theme park.

At **Surfers Paradise**, with its lavish malls, excellent restaurants and good nightlife, and Jupiters Casino at nearby Broadbeach, you can enjoy this seaside Arcadia to the full. A somewhat quieter (and cheaper) ambience can be enjoyed to the south, around Currumbin or at wooded Burleigh Heads, where a discreet national park visitor centre introduces what is left of the coast's natural environment.

SAND FOR SALE
The sands of Fraser Island have a high mineral content that makes them very valuable in certain industrial processes. A notable victory was won here in 1977 by conservationists who succeeded in stopping sand mining and the consequent gradual export overseas of the very substance of the island.

GOLD COAST CONTRASTS
The sprawling Gold Coast is a textbook example of how not to plan an urban environment. The approach from Brisbane, an hour away, is lined with high-rise buildings, varied in shape and decorated in tasteful pastel shades. They jostle each other for a glimpse of the beach, which, because it is to the east and they are too close, is plunged into shade in the course of the afternoon. In stark contrast, the area offers a verdant hinterland (see Lamington National Park on page 220), and wildlife parks such as Currumbin Wildlife Sanctuary near Coolangatta.

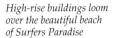
High-rise buildings loom over the beautiful beach of Surfers Paradise

Australia's greatest attraction, the reef stretches for more than 2,000km (1,240 miles) along the east coast from the Gulf of Papua to a point just south of the Tropic of Capricorn (off Gladstone).

REEF FISH
The reef is home to thousands of species of fish, from the greedy potato cod (see picture below), to vibrant parrot fish, graceful rays and poisonous lion fish. It's also home to many types of shark. Attacks are rare, however, and the sharks will probably be more scared of you than you are of them.

Giant potato cod expect to be fed and stroked at Cod Hole, 19km (12 miles) off Lizard Island and one of the world's best diving sites

The coral of the reef's outer rim forms a steep submarine escarpment, dropping abruptly into the abyss of the Pacific; only 30km (19 miles) out from Cairns, this Outer Reef gradually extends farther away from the mainland until, opposite Mackay, it is some 250km (155 miles) off shore. Landward is warm and shallow water, forming a kind of lagoon broken up by more reefs and hundreds of islands, some of them true coral cays, most of them detached fragments of the mainland, cut off when sea levels rose. They vary enormously in character, from exposed and sparsely vegetated cays of sand and coral barely rising out of the water at low tide, to reef-fringed mountain ranges covered in splendid rain forest.

Creatures of the deep Hardly another ecosystem on earth can surpass the reef for sheer beauty or variety. Responsible for its formation are humble polyps, tiny organisms with limestone outer skeletons that form a coral reef's basic building blocks. With wildly differing shapes recalling trees, plates, fungi and even brains, the still-living polyps vividly paint the underwater scene, to which is added a kaleidoscope of other living creatures. These include not only tropical fish of brilliant hue and intriguing personality, but also sponges, starfish, crabs, sharks, turtles, giant clams and an occasional dugong, a large and harmless creature also known as the sea-cow.

Another creature that is drawn to this watery paradise in large numbers is *Homo sapiens*, tourist variety. This medium-sized, sometimes amphibious mammal can be

217

observed gazing at the wonders of the reef from aircraft, wave piercers and vessels of all kinds, including flat-bottomed boats and semi-submersibles, or socializing with its other inhabitants while wearing a snorkel or diving mask. Large numbers of visitors stay on the mainland, venturing out to the Reef on day-trips from the main tourist areas such as Port Douglas, Cairns, Townsville, the Whitsunday region and Bundaberg; others stay on the islands themselves, in exclusive resorts, and crowded hotels and apartments, or the more adventurous camp on tranquil uninhabited isles with no resources whatsoever.

The reef is a great place to learn how to snorkel

Problems of conservation The reef is a World Heritage Area, controlled and managed by the **Great Barrier Reef Marine Park Authority** (www.gbrmpa.gov.au)since 1976. Conservation problems arise not only through the influx of tourists and pressure from developers (who by 1989 had applied for permission to build 250 new resorts along the Queensland coast), but also because of agricultural and other pollutants washed into the sea from the rivers draining the interior. Exploratory drilling in the ocean may have been halted, but the petrochemical industry continues to keep a watchful eye on the reef's potential as an offshore oilfield.

A more immediate threat comes from a natural phenomenon. The crown-of-thorns starfish has a fierce appetite for the coral polyp, which it easily sucks out of its protective skeleton, and in recent years has devastated huge areas of coral. It is thought by some that over-fishing of the starfish's natural predators may have caused its population to explode; other than removing the starfish, scientists are at a loss for a solution.

Butterfly fish: one of the natives of the world's largest living organism

Queensland's islands

▶▶▶ Great Barrier Reef Islands   *201C3*

The following information does not cover all the islands of the reef, but gives details of those that are more popular or more easily accessible, dealing with them from south to north.

Southern Reef At the southernmost end of the reef, **Lady Elliot Island**▶▶ and uninhabited **Lady Musgrave Island**▶▶ are small coral cays right on the reef and both of them offer excellent diving and snorkelling. Lady Elliot Island is accessible by air or boat from Bundaberg (80km/50 miles) or Hervey Bay, while Lady Musgrave Island, which is a national park island with the most basic facilities and a campsite, is reached by launch from Bundaberg (also 80km/50 miles distant).

Heron Island▶▶ is part resort, part national park, famed for its wildlife, with optimal snorkelling and diving, semi-submersibles and reef-walking. Access is by helicopter or launch from Gladstone (72km/45 miles).

Large, wooded **Great Keppel Island**▶▶ is popular with young singles and has glass-bottomed boats, a coral submarine, an underwater observatory, jetskis and water-skiing, bush-walking and nightlife. It has secluded beaches and is accessible by air from Rockhampton (56km/35 miles) or by ferry from Rosslyn Bay.

Whitsunday Islands These hilly, wooded islands, usually fringed with reefs, once formed the tips of ancient mountains and lie scattered to either side of the Whitsunday Passage. Only eight of the 70-plus islands have been developed for tourism, the rest remaining uninhabited. **Brampton Island**▶▶ (a national park and part of the Cumberland group) is loved by honeymooners and other couples for its romantic setting. It has good facilities, including golf and walking tracks, and is accessible by air and launch from Mackay (32km/20 miles).

Numerous high-rise hotels and apartments characterize popular, medium-sized **Hamilton Island**▶▶. It has an airport with flights from most southern Australian cities and Cairns; alternatively, access is by aircraft from Proserpine or Mackay, and by boat from Shute Harbour (16km/10 miles) or Airlie Beach, the area's main town.

Of the other developed Whitsunday Islands, **Hayman Island** is luxurious and expensive, **Lindeman Island**, although a national park, is now a popular Club Med resort, while **South Molle** and **Daydream Island** cater particularly for families. **Hook Island** and **Long Island** are casual and their less expensive resorts are popular with the young, although the latter also has a luxury resort. All offer day trips to the Outer Reef.

North Islands Large **Magnetic Island**▶▶ (off Townsville) has high granite hills, superb sandy beaches, an abundance of koalas and a large national park. Access is by helicopter or ferry from Townsville (9km/5.5 miles); the island has a bus service. Farther north, **Orpheus Island**▶▶, of volcanic origin, is densely wooded, with fine beaches, exceptional coral and biological research station. Access is by air from Townsville (80km/50 miles) or by boat from Lucinda.

Largest and perhaps wildest of the Queensland islands, national park **Hinchinbrook Island**▶▶ has peaks rising through rain forest to 1,142m (3,746ft). The Coastal Walk along the east coast takes experienced hikers several days to complete; access to the island is by launch from Cardwell or seaplane from Townsville (150km/93 miles).

Medium-sized **Dunk Island**▶▶ and smaller **Fitzroy Island**▶▶ both have rain forest-clad hills. The former has wonderful beaches and rich wildlife, and is accessible by air from Townsville (160km/100 miles) and Cairns (120km/75 miles), and by launch from Mission Beach. Fitzroy Island has excellent diving and snorkelling as well as good views from its lighthouse, and is accessible by launch from Cairns (28km/17 miles).

Green Island▶ is easily reached from Cairns (27km/17 miles) by boat and is therefore popular for a day-trip, although the coral cay now has a luxury resort. It has the reef's longest-established underwater observatory.

Exclusive **Lizard Island**▶▶ is sometimes called 'the jewel of the Barrier Reef'. Accessible by air from Cairns (241km/150 miles), it has wonderful bays and fringing coral, and a superb view from Cook's Lookout.

ISLAND ACCOMMODATION
Basic and budget Lady Elliot Island (safari cabins and tents), Lady Musgrave Island (self-sufficient camping with permit from the Queensland Parks and Wildlife Service), Great Keppel Island (family resort and camping), Magnetic Island (backpackers' accommodation), Hinchinbrook Island (camping and an eco resort), Dunk Island (camping with permit) and Fitzroy Island (hostel).
Mid-range and moderate Great Keppel Island (resort and cabins), Brampton, Hamilton, Magnetic, Hinchinbrook and Dunk islands (resorts), Heron Island (three grades of accommodation), Lindeman Island (Club Med) and Fitzroy Island (villas).
Exclusive and expensive Hayman, Orpheus, Bedarra, Green and Lizard islands.

Opposite, above: Blue semicircle angel fish seen around Heron Island

Heron Island becomes a breeding ground for green and loggerhead turtles in October and November

Queensland

220

ABOVE THE RAIN FOREST
Although the Cairns to Kuranda Railway is still the most delightful way to reach this charming village, the Skyrail Rainforest Cableway offers another spectacular option. Opened in late 1995, the cars of this cableway provide a stunning view of the scenery on their 7.5km (4.5-mile) route up the escarpment from Cairns.

THROUGH THE TROPICS BY DUCK
Equally happy climbing a steep jungle track or crossing a turtle-thronged pool, the Kuranda ducks are really 'DUKWs', the code name for a rugged amphibious vehicle developed for army use in World War II.

Lamington National Park, a paradise for hikers and birdwatchers

▶ Innisfail   201D3

A useful gateway to far north Queensland with good access to the Barrier Reef and the Atherton Tableland, the high rainfall area of Innisfail is also well known as a sugar town. Cane was first planted in the 1880s, and the industry was boosted by a wave of Italian immigrants after World War II. Innisfail's Chinese community is of much longer standing; their joss-house (temple) is one of only two still in use in Australia. Another, very different, attraction is the Johnstone River Crocodile Farm.

▶▶ Kuranda   200D2

High up in the Atherton Tableland, this 'village in the rain forest' is popular with visitors, most of whom have taken the spectacular train or cableway ride up from Cairns (see panel). Kuranda is a tourist paradise, with rides in amphibious ex-army 'ducks' (see panel) through the rain forest, a butterfly sanctuary, a vast aviary, a huge open-air market and arts and crafts stores—everything has been accommodated without damaging the town's character too much. Other attractions are a rain forest interpretation centre, walking tours, a fauna sanctuary, Aboriginal activities and a wildlife park. Kuranda is the ideal base for exploring other areas of Atherton Tableland.

▶▶ Lamington National Park   201A4

In contrast to the glitz and concrete of the Gold Coast is its lush hinterland of upland farms and forests. Rising to over 1,100m (3,610ft) on the New South Wales border, the green mountains of Lamington National Park are remarkable for their superb stands of Antarctic beech trees, some of them thousands of years old. The forest, of which they form a part, is best experienced by braving the spectacular treetop walk near O'Reilly's Guesthouse. Between here and Binna Burra Lodge, the other focal point of the park, runs another famous walk, this one 22.5km (14 miles) and with stupendous views over New South Wales border country.

EMERALD SURPRISE

QUEENSLAND KIWI FRUIT

ROUGH AND READY

ROUGH LEAF PINEAPPLES

SUGAR MAKES MANY FOODS MORE ENJOYABLE TO EAT

▶ **Longreach**   *200B2*

Far inland on the Capricorn Highway and railway from Rockhampton, Longreach is the focus for a vast pastoral area of the Outback. It was here that Qantas made its base in the 1920s and here that Australia's first aircraft factory was established. Tourists come here now mostly to visit the splendid **Australian Stockman's Hall of Fame▶▶**; opened for the Bicentenary in 1988, this large and lavish modern building houses every conceivable kind of display on Outback life.

▶ **Mackay**   *201C3*

This city of over 60,000 people prides itself on its important sugar industry, shipping a third of Australia's total production from its deep-water harbour. But tourism is of growing significance, with good access to the adjacent Barrier Reef, mainland beaches and the wonderful **Eungella National Park▶▶** to the northwest. This tract of rain forest-covered upland ('land of the clouds' to the Aborigines) offers a cool contrast to the tropical coast, and has unusual, and often unique, plants, animals and birds like the Eungella honeyeater. You may also catch sight of the normally elusive platypus.

▶ **Maryborough**   *201A4*

Maryborough serves a rich agricultural hinterland. Founded in 1842, it has a good number of 19th-century buildings and examples of the famous 'Queenslander' houses, as well as subtropical parks and gardens.

▶ **Millaa Millaa**   *200D2*

This tiny dairying village is famous for the **Millaa Millaa Falls**, one of several picturesque waterfalls along the scenic route known as the Waterfall Circuit. To the west of the township is the **Millaa Millaa Lookout**, 1,100m (3,610ft) up, with fantastic views over the Atherton Tableland, one of the most densely vegetated areas in Australia.

Quite an experience— inside the 'Big Pineapple'

FLAMBOYANT FRUIT
One of Australia's most emphatic examples of kitsch is the 'Big Pineapple'. Almost 15m (50ft) high, this fibreglass fruit cannot fail to catch your attention as you drive up the Bruce Highway inland from the Sunshine Coast. Advertising the attractions of an extensive pineapple plantation, it has become something of an unofficial emblem of the tropical fruit country focused on the town of Nambour.

Having been logged for its wood, cleared to make way for cane plantations and threatened by roads, airports, reservoirs and tourist developments, Australia's rain forest has finally been recognized as a unique habitat, not only worthy of conservation for its own sake but also for its immense appeal to visitors.

Although it is both shy and rare, the cassowary, Australia's second largest bird, is very powerful

222

ANIMAL LIFE
Rain forest is as abundant in animals as it is in plants. Some of the animals, like varieties of tree kangaroos, ringtail possums or the tiny musky rat kangaroo, are unique to this habitat. One endangered species is the cassowary, a flightless bird related to the emu, whose thuggish habits include a grunting cry, kicking to kill with its sharp toe and an ability to head-butt its way through the densest undergrowth.

Subtropical rain forest in Bunya Mountains National Park

Remnants from the past Scattered along the east coast from Cape York to Tasmania, today's rain forest is a mere fragment of the ancient mosaic of vegetation that covered the whole of the continent millions of years ago. Rain forest flourishes in sheltered, moist conditions, and gradually perished as ancient Australia's climate became drier and drier. But splendid remnants still grace the surface of the land where the complex equation of rainfall, evaporation, soil and temperature balances out. The eastward-facing slopes of north Queensland's coastal mountains, for example, are sheltered by the high ridges of the Great Dividing Range from the parching winds of the interior and enjoy the benefit of moisture-rich onshore breezes. Here are the country's most luxuriant, and perhaps most spectacular rain forests.

Variety A variant, littoral rain forest occurs in unexpected locations close to the sea where sand dunes offer shelter from the scorching effects of salt spray, as on a number of Barrier Reef islands. Farther south, into New South Wales and Victoria, the composition of the rain forest changes; its structure becomes simpler and there are fewer species. Nevertheless, the appearance is still one of great luxuriance. A number of the New South Wales temperate and subtropical rain forests, stretching from the Queensland border to the Newcastle area, have been grouped together to form one of the country's World Heritage areas. This type of forest merges imperceptibly with cool-temperate rain forest, characterized by the trees known as southern beech and Antarctic beech. These trees flourish in the cooler climate of Tasmania, although they can also be seen at high altitude in Queensland's **Lamington National Park** (see page 220).

▶ Mission Beach
201C3

The fine beaches between Tully and Innisfail, known as the Mission Beach area, stretch over 13km (8 miles) along the coast within sight of Dunk Island. Endangered cassowaries frequent the nearby rain forest, and there is spectacular whitewater rafting on the upper reaches of the Tully River.

▶▶ Noosa Heads
201A4

The Noosa Heads area (focused around Noosaville, Noosa, Tewantin and Sunshine Beach) at the northern tip of the Sunshine Coast, 150km (93 miles) from Brisbane, is the place to come if the Gold Coast is not your scene. Noosa offers low-rise hotels and resorts, some excellent restaurants and beautiful beaches. It is the starting point for boat trips up the Noosa River and its lagoons or across the river into the **Cooloola** section of **Great Sandy National Park▶▶**, which also encompasses Fraser Island, where there are beaches and the largest sand dune system in the world. Inland, in the green Blackall Range area, is **Eumundi▶** whose Saturday market is justly famous.

▶ Port Douglas
200D2

This little harbour town and resort 70km (43 miles) north of Cairns exudes a charm all its own, especially on a tropical evening when visitors and locals wander the broad streets, full of excellent restaurants and still lined with old colonial buildings. You can take boat trips out to the Great Barrier Reef or visit the fascinating **Rainforest Habitat Wildlife Sanctuary▶▶**, and near by is a quaint seaside chapel with a view of the Pacific from behind the altar.

▶ Rockhampton
201B4

Australia's 'Beef Capital' lies inland up the Fitzroy River astride the Tropic of Capricorn. A note of distinction is struck by the elegant late 19th-century buildings and tropical trees and shrubs; the Botanic Gardens are among the finest in the country. Near by is the **Dreamtime Cultural Centre▶**, with displays on the life of Torres Strait Islanders and mainland Aborigines.

COAL FROM THE TROPICS
Queensland makes an important contribution to Australia's coal production. In the Bowen Basin and adjoining country inland from Rockhampton, the coal is extracted on the opencast system from huge pits and exported worldwide through Gladstone and special coal ports like Hay Point. Several of the mines (such as Blair Athol at Clermont) welcome visitors although bookings are essential (tel: 07 4980 2444).

223

Cruising home to Port Douglas harbour

Today, steak-happy Australians bite into about half the beef their country produces. The rest is exported, mostly to Canada, the USA, Korea and Japan.

The convicts and soldiers landed from the First Fleet seem to have subsisted on Bengal beef, meat from cattle brought out from India. Later, English breeds were introduced, and the colony became first self-sufficient, then embarrassed by the production of a surplus of beef that could not be consumed locally. Canning and refrigeration eventually solved this problem, enabling Australia to become a major exporter of beef; until the advent of the European Community, a good proportion of the roast beef sold in England started life in the Outback.

Together with sheep, beef cattle were the companions of the white settlers in their conquest of the continent's interior. Some treks were epic: In 1870 cattle thief Harry Redford drove 1,000 stolen animals from Longreach in Queensland to Outback South Australia, and in 1883–85 the Durack family overlanded 10,000 head of stock 5,000km (3,100 miles) from Queensland to the Ord River in the Kimberley, a journey lasting more than two years.

Farming on a grand scale Most of Australia's beef cattle are Herefords or Shorthorns, though there has been cross-breeding with Brahmans in an attempt to increase resistance to extreme heat and pests. Numbers peaked in the 1970s at some 33.5 million, but they have declined and today's total is about 20 million.

The majority of animals graze the arid lands of the middle and north of the country, their thirst slaked by the water pumped up from artesian wells. Because of the poverty of the pasture, stocking rates are incredibly low and cattle stations are huge, some of them the size of European countries. There are few fences to stop the beasts roaming freely until the time comes for round-up. From the stockyard they are taken by mammoth cattle trucks for the rest cure, which puts flesh on their often meagre bones before they are finally slaughtered.

THE ROUND-UP
At muster time the cattle are rounded up by a handful of cattlemen on horseback or, more likely these days, by men on motorbikes or in 4WD vehicles. On the vast stations of the far north helicopters are often used to locate the more wily creatures and drive them from their hiding places.

224

There is some prime beef cattle country in New South Wales

▶▶ Sunshine Coast   201A4

This fabled strip of fine beaches stretches north of Brisbane, for some 64km (40 miles) from Caloundra to Noosa Heads (see page 223) and is popular with those who enjoy a quieter alternative to the Gold Coast. Other attractions include the excellent **Underwater World**▶▶ at Mooloolaba, drives into the scenic hinterland (see page 208), and several major attractions around Caloundra. These include the popular **Australia Zoo**▶▶, home of the world-famous 'Crocodile Hunter' (Steve Irwin) and animals from many countries, and **Aussie World**▶, a large complex with Aboriginal objects, a native reptile display, rides for children and much more.

▶ Toowoomba   201A4

Toowoomba is Queensland's largest inland city, distinguished by wide, tree-shaded streets and attractive parks and gardens. Near by is the **Ravensbourne National Park**▶, rich in birdlife, and **Crows Nest Falls**▶, whose waters crash into a deep granite gorge.

▶ Townsville   201C3

Overlooked by its Castle Hill, Australia's largest tropical city is the outlet for an awesomely vast region stretching inland to Mount Isa and to the distant Gulf of Carpentaria. As well as a university city and a defence centre, it is an important stop-off for tourists heading north or embarking for the Barrier Reef. Townsville has botanic gardens dating from the late 19th century and a number of buildings from the same period, but visitors are likely to be drawn first and foremost to the complex known as the **Reef HQ**▶▶. Here, the glass tunnel of the world's largest coral reef aquarium enables you to marvel at the wonders of the reef without donning wetsuit or snorkel, an experience not to be missed. Almost equally vivid are the films shown on the 360-degree screen of the **IMAX Dome Theatre**▶, while the **Museum of Tropical Queensland**▶ has displays on natural, maritime and social history. Other attractions inlcude Magnetic Island (see page 219) and the interactive **Billabong Sanctuary**—the home of koalas, wombats, kangaroos, crocodiles and other native wildlife.

The Sunshine Coast encompasses dozens of sandy beaches and clear blue waters, like these at the popular resort town of Caloundra

CANE TOADS
Not far behind the rabbit in nuisance value, these unlovely creatures are an example of an introduced animal that has become more of a menace than the pest it was supposed to control. The toad was originally imported from Hawaii in 1935 in the hope that it would eliminate the beetles attacking the cane fields. Unfortunately, it has proved highly successful in reducing the numbers of many kinds of native animals, exuding toxins poisonous enough to kill most of its predators, apart from road vehicles; squashed toads are a common sight along Queensland highways. Unfortunately, cane toads are now spreading south into New South Wales.

Tasmania

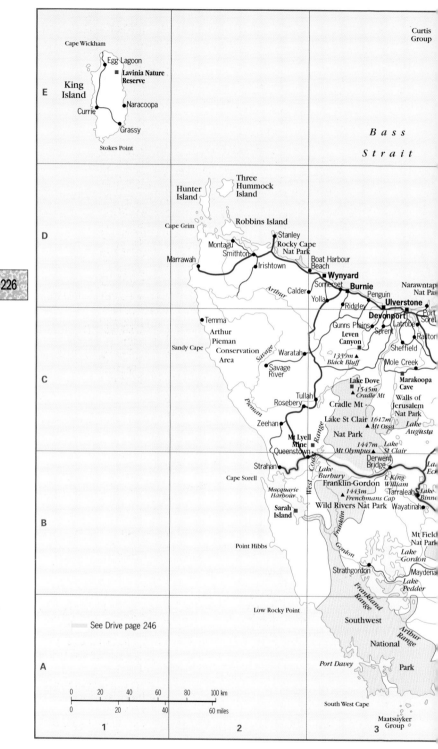

Curtis Group

E King Island

Cape Wickham

Egg Lagoon
■ **Lavinia Nature Reserve**

Currie

● Naracoopa

Grassy ●

Stokes Point

B a s s

S t r a i t

D Hunter Island

Three Hummock Island

Robbins Island

Cape Grim

Stanley ●
Rocky Cape Nat Park

Montagu ●
Smithton

Boat Harbour Beach

Marrawah ●

Irishtown ●

■ **Wynyard**

Somerset

Burnie ●

Narawntapu Nat Pa

Calder

Penguin

Arthur

Yolla

Ridgley ●

Ulverstone

Devonport ●

Port Sorel

Gunns Plains ●

Latrobe ●

Railton

Temma ●

Leven Canyon ■

Sprent ●

Arthur Pieman Conservation Area

Sheffield ●

C Sandy Cape

Savage

Waratah ●

1339m ▲ *Black Bluff*

Mole Creek ●

Marakoopa Cave ■

Savage River ●

Lake Dove ■
1545m ▲ *Cradle Mt*

Pieman

Tullah ●

Cradle Mt ~

Walls of Jerusalem Nat Park

Rosebery ●

Lake St Clair *1617m* ▲ *Mt Ossa*

Lake Augusta

Zeehan ●

Nat Park

West Coast Range

Mt Lyell Mine ■
Queenstown ●

1447m Lake Mt Olympus ▲ *St Clair*

Derwent Bridge

La Ec

Strahan ●

Cape Sorell

Lake Burbury

Franklin-Gordon

L King William

1443m ▲ *Frenchmans Cap*

Tarraleah

Lake Binne

Macquarie Harbour

Wayatinah ●

Wild Rivers Nat Park

B **Sarah Island** ■

Franklin

Mt Field Nat Park

Point Hibbs

Lake Gordon

Gordon

Strathgordon ●

Maydena

Lake Pedder

Frankland Range

Low Rocky Point ●

Southwest

Arthur Range

See Drive page 246

A Port Davey

National

0   20   40   60   80   100 km

Park

0   20   40   60 miles

South West Cape

Maatsuyker Group

1   **2**   **3**

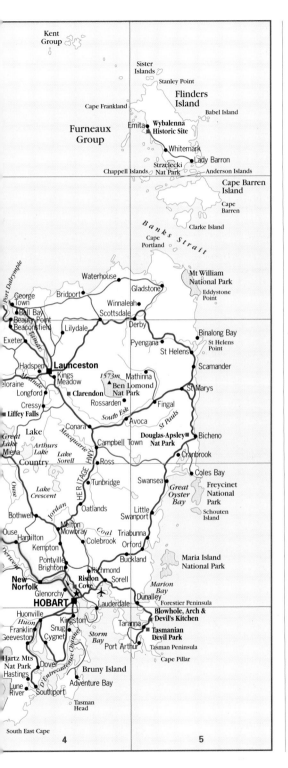

Tasmania

TASMANIA Early explorers assumed Van Diemen's Land (Tasmania's name until 1856) to be part of the mainland, but this error was rectified by George Bass and Matthew Flinders in 1798, and by 1804 Hobart had become the capital of the second British colony to be founded in Australia. This green and mountainous island's intimate links with mainland Australia are celebrated each summer by one of the world's great spectacles of sail, the Sydney–Hobart yacht race, an exciting sprint down the coast of New South Wales and across the often turbulent waters of Bass Strait.

SMALL IS BEAUTIFUL 'Tassie' certainly is different. It's a fully functioning state of the Australian Commonwealth, but everything else about it conspires to distinguish it from the rest of the country. Australia's smallest state, about the size of Ireland, Bavaria or West Virginia, it revels in a temperate climate that nourishes its forests with an abundant rainfall while providing blue skies often enough for the most fanatical of sun-worshippers. In the interior, stone-built bridges, villages, townships and Georgian mansions are set among neat farmlands where hedgerows and deciduous trees recall the early settlers' British origin. Beyond the pastures, vineyards and orchards rise rugged uplands, with clear lakes, rushing rivers and the continent's most magnificent mountain scenery, some of it still hardly explored. The three great national parks of Tasmania's southwest have been declared a World Heritage Area, a wilderness of high peaks, deep gorges and dense rain forest of unequalled grandeur.

VISITORS WELCOME Tasmania's relatively long history has left an exceptional wealth of old settlements and historic buildings, including what for many people is one of the most compellingly poignant of all Australia's

CONFLICT
In recent decades bitter conflict has arisen between narrowly conceived economic interests and environmental groups. Unique Lake Pedder was destroyed by the construction of a dam, but public opinion saved the Franklin and Gordon rivers from going the same way. At the moment, the environment seems to be winning.

228

NEXT
3 km

monuments to convict days, the Port Arthur complex in its evocative setting of sea inlet and parkland. Although small, Hobart, Tasmania's capital, is a city of European style and dignity, its deep-water harbour opening on to the broad River Derwent against a backdrop of splendid green hills and mountains.

Perhaps it is the island's small size and relative isolation that have made it a welcoming place, even by the exceptional standards of Australian friendliness. The pace of life is slow, the locals are usually happy to pass the time of day with a stranger; 'no worries' is even more applicable here than in the rest of the country. (This openness has not stopped Tassie's 485,000 or so inhabitants becoming the butt of jokes for other Australians.)

All this, together with generally lower prices, has made tourism an important bastion of the local economy, though surprisingly few foreigners make the short journey (240km/150 miles) from the mainland. Visitors' dollars are particularly welcome; the island faces the perennial problems of an economy based mostly on primary products, and its unemployment rate has remained consistently higher than that of the mainland. Agriculture thrives in the Midlands, the southeast and along river valleys, though orcharding was dealt a devastating blow when the European Common Market, seeking to trade primarily with other EC member countries, began to exclude Australian products. Mining of metal ores continues in the west, and around Queenstown has left a severely denuded landscape. Forestry is a major industry, though its scope is increasingly restricted by awareness that trees have an ecological and scenic value as well as a short-term financial one. Much wild nature survives to attract the visitor, however—around a third of the state is protected and there are 19 national parks.

It is easy to find historic corners in Launceston

229

TOURING ON FOOT
Anyone who comes to Tasmania should be prepared to walk, even if it is only for a short distance along the numerous marked boardwalks and nature trails. The adventurous can climb the more accessible peaks like Cradle Mountain, walk the five- to ten-day Overland Track or enjoy a guided adventure rafting down the Franklin River.

Lovely Freycinet National Park, on the east coast

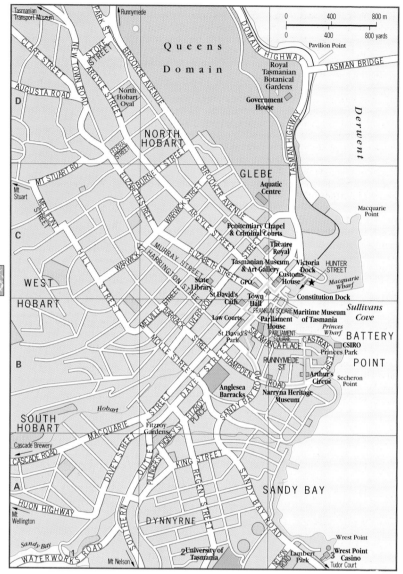

Hobart

The second oldest city in Australia (after Sydney), Hobart is the country's smallest state capital. It stretches out along both shores of the broad estuary of the River Derwent, one of the deepest harbours in the world, linked by the 103m (338-ft) span of the Tasman Bridge.

The old city, with its wealth of colonial buildings, clusters compactly around **Sullivans Cove** on the west bank, backed by wooded slopes rising to the often snow-capped peak of 1,271m (4,170-ft) high Mount Wellington. Its rich architectural heritage and incomparable setting make Hobart a delight to explore.

HISTORY The city was founded by Lieutenant-Governor David Collins in 1804, after the first attempt at settlement the previous year at Risdon Cove just upstream had failed. For many years the population consisted mostly of convicts and their overseers, though the harbour soon became a base for the whalers and sealers pursuing their prey in the Antarctic and South Pacific.

The city spread inland along the grid of streets leading uphill from the wharves and warehouses of Sullivans Cove, leaving a legacy of fine building; individual monuments abound, but it is the almost European quality of the townscape as a whole that makes Hobart virtually unique in Australia. Streets dominated by imposing Victorian structures like the town hall or the Theatre Royal of 1837 contrast with the delightful informality of the village suburb of **Battery Point**.

LAID-BACK LIFESTYLE Life in Hobart proceeds at an easy pace, leavened by the good temper of its inhabitants, who seem perfectly content to live in this least metropolitan of capital cities. This is not to say that amenities are lacking; today's Hobart has a full range of facilities to keep both locals and visitors stimulated and entertained. Its hotels and eating places equal those found elsewhere, while the casino complex at Wrest Point (Australia's first) introduced a note of sophistication when it first opened. Every Saturday the dignified sandstone warehouses of **Salamanca Place** look down on what is one of the country's liveliest and most vibrant open-air markets, while 31 December and the first week in January are enlivened by the excitement of the Sydney–Hobart yacht race. This is also the time of the Hobart Summer Festival, a month-long event which features entertainment and Tasmania's gourmet foods.

TASMANIA DISCOVERED
Dutch mariner Abel Tasman caught sight of an uncharted shore on 24 November 1642 and named it Van Diemen's Land after Anthony van Diemen, Governor-General of the East Indies. Mounts Heemskerk and Zeehan in the west of the island recall the name of his expedition's two ships. Unaware that his discovery was not part of the mainland, much less that it would eventually bear his name, he sailed off, leaving George Bass and Matthew Flinders to circumnavigate the island more than a century and a half later, in 1798. Evidence of French interest was provided by the scientific voyage of Nicolas Baudin in 1800, and it was partly in order to forestall any French designs on the island that Lieutenant John Bowen was sent to plant the British flag on the shores of Risdon Cove in 1803.

231

Hobart's spectacular harbour

Tasmania

CHURCH LANDMARKS
Hobart's churches were mostly built on prominent sites to act as city landmarks. With its commanding octagonal tower, St. George's Church at Battery Point is no exception, although its Egyptian-style stonework, fashionable during the early 19th-century when the church was built, is most unusual.

232

Hobart's Botanical Gardens have a wide range of native and exotic plants, including ferns and the native Huon pine

▶▶ Battery Point   *230B3*

Its commanding position on the promontory separating Sullivans Cove on the north from Sandy Bay to the south, made this a natural site for the battery of guns placed here in 1818 to protect the approach to the harbour. Today, Battery Point is a delightfully 19th-century townscape. There are cottages and villas, and little terraced houses looking (apart from their tin roofs) as if they have just been transplanted from late-Georgian England. Grander altogether is 'Narryna', a pilastered stone-fronted home of 1836, protected from the street by fine iron railings. Housing the **Narryna Heritage Museum▶**, the interior has been refurnished to evoke the more elegant side of life in 19th-century Hobart, and the gardens and outbuildings are being restored in the same spirit.

▶▶ Harbour area   *230B3*

The true spirit of Hobart can still be sensed along the wharves and quaysides of the harbour fronting Sullivans Cove. Fishing boats and pleasure craft tie up in the twin basins known as Victoria Dock and Constitution Dock, the name of the latter a reminder of the great day in 1853 when the granting of a constitution marked the end of convictism in Tasmania. A venerable Sydney ferry contrasts with trim trawlers and with the spick-and-span survey ship of the Commonwealth Scientific and Industrial Research Organisation (CSIRO) tied up at Battery Point to the south. The buildings around the harbour are some of the best in Hobart; they include the **Customs House**, now part of the museum, and the restored warehouses along Hunter Street.

▶ Maritime Museum of Tasmania   *230B3*
16 Argyle Street (tel: 03-6234 1427)
Open: daily 9–5. Admission: moderate
This small museum has a comprehensive collection of maritime memorabilia that shows how intimately Tasmania's history has been linked with the sea. The excellent displays focus on themes such as shipwrecks, the whaling industry, shipbuilding and trading.

▶▶ Mount Wellington   *off 230A1*
A visit to 1,271m (4,167-ft) high Mount Wellington is on most visitor's itineraries. Forming a dramatic backdrop to the city and often snow-capped in winter, this massive dolerite peak offers superb views of Hobart and its suburbs, the River Derwent and surrounding countryside. The mountain, just 20 minutes southwest of the city, is reached by a road constructed in 1937, and there are boardwalks, an interpretative shelter and many marked walking tracks.

▶ Royal Tasmanian Botanical Gardens   *230D3*
Queens Domain (tel: 03-6236 3075)
Open: daily 8–dusk. Admission: Gardens free, Conservatory and Botanical Discovery Centre donation
Sloping steeply down to the Derwent near the Tasman Bridge, these superlative gardens are studded with fine specimen trees and structures like the Fernery and the Conservatory. It's not just botanists who will be fascinated by the carefully maintained array of specifically Tasmanian plants, some still awaiting classification and some under threat of extinction.

▶▶ Salamanca Place   *230B3*
In the 1830s, the slopes of Battery Point were quarried away to build the wharf to the south of Sullivans Cove, and warehouses of magnificently solid appearance were erected to serve the ships docked there. Long since vacated, these superb sandstone structures have happily found new users: craft studios, galleries, restaurants, antique dealers and bookshops. Every Saturday morning the place is transformed by the arrival of an army of stallholders offering wares of incredible variety.

▶▶ Tasmanian Museum and Art Gallery   *230C3*
40 Macquarie Street (tel: 03-6211 4177 or 03-6211 4114—recorded information)
Open: daily 10–5. Admission free
Part of the museum complex, 40 Macquarie Street is supposedly the oldest continuously occupied building in Australia, having been erected in 1808. The natural history section has displays on Tasmanian creatures (and their ancestors, the megafauna of Pleistocene times that included 3m (10-ft) kangaroos and giant wombats); the Tasmanian Aboriginal Gallery tells the sad story of the island's Aborigines; and the colonial history's exhibits bring to life the decades dominated by convictism. The gallery is known for its colonial art; of more than passing interest are John Glover's depictions of Tasmania as a paradise populated by Aborigines, and the famous *Conciliation* by Benjamin Duterrau, marking the fateful meeting that led to their exile and death.

The 1837 Theatre Royal has been carefully restored

MOUNT NELSON
In clear weather both Mount Nelson and Mount Wellington (see main entry) give sensational views of Hobart in its incomparable setting. Mount Nelson (340m/ 1,115ft), the residences of the privileged dotting its slopes, rises over Sandy Bay; a little signal station still stands at the summit, though the signalman's house has become a restaurant.

Constitution Dock, mooring point for sailboats in the Sydney–Hobart yacht race

Walk

Sullivans Cove to Battery Point

This walk from Sullivans Cove begins at the north end of the harbour by the memorial commemorating the city's foundation in 1804, and links Hobart's waterfront to the charming old quarter of Battery Point.

The handsome old warehouses flanking Hunter Street contrast with the modern hotel overlooking Victoria Dock. Take time to enjoy the activity around the **harbour**. Inland are the old buildings of the **Maritime Museum** and **Tasmanian Museum and Art Gallery** whose entrance is around the corner in Macquarie Street, where you will also find the 1864 Town Hall and the tall-towered **General Post Office** of 1905. Now planted with fine trees and with a fountain at its heart, **Franklin Square** was once a parade ground fronting the first Government House. The intersection formed by Murray Street and Macquarie Street is unique

in Australia in having retained all its early buildings: **St. David's Cathedral**, the old **Law Courts** and a number of mid-19th-century terraced houses.

Opposite St. David's Park is a real curiosity, a royal-tennis court, still in use by players of what has become a very exclusive indoor game. The park itself, with its sweeping lawns and fine native and exotic trees, was once the city's cemetery. A memorial recalls John Woodcock Graves, author of the song 'Do ye ken John Peel?', who visited Tasmania in 1886.

Beyond Harrington Street is **Hampden Road**, the artery of Battery Point, with a pleasingly variegated collection of 19th- and early 20th-century buildings. To the left, **Arthurs Circus** is a delightful enclave of quaint 1840s and 1850s cottages, then Runnymede Street leads you to Princes Park, that descends abruptly to the 1818 **Signal Station**. Beyond Castray Esplanade, the CSIRO laboratories occupy the headland, but it is still possible to find a way through and enjoy views across the Derwent. The Esplanade leads back towards the middle of town. Inland from Princes Wharf is the magnificent set of 19th-century warehouses fronting **Salamanca Place**, a fine conclusion to your walk.

How to travel

By air Tasmania is linked to the mainland by services from airports such as Hobart, Launceston, Burnie/Wynyard and Devonport. There are also more limited charter services to airfields at Queenstown, Smithton and Strahan, as well as to Flinders and King Islands in Bass Strait. Regular internal flights between all these airfields are supplemented by local firms operating tourist flights; of these, the seaplane from Strahan to fly over Macquarie Harbour and Frenchman's Cap to land in the gorge of the Lower Gordon River cannot be recommended too highly.

By sea Bringing passengers and their vehicles from the mainland to Devonport, the *Spirit of Tasmania* ships operate services from Melbourne (daily) and Sydney (twice weekly in winter, three times weekly at other times). The journey takes around 10 hours (generally overnight) from Melbourne and 20 hours from Sydney.

By car Many visitors bring their own vehicle with them, but most rent a car once here. Distances are relatively short and roads mostly good, though logging trucks delivering their load can on occasion slow traffic down. The freedom you get from your own car is particularly useful in Tasmania where there is really only the skeleton of a public transportation system.

By train Although a narrow-gauge network still exists, passenger trains (except for enthusiasts' and tourist specials—see Devonport and Queenstown) stopped running many years ago.

By bus Every settlement of any size has its bus service, though its frequency may be strictly limited. There are two main operators: **Tasmanian Redline Coach Services**, who issue a 'Tassie Pass' that is valid for varying periods, and **TassieLink/TigerLine Travel**, which offers an 'Explorer Bus Pass' and provides sightseeing tours, as well as regular bus services that include links to wilderness areas. Buses operate to and from the major national parks and bushwalking start and finish points.

MORE HOBART ATTRACTIONS
Hobart's many other attractions include cruises on the River Derwent, a visit to The Lark Distillery, and tours of the famous Cascade Brewery, established in 1824 and Australia's oldest. Another excursion takes in the processes and produce of the Cadbury factory—a must for chocaholics—and you can also experience a ghost tour of the 1830s Penitentiary Chapel.

235

Prime bushwalking country

236

*The Franklin River is
ideal for exciting white-
water rafting*

National parks

Around a third of Tasmania is designated as national
parks, state reserves or marine reserves.

World Heritage Area The largest tract of protected land
(about 20 per cent of the island) was declared a World
Heritage Area in the 1980s, and stretches from Cradle
Mountain to South West Cape, taking in several parks and
reserves. One of the world's last great temperate wildernesses, its rivers, rain forest and mountain ranges can be
appreciated from the Lyell Highway or by flights and
cruises from Strahan, but its deepest secrets are only
revealed to the dedicated bushwalker or whitewater rafter.
Cradle Mountain–Lake St. Clair, the Franklin–Gordon
Wild Rivers and the Southwest national parks are all
described separately below, but the wild heart of the island
also includes the great natural amphitheatre of the **Walls of
Jerusalem** as well as the 'land of a thousand lakes', as the
Central Plateau area is sometimes known. Through it
passes the Lake Highway linking Deloraine with Melton
Mowbray, a fascinating and unhurried alternative to the
usual Heritage Highway for north–south journeys.

Beautiful and protected National park or reserve
designation applies to many of Tasmania's natural landscapes: beaches, caves, lakes and forests. The granite hills of
Freycinet National Park and the alpine moorlands, tree
ferns and waterfalls of **Mount Field** were the first to be listed
as national parks. In the northeast of Tasmania rise the bare
ridges of **Ben Lomond**, its ski slopes reached by a twisting
mountain road. The eucalypts of the island's last major tract
of dry sclerophyll forest are protected in the **Douglas-Apsley
National Park**. Most of the smaller islands have important
conservation areas: King Island's **Lavinia Nature Reserve** is
home to endangered orange-bellied parrots, while
Wybalenna Historic Site on Flinders Island preserves what
is left of the ill-fated attempt to re-settle the last of
Tasmania's full-blooded Aborigines (1831–47).

*The lush rain forest of
the Franklin-Gordon
Wild Rivers
National Park*

The spectacular alpine scenery of Cradle Mountain

►► Bicheno   227C5

Pronounced Bee-sheno, this east-coast town was once a base for sealers and whalers as well as a port for exporting coal from the nearby mines. Nowadays, its boats bring in crayfish and abalone, and it is popular with fishermen, artists and beach-lovers, attracted by the mild climate, beautiful beaches and superb scenery. The nearby **Douglas-Apsley National Park►** is excellent for walking.

► Bothwell   227B4

Pleasantly set in the beautiful Clyde Valley, Bothwell is of considerable historic interest, containing numerous colonial buildings and the **Australasian Golf Museum►**, as well as being the southern gateway to the Central Highlands.

► Burnie   226D3

Most visitors hurry through Tasmania's fourth largest town, but workaday Burnie makes an interesting contrast to the rather self-conscious rusticity of much of the island. There are industrial plants, the **Pioneer Village Museum►**, a cheese factory and magnificent gardens.

►►► Cradle Mountain–Lake St. Clair
National Park   226C3

Part of Tasmania's World Heritage Area, this national park of rugged mountain peaks and high moorlands is one of the great landscapes of Australia. The gateways to the park are **Cradle Valley►►►** to the north and Lake St. Clair near the Lyell Highway in the south. At Cradle Valley the spacious visitor centre introduces the national park to its public with displays, talks and events; a boardwalk penetrates the depths of the rain forest and gives a fine view of the Pencil Pine Falls. A number of shorter or longer walks radiate from the middle, but most visitors will want to press on up the gravel road to the north shore of **Dove Lake►►►**. Bearing in mind that the park generally receives no less than 261cm (103in) of rain each year and that most days will bring at least some, let us hope that you will see the unforgettable outline of Cradle Mountain reflected in the clear waters of the lake.

Source of the River Derwent, **Lake St. Clair►►►** is the deepest (almost 200m/650ft) body of freshwater in Australia and certainly one of the clearest. It is easy to escape into wild nature, even if it is only as far as Watersmeet, confluence of the Cuvier and Hugel rivers.

237

WEINDORFER'S 'HOME IN THE WOODS'
In 1912, deep in the primeval woodland, an Austrian called Gustav Weindorfer built himself a chalet of King Billy pine and named it 'Waldheim' (Forest Home). It was Weindorfer's enthusiasm that was largely responsible for the area's designation, first in 1922 as a scenic reserve, then later as a national park. Waldheim still stands, albeit rebuilt, but it has been joined by other forms of accommodation ranging from the comfort of Cradle Mountain Lodge to the more basic amenities of a campsite, all designed to harmonize with their incomparable surroundings.

THE OVERLAND TRACK
The route from Cradle Valley to Cynthia Bay on Lake St. Clair is 85km (53 miles) long. Walking it is perhaps the best way to enjoy the varied landscapes of the national park—wild open heaths, forested valleys, deep gorges, lakes and tarns, and rocky peaks, among them Mount Ossa (1,617m/5,305ft), Tasmania's highest point. The trek takes a minimum of five days, but it is better to allow longer (up to ten days) to avoid rushing and to be able to explore a little at will. There are huts along the way, but their capacity is limited and you should be prepared to camp, unless on a guided walk. Always check with a ranger before setting off into the wilderness.

With its abundant rainfall and mountainous terrain, Tasmania's potential for the generation of hydroelectricity is easily the greatest of all the Australian states.

GORDON DAM

One of the many Tasmanian dams

WATER POWER
Tasmania developed its hydroelectric power supplies partly so that it could expand its aluminium processing industry. It takes huge quantities of electricity to turn aluminium ore (bauxite) into the metal. Hydroelectric power is economical, so it must have seemed the ideal solution. Bell Bay, near George Town in northern Tasmania, was selected as a suitable site for an aluminium plant in the 1950s, lying as it does between the cheap power produced in Tasmania's interior and Queensland's large deposits of bauxite.

Early developments The first projects were built before World War I, but it was in the interwar period that grandiose visions were expounded of Tasmania becoming Australia's Ruhr, whose new industries would feed off cut-price electricity and solve the island's economic problems forever. Founded in 1930, the **Hydro-Electric Commission** (HEC) became a kind of state-within-a-state, Tasmania's biggest employer, capable of overcoming whatever technical challenges might be involved in wresting power from the trackless wilderness.

By the late 1960s, the HEC had its eye on glacial **Lake Pedder**, and was able to flood this unique ecosystem in the face of gathering protests from a growing minority of people concerned about the impact of hydro-power on the environment. The destruction of Lake Pedder was described by UNESCO as 'the greatest ecological tragedy since European settlement in Tasmania'.

Power or greenery The HEC's next major proposal was the transformation of the Franklin and Lower Gordon rivers and the surrounding temperate rain forest.

Tasmanian society was bitterly divided, but opposition was better organized this time in the shape of the **Tasmanian Wilderness Society**. A referendum showed the extent of concern, the construction site was blockaded, 1,500 arrests were made, and the project was finally halted in 1983 by a newly elected Federal Labor government anxious to cultivate the 'Green vote'. The wild rivers of the southwest, once described by Premier Gray as 'brown and leech-ridden', were saved; in the end it may well be that Tasmania will gain more from visitors drawn to one of the world's great wildernesses than from any extra wattage that might have been generated.

►► Deloraine
227C4

This attractive old township lies in fertile country on the Meander River halfway between Launceston and Devonport. In and around the town are any number of interesting colonial buildings, including Bonney's Inn (1831), and the area is famous for its arts and crafts.

► Devonport
226D3

Devonport is one of the principal gateways into Tasmania. It is here that the overnight *Spirit of Tasmania* vehicle ferries tie up after arriving from Melbourne and Sydney on the mainland; and there is an airfield, too. Just inland from the 1889 lighthouse, on the rocky promontory of Mersey Bluff, is the **Tiagarra Aboriginal Cultural Centre►**, with excellent displays on the life led by the first Tasmanians, as well as a walk around the collection of over 250 enigmatic carvings that are a feature of the area. Other places to visit include the Maritime Museum and excellent Devonport Gallery and Arts Centre, as well as National Trust-listed 1916 **Home Hill►**, the white house that belonged to Joseph Lyons, the only Australian to have been both State Premier and Prime Minister. Outside the town to the west is the terminus of the **Don River Railway►** where you will find Tasmania's largest collection of veteran locomotives and rolling stock. Vintage trains run regularly, and the museum is quite fascinating.

►► Flinders Island
227E5

Guarding the eastern end of Bass Strait, Flinders is the largest island of the Furneaux Group. Once the abode of sealers, then the site of G. A. Robinson's ill-fated Aboriginal refuge (see page 241), it is a lonely place, with an agricultural and fishing population of just over 1,000. But there is an abundance of wildlife (including the famed muttonbirds—see panel), as well as splendid white beaches contrasting with the rugged granite outcrops of the **Strzelecki National Park►►**.

MUTTONBIRDS
The islands of Bass Strait are the breeding ground of the short-tailed shearwater or 'muttonbird', a rather nondescript brown bird that migrates in a clockwise direction around the Pacific. The nestlings, chubby creatures rich in fat and oil, are bred in meter- (yard-) long burrows, then left to their own devices by their parents. This made them easy prey for the Aborigines, who harvested them in huge numbers.

239

The beautiful Liffey Falls to the south of Deloraine are well worth a visit

The beautiful beaches of the unspoiled Freycinet Peninsula

HUON PINES
Easily identified because of its feathery foliage and trailing branches, this is a uniquely Tasmanian conifer, occurring mainly in the wetter areas of the far southwest. Extraordinarily slow-growing, it is also extraordinarily long-lived; some specimens still alive may go back to the pre-Christian era. Respect for age meant little in colonial days, when the 'piners' prized the Huon for its exceptionally resilient timber. Today, it is valued more for its beauty when converted into ornamental objects such as fruitbowls, and has become a mainstay of the Tasmanian woodcraft and souvenir industries.

►►► Franklin–Gordon Wild Rivers National Park
226B3

This glorious tract of rain forest, wild rivers and rugged uplands extends from the sheltered waters of Macquarie Harbour to the Lyell Highway, forming the central portion of Tasmania's World Heritage Area. Its highest point (1,443m/4,734ft) is the spectacular quartzite monolith known as **Frenchmans Cap►►►**, whose sheer eastern face drops an alarming 300m (985ft). Experienced bushwalkers can make the round trip to Frenchmans Cap in four to five days; others must content themselves with views from the highway. The adventurous can go whitewater rafting on the **Franklin River**, a rewarding trip through gorges and over rapids that takes more than a week to reach the little jetty near the mouth of the Gordon. This point is also accessible by launch from **Strahan** or, more excitingly, by a seaplane that drifts down the gorge to land gracefully on the limpid, brown stream. A boardwalk leads deep into the damp and mossy forest where, among the tree ferns, Huon pines and Antarctic beeches, a waterfall crashes into its pool.

►► Freycinet National Park
227B5

Approached via the fishing township of Coles Bay, the Freycinet Peninsula extends southwards into the azure waters of the Tasman Sea towards little Schouten Island. With its backbone of pink granite peaks, immaculate beaches of white sand, forests of eucalyptus, and wealth of wildflowers and wildlife, this was one of Tasmania's first national parks and has long been popular with locals.

► Geeveston
227A4

Forests and mountains are the main attractions around this old timber town, 61km (38 miles) southwest of Hobart. The **Tahune Forest AirWalk►►** takes visitors almost 600m (1,970ft) up over the forest, scenic **Arve Road Forest Drive►►** has picnic areas and lookouts, and farther inland **Hartz Mountains National Park►►**, a rugged alpine region, is part of the state's World Heritage Area.

In December 1642, the crew of Captain Abel Tasman's Heemskerk *heard voices calling in the forest fringing their landing place near Cape Sorell on the west coast. The owners of the voices failed to show themselves; perhaps they had premonitions about the fate of their descendants at the hands of later colonists.*

Aboriginal rock carving in Devonport (above)

Early conflict Tasmanian Aborigines were quite distinct in character from their mainland counterparts. Thinly spread around the island, they totalled an estimated 4,000 to 5,000 at the start of white settlement in 1803. The usual complicated relationships arose between the two races. There was plenty of cooperation; Aboriginal women in particular gave freely of their skills in the seal hunts that formed such a staple of Tasmania's early economy. But conflict inevitably grew, in spite of earnest professions of concern on the part of white officialdom; the natives' living patterns were disrupted as their hunting grounds were turned into fenced-off farmland. In the face of the destruction of their way of life, some resisted violently, to be met with more effective violence by the settlers. Within 20 years, Aboriginal numbers had been halved.

LOST BUT NOT FORGOTTEN
The disappearance of Tasmania's full-blooded Aborigines is often characterized as genocide, though the processes involved were essentially the same as those at work on the mainland. Many people of mixed blood remain, however.

241

The end of a race Ironically, the most fateful episode was reconciliation. The undoubtedly well-meaning George Augustus Robinson journeyed around the island, making contact with all remaining Aborigines, winning their trust and persuading them to settle in a kind of Christian protectorate on Flinders Island. Here, religion, homesickness, disease and the loss of their land and culture gradually destroyed those who had survived thus far. The last full-blooded Tasmanian Aborigine, a woman called Truganini, died in 1876.

John Glover's 1836 painting, The Last Muster

Hazards aplenty presented themselves to early mariners negotiating the uncharted coastal waters of the great southern continent: vicious storms, unexpected islands, hidden reefs and no hope of succour from land. Even the skilful navigator Captain Cook ran aground on the coral of the Barrier Reef, though his disciplined crew was able to refloat the stranded Endeavour *on the next high tide.*

242

CAPTAIN BLIGH

Often called 'Bligh of the Bounty', the naval officer William Bligh (1754–1817) was also known to his contemporaries as 'Breadfruit Bligh', since one of his tasks had been to introduce that fruit to the West Indies. Strict to the point of harshness and beyond, he had the misfortune to suffer not one, but two mutinies. The first, aboard the *Bounty*, is part of popular history. The second rebellion against his rule, in 1808, was led by the officers of the 'Rum Corps', as the New South Wales Corps was disparagingly known. Bligh, as Governor of the colony, had attempted to curb what he saw as the Corps' excessive influence over the colony's commercial life (including a monopoly on the sale of spirits, particularly rum). A *coup d'état* was staged, and Bligh was arrested by his own guards. Undaunted, he refused to return to London as a prisoner, and was later completely cleared by the British government of any misconduct.

A Dutch disaster The first to experience the inhospitable aspect of Australia were the Dutch, who preferred an indirect but rapid route to their possessions in the East Indies. This led them around the Cape of Good Hope, then swiftly eastwards with the winds of the Roaring Forties filling their sails, turning north before reaching the coast of Western Australia (which they named Nova Hollandia—New Holland).

However, not every captain made the turn in time, among them Commander Pelsaert; his vessel the *Batavia* was named after the chief town of a Dutch colony (now Jakarta) and her cargo included carefully chiselled stones for the town's main gate. On a fateful morning in 1629, the *Batavia* ran aground on one of the low coral atolls of the Houtman Abrolhos Islands, some 60km (37 miles) off Geraldton. Crew and passengers struggled ashore, rescuing what provisions they could.

Once a degree of organization had been established, Pelsaert set sail for distant Java in a small boat to fetch help. His departure gave the signal for the mutiny that had long been brewing aboard the *Batavia*. Disaffected sailors and marines set up a reign of terror; rape and casual murder became the order of the day, though some were able to flee to nearby islands and hold out against the mutineers. By a miracle, Pelsaert's frail craft managed to survive the ocean voyage. He returned to the Houtman Abrolhos Islands and arrested the rebels, executing the ringleaders on the spot.

This improbable tale is told in full detail in the **Western Australian Maritime Museum** at Fremantle. Many of the *Batavia's* timbers have been recovered, and enough of them put together again to make up her stern, a most impressive and evocative sight. Here, too, the ready-cut masonry from her hold has been erected to form the classical gateway once intended to adorn the approach to the city of Batavia.

The Shipwreck Coast The *Batavia* was not alone in coming to grief off Western Australia, but it is probably Bass Strait between Victoria and Tasmania that has been responsible for the greatest number of Australian shipwrecks. In the 19th century, the stormy waters of the Strait formed the principal approach for vessels making for eastern Australia; King Island was only provided with a lighthouse in 1861, and until then ships

would hug the coast of the mainland, and they frequently ran aground on hidden rocks.

The most famous wreck occurred in 1878, when the iron clipper *Loch Ard* foundered on rocks near Port Campbell in Victoria. Of the 50 or so souls aboard, only two survived. Apprentice-boy Tom Pearce clung to a lifeboat and was swept into a narrow cliff-bound gorge. Badly knocked about, he was nevertheless able to rescue young Eva Carmichael, whom the current had also brought into the gorge. Leaving the semi-conscious Eva on the beach, Tom somehow managed to climb the cliff and stagger for help. Only four bodies were recovered from the *Loch Ard*; their graves are in the nearby cemetery, one of several containing the remains of victims of this treacherous shore, which bears the name of the Shipwreck Coast.

Between Princetown in the east and Port Fairy in the west, the historic Shipwreck Trail has markers and information boards indicating the locations of 25 wrecks of coasters, cargo boats and ships full of hopeful immigrants. At Warrnambool is **Flagstaff Hill Museum**, with a **Loch Ard** sound and light show and many objects recovered from these wrecks, and there are other maritime displays at the **Old Cable Station Museum** at Apollo Bay.

The rugged cliffs of Cape Raoul on the Tasman Peninsula (above)

243

The waters around Flinders Island are treacherous (below left)

Precious objects have been salvaged from the 17th-century Batavia *(above and below)*

244

An old windmill attracts visitors in Launceston

► George Town   227D4

With historic sites, unspoiled beaches and gentle scenery, George Town stands near the mouth of the beautiful Tamar River, the 56km (35-mile) long combined estuary of the North Esk, South Esk and Macquarie rivers. One of the oldest towns in Australia, it has several early colonial buildings, including the elegant Georgian house known as **The Grove►**, built in the early 1830s for port officer and magistrate Mathew Curling Friend.

► Hamilton   227B4

A useful stopping point on the way to the west from Hobart, this charming little place of sandstone cottages and a few larger buildings never realized the ambitions of those early colonists who predicted a great future for it. The town offers quality arts and crafts, and trout fishing in the Clyde River.

►► King Island   226E1

Far out in the stormy waters of Bass Strait, verdant King Island has an enviable reputation for dairy products and gourmet foodstuffs, though much of the 58km (36-mile) long island consists of unpopulated bushland teeming with wildlife. Visit **Lavinia Nature Reserve**, an important bird habitat; go walking, fishing, scuba diving or horseriding; or sit back and sample the island's famous produce, including cheeses, crayfish and tender beef.

►► Launceston   227C4

At the point where the North and South Esk Rivers combine to form the beautiful Tamar, Tasmania's second city is the unofficial capital of the northern part of the island. It has retained much of its Victorian and Edwardian heritage and offers continuous pleasures to the urban stroller.

The city was laid out on the usual grid pattern of streets, some of which, like the Mall and Civic Square, have been pedestrianized. In Civic Square is an intriguing sculpture of Tasmanian wildlife, including tail-biting thylacines (tigers—see panel opposite), as well as the 1830 **Macquarie House►**, housing a restaurant. Near by are other reminders of the past—the Queen Anne-style post office and the Italianate town hall, while the Old Umbrella Shop in George Street, now the National Trust store and information centre, has its authentic 1860s frontage.

Other central attractions include the Design Centre of Tasmania and its superb Tasmanian Wood Design Collection, and the **Queen Victoria Museum and Art Gallery**, in a prettily landscaped setting and rivalling Hobart's Tasmanian Museum for the interest of its collections and innovative displays. There is another section of the Queen Victoria Museum across the river at **Inveresk**. This area, once the site of railway workshops, is also the setting for parkland, walkways, bicycle paths, the Academy of the Arts, cafés and restaurants.

Don't miss a visit to **Cataract Gorge Reserve**, a superb riverside recreation area containing a rocky canyon crossed by a chairlift and suspension bridge, parkland, walking tracks and a swimming pool.

There is a great deal to see and do around Launceston. Scenic cruises operate on the Tamar; and there are many excellent wineries, such as the acclaimed Pipers Brook Vineyard, to visit on both banks of the river. A collection of fine country houses graces the hinterland.

Finely proportioned **Franklin House▶** near Kings Meadow would not have been out of place in the countryside of Georgian England, while **Clarendon▶**, behind its restored Ionic portico, is on a grander scale altogether, one of the great rural residences of Australia, overlooking its grounds and the South Esk River with a haughty eye.

▶ Maria Island National Park   227B5

Reached by ferry from near Triabunna, this east-coast island will appeal to those seeking scuba diving, snorkelling, walking and undisturbed nature. Though pre-dating Port Arthur as a penal settlement—convicts were first sent to Maria Island in 1825—and once exploited for various commercial purposes, the island is now an oasis of tranquillity, with an abundant wildlife enjoying total freedom from motor vehicles. Visitors will need to take their own staples, as there are no stores or electricity on the island.

▶ Mole Creek   226C3

The limestone rock around this tiny township is riddled with caves, protected within the World Heritage-listed Mole Creek Karst National Park. Two of the more spectacular are **King Solomon Cave▶**, where a limestone formation recalls the biblical monarch, and the longer **Marakoopa Cave▶**, watered by two streams and lit by glow-worms.

...AND TIGERS
Devils are not an endangered species, but the thylacine or Tasmanian tiger is officially extinct. What is generally thought to have been the last of the race died in Hobart Zoo in 1936, ironically within three months of tigers being declared a protected species. Thylacines were wolf-like marsupials, with stripy backs and wide-opening jaws; their liking for sheep and lambs didn't endear them to farmers. The question of whether the tiger lives on in seclusion somewhere has divided Tasmanians into believers and sceptics; there have been plenty of supposed sightings, but no definite proof.

245

The delights of Cataract Gorge in Launceston'

Drive

Through the wilderness on the Lyell Highway ('The Wild Way')

See map on pages 226–227.

Allow a day for this trip from Hobart across the mountain core of Tasmania on the Lyell Highway to the remote fishing port and resort of Strahan.

The first section of the drive runs up the valley of the Derwent, through well-tamed countryside of fields and

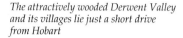

The attractively wooded Derwent Valley and its villages lie just a short drive from Hobart

farms and pleasant towns like English-looking **New Norfolk** and historic **Hamilton**. More rugged country follows, with evidence of Tasmania's highly developed hydroelectricity industry; signs point down side-roads to dams, there is a surprise of a canal, and huge pipelines snake up and down the slopes. After the resort of **Tarraleah**, formerly a village for Hydro-Electric Commission workers, and Lake Binney, the forest thins and gives way to button-grass plains.

Shortly before Derwent Bridge, **Mount Olympus** comes into view; this grand mountain overlooks the clear waters of **Lake St. Clair**, which is reached via a short side-road from Derwent Bridge. The ranger station at Cynthia Bay marks one end of the famous Overland Track between here and Cradle Mountain (see page 237). The recommended time to complete this famous trek is at least five days, but there are plenty of shorter hikes in the area—from a nature stroll on the level to relatively easy day walks.

One of the world's great mountain roads, the Lyell Highway was only completed in 1932. There are several, mostly well-marked stopping points along the way between Derwent Bridge and Queenstown: King William Saddle marks the watershed between the Derwent and Franklin–Gordon river systems, while Surprise Valley Lookout has a view of the imposing 1,443m (4,734-ft) peak, **Frenchmans Cap**. A number of short walks can be made from the Franklin River Bridge along part of the Frenchmans Cap Walking Track to the Donaghy's Hill Wilderness Lookout, to the Alma River Crossing or to Nelson Falls.

The road then skirts round the flooded valley bottom of the HEC's **Lake Burbury**, a mountain scene of incomparable grandeur. Equally extraordinary, albeit in an utterly different way, are the denuded and devastated uplands around the mining town of **Queenstown**. The final leg of the journey is along the twisting but otherwise uneventful road through the forest and down into the little port of **Strahan**, one of the best starting points for further exploration of the wild western coast or the rain forest, rivers and mountains of the interior.

▶ New Norfolk   *227B4*

Upstream from Hobart, the Derwent Valley recalls the landscapes of southern England, with rolling hills as a background to a countryside of big deciduous trees and, around historic New Norfolk, hop fields and their attendant oast houses, one of which is now a museum.

▶ Oatlands   *227B4*

Extension of British power into the interior of Tasmania was marked by the construction of highways; one of the most important was the road now known as the Heritage Highway, linking Hobart with Launceston. A small number of strategic settlements were planned along the route, of which Oatlands was one. First surveyed in 1832, the township is no bigger than a modest village, but nevertheless boasts a number of fine colonial buildings.

▶▶▶ Port Arthur Historic Site   *227A5*

Port Arthur (tel: 1800 659 101). Open: buildings and tours daily 9–5, grounds daily 8.30–dusk. Admission: expensive

Port Arthur is the most evocative of all the places recalling the days of the convict system, offering an experience that no visitor should miss.

The first prisoners were brought here in 1830 to fell and saw the wood that formed the basis of the first of Port Arthur's thriving industries. As more convicts and those sent to guard them arrived, a vast range of activities began to flourish. In time, the place became virtually self-sufficient, supporting a population of more than 2,000, housed, working and worshipping in an array of handsome brick and stone structures. To make officials feel more at home, touches of Old England were contrived; oaks and elms were planted and blackbirds released to sing from their branches.

Both extreme cruelty and weird forms of enlightenment were features of life at Port Arthur. Floggings were given for the slightest offence, but it was also here, at Point Puer, that juvenile delinquents received the first compulsory education in the world. By the mid-19th century, the desire to reform rather than punish led to the building of the Model Prison, whose inmates spent their time in total 'solitary'. However, madness rather than rehabilitation was the frequent outcome.

With the end of the convict era, Port Arthur was closed down as a penal colony, and in the late 19th century became a tourist attraction. Many of the 40ha (99-acre) site's more substantial structures remain. They include the 1842 building used as a penitentiary from 1857, guard towers, the sinister Model Prison and, looking down on the site from landward, the fine church with tower and pinnacles. If you're staying overnight in the area, an evening 'Ghost Tour' is recommended.

NEW NORFOLK FIRSTS
The town boasts a number of 'firsts'. The 1823 St. Matthew's, the island's oldest surviving church; the 1815 Bush Inn, Australia's oldest continuously licensed inn (you are likely to come across several of these); and the Salmon Ponds and Museum of Trout Fishing at nearby Plenty, where a batch of ice-packed eggs survived the long trip from England to hatch into the first trout and salmon to swim the streams of the southern hemisphere.

247

THE TASMAN PENINSULA
In addition to Port Arthur, the peninsula has many other attractions, including the dramatic coastal scenery of Tasman National Park. At Taranna there's wildlife at the Tasmanian Devil Park while sea kayaking, scuba diving and scenic seaplane flights are also available.

Port Arthur, a legacy of the convict era

Eroded hills behind Queenstown

THE GENTLEMAN BUSHRANGER
Filled with 'a deep and concentrated hatred of that power which was undeservedly persecuting me', the Irish convict Martin Cash and two companions braved the sharks in about 1840 by swimming to freedom from the Tasman Peninsula. Recognized in the course of an overconfident visit to a lady friend in Hobart in 1843, Cash shot a police constable while being re-arrested, but avoided execution and eventually settled down to the life of a farmer.

LEATHERWOOD HONEY
One of Tasmania's most distinctive trees is *Eucryphia lucida*, or leatherwood, a characteristic species of the temperate rain forest. For many years, local beekeepers have hung hives in the vicinity of leatherwoods in order to take advantage of the bees' liking for the nectar-rich flowers that bloom in spring and early summer. The nectar is converted into a particularly delicious honey.

▶▶ **Queenstown**   226B2

There are few scenes of industrial devastation quite as spectacular as the bare highlands surrounding this mining town in western Tasmania. For visitors approaching from the east, the contrast between the vast tracts of luxuriant rain forest to either side of the Lyell Highway and the denuded slopes around Queenstown could not come as more of a surprise.

The miners who came here from the early 1880s onwards were prospecting for gold, but it was not long before copper extraction began. The copper smelters' insatiable demand for fuel was responsible for the wholesale clearance of the rain forest all around, while their emissions poisoned any regrowth that might have occurred. With no vegetative cover to bind it together, the soil was quickly washed away by the abundant rainfall (up to 300cm/118in yearly), leaving deep gullies and bare rock faces which are now being slowly revegetated.

Copper and silver are still processed around Queenstown and, not surprisingly, most of the area's attractions are mining related. There are one-hour surface tours of the **Mount Lyell Mine**, as well as longer underground tours that explain many aspects of modern mining. You can also take a spectacular chairlift ride, visit the **Eric Thomas Galley Museum**, with its extraordinary collection of old photographs, and ride the steam trains of the restored 1896 rack and pinion **West Coast Wilderness Railway** to Strahan.

▶▶ **Richmond**   227B4

For Tasmanians, tiny Richmond embodies all that is 'historical' about their island. Along the township's main street are a number of fine buildings from colonial days, some of them dating from the 1820s. Two attractions in particular capture the imaginations: the 1825 jail, erected to house convicts engaged in public works, and the convict-built bridge, Australia's oldest road bridge, which was constructed from local sandstone between 1823 and 1825. More recent attractions include the **Richmond Food and Wine Centre▶▶**, the **Richmond Maze▶** and **Old Hobart Town▶**, a historical model village.

▶▶ Ross 227C4

Driving the Heritage (Midland) Highway is an almost continuous pleasure; the well-engineered road speeds you past a background of blue hills through a countryside that was remade by the early settlers into a facsimile of the England they had left behind.

Ross is one of a number of strategic settlements established along the route in the 1820s to act as staging posts for travellers. The town is particularly famous for its bridge, dating from 1836 and decorated with extraordinary carvings, and charming old stone buildings. Also worthwhile is a visit to the **Tasmanian Wool Centre**, which sells fine woollen products in addition to revealing the history of both Ross and the state's sheep and wool industry.

▶ St. Helens 227C5

The most populous place on Tasmania's east coast, this fishing port is also the most popular, with visitors outnumbering locals five to one in the height of summer. As well as attracting game fishermen, the port makes an excellent base from which to explore the magnificent northeastern coast, particularly in **Mount William National Park**, where there are splendid sand dunes, white sandy beaches and bands of Forester kangaroos.

▶▶ Southwest National Park 226A3

Forming the southern part of Tasmania's World Heritage Area, this is a vast wilderness of mountain ranges rising from virgin forest of southern beech and Huon pine, with great sweeps of buttongrass, glacial lakes and wild rivers, and a wonderful coastline of deserted sandy beaches.

Until quite recently only the more hardy type of bushwalker, mountaineer or canoeist ventured into this remote and unspoiled world. But in the late 1960s, Tasmania's Hydroelectric Commission drove a road deep into the heart of the area, a harbinger of its plan to drown Lake Pedder beneath an artificial water body 20 times its size. The outrage this provoked, not only among conservationists but also in a wider public, turned out to be in vain; Lake Pedder, with its unique fauna and beach of brilliant sand, was duly submerged in the interest of generating marginally cheaper electricity.

However, the advantage for the visitor is that it is now possible to taste, if not fully experience, something of one of the world's last temperate wildernesses by driving up the Gordon River and Scotts Peak roads. Both routes give spectacular views of Lake Pedder in its rugged setting.

For those wishing to penetrate even further into the wilderness, the Port Davey and South Coast tracks from Scotts Peak Dam to Cockle Creek will take a minimum of ten day's strenuous trekking; there are several specialist tour operators in the area.

▶ Stanley 226D2

On its peninsula protruding into Bass Strait, this historic port and holiday town nestles beneath its famous landmark, The Nut; properly known as **Circular Head**, this 150m (490-ft) basalt outcrop is the core of an ancient volcano. Walk or take the chairlift to the breezy summit for terrific views along the northwest coastline.

FISHING IN TASMANIA

Fishing is one of Tasmania's main industries, and fresh seafood—including oysters, scallops, abalone and crayfish—is one of the delights of eating out on the island. There are plenty of opportunities for visiting enthusiasts to go sea fishing, particularly for tuna and marlin from the little ports of the east coast. But it is probably the lure of the trout that will most entice the angler from abroad. Ever since trout spawn from England was successfully hatched in 1864 in the famous Salmon Ponds hatchery near New Norfolk, the island's unpolluted streams and lakes have proved an excellent habitat for both brown and rainbow trout.

249

Catching tuna the 'kind' way off the Tasman Peninsula

▶▶ Strahan   226B2

A small settlement on the inland sea of Macquarie Harbour, Strahan (pronounced 'Strawn') grew to export the wood and minerals of the western interior. Its main functions today are fishing, forestry and tourism. The **West Coast Visitor Centre▶▶** on the waterside has deliberately tendentious displays on the history of the area.

Hell's Gates, as the narrow and dangerous entrance to Macquarie Harbour is known, were so named because they guarded **Sarah Island▶▶**, from 1822 to 1834 one of Britain's most brutally administered penal colonies. Strahan is also the base for exploring the Gordon River, either by cruise boat or by seaplane.

▶ Swansea   227B5

From the beach there is a wonderful prospect across Great Oyster Bay towards the Freycinet Peninsula. One of the best places to stay along the 'Sun Coast', Swansea has such visitor attractions as the 1885 Bark Mill, now housing the Wine and Wool Centre, a coastal reserve and vineyards.

▶ Wynyard   226D3

Linked to the mainland by flights from its own airport, this fishing port at the mouth of the Inglis River is a useful gateway to Tasmania's scenic northwest coast. To the east are the wonderful white sands of **Boat Harbour** and **Sisters Beach**, as well as the rugged coastline of the **Rocky Cape National Park▶▶**. The headland at Table Cape has a lighthouse and offers splendid views.

▶ Zeehan   226C2

Named after one of Abel Tasman's ships, this isolated mining town in Tasmania's far west saw both boom and bust before beginning a modest recovery, brought about by the reopening of a tin and nickel mines in recent years. Legacies of early 20th-century prosperity based on silver-lead extraction include the **Gaiety Theatre** and the **West Coast Pioneers Memorial Museum▶** (see panel).

RAILWAY DELIGHTS
The West Coast Pioneers Memorial Museum in Zeehan is home to a comprehensive array of local exhibits and an acclaimed collection of minerals, as well as locomotives built long ago in Glasgow, Manchester and Germany. These were shipped across the seas to work the ore trains of one of the most mineralized areas on earth.

250

Georges Bay at St. Helens is a bustling fishing port

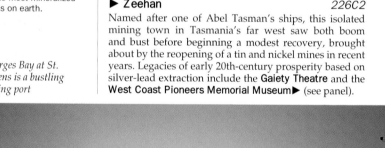

Travel Facts

Arriving and departing

All visitors to Australia must have a valid passport and, with the exception of New Zealanders, a visa or an Electronic Travel Authority (ETA). These must be obtained in advance from an Australian High Commission, Embassy or Consulate: visit their website for more information (www.immi.gov.au).

However, visa requirements can change, so check with the Australian Embassy in your home country in good time before your visit.

By air Most Australian state and territory capitals (not Canberra or Hobart) have direct connections with destinations abroad, and there are also international flights into the Gold Coast and Cairns. There are many opportunities for combining a visit to Australia with stop-overs at intermediate destinations or by buying a 'round-the-world' flight. Many visitors will want to take advantage of the option of arriving at one point in Australia and departing from another.

Fares vary considerably among the many international airlines serving Australia and also fluctuate according to the time of year; the cheapest fare may turn out to be a false economy if it involves an exhaustingly long flight with several stops. Check prices and availability well in advance through a travel agent or reputable media outlets; there are some real bargains, particularly in charter flights.

By sea Those with time to spare can travel to Australia on board the cruise ships of operators such as Cunard, P & O and Princess Cruises, albeit at a price. Some freighters carry a small number of passengers too, but this is by no means a cheap alternative.

Camping

Discounting the risks of insect nuisance, Australia is a wonderful land in which to camp, not just because of its climate but also because of its exceptionally generous and varied provision of places to pitch your tent, both on the edge of town and in the bush. Site equipment is generally good, and might include electricity hook-up, hot and cold water, showers, lavatories and laundry. Some sites offer pre-erected tents, and many more have caravans and cabins for rent. Operators range from town councils to commercial chains or national park authorities. Some of the national park sites are 'basic'. Camping on your own in the wild is also possible, but discretion is advisable; check that your presence will not annoy a landowner.

Motor-homes (RVs) are increasingly popular with Australians exploring their own country in a leisurely way. Such a vehicle should be considered by visitors who intend to spend most or part of their time touring rather than visiting city sights.

Car breakdown

When renting a car, check with the company about breakdown arrangements; they will normally organize help for you. Membership of a motoring club in your own country will in many cases give you access to the facilities of the various state motoring

252

253

The Overland Train runs between Adelaide and Melbourne

clubs (contact the National Roads and Motorists Association for details).

Breaking down in the Outback is potentially fatal and should be avoided by making sensible preparations for your journey (see Driving tips on pages 257–258).

● National Roads and Motorists Association, 74–76 King Street, Sydney, NSW 2000 (tel: 02-8741 6000 or 13 1122), www.nrma.com.au

Car rental
Vehicles are available from a range of agencies (both international and local) at most airports as well as from towns and cities. To rent a car you will need to have a valid driver's licence and normally be aged over 21 years old. One-way rentals between major cities are possible, but they are not cheap. The total cost of the rental will consist of the basic daily or weekly rate plus various additions like collision damage waiver and possibly a kilometrage charge. Choice of vehicle is very much an individual matter; 4WDs and motor-homes are available, and you might find a six-cylinder home-grown saloon more restful for long trips than a zippy

hatchback. There may be restrictions on taking a vehicle over a state boundary, into 'country' or 'remote' areas, or driving it on unsealed roads.

Climate
As befits a country which is also a continent, Australia has a variety of climates. Visitors from the northern hemisphere will, of course, need to get used to the seasons being reversed (summer is from December to February, and winter is from June to August).

In general terms, the southwest and southeast (southwest Western Australia, much of South Australia, Victoria, much of New South Wales, Australian Capital Territory and Tasmania) are best in spring and summer (September to April), though midsummer temperatures can get very high. Winters can be dull and rainy, but frost is rare except at high altitudes where snow can be expected—as in the Snowy Mountains.

Many Australians enjoy a winter holiday, between May and October, in the Red Centre or northwestern Western Australia, where there is

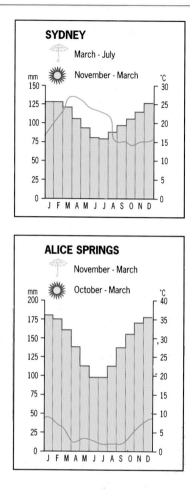

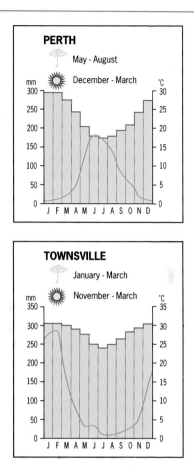

likely to be an endless succession of bright sunny days with temperatures around the 20–25°C (68–77°F) mark, although nights will be cold in the Centre. Summer in these areas can be unbearably hot, with temperatures of 45°C (113°F) not uncommon.

The subtropical and tropical parts of the country (much of Queensland, Western Australia and the Northern Territory) are at their least comfortable in the wet season (Nov–Apr), with heavy rainfall and high humidity. This is also the season when box jellyfish make the sea unsafe for swimmers and roads may be washed away. In the dry season (May–Oct) conditions are much more pleasant, with warm (but not too hot), sunny days.

Crime

Political and business scandals and the activities of a well-organized criminal underworld dominate the headlines in Australia more than casual offences. Thieves and muggers do exist, but Australian cities are still among the safest in the world, and no more than the normal precautions against pickpockets and car thieves are usually necessary.

Customs regulations

Personal effects can be brought into Australia without payment of duty, as can 250 cigarettes (or 250g of tobacco product) and 2.25 litres of alcohol (beer, wine or spirits), and gifts up to a value of A$900. There are tough penalties for importing weapons, drugs (soft or hard), and for attempting to bring in quarantinable

CONVERSION CHARTS

FROM	TO	MULTIPLY BY
Inches	Centimetres	2.54
Centimetres	Inches	0.3937
Feet	Metres	0.3048
Metres	Feet	3.2810
Yards	Metres	0.9144
Metres	Yards	1.0940
Miles	Kilometres	1.6090
Kilometres	Miles	0.6214
Acres	Hectares	0.4047
Hectares	Acres	2.4710
Gallons	Litres	4.5460
Litres	Gallons	0.2200
Ounces	Grams	28.35
Grams	Ounces	0.0353
Pounds	Grams	453.60
Grams	Pounds	0.0022
Pounds	Kilograms	0.4536
Kilograms	Pounds	2.205
Tons	Tonnes	1.0160
Tonnes	Tons	0.9842

MEN'S SUITS

UK	36	38	40	42	44	46	48
Europe	46	48	50	52	54	56	58
US	36	38	40	42	44	46	48
Australia	92	97	102	107	112	117	122

DRESS SIZES

UK	8	10	12	14	16	18
France	36	38	40	42	44	46
Rest of Europe	34	36	38	40	42	44
US	6	8	10	12	14	16
Australia	8	10	12	14	16	18

MEN'S SHIRTS

UK	14	14.5	15	15.5	16	16.5	17
Europe	36	37	38	39/40	41	42	43
US	14	14.5	15	15.5	16	16.5	17
Australia	36	37	38	39	41	42	43

MEN'S SHOES

UK	7	7.5	8.5	9.5	10.5	11
Europe	41	42	43	44	45	46
US	8	8.5	9.5	10.5	11.5	12
Australia	7	7.5	8.5	9.5	10.5	11

WOMEN'S SHOES

UK	4.5	5	5.5	6	6.5	7
Europe	38	38	39	39	40	41
US	6	6.5	7	7.5	8	8.5
Australia	6.5	7	7.5	8	8.5	9

articles, particularly plants that may be disease-carriers.

The import of wildlife souvenirs sourced from rare or endangered species may be either illegal or require a special permit. Before purchase you should check your home country's customs regulations (www.customs.gov.au).

Visitors with disabilities

Conscientious efforts are made by public bodies and by the tourist industry to make life easier for people with disabilities. Modern buildings and facilities are designed to high standards of accessibility for wheelchairs, pedestrian crossings have audible signals when the way is clear and many national parks have specially laid-out trails. Visitors with disabilities will find Australia one of the most helpful countries to visit in this respect, although it would be wise to give advance notice when planning your itinerary. NICAN (PO Box 407, Curtin, ACT 2605, tel: 02-6285 3713; www.nican.com.au) will provide detailed information about facilities.

255

Renting a 4WD is sensible if you wish to journey into the Outback

Domestic travel

By air As you would expect in such a huge country, Australia is very air-minded, with more than 75 per cent of all long-distance journeys made by plane. There are few places that cannot be reached by aircraft, whether in the cabin of a large modern jet or riding the thermals next to the pilot during an Outback joyride or remote-area flight.

Internal airlines are now deregulated, with benefits to passengers in terms of value for money and availability of services. In addition to a number of regional airlines, the main carriers are Virgin Blue and Qantas Airways; the latter offers discounted fares and air passes to visitors from abroad. Visitors using Qantas to get to Australia can usually make discounted internal flights with that company. Check what offers are available when planning your journey and bear in mind that flights fill up quickly during the main holiday periods. Student discounts are available, as are cheap standby and internet fares. Smoking is not permitted on internal flights.

● Virgin Blue Airlines, PO Box 1034, Spring Hill, QLD 4004 (tel: 07-3295 2296 or 13 6789) www.virginblue.com.au
● Qantas Airways, 203 Coward Street, Mascot, NSW 2020 (tel: 02-9691 3636 or 13 1313) www.qantas.com.au

By car Australia's roads are of variable quality. In the metropolitan areas around the great cities they compare well with those anywhere in the developed world, while in remote areas they may consist of dirt tracks liable to disappear altogether in the Wet. Motorways are confined to relatively short sections leading out of the major cities. Most main roads have two lanes, although some still consist of a single strip of bitumen with gravel shoulders and others are made entirely of gravel. The asphalting of main roads in Western Australia and the Northern Territory has made it possible to drive right round the country 'on the bitumen'.

Having your own vehicle offers the usual flexibility and independence, but you should never forget the great distances likely to be involved in any extensive driving around Australia.

Trams are a convenient way of getting around town

Australia is great for backpackers

The great majority of the popular tourist areas can be reached in an ordinary car; a 4WD vehicle will only be necessary if you are contemplating driving extensively on dirt roads in the Outback—for example, on one of the South Australian 'tracks' (see page 143). A motor-home or similar vehicle offers even more flexibility.

An alternative to renting a vehicle (see Car rental on page 253) is to buy one, especially if your stay is going to be a long one. Second-hand vehicles can be obtained in the usual ways (dealers, auctions and so on), or from your fellow visitors. Noticeboards in backpackers' lodges may be a useful source of information here, and in some places dusty motor-homes displaying hopeful prices are lined up on the street. The stress of disposing of your vehicle at the end of your stay can be alleviated by purchasing it from a dealer who offers a guaranteed buy-back, although obviously this will not be the cheapest way.

By train A rail map of Australia seems incomplete, with huge areas empty of any trace of tracks. However, the big cities are all accessible by train, and some Australian rail journeys count among the great railway experiences of the world. Among them are the three-night transcontinental trip aboard the *Indian Pacific* between Sydney (or Adelaide) and Perth across the Nullarbor Plain, and the famous *Ghan*, an exciting foray from Adelaide (with services connecting here from Sydney and Melbourne) to Alice Springs and Darwin. These, together with trains like the fast Tilt Train (Brisbane–Cairns), are a relaxing way of appreciating the vastness and diversity of Australia in great comfort (ingeniously luxurious sleeping compartments, gourmet dining, attentive service and showers). Other rail services are best developed in the east and southeast of the country, with extensive metropolitan networks around Sydney, Melbourne, Brisbane and Adelaide. Europeans, used to frequent services, may be surprised to find that trains may run only once a day. Speeds are less impressive than standards of comfort.

Visitors can buy good-value rail passes (only outside Australia), including the **Austrail Flexipass**, permitting widespread travel and stopovers within a six-month period, and the **East Coast Discovery Pass**, for travel between Melbourne, Sydney and far north Queensland (www.railaustralia.com.au).

Driving tips
Road safety is improving and Australia has a fairly low road fatality rate compared to vehicle numbers. Drinking and driving were once very much part of ordinary life, and may still be so in Outback areas, but police crackdowns are having a useful effect in major cities. The legal permitted limit for alcohol is 0.05 per cent blood alcohol level in all states and territories.

In principle, Australians drive on the left and overtake on the right. However, this may not immediately be obvious on a multiple-lane highway where many drivers prefer to stay in the right-hand lane, impervious to the traffic passing them on the left. Driving down the central strip of bitumen on a part-surfaced highway is acceptable, but it can turn into a test of nerves as oncoming traffic approaches. The monstrous 'road trains' to be encountered in Western Australia, Queensland and the Northern Territory expect you to give way to them at all times and have no strategy for coping if you don't. Overtaking a road train which may be 50m (165 feet) or more long and throwing up clouds of dust can be tricky; if you can't see a long way ahead, give up altogether.

Driving on unsurfaced roads requires special skills that you are unlikely to have time to acquire. It's best to avoid them or take very special care. At dawn, dusk and at night many animals stray on to the highway; 'roo bars' are not fitted to vehicles just for macho reasons but to minimize the damage that a collision with a large kangaroo can cause. Don't drive in the country at night if you can avoid it.

Road signs in Australia differ from those in other countries, but their meaning is clear!

Speed limits are a maximum of 40–60kph (25–37mph) in urban areas and 100/110kph (62/68mph) elsewhere unless indicated; seatbelts must be worn in both front and back seats. Some road signs are peculiar to Australia, but most of these will be immediately understandable to visitors. On some stretches of winding road, long lay-bys (turnouts) are provided which should be used by slow traffic to enable other drivers to overtake, but remember that the overtaking traffic has the right of way.

Visitors from abroad must have a valid driver's licence with a translation if the licence is not in English or, better still, an international driving licence in addition to a valid driver's permit. Fuel is sold (by the litre) in unleaded, premium unleaded and diesel grades. Filling stations are fairly numerous but tend to have restricted opening hours in remote areas.

Adequate preparations must be made for driving in the Outback. The vehicle must be in good condition and it is sensible to carry a selection of spare parts, including an emergency plastic windscreen. Enough fuel and water (4 litres/8 pints of drinking water a day) to see you through is essential. On some routes you may be required to complete a police form, giving your itinerary and estimated time of arrival.

In case of breakdown it is vital that you stay in or near your vehicle as it will offer shade and protection, and will also be much more visible than if you are on your own.

Electricity
Current emerges at 220–240 volts AC from Australian sockets, these being of a three-pin type unlike those used in most countries. You will either need to bring an adaptor for your appliances, or you can simply fit them with an Australian plug on arrival. Most shaver points are of the universal type.

Embassies and consulates
● British High Commission, Commonwealth Avenue, Yarralumla, Canberra (tel: 02-6270 6666).
● Canadian High Commission,

The best way to explore Simpsons Gap is on foot, but go prepared

Commonwealth Avenue, Yarralumla, Canberra (tel: 02-6270 4000).
● New Zealand High Commission, Commonwealth Avenue, Yarralumla, Canberra (tel: 02-6270 4211).
● United States Embassy, 21 Moonah Place, Yarralumla, Canberra (tel: 02-6214 5600).
   The USA is also represented in Sydney, Melbourne and Perth and the UK in the same cities, as well as Brisbane, Adelaide and Hobart.

Emergency telephone numbers
For police, ambulance or fire brigade services, dial 000.

Health
No special health precautions are required before visiting Australia. Standards of hygiene are high, and food and drinking water are safe. Sunburn is a common hazard; wear a broad-brimmed hat, a shirt with a collar and apply plenty of sunscreen.
   Free hospital medical treatment under the Australian Medicare scheme is available to visitors from the United Kingdom, Republic of Ireland, New Zealand and other countries, although ambulance charges and the cost of medicines must be met. For UK visitors, Medicare also covers the bulk of the cost of a visit to a doctor. Visitors from most other countries will need full medical insurance. Dental treatment is paid for in full (www.medicareaustralia.gov.au).

Language
The peculiarities and delights of Australian English are widely known in the English-speaking world, not least through the efforts of the humourist Barry Humphries, creator of Dame Edna Everage, Sir Leslie Patterson and Barry McKenzie.
   Having some affinities with Cockney, the rather nasal Australian accent is, however, quite distinctive and is spoken without any real regional variation throughout the whole country. Differences in speech are likely to be more a matter of occasion or class; the types you might meet in a country bar would probably pour scorn on a 'posh' Australian city voice. In turn, their speech might present difficulties to a non-native English speaker who has learned the 'standard' language. Many Australians speak with a rising intonation which makes their sentences sound like questions.

Enjoying a beaut barbie down under with a few mates

The Australian vocabulary contains a number of words of Aboriginal origin (mallee, didgeridoo and kangaroo), as well as plenty of invented terms to describe characteristic Australian phenomena (Outback, bottlebrush and bloodwood), and not a few English words that have changed their original meaning (creek means river, mountain ash is a kind of eucalyptus and mob is a group of people or animals). But the real joy of 'Strine' (Australian) is its slang. Anything that can be reduced to a more or less affectionate diminutive is ('barbie' means barbecue, 'cossie' is a swimming costume, and 'garbo' is a garbage collector), and there are any number of quirky inventions (dunny is an outside toilet, while bludger is a scrounger) that may be the remnants of the slang of Georgian England. A lot of slang is sexual, scatological or connected with heavy drinking. Terms evocative of throwing up after a binge are plentiful ('to chunder', 'have a liquid laugh', 'speak into the big white telephone'). Insults are common, sometimes delivered with

affectionate intent ('you old bastard'); a university course instructed 'New Aussies' on how to swear acceptably.

Although Strine is based on British English, the biggest influence on it today is American English—in terms of pronunciation ('quarder' instead of quarter), of vocabulary ('take on board' and 'yuppie'), and in spelling ('program'), although the ALP has used the American spelling of 'Labor' since its foundation in the late 19th century.

The following is a highly selective list of words, phrases and abbreviations a visitor might encounter:

ABC	Australian Broadcasting Corporation
ACT	Australian Capital Territory (Canberra area)
The Alice	Alice Springs
ALP	Australian Labor Party
ANZAC	Australian and New Zealand Army Corps
arvo	afternoon
barbie	barbecue
beaut	wonderful
big smoke	the city

billy	tin for brewing tea
bloke	man
bludger	scrounger
blue	a fight, a redhead
bottle shop	liquor store
bush	countryside
bushranger	outlaw
BYO	bring your own (drink to a restaurant)
cask	wine-box
chook	chicken
chunder	to vomit
crook	ill, no good
dag, daggy	tangled dirty wool at rear end of a sheep, used abusively (or affectionately) of persons or things
daks	trousers
dead set	correct, spot on
dinkum	genuine
drongo	a slow-witted person
Dry	the dry season
dunny	outside lavatory
fossicking	hunting, as in for precious stones
galah	a kind of parrot, an idiot
garbo	garbage collector
g'day	good morning, good afternoon, hello
greenie	conservationist
hoon	hooligan
international	foreign (as in 'international visitors')
interstate	anything to do with the other Australian states ('he's interstate' means the person referred to is away from his home state)
journo	journalist
larrikin	rogue, hoodlum
mate	universal greeting
mob	group of persons or animals, for example sheep

mozzie	mosquito
Never-Never	the far-off Outback
ocker	Australian male of crude manners
pokie	poker machine, fruit machine
Pom, Pommie	English person
postie	postman or woman
property	farm
rort	rowdy party or scam
RSL	Returned Servicemen's League
salties	saltwater crocodiles
semi-trailer	articulated truck
servo	service/petrol station
she'll be right	it'll all be OK
shout	a treat, as in buying a round of drinks
slab	24-pack of beer
smoko	work break
station	extensive farm
stingers	jellyfish
strides	trousers (pants)
swag	gear or personal belongings
ta	thank you
tea	evening meal
thongs	flip-flops
tucker	food
uni	university
ute	pickup truck
Wet	the rainy season
wowser	puritan, killjoy
yakka	work
youse	plural of you

The best food in town next to the river!

261

Media
Newspapers and periodicals A glance inside a newsagent (newsstand) will convince you that Australians are great readers. The array of publications includes national and regional daily broadsheets, lurid tabloids with screaming headlines, local newspapers and magazines dealing with every conceivable interest.

The Australian was founded in 1964 by media tycoon Rupert Murdoch to perform the role of a national general interest daily paper, supplementing the less popular *Australian Financial Review*. Regionally produced papers like the Melbourne *Age* and *Sydney Morning Herald* are considered superior by many readers, although visitors from abroad may find coverage of non-Australian news rather selective (but check how well your home paper covers Australian affairs).

The Abbey Church at New Norcia, Western Australia

Australian tabloids, like most such newspapers, are not of the highest standard. Most ethnic groups have dailies or weeklies in their own languages.

Television and radio Radio recalls newspapers in its divisions. The ABC (Australian Broadcasting Corporation) has countrywide coverage and offers by far the best mix of broadcasting, with excellent news coverage and magazine broadcasts. In contrast are the numerous commercial stations, many of which run on a shoestring, plugging out pop music, phone-ins, traffic reports and similar time-fillers. In addition, there are a number of special interest and community radio stations.

Commercial television suffers from a surfeit of advertising and a reliance on imported programmes (though this may enable foreign visitors to catch up on the popular soaps). ABC TV maintains high standards generally and some of the schedule of SBS (Special Broadcasting Service, not available over the whole country) is devoted to ethnic minorities in their own languages.

Money matters
The Australian currency was decimalized in 1966, when sterling (pounds, shillings and pence) was replaced by dollars and cents (100¢ = $1). Coins come in 5¢, 10¢, 20¢, 50¢, $1 and $2 denominations, and notes (bills) in amounts of $5, $10, $20, $50 and $100. These are made of durable polymer. You can take as much money as you want into and out of the country, although amounts over A$10,000 must be declared to Customs.

Changing money is rarely a problem, with plenty of exchange bureaux at places where tourists congregate, as well as at banks. Bank hours are usually 9.30–4 Monday to Thursday, and 9.30–5 on Friday. Traveller's cheques made out in Australian dollars are likely to be dealt with more speedily. Credit cards are widely in use, but may not be particularly welcome in remote areas or in small shops. ATMs are plentiful.

Australia Day celebrations, Sydney

National holidays

Day

- New Year's — 1 January
- Australia Day — 26 January (commemorates the landing of the First Fleet in 1788)
- Labour Day — Varies from state to state (commemorates achievement of the 8-hour day)
- Good Friday
- Easter Monday
- Anzac Day — 25 April (commemorates Gallipoli landings in 1915)
- Queen's Birthday — Second Monday in June (except WA)
- Christmas Day — 25 December
- Boxing Day — 26 December (28 December in South Australia)

Opening hours

Shops These are generally open 9–5 (or 5.30) Monday to Friday and 9–4 on Saturday (and Sunday in the capital cities), with late-night shopping on Thursday or Friday until 8 or 9. Corner shops keep longer hours and also open on Sundays.
Offices Open Monday to Friday 9–5.

Museums and galleries Usually closed on Christmas Day and Good Friday, with some also closed on Anzac Day. Major institutions are usually open 9 or 10–5 daily. Many smaller museums open only at weekends or during school or public holidays, so the best advice is to check before you set out.

Pharmacies

Called both pharmacies (as in the US) and chemists (as in the UK), these dispense a range of medicines and products which will probably be familiar to you. Many are open long hours, and you will find a 24-hour service in big cities. Prescriptions must be written by an Australian-registered doctor. Prices of pharmaceuticals are fairly high.

Places of worship

Most religions are represented in Australia, although outside the big cities only the major Christian denominations have places of worship. The Roman Catholic Church and the Anglican Church have roughly the same number of adherents; their cathedrals were once among the dominant buildings of the cities. The Uniting Church was formed in 1977 as a union of Methodists and Congregationalists. Islam was introduced by the Afghan camel drivers in the 19th century and there are now many mosques throughout the country. Synagogues

Fly-fishing is a popular pastime at London Lakes in Tasmania

and Buddhist temples are concentrated in the state capitals.

Police

Australia has both state and federal police, the latter (the AFP) being responsible for the investigation of major crimes, intelligence work and anti-terrorist activities, as well as for policing the Canberra area (ACT).

The men and women in blue are usually extremely helpful to visitors from abroad, but don't expect any special privileges if you break the law (see Driving tips on pages 257–258). In the unlikely event that you are arrested, you must give your name and address, but are then entitled to say nothing until you have contacted a friend or legal representative. In this situation, the best thing to do is to ask to be put in touch with your consul (see Embassies and consulates on pages 258–259).

Post offices

The offices of Australia Post are to be found in cities, suburban areas and all over the country, often combined with a general store in smaller places. Larger offices have a wide range of services available to the public like fax and electronic post.

Services are reasonably efficient. Airmail letters can arrive in the UK or US after a few days, provided the cor-rect rate has been paid and the letter or postcard is clearly addressed. A parcel sent by sea mail to Europe will undergo an interminable sea voyage. An alternative to paying the full air-mail charge in this case is to send it Economy Air which should ensure its arrival in the UK or US after about two weeks. Post offices usually have a good range of stationery and pack-aging material for sale, and *poste restante* facilities are also available. Australia's rectangular mail boxes are painted red with a white stripe or yellow for the special express post service.

Public transport

The sprawl of low-density suburbs surrounding major cities is not con-ducive to the operation of an effective public transportation system, and Australians have become very depen-dent on cars for work, shopping and recreational trips. However, city public transportation services based on bus, rail, tram (Melbourne) and ferry (Sydney, Perth and Brisbane) are generally extensive, frequent and efficient, albeit a heavy drain on the public purse. Most systems offer spe-cial deals that are likely to be of interest to a tourist (day tickets covering the whole network, reduced fares for travel outside the rush hour and so on). Further details are in the travel sections within each chapter. For long-distance transport, see Domestic travel on pages 256–257.

Student and youth travel

There are relatively few official concessions for young visitors from abroad. Accommodation is provided by countless hostels and backpackers' lodges. Membership of your national Youth Hostels Association may get you the occasional discount and also entitles you to use Australian youth hostels. Long-distance travel by bus is not expensive, and hitch-hiking is easier than in many countries, although not entirely without danger. The noticeboards in lodges and hostels are good sources of information on car-sharing and on what is on offer in terms of meals, excursions and entertainment.

Working holidays are available for the 18–30 age group and are very popular. STA Travel, a specialist in youth travel, may be able to help here, as well as with other travel arrangements; they have offices in the UK and the US, as well as in Australia (www.statravel.com.au).

Taxes

Australia has a Goods and Services Tax (GST) of 10 per cent (included in prices). Departing visitors may be able to claim a refund for GST on goods purchased in Australia (check www.customs.gov.au).

Telephones

The public telephones of Telstra are easy to find in most places. Long-distance or STD (Subscriber Trunk Dialling) calls can be made from most telephone boxes and international calls from boxes designated ISD (International Subscriber Dialling). Most machines take phone or credit cards. Local calls have no time limit, while interstate calls are relatively inexpensive given the distances involved. Cheap rates apply 7pm–midnight (4pm–midnight on Saturday). Hotels frequently double the cost of any calls that are made from your room.

To call an Australian number from overseas, dial the international access code, the country code for Australia (61), the local code (minus the initial 0), then the subscriber's number. To call an overseas number from Australia, dial the international access code (0011), the country code, the local code (minus its initial 0), then the subscriber's number. It is also worth working out the time disparity between home and Australia (see below).

Time

The enormous width of Australia has resulted in the creation of three time zones. Eastern Standard Time (EST) applies to New South Wales, ACT, Victoria, Tasmania and Queensland; Central Standard Time (CST) applies to South Australia and the Northern Territory; and Western Standard Time (WST) applies to Western Australia. CST is half an hour behind EST, while WST is two hours behind. Daylight saving (Summer Time) is practised in all states except Queensland, the NT and Western Australia from late October to late March, when clocks are advanced by one hour. Eastern Standard Time is 10 hours ahead of Greenwich Mean Time.

Paddling on Bondi Beach

Tipping
Hotel porters can be tipped at your discretion. Service charges are not normally added to restaurant bills; given exceptionally good service you might leave a tip of 10 per cent.

Toilets
Australian cities are well provided with (usually clean) public lavatories. City plans often make a point of identifying their location.

Visitor information
Tourism Australia provides information on individual states as well as on the country as a whole from its website and offices abroad (see opposite), while each state has its own Tourism Board with headquarters in its own state capital, and offices in some other state capitals.

Other useful sources of information are motoring organizations, which give free maps to visitors who belong to allied organizations abroad, and visitor centres or offices of the various state national parks services.
Tourism Australia:
● New Zealand
Level 3, 125 The Strand, Parnell, Auckland (09 915 2826).

● UK
Australia Centre, Australia House (6th floor), Melbourne Place/Strand, London WC2B 4LG
(020 7438 4601).
● USA 6100 Center Drive, Suite 1150, Los Angeles, CA 90045
(310/695-3200).
● www.australia.com is a useful website for general information.

Other useful websites
Brisbane Marketing:
www.ourbrisbane.com
Australia Capital Tourism:
www.visitcanberra.com.au
Tourism Northern Territory:
wwwtravelnt.com
South Australian Tourism Commission:
www.southaustralia.com
Tourism Queensland:
www.queenslandholidays.com.au
Tourism Tasmania:
www.discovertasmania.com
Tourism Victoria:
www.visitvictoria.com
Tourism Western Australia:
www.westernaustralia.com
Tourism New South Wales:
www.visitnsw.com.au

The Devils Marbles in the Northern Territory

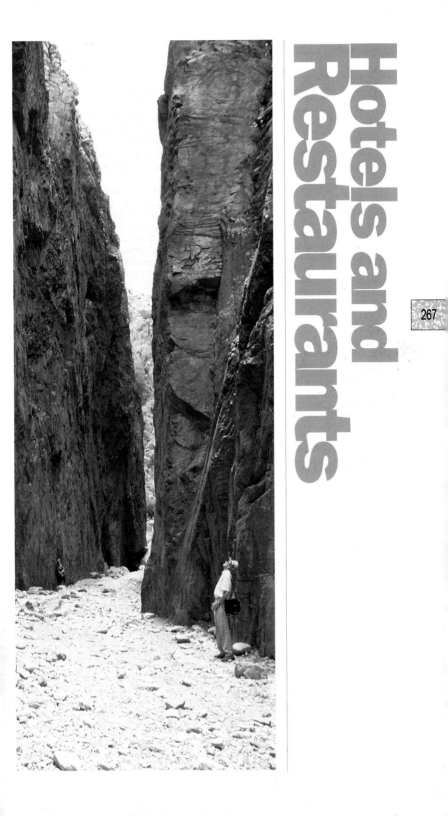

Hotels and Restaurants

HOTELS

Australia's accommodation ranges from some of the world's finest and most luxurious hotels through motels, 'units' (equipped apartments), 'hotels' (which may be the most basic of inns), to backpackers' hostels. You are unlikely to have difficulty in finding somewhere to stay, although it's advisable to book ahead during peak seasons (Jul–Sep in northern Australia and Dec–Feb generally). Prices compare well with those in other developed parts of the world, and discounts can often be obtained for internet bookings or longer stays or if you use hotels in a particular chain.

The following recommended hotels have been divided into three price categories:

($) = inexpensive
($$) = moderate
($$$) = expensive

SYDNEY

Aarons Hotel ($$)
37 Ultimo Road, Haymarket
tel: 02 9281 5555, fax: 02 9281 2666
www.aaronshotel.com.au
Better than average moderate accommodation near Darling Harbour and Chinatown.
Blue at Woolloomooloo Bay ($$$)
The Wharf, 6 Cowper Wharf Road, Woolloomooloo
tel: 02 9331 9000, fax: 02 9331 9031
www.tajhotels.com
This expensive and very stylish boutique hotel is located in a heritage-listed wharf, between the city centre and Kings Cross.
Bondi Beachouse YHA ($)
Corner of Fletcher and Dellview Streets, Bondi Beach
tel: 02 9365 2008, fax: 02 9365 2177
www.yha.com.au/hostels
This excellent budget hotel at Bondi Beach is not just for backpackers: it caters for everyone, with shared, single, double and family rooms, some with private bathrooms.
Cremorne Point Manor ($–$$)
6 Cremorne Road, Cremorne Point
tel: 02 9953 7899, fax: 02 9904 1265
www.cremornepointmanor.com.au
A charming old mansion with 30 rooms just a short ferry ride from the middle of town. Good value.
Crowne Plaza Coogee Beach ($$)
242 Arden Street, Coogee
tel: 02 9315 7600, fax: 02 9315 9100
www.ichotelsgroups.com
On the waterfront of one of Sydney's most popular beaches, this is an excellent alternative to a city hotel.
De Vere Hotel ($$)
44–46 Macleay Street, Potts Point
tel: 02 9358 1211, fax: 02 9358 4685
www.devere.com.au
A good-value hotel in the Kings Cross area. Self-contained studio apartments are also available.
Harbour Rocks Hotel ($$–$$$)
34 Harrington Street, The Rocks
tel: 02 8220 9999, fax: 02 8220 9998
www.harbourrocks.com.au

This medium-sized hotel, with 55 rooms, is in in the heart of The Rocks.
Hilton Sydney ($$$)
488 George Street
tel: 02 9266 2000, fax: 02 9265 6065
www.hiltonsydney.com.au
Totally renovated in 2005, Sydney's famous Hilton now offers almost 600 tastefully decorated rooms and suites, a swimming pool, spa, health club and some excellent dining options.
Holiday Inn Potts Point ($$)
203 Victoria Street, Potts Point
tel: 02 9368 4000, fax: 02 8356 9111
www.ichotelsgroups.com
In the heart of the Kings Cross dining and nightlife precinct, the Holiday Inn has good facilities, a restaurant and bar, and excellent city and harbour views.
Hotel Altamont ($$)
207 Darlinghurst Road, Darlinghurst
tel: 02 9360 6000, fax: 02 9260 7096
www.eighthotels.com
Reasonably priced modern accommodation in a former Georgian mansion, close to Kings Cross.
Hotel Ibis Darling Harbour ($$)
70 Murray Street, Pyrmont
tel: 02 9563 0888, fax: 02 9563 0899
www.accorhotels.com.au
Good value accommodation on the western side of Darling Harbour. The hotel has good views, as well as its own restaurant and bar.
Hotel Inter-Continental Sydney ($$$)
Corner of Bridge and Phillip streets
tel: 02 9253 9000, fax: 02 9240 1240
www.sydney.intercontinental.com
Partly housed in the restored 1851 Treasury Building, the hotel is close to Circular Quay and the Opera House.
The Hughenden Boutique Hotel ($$)
14 Queen Street, Woollahra
tel: 02 9363 4863, fax: 02 9362 0398
www.hughendenhotel.com.au
A charming old Victorian manor house that offers good-value accommodation in the trendy Paddington/Woollahra area. Breakfast is included.
Manly Pacific Sydney ($$–$$$)
55 North Steyne, Manly
tel: 02 9977 7666, fax: 02 9977 7822
www.accorhotels.com.au
This hotel is on the beachfront in Sydney's seaside resort of Manly, only a short ferry trip from the city.
Mercure Hotel Sydney Airport ($$)
20 Levey Street, Wolli Creek
tel: 02 9518 2000, fax: 02 9518 2002
www.mecuresydneyairport.com.au
Just five minutes from Sydney Airport, the Mercure is the ideal choice for travellers with early flights. There are more than 250 comfortable rooms and suites, a restaurant and good leisure facilities.
Metro Apartments on Sussex ($$)
132–136 Sussex Street
tel: 02 9290 9200, fax: 02 9290 3032
www.metrohotels.com.au
Fully serviced one-bedroom suites and apartments in two convenient central locations.

The Observatory Hotel ($$$)
89–113 Kent Street
tel: 02 9256 2222, fax: 02 9256 2233
www.observatoryhotel.com.au
Close to The Rocks area, this is one of Sydney's most luxurious boutique hotels.

Park Hyatt Sydney ($$$)
7 Hickson Road, The Rocks
tel: 02 9241 1234, fax: 02 9256 1555
www.sydney.park.hyatt.com
Sydney's most expensive hotel is in a superb location around the edge of the harbour.

The Russell Hotel ($$)
143a George Street, The Rocks
tel: 02 9241 3543, fax: 02 9252 1652
www.therussell.com.au
In a charming 19th-century Rocks building, this small guest house-style hotel is known for its good service and beautifully decorated rooms.

Rydges Jamison Sydney ($$–$$$)
11 Jamison Street
tel: 02 9696 2500, fax: 02 9696 2600
www.rydgesjamison.com
This boutique-style hotel in the city has an elegant modern interior, a day spa, a pool, two bars and two restaurants.

Sydney Central YHA ($)
Corner of Pitt Street and Rawson Place
tel: 02 9218 9000, fax: 02 9218 9099
www.yha.com.au/hostels
Close to Central Station, this is the world's biggest youth hostel (530 beds). It has a licensed café and rooftop pool/barbecue area.

The Westin Sydney ($$$)
1 Martin Place
tel: 02 8223 1111, fax: 02 8223 1222
www.westin.com.au
Once Sydney's grand Victorian GPO building and now one of the city's finest hotels. Rooms in the original structure and the new tower.

CANBERRA (ACT)

The Brassey of Canberra ($$)
Belmore Gardens, Barton
tel: 02 6273 3766, fax: 02 6273 2791
www.brassey.net.au
Established in 1927, and set in attractive gardens, this elegant hotel is close to Parliament House and the attractions south of the lake.

Forrest Inn and Apartments ($–$$)
30 National Circuit, Forrest
tel: 02 6295 3433, fax: 02 6295 2119
www.forrestinn.com.au
Reasonably priced motel rooms and comfortable serviced apartments, close to the popular Manuka restaurant precinct.

Hyatt Hotel Canberra ($$$)
Commonwealth Avenue, Yarralumla
tel: 02 6270 1234, fax: 02 6281 5998
www.canberra.park.hyatt.com
Canberra's best hotel. Excellent service and full facilities in this restored art deco building.

The Olims Hotel Canberra ($$)
Corner of Ainslie and Limestone avenues, Braddon
tel: 02 6243 0000, fax: 02 6243 0001
www.olimshotel.com
Good quality accommodation at a reasonable price, and close to the middle of town.

Rydges Lakeside Canberra ($$–$$$)
London Circuit, Canberra City
tel: 02 6247 6244, fax: 02 6257 3071
www.rydges.com/canberra
A central hotel with great views.

Saville Park Suites ($$)
84 Northbourne Avenue
tel: 02 6243 2500, fax: 02 6243 2599
www.savillesuites.com
A central hotel, with standard rooms and one- or two-bedroom apartments. There is also a gym, pool, sauna, restaurant and bar.

NEW SOUTH WALES

Blue Mountains

The Carrington ($$–$$$)
15–47 Katoomba Street, Katoomba
tel: 02 4782 1111, fax: 02 4782 7033
www.thecarrington.com.au
One of the region's original grand hotels now offers a day spa and 66 rooms and suites.

Jemby Rinjah Eco Lodge ($$)
336 Evans Lookout Road, Blackheath
tel: 02 4787 7622, fax: 02 4787 6230
www.jembyrinjahlodge.com.au
The timber cabins, some of which are self-catering, and the larger lodges are right next to the Blue Mountains National Park; excellent restaurant.

Jenolan Caves Resort ($–$$$)
Jenolan Caves
tel: 02 6359 3322, fax: 02 6359 3227
www.jenolancavesrresort.com.au
A range of accommodation—from historic Caves House and the comfortable Mountain Lodge to the less expensive Cottage and budget Gatehouse.

Mercure Grand Hydro Majestic ($$$)
Great Western Highway, Medlow Bath
tel: 02 4788 1002, fax: 02 4788 1063
www.hydromajestic.com.au
First opened in 1904, this imposing hotel has been renovated to its former splendour. There are more than 60 rooms, the atmospheric Grand Dining Room and good facilities.

The Mountain Heritage ($$–$$$)
Corner of Apex and Lovel streets, Katoomba
tel: 02 4782 2155, fax: 02 4782 5323
www.mountainheritage.com.au
A charming old-style hotel, with log fires, comfortable rooms and some excellent views.

Peppers Fairmont Resort ($$$)
1 Sublime Point Road, Leura
tel: 02 4784 4144, fax: 02 4784 1685
www.peppers.com.au/fairmont
Excellent accommodation with wonderful clifftop views as well as good recreation facilities.

Hunter Valley

Peppers Guest House Hunter Valley ($$–$$$)
Ekerts Road, Pokolbin
tel: 02 4993 8999, fax: 02 4998 7739
www.peppers.com.au/guesthouse
The colonial-style Peppers consistently receives awards for its comfort, facilities, hospitality and the excellent food in its restaurant.

Pokolbin Village Resort ($$)
188 Broke Road, Pokolbin
tel: 02 4998 7670, fax: 02 4998 7377
www.pokolbinvillage.com.au
This resort-style accommodation has a variety of
room styles, a restaurant, tennis court, swimming
pool and landscaped grounds.

Vineyard Hill ($$)
Lovedale Road, Lovedale
tel: 02 4990 4166, fax: 02 4991 4431
www.vineyardhill.com.au
With great views of the valley, Vineyard Hill offers
eight one- or two-bedroom villas, each of which
has its own private deck and is fully equipped.

Southern Highlands

Links House Country Guesthouse ($$)
17 Links Road, Bowral tel: 02 4861 1977,
fax: 02 4862 1706; www.linkshouse.com.au
In a quiet position opposite the local golf course,
this friendly hotel has a garden and tennis court,
pleasant rooms, two lounge areas with log fires
and a popular restaurant.

Peppers Manor House Southern Highlands ($$$)
Kater Road, Sutton Forest
tel: 02 4860 3111, fax: 02 4868 3257
www.peppers.com.au/manorhouse
A delightful boutique hotel with spacious rooms
and suites and a fine restaurant. The property,
surrounded by gardens, is next to a golf course.

Treetops Country Guesthouse ($$)
101 Railway Avenue, Bundanoon
tel: 02 4883 6372, fax: 02 4993 6176
www.treetopsguesthouse.com.au
In the delightful village of Bunadoon, this is one of
the region's original guesthouses. The accommo-
dation includes spa suites and family suites.

VICTORIA

Melbourne

The Adelphi Hotel ($$$)
187 Flinders Lane
tel: 03 9650 75555, fax: 03 9650 2710
www.adelphi.com.au
With only 30 or so rooms, the boutique Adelphi
offers exceptional personal service. There is also
a restaurant and rooftop lap pool.

The Albany Melbourne ($$)
Corner of Toorak Road and Millswyn Street, South
Yarra tel: 03 9866 4485, fax: 03 9820 9419
www.thealbany.com.au
Good-value accommodation in the normally more
expensive South Yarra area of the city.

Batmans Hill on Collins ($$)
6623 Collins Street
tel: 03 9614 6344, fax: 03 9614 1189
www.batmanshill.com.au
Opposite Southern Cross Station behind a fully
restored historic façade.

City Limits Motel ($$)
20–22 Little Bourke Street
tel: 03 9662 2544, fax: 03 9662 2287
www.citylimits.com.au
In the heart of the city, this economical hotel has
good-value rooms and apartments.

City Park Hotel ($$)
308–310 Kingsway, South Melbourne
tel: 03 9686 0000, fax: 03 9699 9224
www.cityparkhotel.com.au
Reasonably priced accommodation, close to the
city's Botanic Gardens.

Georgian Court Bed & Breakfast ($–$$)
21–25 George Street, East Melbourne
tel: 03 9419 6353, fax: 03 9416 0895
www.georgiancourt.com.au
In the exclusive and attractive area of East
Melbourne, and close to the middle of town.

Grand Hyatt Melbourne ($$$)
123 Collins Street tel: 03 9657 1234, fax: 03
9650 3491; www.melbourne.hyatt.com
Probably the most luxurious hotel in the city, the
Hyatt offers a full range of facilities.

Hotel Lindrum ($$$)
26 Flinders Street
tel: 03 9668 1111, fax: 03 9668 1199
www.hotellindrum.com.au
This central establishment, in an old billiard hall,
is one of Melbourne's most atmospheric and
sophisticated hotels.

The Hotel Y ($$)
489 Elizabeth Street
tel: 03 8327 2777, fax: 03 9329 1469
www.hotely.com.au
One of Melbourne's best moderately priced
hotels, opposite Queen Victoria Market.

The Lyall Hotel ($$$)
14 Murphy Street, South Yarra
tel: 03 9868 8222, fax: 03 9820 1724
www.thelyall.com
Luxurious one- and two-bedroom suites at a prestigious South Yarra address. Spa, bar and bistro.

Magnolia Court Boutique Hotel ($$)
101 Powlett Street, East Melbourne
tel: 03 9419 4222, fax: 03 9416 0841
www.magnolia-court.com.au
Small but elegant hotel just to the east of the
city, close to the Melbourne Cricket Ground.

Melbourne Marriott Hotel ($$$)
Corner of Exhibition and Lonsdale streets
tel: 03 9662 3900, fax: 03 9663 4297
www.marriott.com
Melbourne's most luxurious boutique hotel.
Excellent facilities include elegant bars and restaurants.

Metro Apartments on Bank Place ($$)
18 Bank Place
tel: 03 9604 4321, fax: 03 9604 4300
www.metrohotels.com.au
This heritage-listed building has 60 good-value
serviced apartments and studio rooms.

Novotel St. Kilda ($$)
16 The Esplanade, St. Kilda
tel: 03 9525 5522, fax: 03 9525 5678
www.accorhotels.com.au
Overlooking Port Phillip Bay in the cosmopolitan
suburb of St. Kilda, this 200-room hotel's
facilities include a pool, spa and gymnasium.

Punt Hill Apartments ($$)
267 Flinders Lane
tel: 03 9631 1111, fax: 03 9650 4409
www.punthill-apartments.com.au
Fully equipped one-, two- or three-bedroom apart-
ments or studios in several locations.

270

Quest Fairfax House ($$)
392 Little Collins Street
tel: 03 9642 1333, fax: 03 9642 4607
www.questapartments.com.au
A good city centre hotel in a large Victorian building, with one-, two- and three-bedroom apartments.

St. Kilda Road Parkview Hotel ($$–$$$)
562 St. Kilda Road, St. Kilda
tel: 03 9529 8888, fax: 03 9525 1242
www.viewhotels.com.au
A boutique-style hotel with large rooms and excellent service. A short tram ride from the middle of town, this hotel is in one of Melbourne's most interesting inner suburbs.

Somerset Gordon Place ($$–$$$)
24 Little Bourke Street
tel: 03 9663 2888, fax: 03 9639 1537
www.somersetgordonplace.com
These luxuriously appointed apartments open on to a vine-clad interior courtyard with a huge palm tree. The historic building also offers a heated pool, a bar and a restaurant.

The Victoria Hotel ($$)
215 Little Collins Street
tel: 03 9669 0000, fax: 9669 0001
www.victoriahotel.com.au
This comfortable early 20th-century hotel, right in the city, has become a Melbourne institution.

The Windsor ($$$)
103 Spring Street
tel: 03 9633 6000, fax: 03 9633 6001
www.thewindsor.com.au
This grand old hotel has been splendidly restored and has been classified by the National Trust.

Ballarat

The Ansonia ($$)
32 Lydiard Street South
tel: 03 5332 4678, fax: 03 5532 4698
www.ansonia.com.au
This beautiful Victorian building is home to 20 guest suites on two levels. There is also a cosy guest lounge, a restaurant and sunny courtyard.

Sovereign Hill Lodge ($$)
Magpie Street
tel: 03 5333 3409, fax: 03 5533 5861
www.sovereignhill.com.au
Stay next door to Sovereign Hill, Ballarat's main attraction. The lodge has both motel and heritage-style rooms, as well as a lounge and bar area.

Great Ocean Road

Cumberland Lorne Resort ($$$)
150 Mountjoy Parade, Lorne
tel: 03 5289 2400, fax: 03 5289 2256
www.cumberland.com.au
An award-winning luxury apartment resort in the heart of this well-established seaside resort.

Mantra Erskine Beach Resort ($$)
Mountjoy Parade, Lorne
tel: 03 5289 1209, fax: 03 5289 1185
www.stellaresorts.com.au
Refurbished in 2005, this beachfront resort features more than 280 apartments, a restaurant and café and facilities such as a pool and gym.

Seacombe House ($–$$)
Corner of Cox and Sackville streets, Port Fairy
tel: 03 5568 1082, fax: 03 5568 2323
www.seacombehouse.com.au
Seacombe House offers motel units, executive suites, self-contained heritage cottages and rooms in the original 1847 hotel.

Sea Foam Villas ($$)
14 Lord Street, Port Campbell
tel and fax: 03 5598 6413
www.seafoamvillas.com.au
These luxury apartments in Port Campbell's main street have superb ocean views, balconies and modern facilities.

Northeast Victoria

Finches of Beechworth ($$)
3 Finch Street, Beechworth
tel: 03 5728 2655, fax: 03 5728 2656
www.beechworth.com/finches
This beautifully restored Victorian home offers six charming rooms and extensive gardens.

Mount Buffalo Chalet ($$)
Mount Buffalo National Park
tel: 03 5755 1500, fax: 03 5755 1892
www.mtbuffalochalet.com.au
An old-fashioned Alpine-style establishment in the exhilarating surroundings of this national park.

Mount Buller Chalet ($$$)
Summit Road, Mount Buller
tel: 03 5777 6566, fax: 03 5777 6455
www.mtbullerchalet.com.au
Open all year and an ideal base for winter skiing or summer alpine walking, this 65-room hotel has top facilities, including a sports complex and cocktail bar.

Silverwater Cottages ($)
4 South Crescent, Eildon
tel: 03 5774 2050, fax: 03 5774 2855
www.cute.com.au/silverwater
There are nine cottages, set in quiet surroundings near Lake Eildon. Pool and tennis court.

SOUTH AUSTRALIA

Adelaide

Holiday Inn Adelaide ($$–$$$)
65 Hindley Street
tel: 08 8231 5552, fax: 08 8237 3800
www.holidayinn.com.au
A good-quality hotel with spa and restaurant, on one of the main restaurant and nightlife streets.

Hotel 208 ($–$$)
208 South Terrace
tel: 08 8223 2800, fax: 08 8224 0519
www.hotel208.com
This good-value hotel offers a variety of room styles and prices, as well as a restaurant, bar and pool.

Hotel Adelaide International ($$)
62 Brougham Place, North Adelaide
tel: 08 8267 3444, fax: 08 8239 0189
www.goodearth.com.au
A short walk from the heart of the city and the O'Connell Street café and shopping strip, this good value hotel also has excellent city views.

Hotels and Restaurants

Hyatt Regency Adelaide ($$$)
North Terrace
tel: 08 8231 1234, fax: 08 8231 1120
www.adelaide.regency.hyatt.com
Decorated with stunning works of art, the Hyatt is the city's most sumptuous hotel, and is near major attractions.

Majestic Tynte Street Apartments ($$)
82 Tynte Street, North Adelaide
tel: 08 8334 7783, fax: 08 8334 7788
www.majestichotels.com.au
In leafy North Adelaide, these one-bedroom and studio apartments represent very good value.

Medina Grand Adelaide Treasury ($$$)
2 Flinders Street
tel: 08 8112 0000, fax: 08 8112 0199
www.medinaapartments.com.au
Adelaide's heritage-listed Treasury building is now a superb 80-room apartment hotel with excellent facilities and service.

North Adelaide Heritage Group ($$–$$$)
tel: 08 8272 1355, fax: 08 8272 1355
www.adelaideheritage.com
A superb collection of self-contained heritage apartments in the refined suburb of North Adelaide. The choices include everything from intimate cottages to an old chapel, and even an imaginatively renovated fire station.

Oaks Embassy Adelaide ($$$)
96 North Terrace tel: 08 8124 9900, f
ax: 08 8124 9901; www.theoaksgroup.com.au
Elegant apartment-style hotel, with balconies, gym, lap pool, wine bar and two dining rooms.

Oaks Plaza Pier Apartment Hotel ($$–$$$)
16 Holdfast Promenade, Glenelg
tel: 08 8350 6688, fax: 08 8350 6699
www.theoaksgroup.com.au
The best hotel in Adelaide's most famous beach suburb, a short and pleasant tram ride from the heart of town.

Quest Mansions ($$)
21 Pulteney Street
tel: 08 8232 0033, fax: 08 8223 4559
www.questmansions.com.au
A well-located hotel with self-contained apartments in an interesting old building.

Adelaide Hills

Adelaide Hills Country Cottages ($$)
Oakwood Road, Oakbank
tel: 08 8388 4193, fax: 08 8388 4633
www.ahcc.com.au
Choose from five delightful self-contained cottages, set among gardens and native bushland in the heart of the Hills.

Grand Mercure Mount Lofty House ($$$)
74 Summit Road, Crafers
tel: 08 8339 6777, fax: 08 8339 5656
www.mtloftyhouse.com.au
Luxury country house living, South Australian style. Just below the summit of Mount Lofty and only a short drive from the city. There is also a gourmet restaurant.

Hahndorf Resort ($–$$)
145 Main Street, Hahndorf
tel: 08 8388 7921, fax: 08 8388 7282
www.hahndorfresort.com.au
With both motel-style units and spacious chalets, plus large grounds that include a pool, tennis courts and lake, this is a good choice for a Hahndorf stay.

Barossa Valley

Collingrove Homestead ($$–$$$)
Eden Valley Road, Angaston
tel: 08 8564 2061, fax: 08 8564 3600
www.collingrovehomestead.com.au
A fine National Trust property on the edge of the Barossa. Dinner is available by arrangement.

Lanzerac Country Estate ($$)
Lot 5, Menge Road, Tanunda tel: 08 8563 0499,
fax: 08 8563 3652; www.lanzerac.com.au
Surrounded by vineyards, this French-style guest-house features seven luxurious rooms, some with spa baths.

Novotel Barossa Valley Resort ($$–$$$)
Golf Links Road, Rowland Flat
tel: 08 8524 0000, fax: 08 8524 0100
www.accorhotels.com.au
Facilities include a restaurant, two bars, a pool, tennis courts and access to an 18-hole golf course.

Tanunda Hotel ($)
51 Murray Street, Tanunda
tel: 08 8563 2030, fax: 08 8563 2165
www.tanundapub.com
Budget accommodation in a historic pub in the often expensive Barossa Valley area.

WESTERN AUSTRALIA

Perth

Aarons Hotel Perth ($$)
70 Pier Street
tel: 08 9325 2133, fax: 08 9221 2936
www.aaronsperth.com.au
Reasonably priced accommodation in the heart of the city. The hotel includes a restaurant and bar.

Baileys Motel ($)
150 Bennett Street
tel: 08 9325 3788, fax: 08 9221 1046
www.baileysmotel.com.au
Central budget-priced self-contained units, including family units and suites.

City Waters Lodge ($–$$)
118 Terrace Road
tel: 08 9325 1566, fax: 08 9221 2794
www.citywaters.com.au
Self-contained apartments by the Swan River.

The Commodore Hotel ($$)
417 Hay Street
tel: 08 9238 1888, fax: 08 9238 1999
www.thecommodorehotel.com.au
Good quality accommodation at a reasonable price close to the city's business district. The hotel has a fitness centre and restaurant.

Cottesloe Beach Hotel ($–$$)
104 Marine Parade, Cottesloe
tel: 08 9383 1100, fax: 08 9385 2482
www.cottesloebeachhotel.com.au
This beachside pub is just 15 minutes drive from the city; good-value accommodation, bars and a café.

Goodearth Hotel Perth ($$)
195 Adelaide Terrace
tel: 08 9492 7777, fax: 08 9221 1956
www.goodearthhotel.com.au
A good mid-range city centre hotel with rooms, self-contained apartments and a café.

Hyatt Regency Perth ($$$)
99 Adelaide Terrace, East Perth
tel: 08 9225 1234, fax: 08 9325 8899
www.perth.regency.hyatt.com
One of the city's best hotels, the Hyatt Regency is just to the east of central Perth and overlooks the Swan River.

Intercontinental Burswood Resort Perth ($$$)
Great Eastern Highway, Burswood
tel: 08 9362 7777, fax: 08 9470 2553
www.burswood.intercontinental.com
This luxurious resort on the banks of the Swan River is part of the vast Burswood Entertainment Complex, featuring parklands, a casino, a golf course and many other leisure facilities.

Mounts Bay Waters Apartment Hotel ($$)
112 Mounts Bay Road tel: 08 9213 5333,
fax: 08 9486 7998; www.mounts-bay.com.au
With 200 one- and two- and three-bedroom apartments, this hotel (adjacent to Kings Park) also has two swimming pools, tennis courts and a restaurant.

Parmelia Hilton Perth ($$$)
14 Mill Street tel: 08 9215 2000,
fax: 08 9215 2001; www.perth.hilton.com
One of the most individual of all the hotels in the Hilton chain, right in the heart of the city.

Rendezvous Observation City Hotel ($$$)
The Esplanade, Scarborough
tel: 08 9245 1000, fax: 08 9245 1345
www.rendezvoushotels.com/perth
A luxurious five-star resort on the beach, just a 15-minute drive from the city.

The Richardson Hotel, Suites and Spa ($$$)
32 Richardson Street, West Perth
tel: 08 9217 8888, fax: 08 9214 3931
www.therichardson.com.au
Near Kings Park, this ultramodern 74-room establishment is one of Perth's newest and best hotels.

Riverview on Mount Street ($$)
42 Mount Street
tel: 08 9321 8963, fax: 08 9322 5956
www.riverview.au.com
Self-contained studio apartments, complete with cooking facilities. Close to Kings Park.

Sullivans Hotel ($$)
166 Mounts Bay Road
tel: 08 9321 8022, fax: 08 9481 6762
www.sullivans.com.au
A small, friendly hotel that is at the edge of Kings Park. Some rooms have river views.

Fremantle

Esplanade Hotel Fremantle ($$$)
Corner of Marine Terrace and Essex Street
tel: 08 9432 4000, fax: 08 9430 4539
www.esplanadehotelfremantle.com.au
International-standard hotel in the heart of historic Fremantle. Rooms, studios and suites are available, and the hotel also has excellent recreation and dining facilities.

Tradewinds Hotel ($$)
59 Canning Highway, East Fremantle
tel: 08 9339 8188, fax: 08 9339 2266
www.tradewindshotel.com.au
Overlooking the Swan River, a short walk from central Fremantle, this hotel provides self-contained apartments that are serviced daily.

Kalgoorlie–Boulder

All Seasons Plaza Hotel Kalgoorlie ($$)
45 Egan Street, Kalgoorlie
tel: 08 9021 4544, fax: 08 9091 2195
www.accorhotels.com.au
All Seasons is one of the best hotels in town. Good comforts and facilities. Reasonably central.

Broadwater Resort Hotel Kalgoorlie ($$–$$$)
21 Davidson Street, Kalgoorlie
tel: 08 9080 0800, fax: 08 9080 0900
www.broadwaters.com.au
Kalgoorlie's most elegant hotel offers luxurious studios and one- or two-bedroom apartments, as well as a pool and spa.

Hannan's View Motel ($$)
430 Hannan Street, Kalgoorlie
tel: 08 9091 3333, fax: 08 9091 3331
www.hannansview.com.au
Recommended central motel.

273

NORTHERN TERRITORY

Darwin

Capricornia Hotel/Motel ($)
3 Kellaway Street, Fannie Bay
tel: 08 8981 4055, fax: 08 8981 2031
email: capricorniahotel@bigpond.com
Comfortable and well-priced units, on the edge of town. The motel has a barbecue area and a pool.

City Gardens Apartments ($$)
93 Woods Street
tel: 08 8941 2888, fax: 08 8981 2934
www.citygardensapts.com.au
Central complex, with apartments and family units, as well as a pool, gardens and barbecues.

Holiday Inn Esplanade Darwin ($$–$$$)
The Esplanade tel: 08 8980 0800,
fax: 08 8980 0888; www.ichotelsgroup.com
Housed in a pink and blue postmodern complex on Darwin's Esplanade, the luxury Holiday Inn is one of the more striking additions to the city's post-Tracy skyline. Comfortable rooms, excellent service and good restaurants here.

Novotel Atrium Darwin ($$)
Corner of Peel Street and The Esplanade
tel: 08 8941 0755, fax: 08 8981 9025
www.novoteldarwin.com.au
This medium-sized modern hotel offers all the facilities and service you would expect from this international chain. The rooms vary from standard to deluxe suites. A great position.

Palms City Resort ($$)
64 The Esplanade
tel: 08 8982 9200, fax: 08 8981 9575
www.palmscityresort.com
A tropical-style waterfront resort, offering good-value accommodation in a landscaped garden setting.

Hotels and Restaurants

Saville Park Suites ($$–$$$)
88 The Esplanade
tel: 08 8943 4333, fax: 08 8943 4388
www.savillesuites.com
This award-winning four-star hotel on Darwin's waterfront has 140 apartments of various sizes, 64 hotel rooms, a restaurant, bar and swimming pool.

Skycity Darwin Hotel ($$$)
Gilruth Avenue, The Gardens
tel: 08 8943 8888, fax: 08 8943 8999
www.skycitydarwin.com.au
This deluxe hotel that is part of Darwin's casino complex has a good location on the beach, just out of the city.

Alice Springs

Alice Springs Resort ($$–$$$)
34 Stott Terrace
tel: 02 8296 8010, fax: 02 9299 2103
www.voyages.com.au
This attractive resort-style accommodation has studio, standard and deluxe categories.

Alice Tourist Apartments ($–$$)
Corner of Gap Road and Gnoilya Street
tel: 08 8952 2788, fax: 08 8953 2950
www.aliceapartments.com.au
Good-value one- and two-bedroom apartments set in a small complex, just out of town. There is a pool, and all apartments have full cooking facilities.

All Seasons Diplomat Alice Springs ($–$$)
Corner of Gregory Terrace and Hartley Street
tel: 08 8952 8977, fax: 08 8953 0225
www.accorhotels.com.au
This central hotel offers superior motel-style accommodation laid out on two levels. Executive suites with spa baths are also available.

All Seasons Oasis Alice Springs ($$)
10 Gap Road
tel: 08 8952 1444, fax: 08 8952 3776
www.accorhotels.com.au
Well-located accommodation with good facilities, including pool and gardens.

Aurora Alice Springs ($–$$)
11 Leichhardt Terrace
tel: 02 8950 6666, fax: 02 8952 7829
www.auroraresorts.com.au
With more than 100 air-conditioned rooms and good facilities, this is one of the best central accommodation options in Alice Springs. The complex includes the popular Red Ochre Grill restaurant.

Crowne Plaza Hotel Alice Springs ($$$)
82 Barrett Drive
tel: 08 8950 8000, fax: 08 8952 1373
www.ichotelsgroup.com
Just a short distance to the south of town, the Crowne Plaza provides resort-type luxury at the foot of the stark MacDonnell Ranges.

Lasseters Hotel Casino ($$–$$$)
93 Barrett Drive
tel: 08 8950 7777, fax: 08 8953 1680
www.lassetershotelcasino.com.au
This is one of the town's best hotels, and is part of the Alice Springs casino development. Both rooms and suites are available.

Uluru

All accommodation and most other facilities at Uluru are provided outside the National Park at Ayers Rock Resort. You can stay in luxury at the superbly landscaped **Sails in the Desert Hotel**, in comfort at the **Desert Gardens Hotel, Lost Camel Hotel** and **Emu Walk Apartments**, and the plainer but very affordable **Outback Pioneer Hotel**. All of these can be contacted via central reservations —tel: 02 8296 8010, fax: 02 9299 2103, www.voyages.com.au. Backpackers and campers are also welcome. There are also many restaurants and cafés, with prices to suit all budgets.

QUEENSLAND

Brisbane

Brisbane Marriott Hotel ($$$)
515 Queen Street tel: 07 3303 8000,
fax: 07 3303 8088; www.marriott.com.au
Luxury and class characterize this superb 267-room hotel, with an interior of marble, timbers and parquetry. The facilities are excellent.

Conrad Treasury Brisbane ($$$)
130 William Street
tel: 07 3306 8888, fax: 07 3306 8880
www.conrad.com.au/treasury
An elegant heritage hotel just a short stroll from the Brisbane River and South Bank.

Goodearth Hotel Brisbane ($$)
345 Wickham Terrace, Spring Hill
tel: 07 3831 6177, fax: 07 3832 5919
www.goodearth.com.au
The most prominent among the cluster of hotels on the leafy heights overlooking the city.

Holiday Inn Brisbane ($$)
Roma Street tel: 07 3238 2222,
fax: 07 3238 2288; www.ichotelsgroup.com
Extra-large rooms, a restaurant, bars and spa, sauna and gym, all in the heart of the city.

Mercure Hotel Brisbane ($$)
85–87 North Quay
tel: 07 3237 2300, fax: 07 3236 1035
www.mercurebrisbane.com.au
Overlooking the river and South Bank Parklands, this central hotel has excellent facilities.

Metro Hotel Tower Mill ($$)
239 Wickman Terrace
tel: 07 3832 1421, fax: 07 3835 1013
www.metrohospitalitygroup.com
A good-value hotel with a rooftop restaurant and bar; walking distance of the city and South Bank.

Pacific International Apartments ($$)
570 Queen Street
tel: 07 3234 8888, fax: 07 3236 9637
www.pacificinthotels.com
This central hotel offers rooms and one- and two-bed apartments with balconies and kitchens.

Sofitel Brisbane ($$$)
249 Turbot Street
tel: 07 3835 3535, fax: 07 3835 4960
www.sofitelbrisbane.com.au
With more than 400 rooms, a rooftop pool and spa, three dining venues and a central position, this is one of Brisbane's best hotels.

Sunshine Coast

Breakfree Noosa International Resort ($$)
Edgar Bennett Avenue, Noosa Heads
tel: 07 5447 4822, fax: 07 5447 2025
www.stellaresorts.com.au
On a hillside above Noosa. Spacious apartments, restaurant and landscaped pool with a swim-up bar.

Hyatt Regency Coolum ($$$)
Warran Road, Coolum Beach
tel: 07 5446 1234, fax: 07 5446 2957
http://coolum.regency.hyatt.com
A self-contained, luxury resort with a championship golf course, spa and a wide range of recreational facilities. Between the green hinterland and the glorious sands of the Sunshine Coast.

Netanya Noosa ($$)
75 Hastings Street, Noosa Heads
tel: 07 5447 4722, fax: 07 5447 3914
www.netanyanoosa.com.au
A delightful resort right on the boardwalk. All suites have a balcony and kitchenette, and the hotel is close to a selection of restaurants.

The Sebel Maroochydore ($$–$$$)
20 Aerodrome Road, Maroochydore
tel: 07 5479 8000, fax: 07 5479 8100
www.mirvachotels.com.au
Ultramodern one- and two-bedroom apartments, with superb views of the southern Sunshine Coast. Facilities include a pool, rooftop barbeque area and a restaurant.

Sheraton Noosa Resort and Spa ($$$)
Hastings Street, Noosa Heads
tel: 07 5449 4888, fax: 07 5449 2230
www.starwoodhotels.com/sheraton
High-class accommodation in a well-designed, low-rise resort. Its spacious rooms all have spas and kitchenettes.

Noosa has a variety of accommodation, mostly in pleasing modern buildings. Details can be obtained from: **Accom Noosa**, PO Box 694, Noosa Heads, Queensland 4567 (tel: 07 5447 3444, www.accomnoosa.com.au).

Gold Coast and Hinterland

Conrad Jupiters ($$$)
Broadbeach Island
tel: 07 5592 8130, fax: 07 5592 8219
www.conrad.com.au/jupiters
With its 590-plus rooms and a 24-hour casino, this is a prime place to see and be seen.

Couran Cove Island Resort ($$–$$$)
South Stradbroke Island, via Hope Harbour
tel: 07 5509 3000, fax: 07 5597 9090
www.couran.com
Just 30 minutes from the Gold Coast, this eco-tourism resort has everything from deluxe suites to bush cabins. It is surrounded by bushland and beaches and offers an extraordinary range of sports and activities.

Hotel Watermark Gold Coast ($$)
3032 Surfers Paradise Boulevard,
Surfers Paradise
tel: 07 5588 8333, fax: 07 5588 8300
www.hotelwatermark.com.au

Between the beach and the Nerang River, this modern hotel has stylish accommodation and excellent facilties.

Phoenician Resort Apartments ($$–$$$)
24–26 Queensland Avenue, Broadbeach
tel: 07 5585 8888, fax: 5585 8880
www.phoenician.com.au
Good-value apartments at lively Broadbeach. The complex includes a spa and health centre, two pools and a gym.

Sheraton Mirage Resort & Spa Gold Coast ($$$)
Sea World Drive, Main Beach
tel: 07 5591 1488, fax: 07 5591 2299
www.sheraton.com/miragegoldcoast
The Sheraton is a tasteful and luxurious low-rise complex of buildings. The famous eat at the prestigious Horizons Restaurant.

In the green hills beyond the coast

Binna Burra Mountain Lodge ($$$)
Beechmont, via Nerang
tel: 07 5533 3622, fax: 07 5533 3747
www.binnaburralodge.com.au
A good alternative to O'Reilly's (see below).

O'Reilly's Rainforest Guesthouse ($$)
Lamington National Park, via Canungra
tel: 07 5544 0644, fax: 07 5544 0638
www.oreillys.com.au
O'Reilly's Guesthouse has been welcoming people into the mountains since 1926. Prices include accommodation, meals and activities.

Cairns and the Far North

Cairns Colonial Club Resort ($$)
18–26 Cannon Street, Manunda, Cairns
tel: 07 4053 5111, fax: 07 4053 7072
www.cairnscolonialclub.com.au
A resort-style complex a short drive from town. Facilities include tennis courts, pools, three restaurants and extensive gardens.

Cairns Resort by Outrigger ($$–$$$)
53–57 The Esplanade, Cairns
tel: 07 4046 4141, fax: 07 4046 4242
http://outrigger.com/hotels
Right on the Cairns waterfront, this stylish hotel incorporates the old Cairns Courthouse, now a bistro and bar.

Ferntree Rainforest Lodge ($$$)
Cape Tribulation
tel: 02 8296 8010, fax: 02 9299 2103
www.ferntreelodge.com.au
A unique resort in wonderful rain forest and tropical beach surroundings.

Daintree Cape Tribulation Heritage Lodge ($$)
Turpentine Road, Cooper Creek, via Mossman
tel: 07 4098 9138, fax: 07 4098 9004
www.heritagelodge.net.au
A range of stylish modern units designed to blend with their rain-forest surroundings.

Garrick House ($$)
11–13 Garrick Street, Port Douglas
tel: 07 4099 5322, fax: 07 4099 5021
www.garrickhouse.com.au
High-standard apartment units with all amenities in a quiet street in delightful Port Douglas.

Hotels and Restaurants

Hibiscus Gardens Spa Resort ($$$)
22 Owens Street, Port Douglas
tel: 07 4099 5315, fax: 07 4099 4678
www.hibiscusportdouglas.com.au
Award-winning Balinese-style resort with tropical gardens, statues, pools, spa and a restaurant.

Rydges Tradewinds Cairns ($$)
137 The Esplanade, Cairns
tel: 07 4053 0300, fax: 07 4051 8649
www.rydges.com
An attractive and central hotel with views of Trinity Bay, gardens or the swimming pool.

The Sebel Reef House and Spa ($$$)
99 Williams Esplanade, Palm Cove
tel: 07 4055 3633, fax: 07 4055 3305
www.reefhouse.com.au
On a beach north of Cairns, this is a tropical-style resort with the best facilities and a high reputation.

Sofitel Reef Hotel Casino ($$$)
35–41 Wharf Street, Cairns
tel: 07 4030 8888, fax: 07 4030 8777
www.reefcasino.com.au
This sophisticated hotel is part of the Cairns casino development. The Reef offers butler service, fine restaurants and the ultimate in comfort.

TASMANIA

Hobart

Battery Point Guest House ($$)
7 McGregor Sstreet, Battery Point
tel: 03 6224 2111, fax: 03 6224 3648
www.batterypointguesthouse.com.au
This National Trust classified 1880s house offers six comfortable rooms with modern amenities, a sunny breakfast room and log fires in winter.

Corinda's Cottages ($$)
17 Glebe Street, Glebe
tel: 03 6234 1590, fax: 03 6234 2744
www.corindascottages.com.au
Near the Botanical Gardens. Delightful 1850s fully self-contained cottages are furnished with antiques.

The Lodge on Elizabeth ($$)
249 Elizabeth Street
tel: 03 6231 3830, fax: 03 6234 2566
www.thelodge.com.au
At the top end of town is the oldest residential building in Hobart, tastefully converted.

The Old Woolstore ($$–$$$)
1 Macquarie Street
tel: 03 6235 5355, fax: 03 6234 9954
www.oldwoolstore.com.au
This luxurious apartment hotel, in a heritage building, has a range of suites and apartments.

Salamanca Inn ($$–$$$)
10 Gladstone Street
tel: 03 6223 3300, fax: 03 6223 7167
www.salamancainn.com.au
Integrated with unusual sensitivity among the old warehouses of Salamanca Place, the Salamanca is a luxury apartment hotel.

Motel 429 ($–$$)
429 Sandy Bay Road, Sandy Bay
tel: 03 6225 2511, fax: 03 6225 4354
www.motel429.com.au
Near the casino in this waterside suburb, this moderately priced motel represents good value.

Somerset on the Pier ($$$)
Elizabeth Street Pier
tel: 03 6220 6600, fax: 03 6224 1277
www.somersetonthepier.com.au
On a renovated 1930s pier, this all-suite apartment hotel has loft-style bedrooms.

Woolmers Inn ($$)
123 Sandy Bay Road, Sandy Bay
tel: 03 6223 7355, fax: 03 6223 1981
www.woolmersin.com
Just a ten-minute walk from the heart of the city, this comfortable hotel offers self-contained studio, twin and two-bedroom apartments.

Cradle Mountain

Accommodation for visitors to the national park ranges from campsites to the luxurious **Cradle Mountain Lodge** ($$–$$$) *(PO Box 153 Sheffield, tel: 02 9364 8900, www.cradlemountainlodge.com.au)*. Other options are the cabins of **Cradle Mountain Wilderness Village** ($$) (tel: 03 6492 1018, www.cradlevillage.com.au) and the rustic **Waldheim Cabins** ($) (tel: 03 6492 1110, www.parks.tas.gov.au).

Launceston

Ashton Gate Guest House ($$)
32 High Street
tel: 03 6331 6180, fax: 03 6334 2232
www.ashtongate.com.au
This elegantly restored Victorian home is a short walk from the heart of the city, and overlooks St. George's Square Park. Good value.

Hatherley House ($$$)
43 High Street
tel: 03 6334 7727, fax: 03 6334 7728
www.hatherleyhouse.com.au
This 1830s mansion has been transformed into a contemporary hotel, with deluxe, individually themed and ultra-modern suites.

Kilmarnock House ($$)
66 Elphin Road
tel: 03 6334 1514, fax: 03 6334 4516
www.kilmarnockhouse.com
With National Trust classification, this splendid large villa has been carefully refurbished to evoke the atmosphere of the night in 1904 when it was patronized by the Prince of Wales.

The Old Bakery Inn ($$)
270 York Street
tel: 03 6331 7900, fax: 03 6331 7756
www.plazahotels.com.au
This well-restored old inn offers accommodation along traditional lines.

Peppers Seaport Hotel ($$$)
28 Seaport Boulevard
tel: 03 6345 3333, fax: 03 6345 3300
www.peppers.com.au
Modern alternative, offering stylish rooms and apartments, just five minutes from the city centre.

RESTAURANTS

Eating out is relatively inexpensive in Australia, with a wide choice of ethnic cuisines and generally excellent ingredients. Costs can be further trimmed if you BYO—bring your own (wine or other liquor)—which is allowed by many establishments. The 'counter meals' served in many pubs are usually excellent value, and most places where tourists congregate have a reasonable variety of takeaway outlets.

The following recommended restaurants have been divided into three price categories:

($) = inexpensive
($$) = moderate
($$$) = expensive

SYDNEY

Aqua Dining ($$–$$$)
Paul Street, Milsons Point
tel: 02 9964 9998
Overlooking North Sydney's famous Olympic pool, the harbour and Opera House, this is a great spot for lunch or dinner.

Balkan Seafood ($$)
217 Oxford Street, Darlinghurst
tel: 02 9331 7670
This busy, long-established restaurant specializes in seafood and mixed meat or seafood platters.

Bayswater Brasserie ($$–$$$)
32 Bayswater Road, Kings Cross
tel: 02 9357 2177
The best and most stylish brasserie in town. A three-course meal tends towards the expensive, but there are cheaper alternatives.

bills ($–$$)
433 Liverpool Street, Darlinghurst
tel: 02 9360 9631
A popular café in the Kings Cross area serving everything from breakfasts to Modern Australian-style lunches and dinners.

Chinta Ria Temple of Love ($$)
Roof Terrace, Cockle Bay Wharf, Darling Harbour
tel: 02 9264 3211
With its dramatic Asian interior and good-value Malaysian food, Chinta Ria is one of the stars of the smart Cockle Bay Wharf complex.

Doyle's On the Beach ($$$)
11 Marine Parade, Watsons Bay
tel: 02 9337 2007
Classic fish and chips served to up to 700 diners in one of the world's most famous fish restaurants, with great views of the harbour. There are other branches at Circular Quay West (tel: 02 9252 3400) and the Sydney Fish Market (tel: 02 9552 4339).

East Ocean ($–$$$)
Level 1, 421–429 Sussex Street, Haymarket
tel: 02 9212 4198
From inexpensive *yum cha* to à la carte seafood dishes, the East Ocean serves some of Chinatown's best food. The restaurant is famous for its large tanks containing fish and crustaceans.

Guillaume at Bennelong ($$$)
Sydney Opera House, Bennelong Point
tel: 02 9241 1999
The best of the Opera House's food and drink outlets, with excellent Modern Australian food. The restaurant has 180-degree views over the harbour.

Hyde Park Barracks Café ($–$$)
Queens Square, Macquarie Street
tel: 02 9222 1815
Set in the grounds of the historic Hyde Park Barracks, this long-established café is excellent for lunch or daytime snacks (closed evenings).

Jordons Seafood Restaurant ($$)
197 Harbourside, Darling Harbour
tel: 02 9281 3711
Good seafood and an excellent atmosphere with views of the water.

The Malaya ($$)
39 Lime Street, King Street Wharf
tel: 02 9279 1170
One of Sydney's best Asian restaurants, specializing in Malaysian and Chinese cuisine, and in a great waterfront location.

Marigold Citymark ($$)
683–689 George Street, Haymarket
tel: 02 9281 3388
This large restaurant in the Chinatown area offers a wide range of predominantly Cantonese dishes. A great spot for weekend *yum cha.*

MCA Café ($$)
140 George Street, The Rocks
tel: 02 9241 4253
In the Museum of Contemporary Art, with a terrace and a view of Circular Quay and the Opera House. Reasonably priced Modern Australian cuisine.

Nelson's Brasserie ($$)
Lord Nelson Brewery Hotel, 19 Kent Street, Millers Point
tel: 02 9251 4044
Good-value contemporary cuisine at one of Sydney's oldest pubs, dating from the 1830s.

Pier ($$$)
594 New South Head Road, Rose Bay
tel: 02 9327 6561
One of Sydney's most acclaimed seafood restaurants, right on the harbour in the Eastern Suburbs. Expensive, but perfect for a night out.

Quay ($$$)
Overseas Passenger Terminal, Circular Quay West: tel: 02 9251 5600
This much-awarded restaurant serves expensive Modern French and Australian fare in a superb setting opposite the Opera House.

Ravesi's ($$–$$$)
Corner of Campbell Parade and Hall Street, Bondi Beach tel: 02 9365 4422
Another great brasserie, this restaurant can be found in the boutique-style Ravesi's Hotel overlooking Bondi Beach.

Rockpool ($$$)
107 George Street, The Rocks
tel: 02 9252 1888
Owned by Sydney's most famous chef and restaurateur, Neil Perry, this restaurant is renowned for its Modern Australian cuisine.

Sailors Thai ($–$$$)
106 George Street, The Rocks
tel: 02 9251 2466
There are two superb options at this restaurant—a noodle bar with communal cafeteria-style seating,

277

or a much more exclusive (and more expensive) downstairs restaurant.

Summit Restaurant ($$)
Level 47, Australia Square, 264 George Street
tel: 02 9247 9777
This revamped 1960s revolving restaurant and cocktail bar now has a menu good enough to match the magnificent views.

Sydney Cove Oyster Bar ($$)
1 East Circular Quay
tel: 02 9247 2937
Specializing in oysters and other seafood, but also serving meat and chicken dishes, this place has some of the best harbour views in Sydney.

Sydney Fish Market ($–$$)
Bank Street, Pyrmont
tel: 02 9004 1100
There's a good range of cafés and restaurants at the famous Sydney Fish Market—serving everything from fish and chips to sushi and oysters.

The Tearoom ($$)
Level 3, Queen Victoria Building,
455 George Street
tel: 02 9269 0774
The magnificent former QVB Grand Ballroom is famous for its traditional morning and afternoon teas. There are also à la carte lunches and the desserts are particularly recommended.

Tetsuya's ($$$)
529 Kent Street tel: 02 9267 2900
One of Sydney's very best restaurants, Tetsuya's blends Australian, French and Japanese cuisines in stunning combinations.

CANBERRA (ACT)

The Boat House by the Lake ($$–$$$)
Greville Park, Minindee Drive, Barton
tel: 02 6273 5500
With superb views of Lake Burley Griffin, The Boat House specializes in fine Modern Australian cuisine, as well as a tapas-style lunch menu. There is an extensive wine list.

The Chairman and Yip ($$$)
108 Bunda Street, Canberra City
tel: 02 6248 7109
A popular modern Asian restaurant that manages to blend tastes from East and West.

Gus' Cafe ($)
Shop 8, Garema Place, Canberra City
tel: 02 6248 8118
A good-value central café with hearty breakfasts, great coffee and an all-day menu that includes pastas, salads and steaks.

Ottoman Cuisine ($$$)
Corner of Broughton and Blackall streets, Barton
tel: 02 6273 6111
Probably Canberra's best restaurant—in a renovated art deco building and serving superb modern Turkish food.

NEW SOUTH WALES

Blue Mountains

The Paragon Restaurant ($$)
65 Katoomba Street, Katoomba
tel: 02 4782 2928

In a National Trust-classified building, dating from 1916, the Paragon is worth visiting.

Silks Brasserie ($$–$$$)
128 The Mall, Leura
tel: 02 4784 2534
This brasserie has a deservedly high reputation for its Modern Australian menu.

Solitary ($$–$$$)
90 Cliff Drive, Leura Falls
tel: 02 4782 1164
An excellent Modern Australian restaurant with the bonus of superb mountain and valley views.

Victory Café ($$)
17 Govetts Leap Road, Blackheath
tel: 02 4787 6777
An excellent daytime café, part of an antiques centre, that serves huge breakfasts, very good coffee and a wide range of lunches and snacks.

VICTORIA

Melbourne

Arrivederci ($$)
191 Nicholson Street, Carlton
tel: 03 9347 8252
Authentic, provincial Italian fare is served in this popular restaurant, just north of the city.

BearBrass ($$)
River Level, Southgate, Southbank
tel: 03 9682 3799
The casual café at Southgate serves breakfasts, pizzas, tapas and a good range of main courses—all at very reasonable prices.

Bistrot d'Orsay ($–$$)
184 Collins Street tel: 03 9654 6498
This tiny café is famous for its excellent coffee and reasonably priced meals—including pasta and spicy sausages with mashed potato.

Colonial Tramcar Restaurant ($$$)
Departs from Normanby Road, South Melbourne
tel: 03 9696 4000
Dine on Australian fare while this beautifully renovated old tram car travels through the city.

Dogs Bar ($–$$)
54 Acland Street, St. Kilda tel: 03 9534 3075
Great for coffee and cake or a good-value meal.

Donovans ($$$)
40 Jacka Boulevard, St. Kilda
tel: 03 9534 8221
Great Italian and seafood served in a splendidly restored bathing pavilion overlooking the bay.

Flower Drum ($$$)
17 Market Lane tel: 03 9662 3655
An exceptionally good Cantonese restaurant.

Lemongrass ($$$)
176 Lygon Street, Carlton tel: 03 9662 2244
An unusual find in the heart of Melbourne's 'Little Italy', this attractive restaurant serves a fine range of Thai dishes.

Nudel Bar ($)
76 Bourke Street tel: 03 9662 9100
A central café that serves a range of noodles, from pasta to fried Thai varieties, with a choice of sauces. Great value.

Republic Café & Bar ($$–$$$)
299 Queen Street tel: 03 9670 2999
This stylish restaurant serves an innovative

278

Modern Australian menu. The bar is a popular drinking spot.

Taxi ($$)
Transport Hotel, Federation Square
tel: 03 9654 8808
At the heart of happening Federation Square, this pub dining room serves everything from sushi and other Asian dishes to Modern Australian fare.

Thy Thy ($)
First floor, 142 Victoria Street, Richmond
tel: 03 9429 1104
Excellent and very inexpensive Vietnamese food. It is also worth trying the other branch of Thy Thy just down the street (116 Victoria Street, Richmond
tel: 03 9428 5914).

Vue de Monde ($$$)
Normanby Chambers, 430 Little Collins Street
tel: 03 9691 3888
One of Melbourne's best fine dining restaurants, Vue de Monde is known for its acclaimed Modern french cuisine in very elegant surroundings.

SOUTH AUSTRALIA

Adelaide

Blake's Restaurant & Wine Bar ($$$)
Hyatt Regency Adelaide, North Terrace
tel: 08 8238 2381
This elegant hotel restaurant serves innovative Modern Australian food, with a strong emphasis on South Australian produce and wines. The ideal place for a really special night out.

Cibo Ristorante ($–$$)
10 O'Connell Street, North Adelaide
tel: 08 8267 2444
A popular Italian café, with an outdoor terrace, serving wood-fired pizzas, pasta and great coffee.

Eros Ouzeri ($$$)
277 Rundle Street
tel: 08 8223 4022
Adelaide's best Greek restaurant offers both traditional and innovative dishes. The service is particularly good.

Jolleys Boathouse Restaurant ($$)
Jolleys Lane
tel: 08 8223 2891
This refurbished boathouse on the River Torrens serves mainly Modern Australian food.

The Lion Hotel ($–$$$)
Corner of Melbourne and Jerningham streets, North Adelaide
tel: 08 8367 0222
The Lion's restaurant serves excellent Modern Australian dishes, while the less expensive café is another good option.

Magill Estate Restaurant ($$$)
78 Penfold Road, Magill
tel: 08 8301 5551
It's worth the trip to this superb restaurant, which serves fine wines and Modern Australian cuisine.

Nu Thai ($$)
117 Gouger Street
tel: 08 8410 2288
A busy central restaurant that serves excellent Thai food at reasonable prices. Dine inside or outdoors.

Rundle Noodle Bar & Restaurant ($)
287 Rundle Street tel: 08 8223 7575
Great-value noodles and other Asian dishes at this popular East End eatery.

The Stag Hotel ($–$$)
299 Rundle Street tel: 08 8223 2934
A beautifully renovated old pub serving Modern Australian fare, bistro meals and coffee.

Universal Wine Bar ($$–$$$)
285 Rundle Street tel: 08 8232 5000
A trendy East End wine bar and bistro, famous for its extensive wine list and modern menu.

Vietnam Palace ($)
132 Gouger Street tel: 08 8212 1968
This long-established Vietnamese restaurant offers delicious fresh meals at affordable prices.

Adelaide Hills

The Summit ($–$$)
Summit Road, Mount Lofty tel: 08 8339 2600
This modern restaurant serves everything from snacks and coffee to lunches, dinner and wine.

Barossa Valley

1918 Bistro & Grill ($$)
94 Murray Street, Tanunda tel: 08 8563 0405
Imaginative modern regional cuisine is the speciality of this fine Barossa restaurant.

WESTERN AUSTRALIA

Perth

44 King Street ($$)
44 King Street tel: 08 9321 4476
This city brasserie serves a great range of snacks and ethnically inspired meals.

Fraser's Restaurant ($$–$$$)
Fraser Avenue, Kings Park tel: 08 9481 7100
Fine Western Australian produce means the food it always good at this eatery. Good views.

Globe Bar & Restaurant ($$–$$$)
Parmelia Hilton, Mill Street tel: 08 9215 2421
The acclaimed Modern Australian menu make this stylish restaurant one of the most popular in Perth.

Grand Palace ($–$$$)
3 The Esplanade
tel: 08 9221 6333
One of Perth's best Chinese restaurants, complete with a bar. In a historic parkside building.

Indiana Tea House ($$)
99 Marine Parade, Cottesloe
tel: 08 9385 5005
This award-winning establishment serves Asian-style Modern Australian food in casually elegant surroundings. Excellent service and great ocean views.

The Loose Box Restaurant ($$$)
6825 Great Eastern Highway, Mundaring
tel: 08 9295 1787
This restaurant has one of the best reputations in Western Australia, and is worth the half-hour drive out of Perth into the Darling Range.

Maya Masala ($$)
49 Lake Street, Northbridge tel: 08 9328 5655
A lively restaurant that serves good-value Indian food, from tandoori dishes to delicious desserts.

279

Hotels and Restaurants

The Old Swan Brewery Restaurant ($$–$$$)
173 Mounts Bay Road
tel: 08 9211 8999
Modern Australian restaurant beside the Swan River. Also a café and its own microbrewery.
Verve ($$)
Wooodside Plaza, 240 St Georges Terrace
tel: 08 9226 3636
This city-centre bar/restaurant serves good Modern Australian food. There is an extensive wine list and live jazz on Friday nights.

Fremantle

George Street Bistro ($$)
71–73 George Street, East Fremantle
tel: 08 9339 6352
This all-day bistro offers a great range of dishes, plus brunch buffet on Sundays.
Little Creatures Brewery ($$)
40 Mews Road
tel: 08 9430 5555
In a vast old boat shed, this brewery also serves excellent pizzas, seafood and other reasonably priced meals.
The Red Herring ($$)
26 Riverside Road, East Fremantle
tel: 08 9339 1611
A chic riverside eatery, which serves an extensive Modern Australian menu, focusing on seafood.

Kalgoorlie–Boulder

Judds Restaurant ($$)
The Kalgoorie Hotel, 319 Hannan Street
tel: 08 9021 3046
A pub restaurant that serves good-value meals. Their woodfired pizza is especially good.
Top End Thai ($$)
71 Hannan Street tel: 08 9021 4286
Excellent Thai restaurant.

NORTHERN TERRITORY

Darwin

Cornucopia Museum Café ($$)
Conacher Street, Bullocky Point
tel: 08 8981 1002
At Darwin's museum, this café/restaurant serves innovative Modern Australian food, with a great view from the outside tables.
The Darwin Sailing Club ($–$$)
Aitkins Drive, Vesteys Beach tel: 08 8981 5153
Darwin's sailing club's Waterfront Bistro has a good Australian, Asian and seafood menu.
Dragon Court ($$)
Skycity Darwin Hotel, Gilruth Avenue,
The Gardens
tel: 08 8943 8888
Excellent Chinese fare, using local produce at this ppopular hotel restaurant.
The Hanuman ($$–$$$)
28 Mitchell Street tel: 08 8941 3500
Arguably Darwin's finest restaurant—the food consists of Thai and Malaysian Nonya dishes.
The Magic Wok ($$)
48 Cavenagh Street tel: 08 8981 3332

Wok meals using buffalo, crocodile, deer and camel as well as seafood and vegetables.
Pee Wee's Beach Front Café ($$$)
Alec Fong Lim Drive, East Point
tel: 08 8981 6868
On the beachfront, this tropical-style restaurant serves some of Darwin's best à la carte dining. Great views of the city.

Alice Springs

Bar Doppio ($)
Fan Arcade, Todd Mall
tel: 08 8952 6525
This casual and friendly café with indoor and out-door dining, specializes in delicious, wholesome food and good coffee.
Bluegrass Restaurant ($$)
Corner of Todd Street and Stott Terrace
tel: 08 8955 5188
Steaks, kangaroo, seafood, pastas, vegetarian dishes and over 100 different labels on their wine list.
Bojangle's Saloon & Restaurant ($$)
80 Todd Street
tel: 08 8952 2873
Emu, kangaroo and camel feature on the menu of this cheerful establishment. Live entertainment.
Samphire Restaurant ($$)
Lasseters Hotel Casino, 93 Barrett Drive
tel: 08 8950 7777
Open for breakfast, lunch and dinner, this hotel restaurant is a good dining option.

Uluru
See hotel listings on page 274.

QUEENSLAND

Brisbane

Breakfast Creek Hotel ($–$$)
2 Kingsford Smith Drive, Albion
tel: 07 3262 5988
Brisbane's best-known pub serves fine beers and wines in addition to good-value steaks and other bistro-style meals.
Brett's Wharf ($$$)
499 Kingsford Smith Drive, Hamilton
tel: 07 3868 1717
Beside the Brisbane River, Brett's Wharf has great views and ambience, and excellent seafood.
City Gardens Café ($–$$)
City Botanic Gardens, Alice Street
tel: 07 3229 1554
In the city's botanical gardens, this café serves delicious snacks and full meals at lunchtime.
E'cco Bistro ($$$)
100 Boundary Street
tel: 07 3831 8344
This internationally acclaimed bistro offers one of Brisbane's finest dining experiences. Try to visit it at least once.
Green Papaya North Vietnamese Restaurant ($$)
898 Stanley Street, East Brisbane
tel: 07 3217 3599
Innovative Vietnamese dishes in one of Brisbane's best Asian restaurants.

James Street Bistro ($$)
39 James Street, Fortitude Valley
tel: 07 3852 5155
A bustling bistro, with a long communal table and a predominantly Mediterranean menu.

Pier Nine ($$–$$$)
Eagle Street Pier, 1 Eagle Street
tel: 07 3226 2100
Here, riverside views and menus reflect the availability of delicious seafood.

River Canteen ($$–$$$)
Boardwalk, South Bank tel: 07 3846 1880
Sample Modern Australian cuisine while enjoying the excellent city views.

Summit Restaurant ($$–$$$)
Sir Samuel Griffith Drive, Mount Coot-tha
tel: 07 3369 9922
Good food and stunning views out to Moreton Bay from this mountaintop restaurant.

Sunshine Coast

Lindoni's Ristorante ($$)
13 Hastings Street, Noosa Heads
tel: 07 5447 5111
Delicious Italian food and excellent service.

The Spirit House ($$)
20 Ninderry Road, Yandina tel: 07 5446 8994
A drive inland from the coast is well worthwhile to sample the delectable contemporary Asian offerings of this restaurant in the rain forest.

Gold Coast and Hinterland

Absynthe ($$)
Shop 4, Q1, Gold Coast Highway, Surfers Paradise tel: 07 5504 6466
This stylish restaurant serves superb French-style food, created by an award-winning chef.

Ristorante Fellini ($$)
Marina Mirage, Seaworld Drive, Main Beach
tel: 07 5331 0300
This popular family-run Italian restaurant serves handmade pasta, seafood and meat dishes, plus wonderful views.

Cairns and the Far North

2 Fish Seafood Restaurant ($$–$$$)
7/20 Wharf Street, Port Douglas
tel: 07 4099 6250
Delicious fresh seafood is the specialty of this popular Port Douglas eatery. There is a sister restaurant in Cairns (tel: 07 4041 5350).

Barnacle Bills Seafood Inn ($$)
65 The Esplanade, Cairns
tel: 07 4051 2241
A popular seafront seafood-eating emporium: an essential experience for any visitor.

Nautilus Restaurant ($$$)
17 Murphy Street, Port Douglas
tel: 07 4099 5330
Enjoy Asian-style seafood at this delightful open-air restaurant in Port Douglas.

Red Ochre Grill ($$)
43 Shields Street, Cairns tel: 07 4051 0100
Native Australian food, such as emu or eucalypt-smoked fish dishes, is the main attraction.

TASMANIA

Hobart

Annapurna ($–$$)
305 Elizabeth Street, North Hobart
tel: 03 6236 9500
Excellent Indian meals, including many vegetarian options, at very reasonable prices. Always popular, so booking is advisable.

Fish Frenzy ($–$$)
Elizabeth Street Pier, Sullivans Cove
tel: 03 6231 2134
A good-value seafood restaurant on the waterside. Open for lunch and dinner.

Lebrina ($$$)
155 New Town Road, New Town
tel: 03 6228 7775
Acclaimed French- and Italian-based food at this smart restaurant, just north of the city.

Maldini ($$)
47 Salamanca Place
tel: 03 6223 4460
A popular restaurant and café that serves great coffee and a good variety of Italian meals.

Mures Upper Deck ($$–$$$)
Victoria Dock
tel: 03 6231 1999
From its glazed second-floor pavilion, Mures serves seafood with great flair. Reservations recommended.

Restaurant Gondwana ($$)
Corner Hampden Road and Francis Street, Battery Point
tel: 03 6224 9900
In a lovely old building in historic Battery Point, this restaurant serves excellent Modern Australian cuisine, featuring fine local produce.

Vanidol's ($$)
353 Elizabeth Street, North Hobart
tel: 03 6234 9307
This excellent restaurant, in the popular North Hobart dining strip, serves a wide variety of Thai, Indian and other Asian cuisines.

Cradle Mountain
See hotel listings on page 276.

Launceston

Fee and Mee ($$–$$$)
190 Charles Street
tel: 03 6331 3195
One of the best restaurants in Tasmania, specializing in fine Modern Australian cuisine.

Mud Bar and Restaurant ($$)
28 Seaport Boulevard
tel: 03 6334 5066
Italian-influenced Modern Australian dining in a casual setting, which includes a bar and large outdoor area.

Stillwater River Cafe ($$)
Ritchies Mill, Paterson Street
tel: 03 6331 4153
In a historic flour mill, this delightful riverside restaurant serves acclaimed Modern Australian cuisine.

Index

282

283

Index

Index

286

Acknowledgements

The Automobile Association would like to thank the following photographers, libraries and associations for their assistance in the preparation of this book.
ACT TOURISM 82. ALLSPORT UK LTD 166. ARDEA LONDON 88a (V Taylor), 88c (C J Mason), 228–229 (Jon P Ferrero), 236b (Jon P Ferrero), 238b (Jon P Ferrero), 242–243 (Jon P Ferrero). BRIDGEMAN ART LIBRARY, LONDON 19 Dog & Duck Hotel by Sidney Nolan (1917–1992), Roy Miles Gallery, 29 Bruton Street, London W1. DEPARTMENT OF MARITIME ARCHAEOLOGY, WA MARITIME MUSEUM 243a, 243c. MARY EVANS PICTURE LIBRARY 26a, 26b, 27, 28–29, 30b, 76, 77, 161b. CHRIS FAIRCLOUGH COLOUR LIBRARY 166–167, 194, 195. CORBIS 17, 45 (Nick Rains). FFOTOGRAFF 24a, 174, 241. FOOTPRINTS 216–217 (A Dalton), 216 (N Hanna), 217b (Carlos Lima), 218 (A Dalton), 219 (N Hanna). RONALD GRANT ARCHIVES 18c. INTERNATIONAL PHOTOBANK 12a, 13, 14a, 24b, 29, 31, 32, 34, 82–83, 90, 97, 114, 114b, 127, 134, 135, 137, 140–141, 140, 142, 175b, 177, 178, 184, 185b, 200, 208, 209b, 210, 211, 213, 217a, 252, 253, 257, 267a. MICHAEL IVORY 8b, 25. NATURE PHOTOGRAPHERS LTD 121 (R Tidman), 222b (S C Bisserot). NORTHERN TERRITORY TOURIST COMMISSION 181, 182, 190, 191, 198, 255, 259. CHRISTINE OSBORNE PICTURES 53, 224b. PHOTO INDEX 159. PICTURES COLOUR LIBRARY 138. ANDY PRICE 18a, 21a, 178–179, 192b, 193, 194–195. QUEEN VICTORIA MUSEUM & ART GALLERY 241b, ROYAL GEOGRAPHICAL SOCIETY 23. SPECTRUM COLOUR LIBRARY 79, 99, 103, 120, 203b, 215, 220, 222a, 222c, 223, 225, 235, 237, 247, 250. TOURISM SOUTH AUSTRALIA 130, 131, 132, 133, 139. TOURISM TASMANIA 236a, 240, 243, 246, 248, 249, 264. WESTERN AUSTRALIAN TOURISM COMMISSION 148, 151, 157b, 160, 167, 168, 170, 173a, 173b, 175a, 262. ZEFA PICTURE LIBRARY (UK) LTD 224a.

All remaining pictures are held in the Association's own picture library (AA PHOTO LIBRARY) with contributions from:
BILL BACHMAN 108, 118, 189b, 256. ADRIAN BAKER 2, 5b, 5c, 6a, 7a, 7b, 8a, 10–11, 10, 11, 15, 20, 21b, 22–23, 22, 23, 28, 30a, 33a, 35, 47, 48, 49, 52a, 54, 55b, 60, 64–65, 66, 67a, 69, 70, 71, 72, 73, 75, 76–77, 78, 83, 85, 87, 88b, 89, 92a, 92–93b, 98, 100a,100b,102b, 106, 107, 109, 111, 112–113, 112, 113, 115, 117, 119, 120b, 122, 123, 126–127, 136, 143a, 143b, 145, 146, 149, 152, 153, 154, 156, 157a, 158, 161a, 162, 163, 164, 165, 169a, 169b, 169c, 171, 172, 185a, 186, 187, 188–189, 192a, 196a, 196b, 197, 199, 202, 203a, 205, 207, 209a, 212, 221, 228, 229, 231, 232, 233, 234, 238a, 239, 244, 245, 258, 260, 261, 263. PAUL KENWARD Spine, back cover a, b, 3, 4, 5a, 9b, 12b, 14b, 16a, 33b, 39, 40, 40–41, 42, 43, 46a, 46b, 50, 51, 52b, 55a, 58, 59, 61, 62, 67b, 68, 74, 80–81, 84, 86, 183b, 251a, b, 265, 266, 267b. MIKE LANGFORD 188b, 188–189a. CHRISTINE OSBORNE 96a, 96b, 101, 102a, 104, 105, 110, 166. KEN PATERSON 183a.

Contributors

Original copy editor: Sally Knowles Revision verifier: Anne Matthews
Revision edit and design: Bookwork Creative Associates Ltd.